Joseph Brodsky a KT-119-181

Literary criticism of the work of Russian poet Joseph Brodsky has tended to be biographical, stressing the significance of physical or metaphysical exile, estrangement, and alienation in his poetry. In a welcome move away from previous emphases, David MacFadyen argues that Brodsky's corpus was inspired by a Baroque aesthetic.

MacFadyen shows that the works of John Donne, the existential philosophy of Kierkegaard and Šestov, and the cities of St Petersburg and Venice inspired a fundamentally Baroque evolution in Brodsky's development. He provides a compelling and comprehensive examination of Brodsky's poetry and prose in the context of a fascinating overview of some problems of post-Soviet aesthetics. The book concludes with a reassessment of Brodsky's final role, that of cross-cultural, bilingual essayist.

Joseph Brodsky and the Baroque will appeal to students and scholars of Russian literature as well as the growing body of Brodsky's admirers.

DAVID MacFADYEN is assistant professor of Russian studies, Dalhousie University.

Joseph Brodsky
Photo © Annalisa Alleva, 1992

Joseph Brodsky and the Baroque

DAVID MacFADYEN

McGill-Queen's University Press
Montreal & Kingston · London · Ithaca

© McGill-Queen's University Press 1998
ISBN 0-7735-1779-0

Legal deposit fourth quarter 1998
Bibliothèque nationale du Québec

1001579752

Printed in the United States of America on acid-free paper

Published simultaneously in the European Union by Liverpool University Press.

This book has been published with the help of a grant from the Humanities and Social Sciences Federation of Canada, using funds provided by the Social Sciences and Humanities Research Council of Canada.

McGill-Queen's University Press acknowledges the financial support of the Government of Canada through the Book Publishing Industry Development Program for its activities. We also acknowledge the support of the Canada Council for the Arts for our publishing program.

Canadian Cataloguing in Publication Data

MacFadyen, David, 1964–
    Joseph Brodsky and the Baroque
    Includes bibliographical references and index.
    ISBN 0-7735-1779-0
    1. Brodsky, Joseph, 1940–   – Criticism and interpretation. 2. Arts, Baroque. I. Title.
    PG3479.4.R64Z78 1999 891.71'44   C98-900707-3

Typeset in New Baskerville 10/12
by Caractéra inc., Quebec City

Contents

For my parents
For my brother and sister

Acknowledgments

As this book was written in Scotland, America, Russia, and Canada, expressions of gratitude must be directed towards several of "the round earth's imagined corners," in John Donne's words. America is the logical place to start, because *Joseph Brodsky and the Baroque* is founded upon a 1995 doctoral dissertation from the University of California at Los Angeles. I would like to acknowledge the support and enthusiasm of my adviser, Ronald Vroon, which I enjoyed throughout my time at UCLA. Thanks are also due to the other members of my committee, Gail Lenhoff, Michael Heim, and Alessandro Duranti. With regard to the more distant past, I am increasingly appreciative of the introduction to Joseph Brodsky's work given to me by George L. Kline and Anna Ljunggren, long before the book was ever formulated.

As for the broader context in which my American research was done, I am indebted to Margaret Bachtold for her help and hospitality, as well as to the American Council for Teachers of Russian for the opportunity to write in St Petersburg. The kindness and patience of my friends Elena and Iosif during that time proved invaluable.

Once in Canada, work continued apace at Dalhousie University with the support of my colleagues John Barnstead, Yuri and Marina Glazov, Norman Pereira, and Ieva Vitins. Just around the corner, the document delivery section of Dalhousie's Killam Library was very generous with its time and energy in chasing elusive articles.

My greatest thanks, however, are reserved for my parents. The initial books for this research were chosen from the shelves of Edinburgh Central Library with the advice of my father. I am sure that without them both I would not be busy introducing a book.

Joseph Brodsky and the Baroque

Introduction

The Russian poet Joseph Brodsky was born in St Petersburg (then Leningrad) in 1940. Writing verse as a young man, he attracted the attention of the Soviet authorities and was subsequently banished for most of 1964 and 1965 to the emptiness of the Russian north, after a trial that found him guilty of social parasitism. This indictment did little to deter the poet, however, and his expulsion beyond the borders of the Soviet Union began to look increasingly likely. He was exiled in 1972, at which time he chose to go to the United States. Much to the chagrin of the Soviets, no doubt, his successes increased overseas, culminating with the Nobel Prize for Literature in 1987. Other accolades during his twenty-four years in America included awards from the National Book Critics and the MacArthur Foundation. He was appointed poet laureate of the United States in 1992 and was teaching at Mount Holyoke College at the time of his death in New York in 1996.

Brodsky's swift rise to the stature of "some sort of international superstar, the new Elvis Presley of world literature" (Rejn, 1992a: 61), made him the unfortunate object of several well-worn critical and cultural stereotypes. Two points of view in particular were – and continue to be – central to almost all studies of the poet: first, that Brodsky languished in physical or metaphysical exile, away from a lost "home," and second, that key metaphors or motifs may be easily recognized as stable elements of his verse, which are held to be the unchanging foundation of Brodsky's worldview. As a result, little attention has been paid to the changes that the poet's work underwent, especially those indicative of broader, socio-cultural processes. This book goes very much against the grain of existent studies and proposes instead an interpretation of Brodsky's work as a fundamentally Baroque passage.

The term "Baroque" is justifiable on two counts. There are, without doubt, striking typological similarities between seventeenth-century and post-Soviet aesthetics. Over and above this, however, Brodsky's own life brought him into direct and meaningful contact with several phenomena of seventeenth- and early eighteenth-century culture. Most notable were the city of St Petersburg, where the poet was raised, the verse of the English Metaphysical poets, studied whilst in internal exile, and Venetian culture, at the centre of the poet's attention in his later years.

Both uses of the term Baroque need to be clarified before it can be applied as an interpretative model for culture following the demise of the Soviet Union. The first chapter of this book offers, therefore, an overview of some broader, typological aspects of seventeenth-century culture which fuelled the Baroque, aspects that allow one first to define a general *Zeitgeist* and then to draw contemporary parallels which make Brodsky's affinity with the Baroque much clearer. By placing the poet within a general socio-cultural process, which to a large degree is a consequence of post-Soviet existence, similar parallels can be drawn with other contemporary poets. Such parallels show that Brodsky's departure from Russia presaged the creative state in which modern Russian poetry now finds itself. Many young writers also display Baroque elements. As with Brodsky, these consist of both typological similarities and specific references to the period.

Why do such parallel states exist? One explanation comes from the Italian semiotician Omar Calabrese who, at least in the realm of film and television, has decided that there is a predominantly neo-Baroque current in late twentieth-century culture. The work of British sociologist Anthony Giddens offers yet more justification for the term Baroque. Giddens's views outline a modern existential state that neatly parallels a post-Renaissance *Weltanschauung*; this book places an analogous emphasis upon the existential crises of a post-Soviet, "post-traditional" culture – in other words, one that follows after the strict canonical dictates of Soviet art. Confining though such dictates may have been, they nonetheless provided a sense of ontological and teleological security. To reject them is to project oneself into a state of enormous existential responsibility, leading to doubts concerning the potential of one's future agency. As a result of the ongoing flux between confidence and insecurity, the supposedly stable, unchanging metaphors seen in Brodsky's work by other researchers cannot be found. Enormous changes take place in his corpus as it undergoes the constant search for ontological reference points. The power of self-determination in the poet's work is constantly at odds with his views on the inevitable passage of time – as history or cyclical, literary tradition – once he has absorbed various phenomena of seventeenth-century culture.

Once a definition of Baroque has been established, an analysis of Brodsky's output as an aesthetic evolution is possible. The creation of such an aesthetic is the result of two primary influences, the existentialism of Kierkegaard and Šestov, and the verse of John Donne. Donne proposes a brave, empirical "going forth" into what for him is an unknown, post-traditional world, an outlook paralleled in the young Brodsky by his enthusiasm for Kierkegaard and Šestov. Today, however, as part of literary history, Donne's path is seen by a twentieth-century reader as a completed journey. Brodsky knows what the aesthetic and psychological consequences of the Metaphysicals were; they were harbingers of the Baroque. His frequently deterministic views on the evolution of art bring him, therefore, to a paradoxical situation. The Metaphysical poets offer him a sense of self-determination, a liberation from the constraints of the past, whilst simultaneously being part of inescapable, cyclical literary history, part of culture's organic or "catabolic" processes of growth and decay. Metaphysical elements give rise to the burgeoning, more elaborate Baroque, which in turn dissipates, forming the Rococo, Précieux, or Cavalier style, depending on whether the analogy is with pictorial or verbal art. Although the primary analogy of this study is with poetry, with the post-Donnean verse of Richard Crashaw and Abraham Cowley, frequent reference is also made to architecture and painting as Brodsky moves from Baroque to post-Baroque emphases. Such comparisons are justifiable not only in terms of a twentieth-century existential passage, but also by the poet's own references to the philosophical cause and consequence of Baroque and Rococo art.

After describing and defining such a passage, this book concludes with the relevance of a Baroque aesthetic for understanding both Brodsky's last role, as a cross-cultural, bilingual essayist, and a central theme of this bilingual prose: Venice. The art of Venice operates as a symmetrical counterpart to the influence of St Petersburg's art and architecture in Brodsky's earlier work, such that the issues and problems of a return to a source or cyclical, recurrent state that existed in the beginning are uppermost even in his final publications. And they continue to negate the supposed significance of exile, alienation, or estrangement which has been of central importance to other discussions of the poet's œuvre. What now follows, as a response to the supposed significance of exile, is a different, yet vital prolegomenon to the analysis of Joseph Brodsky's work. To show the poet's affinity with a Baroque aesthetic is instructive; to define it as indicative of a widespread social situation is markedly more so. Analysis of Brodsky's verse is therefore not the emphasis of this initial chapter. Instead, the aim is to offer a broad assessment of a social phenomenon, of which Brodsky is one example, and then in following chapters to focus directly upon textual evidence from his corpus.

1 Justification for the Term "Baroque"

In beginning with an overview of pertinent aspects of seventeenth-century culture, one should not propose a complete synonymy of the Baroque with the Counter-Reformation. The new sense of self-determination which emerged in the seventeenth century was just as much a secular force, and was inspired by the demise of ecclesiastical authority. Both spiritual and social hierarchies were, for example, challenged by a new mercantile spirit; scant respect for traditional structures of authority brought great success to nomadic, upstart traders. This commercial explosion, however, moved eventually towards a consolidation of its widespread, unruly influence through an "authoritarian bureaucracy, idealized as the state." The eventual centripetal tendency of seventeenth-century power has led one historian to call disorder, followed by a movement towards central administration, "the most striking development of the period" (Friedrich, 40, 25). The Holy Roman Empire lay in disarray, broken into some two thousand autonomous territories. Subsequent attempts at unity by the house of Habsburg led to the chaos of the Thirty Years' War, and military conflict did little but reinstate the political situation that preceded it, because the Peace of Westphalia, signed in 1648, simply returned authority to German Protestant princes. The peace was one of several postwar settlements, however, including France's acquisition of Alsace, which allowed Richelieu to set in motion Louis xiv's inexorable domination of Europe. In France itself, troubles surrounding the new-found freedoms of the seventeenth century were in general alleviated by a turn towards the unquestionable sovereignty of a given individual, a turn which presaged the emergence of what we now know as the modern state (Blitzer, 42, 56).

In England, matters were a little different. The self-assured designs of James I's "caesaropapism," together with Charles I's constant disso-lution of Parliament, led to the Civil War. Ironically, perhaps, stability (in the form of Parliament) was defended by the very merchants who hade made the traditional authority of the aristocracy so unstable. As a consequence of this more enduring mercantile influence, England avoided the loud expressions of the Baroque used across the Channel to bolster Louis XIV's autocracy.

The situation in Russia was more French than English. There are parallels between Louis's decision to manifest his power by conjuring up Versailles on a "totally undistinguished, dusty plain a few miles outside Paris" (Friedrich, 60) and Peter the Great's erection of his city on "a shore of desolate waves," to quote Puškin, as well as the con-struction of the Peterhof Palace, modelled on Versailles by Leblond and then by Rastrelli. Though Peter's desire to enter the aesthetic and social European arena was fully realized after the 1709 victory against the Swedes at Poltava, the Russian Baroque can be traced back to the Time of Troubles following the death of Boris Godunov. After the narrowly avoided disaster of Polish and Swedish influence upon the Russian throne, the emergence of the Romanov dynasty in 1613 marked a return to the processes of centralization. By the time of Peter I's reign, Russia was "one great regimented society, organized for making war upon its neighbors," in other words, Poland, Sweden and Turkey (250). Even without Russia's interference, the Swedes and the Turks saw their dominions plundered by Louis XIV and the Holy Roman Emperor, Leopold I: it seemed that the ninety-five theses nailed by Luther to the door of the Castle Church in Wittenberg, though inspired by autonomy, had set in motion a chaotic series of events which finally gravitated towards autocracy: "Absolutism became, in theory and in practice, the century's clearest answer to the problem of order" (Blitzer, 56).

THE PHILOSOPHICAL CONTEXT

The speed with which the movement from autonomy to autocracy took place was to a large degree determined by man's explorations and expansionism: seafaring mercantile growth, discovery of the New

World, military conquests. Man was inspired in his power to shape his own society, to control his own destiny. It fell to the realm of science to instill in him a simultaneous sense of impotence. Confidence in the visible world was tempered by an awareness of one's insignificance in the face of a rapidly expanding universe. Not only did studies in astronomy continue the post-Copernican revolution, but developments in the microscope by Anton van Leeuwenhoek and Robert Hooke revealed a new multiplicity of being: bacteria, spermatozoa, protozoa.

The end of scholasticism meant the end of unquestioning faith. Galileo, following his forced recantation, is rumoured to have stamped upon the earth, which the church held to be immobile, and muttered "But it *does* move!" The end of the universe's Ptolemaic stability was also part of the seventeenth century's shift in emphasis "from the contemplation of Being to the observation of Becoming" (Willey, 6), a prospect frightening enough to stop the faculty at Padua from looking through Galileo's telescope. Scientific inquiry to further the aims of science independent of religion was supported by Francis Bacon: "The opposite part of the process – keeping religion pure from science – did not interest him nearly so much" (Willey 29). This disconcertingly subversive empiricism led those such as Sir Thomas Browne to champion a more balanced union of science and religion, of body and soul, which subsequently earned him the epithet "metaphysical." Any rigorous assessment of the English Metaphysical poets will show that their "unified sensibility," to use T.S. Eliot's famous phrase, also results from such a union, from an awkward marriage of potential strength with a disconcerting awareness of human limitations.

René Descartes offered another response to troublesome disorder, to the anxiety caused by this inifinite world: he subjected it to mathematics. The existence of God was to be proven by logical postulates, not piety. Cartesian dualism is a supremely logical inquiry conducted in the realms of the visible and the invisible, with its division of reality into objects, with "extension" in space (and subject to mathematical laws) and the "thinking substance," which finds the proof of existence to be its self (*cogito, ergo sum*). The thinking I is not subject to the constraints of matter as expressed by geometrical laws and enjoys an extra-corporeal existence. Descartes excluded thought from the laws of geometrical *becoming*, a distinction rejected by Thomas Hobbes in his view of philosophy as nothing more than the study of bodies in motion, and consciousness as a nervous reaction, pure and simple. The potentially chaotic, natural rights of individuals to self-preservation and self-assertion were to be subsumed in an ideal social contract overseen by ideal sovereignty, that of an absolute monarch. Hobbes's deterministic outlook and celebration of autocracy mirror the same centripetal processes shown in the consolidation of seventeenth-century imperialism, which fed directly into the aesthetics of an incipient Classicism. Order, clarity, and proportion were restored. They contradicted any post-Renaissance chaos when "beauty was dead, [when] proportion and symmetry had disappeared" (Nicolson, 121–2).

THE ARTISTIC CONTEXT

The period when beauty was pronounced dead, between the Renaissance and Classicism, encompasses the Baroque, a time of unprecedented internationalism in all arts. National variation often vanished in the new cosmopolitan atmosphere. As a consequence, general tendencies can be discerned across Europe, tendencies both secular and ecclesiastical. At the sametime, an art which emerged boldly from the religious constraints of the past was used – in Rome, for example – to further the aims of Jesuit propaganda, hence the frequent analogy of varied forms of Baroque art with rhetoric. Whether facing the dizzying dimensions of the universe shown by the new science, or as the object of fiery Jesuit rhetoric, man's irrational and finite existence was now seen as relative to much grander designs. The Baroque became an expression of the disorder in politics and philosophy. An emphasis fell upon the "fleeting glance, the momentary gesture, the changing aspects of nature," all of which told of "transience, mutability and time's swift flight" (J.R. Martin, 15).

The idea of mutability in Baroque culture describes a similar development in the political and philosophical states. The recent study of the Baroque by John Rupert Martin has attempted to counteract the typical assessment of the period as the sudden appearance of bombast. Martin discerns three fundamental stages of Baroque art. The first he terms naturalistic, as epitomized by Caravaggio. The spiritually driven portraits by both Caravaggio and artists such as Bernini – the quintessential Baroque sculptor – rely upon advances in the science of anatomy, though this naturalism is nevertheless driven by a "fundamentally metaphysical view of the world" (Martin, 13). The union of secular and divine influences appears in both the pitch-black backgrounds of Caravaggio's canvases and the inside of an archetypal Baroque cupola, where naturalistic human figures are suspended, even isolated, in infinite depth, in the boundless perspective of divine dimensions. The still tension of such oppositions in Caravaggio's work is released in the second stage.

Beyond the unified opposites of early naturalism lies what Martin has termed the second stage, the high Baroque. Typical of this period is the sensuous work of Rubens. Though Rubens fell under an Italian influence in the first decade of the seventeenth century, his association with Antwerp was with a region where the prevailing mercantile atmosphere (as in England) tempered the extremes of the Baroque art driven by Jesuit doctrine: Charles I had Rubens brought to his court. To the stark oppositions of Caravaggio, Rubens added movement or a struggle between them, as in his *Battle of the Amazons* (painted around 1618). The drama of Caravaggio's light is possible only when dominated by darkness, which suggests the morose rhetoric from pulpits of the Counter-Reformation. Rubens brings enlightenment to the whole canvas and creates a compositional harmony between fore- and background, not the quintessentially Italian projection of the former at the expense of the latter.

Rubens's technique creates a compositional entirety through the direction of the brush strokes, which force the viewer's eye into constant activity, across a canvas crowded with unreasonable movement: "Rubens' wonderful handling, which *quivers with life*, is not merely a form of sensuality, it is a *dynamic* expression. His brush *moves* from form to form *without ever lingering*, in a kind of *whirling rush*, and out of this nebula of color and light, as his sketches show, a world comes *gradually into being*" (Martin, 66, my emphases).

From the collocation of order and disorder in Rubens's work grows the third and final stage of the Baroque, occurring in France. Poussin represents a turn towards "clarity and composure [from] the growing strength of the classicists" (Martin, 28) emerging in France between 1635 and 1640, perhaps fixed in 1664 when Louis XIV rejected Bernini's plans for the east façade of the Louvre, thus embracing a more orderly aesthetic which Poussin had developed, ironically, in Rome. There the Frenchman "worked out some of the most accomplished forms of Classicism – to some extent a continuation of the Renaissance conception ... Nothing in the whole seventeenth century is so far removed from Caravaggio (whom he detested) as the art of Poussin" (Bazin, 134–5).

If the work of Poussin is so radically different from that of Caravaggio, whilst simultaneously invoking aspects of the Renaissance, it comes as no surprise that theories based upon a binary oscillation in all arts occasionally find great favour. The attractiveness of such theories can be explained by looking at individuals whose lives span such great stylistic shifts, such as Brodsky or, in the seventeeth century, Rembrandt. The coincidence of Rembrandt's output and the course of Baroque art in general has been termed remarkable. Raised in the independent and prosperous United Provinces of Netherlands, he experienced both the freedom of such an environment and the pressures of artistic production without a benevolent court. Isolation caused by the latter condition was exacerbated by the predominance of Calvinism in the Northern Netherlands, which could often be antithetical to the new-found sense of self-determination of the seventeenth century. Following the death of his wife, Rembrandt, who once enjoyed the early freedom of a Baroque aesthetic, moved in general from "the frank and joyful sensuality of his youth to the anxious meditations that characterized his old age" (Bazin, 87). Rembrandt's movement across the Baroque is charted by shifting emphases. There is an emphasis upon the spiritual in his earliest work, followed by the physical, and later a synthesis of the two. The ravages of time, made more poignant by the importance of inevitability in Calvinist doctrine, led to more than fifty self-portraits. His relentless self-evaluation was displeasing to the classically inclined, who saw it as ignorance of proportion or simply as bad taste (R. de Piles [1706], in Koehler, plate 38), elements inherent in the much-disputed etymology of the term Baroque.

THE RELENTLESS INVESTIGATION OF INFINITE TIME AND SPACE

The artist's very act of scrutinizing the fleeting moment is courageous, an admission of finite existence whilst simultaneously creating in order to celebrate (prolong?) its passing glory. The clear gaze of reason upon the passage of time ironically limits the power of reason itself: curiosity drives the intellect into consideration of the new spatio-temporal dimensions of the world, and finds them overwhelming. (A parallel, visual example of the awe felt before the infinite is the overwhelming expanse of sky in seventeenth-century Dutch panoramic painting, a dimension shown at the expense of a flat, low-lying landscape.) Marjorie Nicolson's work on the attraction of these dimensions for verse of the time supports the argument that a new empiricism in the spirit of Bacon meant charting unknown, dangerous realms: "'The human understanding is unquiet,' Bacon had said. 'It cannot stop or rest, and still presses onward. Therefore it is that we cannot conceive of any end or limit to the world, but always as of necessity [!] it occurs to us that there is something beyond'" (Nicolson, 195; my exclamation point).

Nicolson sees these opposing urges as literary content and aspiration. Though one could stay contained within the ontologically pacifying tenets of the past, there existed on the edge of human potential the charm of the dangerous – an aspiration which emphasizes the importance of spatial borders, limits, frames or enclosures for seventeenth-century aesthetics. The influence of exotic ornamentalism in the Baroque, for example, was to a large degree taken from geographical borders where there was actual contact with Europeans and their territory, contact with a looming Turkish presence, for example, or the newly discovered, virgin lands of the New World, where monsters and savage natives lay in wait. Long after the demise of the Baroque, even, the influence of chinoiserie upon the Rococo marks the continuing discovery of lands farther still from home.

The exotic, the ornamental, by its very nature moves beyond boundaries as its extravagant flourishes decentralize a compositional whole. Even entirely "European" expressions of visual art of the period often reach out beyond the frame, such as Rembrandt's *Night Watch*, creating a similar "integration of real and fictive space" (Martin, 157). A known and tangible space is linked with the hypothetical realm conjectured by the artist's imagination, be it out into extended space or time – and sometimes with apocalyptic consequences, for the following reason. Francis Bacon's rejection of scholasticism in favour of induction, of using facts garnered empirically, led to the creation of novel hypotheses about the nature of things. These were then constantly tested and re-tested through further experience; truth, in other words, must be chased, as it lies just beyond the border or frame. Hence the ontological carrot which dangles in front of an artist drags him and his reason headlong into what is unknown and unreasonable, into a chaos which his aspiration leads him to think will be an "apocalyptic cleansing" (40). An initial, bold leap towards the future soon brings about the frantic desire to stop the processes that have been set in motion. With horror, the empiricist recognizes what lies ahead: the fate of those who fly too high such as Icarus and Phaeton. The extravagance of the Baroque is caused in part by fear of an impending descent, by a recurrent and sadly predictable sense of zero self-determination in the face of empirical cycles which are freely begun, yet soon scribed in the designs of "historically limited civilizations and the cosmos" (Gillespie, 66).

The drive towards knowledge, the assertion of the individual, is therefore unfortunately linked to self-obliteration. Violence done to one's well-being is nevertheless still an existential expression of will: the artist "would rather choose the void for his purpose than be void of purpose" (Gillespie, 153). The freely willed, disorderly ascent of seventeenth-century literature instigated its own collapse, a return to the order, clarity, and rules of Neo-Classicism: "When [Baconian] empiricism took over the iconoclastic function of radical Protestantism, our world of 'progress' and 'revision' was born" (140).

TWENTIETH-CENTURY PARALLELS
WITH THE BAROQUE

If Baroque phenomena are recurrent, can such cyclical movements be rolled forward as far as the twentieth century? In the field of Russian studies, the Baroque has at times been called upon to explain the diverse schools and practices of pre-Soviet, twentieth-century literature. It has been compared with the literature of Futurism, on the basis of similar responses to differing historical realia. Parallels have also been extended from seventeenth-century painting to Cubism and then, with a deft sidewards step, once again to Futurism. Both Cubism and Futurism reproduce elements of the Baroque's response to the world because their knowledge of a new aesthetic and of a modern world is also gained empirically, bit by bit, at a time when traditional assumptions about that world are being rejected. Consequently, Cubism emphasizes the "*process* of perceiving and conceiving of reality" (Steiner, 525; my emphasis). No one view of this reality has hegemony, which leads to the style's "polyperspectivism." The consequent absence of stable space in painting has a temporal analogue in Futurist verse. The very epithet chosen by the literary group emphasizes their aspiration to push language beyond its borders, its present form and significance, as the Metaphysicals strove to drive their contradictory experience into their recently discovered realms of infinity. As a result, the "present is experienced in the future and vice versa," a "round trip in time" (I.P. Smirnov, 338).

A recent collection of theses and materials published in Moscow considers similar analogies, this time at the other end of the Soviet Union, at the collapse of Socialist Realism. As Baroque elements were discerned prior to a "New Classicism" in the 1930s, so once again in the present. This leads one commentator to link the fleeting passage of time which informs contemporary, "Baroque" ornamentation to an awareness of man's reduced agency in temporal (specifically agricultural) cycles and the celebratory aspects of the transient, yet recurring *dies festus* (Molon and Ricci, 34). Another researcher links the Baroque eighteenth-century poet Deržavin to the twentieth-century prosaist Sokolov in their similar attempts to exercise a sense of linguistic liberty in the face of the "burden" of historical processes. As these processes become linked more concretely with the arrival and passing of specific periods of constraint or specific regimes, so ostentatious display is repeatedly linked to anxiety at their emergence and celebration at their disappearance. The Baroque *homo ludens* is equated with the *homo politicus* (Benčič, 8). What can be said about contemporary "play" and politics to support this?

A Recent Semiotic Parallel

This contemporary variant of the Baroque, towards which Russian literature may be projecting itself, has been perceived by the Italian semiotician Omar Calabrese as a cultural phenomenon already realized in the West. The inhuman speed with which information now traverses both space and time, and the concomitant sense of disorder, leads Calabrese to define a contemporary Neo-Baroque in opposition to all things classical (15). The former is characterized by "organized variation, polycentrism ..., regulated irregularity, and frantic rhythm" (43). The breakneck speed with which cultural phenomena are thrust upon the perceiver, and then exchanged for other variants, is at first associated with a joyous state, similar to the liberation of seventeenth-century literature: "[The reader] is invited to take pleasure in the sense of vertigo, and in the inability to make decisions about the roles and characteristics of the protagonist that this provokes. The reader, in other words, is practically asked to abandon himself in delerium to the metamorphoses and instability of what is being narrated" (108). The sense of joy, however, is contingent upon an ability to rediscover order, which will allow the Baroque elements to remain a game, a temporary "letting go" by the *homo ludens*. Calabrese maintains that the letting go can, sooner or later, become a desperate chasing after variation which takes place in an avoidance of a looming, inevitable state of entropy:

"The subject, in fact, *knows* of the existence of a residue in the definition of [his] being, but *cannot* express it. And this disequilibrium generates passion. The subject is ... *suspended* between the tension created by two different modalities – for example, between *wanting to know* and *not being able to know,* or between *not wanting to know* and *having to know*" (160; my emphasis).

The problem specific to the late twentieth century, in Russia or elsewhere, is that the mix of self-perpetuating variety and the speed of traffic on the information superhighway leads to a suspicion that "everything has already been said, everything has already been written." If one suspects that art is fast approaching some entropic state, the only way to postpone it is by playing on the ever-diminishing number of variations. Though Calabrese notes that the "pleasure" of artistic creation is derived from "tiny variation[s]" (44), it reduces the number of potential future variations or novelties each time it acts one out. Details and fragments are constantly rearranged as new works, as ever more frantic configurations before which the reader must surrender rationality if he or she is to find some sense of cohesion in the text. The term "pleasure," then, is ironic, as each work of art pushes art as a whole one step further towards a dead-end. The dizziness of freedom goes hand-in-hand with fear as to where it will lead.

A Recent Sociological Parallel

The unavoidable union of power and impotence is also central to a recent study of post-traditional society by Anthony Giddens (1991). As the "new science" of the seventeenth century brought man unnervingly close to the overwhelming aspects of bigger space (new lands, new planets) and longer time (infinity), so the science of the twentieth century means that authoritative events in a global sphere are constantly impinging upon the local. Because centres of such authority are multiplied and themselves constantly challenged, both governance and a stable sense of self are therefore empirical projects attempted between the local and the global, in a relationship of "reflexivity," the "chronic potential revision" of authoritative information. The consequent multiplicity of choices produces existential anxiety over a self-identity that cannot be rationally controlled or caused. One's sense of self is gradually lost to grander processes. "Fear of loss [then] generates effort" (41), the same fear that inspired the increased extravagance of Baroque art.

I.P. Smirnov, comparing the Baroque and 1920s Futurism, saw some common ground between the former movement and fear caused by an inability to distinguish between personal cause and general effect. Giddens sees a similar fear in our late twentieth-century, post-traditional environment: "Human history is created by intentional activities but is not an intended project; it persistently eludes efforts to bring it under conscious direction. However, such attempts are continually made by human beings, who operate under the threat and promise that they are the only creatures who make their 'history' in cognizance of that fact ... I am the author of many things I do not intend to do, and may not want to bring about, but none the less *do*" (Giddens, 1984: 27, 9).

An existential responsibility is the cause of unending concern. To reject any responsibility to oneself is, as in the Baroque, to surrender to a fatalistic outlook. Fatalism is an admission by finitude of its impotence in the face of the infinite; the modern relationship between transience and permanence, between empiricism and determinism, that inspires fatalism is as follows. The finite life of the individual is usually perceived as a linear, empirically understood path. Day-to-day experience, however, is seen as cyclical repetition, as is the *longue durée* of what might be termed institutional time – or, for our purposes, what can be seen as the repetition of generic cycles. Daily routine is by its very nature repetitive. Institutional time, akin to that of tradition, works in the same way, but on a grander scale. Between the two circles is the straight, unrepeatable, irreversible line of the individual's life. Day-to-day and institutional time are reversible, but the life of the individual is not – hence the possibility of equating irreversibilty and ephemerality with anxiety.

THE ISSUE OF POST-SOVIET AESTHETICS

After drawing parallels between seventeenth- and early twentieth-century culture, it remains to bring such attempts up to the present, to the culture of the fading Soviet Union. The famous equation of Soviet Socialist Realism with neo-Classicism by Abram Tertz (i.e., Sinyavsky) is extremely useful here as a starting-point; he suggests that artists unconsciously revive the traditions of their grandfathers, leap-frogging their parents in the process (Tertz, 71). In his ironic role as advocate of one of these traditions, Socialist Realism, Tertz dismisses the anarchic arm-waving of individualism as something antithetical to the "great harmony" of the multitude, which is always close at hand (53). Marxist teleology, whilst admitting that this harmonious goal may not be attainable in the immediate future, nonetheless insists upon its proximity. It is both permanently visible to the initiated and opposed to the ambiguities facing an empirical approach to the future. All moves centripetally towards "the Purpose": "Each work of Socialist Realism, even before it appears, is thus assured of a happy ending" (44). The centrifugal aspects of the early Baroque, the release of individuals from an over-arching ideology, are here reversed.

Only with the death of Stalin, the personification of the Purpose, did dreaded revisionism, the ability to challenge axiomatic Soviet teleology, emerge. Past periods of Russian history were re-examined, leading to more "elastic" interpretations of their lessons. The coordinates, according to which Soviet history was projected towards the Purpose, were questioned. It seemed that so much information had been falsified in the name of the Soviet goal that the very nature of human beings was distorted. The unfamiliar freedoms of revisionism during the post-Stalinist thaw produced not only the rewriting of such distortions, but a simultaneous feeling of guilt at years of silence. The poets born during the 1930s needed to chart a new course, their verse acting as something of an existential travelogue on their way out of that silence. They met the new dimensions of freedom with "youthful verve, their greater willingness to experiment and *go to extremes*" (D. Brown, 107; my emphasis). Soviet short prose produced at the same time talks of a loss of direction: "Characters ...

drift about the country without personal or family ties, changing jobs frequently, driven by a wanderlust whose motivation is not clearly specified ... The general characteristics of these protagonists ... were a degree of restlessness and bewilderment, a lack of self-confidence ..., uncertainty and apprehension about the future" (211, 214). The poetry of the postwar generation was thus released from teleological security into great anxiety, a Baroque state of disillusionment. The pretensions of Soviet ideology towards a grand imperial permanence are mocked in a retrospective, witty poem by Alexej Cvetkov, published in 1985: "From podiums they swore allegiance repeatedly trumpeted / make an effort and time will be no mo." (The word "more" is cut short.)

From the earliest hints of self-determination in the verse of Boris Sluckij, cast as the (Baroque) metaphor of a battle against fate, expressions of a happy freedom are possible to find. However, if we take one such expression of the "joy of freedom ... with no anxiety, sermonizing or lies" in the verse of Vladimir Kornilov, contradictory statements compete in the same poet's work. He waited for freedom for "so many lengthy years, to the point of pain and shaking," but now that freedom has come, he declares "I'm not ready" (cited in G. Smith, 1993: 48). In his poem *Youthful Verse* of 1987, Kornilov says that the lyre may now be freer, but it stands alone in the world and it is more frightened. Abram Tertz's positive hero, who could make out the socialist goal on the road ahead, is replaced by a poet who "strains his hearing" before the end of the world and cries out his loneliness.

Evgenij Rejn, often referred to as Brodsky's mentor, even by Brodsky himself, makes frequent reference in his own verse to a temporal circularity, one which epitomizes the occasional tendency towards fatalism in the work of his generation. The metaphor of a railroad appears more than once, stressing both the inability to deviate from the rails and the fact that a train is obliged to return its point of origin (Rejn, 1990: 44, 74). Choice vanishes in a chain of fleeting seasons. What does manage to emerge from Tertz's "great harmony" is referred to as a savage, clambering out from architectural rubble, or the rambling decoration of jazz (50, 58).

I referred earlier to Rembrandt's *Night Watch* as indicative of the Baroque extension of art beyond its frame or borders, in the merging of real and fictitious space. Rejn's poem of the same name inverts the typical associations of Baroque and disorder. In an atmosphere of demonic possession and pentagrams, he emphasizes the triumph of order. Rejn sees the guards of the painting as stepping forth into a demonic cycle of state surveillance, as it "was yesterday, it is today and soon will be..." (Smith, ed., 1993: 80). Aleksandr Kušner takes the pessimistic view that repetitive "history punishes us, it doesn't instruct, it punishes" (114). He feels that happier poems were written in the days when "everything hindered us" (118). So what of freedom? Kušner in the title poem of his 1966 collection *The Night Watch* juxtaposes the military with the creative potential of the artistic. The poem relates directly to Rembrandt's painting. It dramatizes the dialogue of a captain with another soldier on the "night watch," just as Rembrandt's painting centres on the words spoken between Captain Frans Banning Cocq and another soldier. Kušner's soldier lets out an expression of wonder at the artist's miraculous work at night. Answering the captain's question as to "who isn't extinguishing his light after dark," the soldier is apparently talking of his creator (i.e., the painter) beyond the painting's frame or "walls": "Truth to tell, you won't know, / Having looked from all sides / If we are the night guard / In these walls, or if it is he."

The problems surrounding creative potential in the work of more recent poets have been noted by Mikhail Epstein: "The new poetry arouses in the reader a feeling of aesthetic unease, a loss of orientation .... The fundamental absence of any center, which used to be associated with the lyric 'I.'" Reactions to the true release of Soviet constraints in the last several years find expression in the opposition of two schools: Conceptualism and Metarealism. The former tendency is fascinated with the way that language became semantically exhausted through Soviet propaganda, through serving the Purpose alone. Now, attempts at writing are beset with "self-repetition and tautologies," as well as "tongue-tiedness ..., the alter-ego of grandiloquence" (Johnson and Ashby, ed., 279, 275). Existential aspirations are negated, since the semantics of the Russian language are not the property of the individual, but fossilized in the dead end of their Soviet usage. Such a situation forms one half of a neo-Rococo; everything has been said. The other half is creation through re-ordering, through ornate variations of pre-existing elements. Indeed, Epstein likens the position of a modern conceptualist Russian poet to that of a humble compiler, or composer.

As for Metarealism, it aims at wanton complexity, at frantic citation, likened to a macaronic Postmodernism. Sources of importance, not surprisingly, include the Baroque. Erstwhile Soviet attempts to halt time were cited in Cvetkov's poem; now there is a sense of time rushing by, because such attempts have been abandoned: "This generation, spiritually formed under the conditions of historical stagnation, cannot help but feel the *retarded flow of time* and respond with a heightened sensitivity in the *eternal, recurring situations of being*" (282, my emphases).

In the broadest possible terms, then, contemporary artists find themselves assessed by outsiders as reeling and floundering in an uncertain present. They are victims of a rasterjannost', translated by one journalist as "perplexity, confusion, with a tinge of losing one's head" (Goldberg, A12). Disillusionment comes from the removal of ontological security and the move towards existential anxiety as Soviet tradition evanesces. The resulting new and diverse authorities are themselves constantly usurped. The primary means by which information is now transmitted is visual, and the speed of its transmission and change to a large degree underlies both Calabrese's understanding of the neo-Baroque and poet Nina Iskrenko's investigation of the "acceleration" of perception: "Traditional static perception is perhaps no longer enough. We need an increase in perceptual dexterity and Gestalt-like speed" (Calabrese, 130).

CONCLUSIONS

Why do contemporary artists appeal to an earlier period for vindication or legitimization, specifically to the Baroque? A good place to start is Dmitrij Lixačev's reductionist theory of art's eternally recurring primary and secondary styles, based as it is upon the same opposing dilemmas of the self: unification versus fragmentation, (existential) powerlessness versus (potential) appropriation, authority versus uncertainty. Lixačev sees art history as organized in opposing pairs: Renaissance with Baroque, Classicism with Romanticism, for example. The former are primary styles, the latter secondary, the characteristics of secondary styles being irrationality and decorativeness. Social upheavals constantly produce new pairs, a process which has been repeating ever faster. Primary styles are created (*sozdannyj*); secondary styles are the transformed or reorganized (*preobrazovannyj*) versions of older ones. I am not offering Lixačev's view as one to which I myself subscribe, but its simplicity can at least be married to a brief explanation of the psychology of retrospection: why a past style is invoked and the way in which the invocation of a past style can cultivate a false sense of inescapable generic cycles.

Greater cultural status should be assigned to the primary styles, where, for example, the individual is belittled by the great harmony of Socialist Realism. For the secondary styles to mean anything to the dominant primary styles, they must realize that to mean is to be understood, and that there is no understanding without evaluation (Vološinov, 103, and Bakhtin, 181). The reception, or evaluation, of each style helps to constitute its meaning together with the intention of its producer. Any change in style, for example from primary to secondary, is a deviation, a re-evaluation. The meaning of such a deviation is therefore a negotiated process of speaker intent and hearer receipt. The producer of a statement – Baroque or any other – wants not only that "his actions be unimpeded by others," but also that "his wants be desirable to at least some others" (Brown and Levinson, 62).

What happens next is as follows. Continuing the analogy of dialogical meaning with actual dialogue, the situation starts to reflect the structure of adjacency pairs. These are discursive structures which consist of a first half (request, offer, assessment, etc.) and must be immediately attended to in the discourse with one of two second halves (acceptance or refusal, agreement or disagreement). When the speaker takes the floor to produce the first half, he tries as hard as possible to guarantee the second half he wants. If he is interrupted or finds his agency diminished by the hearer, there occurs a process of greater expressiveness, a verbal equivalent of aesthetic extravagance. This process is called upgrading.

To lose the floor to a subsequent speaker is to lose all influence or agency in the creation of meaning. The loss of agency is the loss of the capability to exercise power. Diminished agency provokes a particular response: "The threat of personal meaninglessness is ordinarily held at bay because routinised activities, in combination with basic trust, sustain ontological security" (Giddens, 1991: 202). The deviant member of the secondary style therefore turns back, as Lixačev says, to that with which he thinks he has an affinity and can therefore enjoy a sense of both solidarity and security. The charcteristics of "high modernity" are similar enough to the seventeenth-century context to make the Baroque an attractive reference point. This not only offers the security of membership, but simultaneously invokes a cyclical impression of genres, styles, and so on. What happens can be termed traditionalization, "an act of authentication, akin to the art or antique dealer's authentication of an object by tracing its provenience" (Bauman, 137).

Meaning is therefore caught in what Vološinov calls "the dialectal generative process" produced by the interplay between subjective intention and objective context, by Giddens's combination of the linear life span of the individual, which is irreversible, and its relationship to reversible institutional time – that is, history, tradition, and so forth. The former always tries to manifest its fleeting presence in the face of the latter. However, because the individual's "actions and works are the product of a *modus operandi* of which he is not the producer and has no conscious mastery, they contain an 'objective intention,' as the Scholastics put it, which always outruns his conscious intentions ... It is because subjects do not, strictly speaking, know what they are

doing, that what they do has more meaning than they know" (Bourdieu, 1977: 79).

Joseph Brodsky's corpus constitutes an attempt to develop a sense
of genuine self-determination in the face of history and tradition's
modus operandi, an attempt that is inspired by the seventeenth-century
poetry of John Donne, and then develops in an analogous fashion to
the processes outlined in this chapter. Brodsky's poetry traces a trajectory from a pre-Baroque (or metaphysical) balance to Baroque imbal-
ance to a Précieux recodification. Within each stage one sees the
workings of historical allusions that connect that particular period to
its typological analogue in the historical Baroque.

2 Kierkegaard and Šestov: Affinities and Influence in Brodsky's Pre-Exile Verse, 1957–1972

Pierre Bourdieu's observations quoted at the close of the preceding chapter do not bode well for free will: "The product of history produces individual and collective practices, and hence history, in accordance with the schemes engendered by history" (1977: 82). Bourdieu maintains that situational constraints generate claims to self-determination which can only ever be realized *within* such constraints. As a result, agents reject what was always impossible and try to justify the inevitable as choice. In his prose and poetry Joseph Brodsky attempts to escape these constraints and develop a sense of genuine self-determination; his literary innovation gradually becomes a faith in language as the means by which freedom is achieved. This faith in innovation's ability to assist in self-realization can be explained as an extension of my arguments concerning the problematic exit from "tradition."

In literature, the competition between attempted innovation and the constraints of tradition is a competition between realities. The arguments in literature over what is true and false are negotiations over the form or character that life takes, over what things *are*; unfortunately, they often become unyielding codifications of reality. The danger of such rigidity exists because when even the most innovative prosaist or poet fashions a new, subjective experience of reality, he works in the same language as those before him. By rejecting an old movement or genre, then, "new" literature becomes an empirical experience of "old" language, a radical reassessment or even a re-creation of reality from existing elements; for Brodsky, it is less a new theology than a new cosmogony that emerges in the process of writing (LTO, 203). Literature becomes the personal task or challenge of constructing something qualitatively new, a truly idiosyncratic or personal faith, not just the modification of an accepted or codified belief system. Even in Brodsky's earliest verse this word- or world-building instigates a growing importance of language, to the status of "deity," as the poet would later admit.

BRODSKY, KIERKEGAARD, AND ŠESTOV

The idea of language as deity will become increasingly important as Brodsky's work progresses. Between 1957 and 1972 much of this progression is attributable to the work of two philosophers: Søren Kierkegaard (1813–55) and Lev Šestov (1866–1938), whom he read close to the time that he encountered the poetry of John Donne. The existentialism of these two men acts as a complement to the influence of the Metaphysical poets, yet no study has been undertaken of how the two philosophers both instigate and clarify Brodsky's teleological progress, nor of how the poet radically re-fashions some of their basic tenets in a manner which is integral to the development of a Baroque aesthetic. Only passing reference has been made to the influence of Kierkegaard and Šestov, hence the following brief introductions, which will begin a comparison of the seventeenth-century Metaphysical poets and nineteenth- or twentieth-century existentialism. In this way the stage will be set for a discussion of Brodsky's earliest work.

Kierkegaard and Nietzsche are the theological and secular precursors of twentieth-century existentialism. The former thinker aims in essence at a rejection of rigidly systematic philosophy. In place of Hegel's objective system of thesis, antithesis, and synthesis, for example, Kierkegaard suggests that truth lies within subjectivity, an empirical development or personal *telos* which can be directed by individual choice. Life's endless choices constitute a dialectic between two world views; the psychic and the pneumatic. The psychic world sees spirit as soul, at one with the tangible, the visible, and the static. It is associated with ancient Greek culture, rigidity, and stasis. The pneumatic view reveals spirit as spirit, in a spoken, literally dialogical and dynamic relationship with the concrete world; it underlies a true Judeo-Christian *Weltanschauung*, because a spoken word can effect a promise or commitment to a Christian teleology. Thus might one's word mature as per the dialogue of material and spiritual which is inherent in the Word.

Any talk of a psychic view invokes the prototypical example of Plotinus (c. 205–70 AD) and his original negation of physicality in favour of the Psyche, a worldview which not only stands in immobile and silent opposition to the physically uttered dialogue of spirit and flesh of a pneumatic *Weltanschauung*, but is also akin to the seventeenth-century split between flesh and spirit in Cartesian dualism, itself a forerunner of any model of psychic exile such as those so often applied to Brodsky's experience. Psychic dualism marks the rational, logical demise of seventeenth-century faith and it is a disconcertingly inevitable state which Brodsky, Kierkegaard, and their witty, Metaphysical forerunners aim to avoid.

The psychic is always an attractive option, though, because it is less risky than the pneumatic, less frightening. A recent analysis of Kierkegaard's applicability to our own age has not only linked the psychic view to (neo)classical aesthetics, but also to a safe haven to which one might return if scared by existential responsibility in the absence of an idealist system, which could be either Hegelian or Marxist. This is the safe option in the face of the existential task of the three stages which constitute Kierkegaard's ideal, subjective *telos*: the aesthetic, the ethical, and finally the religious. The aesthetic individual is dizzy with freedom; he revels in the constant variety of transient sensations, of new phenomena. Since, however, each moment is just that, a moment with no connection to those before or after it, the aesthete is literally hopeless – he can neither plan nor predict anything. He despairs of his tedious life, bound to the world, to what is tangible. He needs to choose something and therefore make an ethical decision, with which he actively submits to the universal dictates of duty, of right and wrong. The declaration to enter the second stage requires the choosing agent to sacrifice some of his agency to ethics, to rules which require everyone to behave the same way. He *says* he will choose the next stage of his life, an act which supports Wittgenstein's view that forms of saying are forms of life: "Modalities of existence – i.e., the aesthetic, the ethical, and the religious – are ultimately modalities of saying" (Hall, 74).

Here there is a parallel with Brodsky's contention that linguistic aesthetics is the mother of ethics (SS1, 19). For Kierkegaard, however, poetry and the poet are often an aesthetic phenomenon, beyond which the spirit might develop. The differences between the two men and their attitude to language is clearer from the third stage, prior to which lies humour, juxtaposed with irony. Whereas irony is born of fear of accepting responsibility for the importance of one's words, humour admits the limits of rational possibility. It is based upon an awareness of man's limitations in the finite, upon the knowledge that what is humorous is unlikely, irrational or absurd. Prior to man's leap into the irrational realm of the religious, humour is an indication of things to come: "By its help ... we can achieve some consciousness of the conflict between time and eternity, and have as it were a presentiment of the paradox and the absurd" (Jolivet, 146).

Faith is an absurdity, its object cannot be logically proven, nor can the freedom which it offers, hence the leap into the unknown which it demands fills the rational, ethical mind with horror. As Abraham had to move beyond ethics to prove his faith to God in his readiness to slay Isaac, so the modern individual must also conceive of a "teleological suspension of the ethical." The leap into faith is made with a freedom that is only granted *after* the leap – an ethically inexplicable situation. Freedom is therefore inextricably bound with necessity; freedom must be surrendered in the faith that it will be regained on a higher plane, but the faith is not truly known until after the surrender.

Each stage is therefore a challenge; if the individual chooses to leap into the next stage, then he has successfully completed the trial of the previous one. Each is a finite exercise as he moves towards a closer relationship with the infinite: "Since a trial is *temporary* it is *eo ipso* qualified by relation to time and must be done away with in time" (SK, 1964: 116). Each is completely isolated, self-contained from the other stages which may lie before or after it. It is therefore impossible to talk of mere development from one stage to another. After the leap to a higher stage "the individual regularly begins anew" (SK, 1957: 26), starting the next, higher one all over again from scratch, even though it is to a large degree a repetition of the last one.

The individual tries to complete the repetition of another stage when he surrenders his subjectivity once more to the unknown, to the dreadful leap. Once the leap is successful, his subjectivity, his life as "the consciousness or thinking or perceiving subject or ego," is returned to him at the very beginning of the next task. Subjectivity is both returned and situated one stage higher, hence Kierkegaard's amazement: "Did I not receive myself again, and precisely in such a way that I must feel doubly the significance of it?" (1964, 14–15). Brodsky surrenders to (or leaps into) language via poetry, in order to gain a revelatory experience, be returned to himself at a higher, revelatory level. Paradoxical though it may sound, the teleology of Kierkegaard's personal, subjective repetition becomes the means of escaping historical repetition – that is, cyclical history, the predictable, objective systems such as Hegel's. The fact that Brodsky's repetition is based upon the linguistic interaction of the agent and patient, self and other, finite and infinite, means that the whole idea of personal repetition is often expressed in terms of a dialogue, ideally with an otherworldly "other." With the addressee's response, or return of the poet's word, a potentially ideal dialogue would begin, either between the poet's faith and the horrors of its loss in an abyss, or later between the opposites which must be held together in faith, such as the finite and infinite, or the human word and the divine Word.

Kierkegaard demands that the individual live (or speak) a similar union of the earthbound and divine, "a contemporaneity with Christ." He must use Christ as the model of his own existence. The life of Christ is an expression of God positing divine content in material form, which the eathbound believer sees as a guarantee of his own ability to use physical form as a vessel for the spiritual. The spiritual and infinite therefore need the physical and finite, but the latter pair first considers and then wills its own demise by entering into a dialogue with spatio-temporal dimensions beyond its abilities or ken. One must begin the dialogue, however, and attempt paradoxically to unify its two halves in imitation of Christ, a unity that has its own inevitable, Golgotha-bound teleology. Yet not only is the God/Man himself the greatest paradox – that of the Logos – but self-willed martyrdom for one's faith is undoubtedly "a kind of usurpation of the rights of God" (Jolivet, 84). Growing faith is growing proximity to God, but to consider or even believe this is absolute arrogance and sacrilege. One therefore sins if one rejects contemporaneity (if one refuses to model one's life on Christ's) and one sins if one accepts it. The awful challenge of faith to the individual, of the infinite to the finite, of the intangible to the tangible, is familiar from the story of Baroque aesthetics. The either/or of one's decision to escape from the aesthetic stage into the ethical is a choice made above a bottomless abyss, the black, perspectiveless expanse of Caravaggio's chiaroscuro. Only by the Kiekegaardian leap into an irrational, Rubensesque disorder and by future, repeated submission to divine magnitude can one avoid the mathematical stasis of a Poussin.

Kierkegaard himself comes late in life to see his own Protestantism as arrogant "worldliness from beginning to end" (Dru, 1938: 1379), which "produced a fundamental confusion in Christianity." Awe before God leads him to consider surrendering arrogant Lutheran individualism to anonymity in Catholicism, a leap some believe he would have taken had he lived longer. Thus Kierkegaard's own passage of faith recapitulates that of the Baroque age whilst trying to avoid its reasonable and logical descent from a dizzying altitude, a descent with an undoubtable air of failure about it.

Kierkegaard believes that if personal repetition fails, if the offence that faith does to reason is not overcome and one does not make the dreadful leap away from finite subjectivity in order to regain it in faith, then one succumbs to "levelling." Levelling is a mathematically determinable, entropic state caused by no individual choosing to rise in faith, a state that "has its profound importance in the ascendancy of the [temporal] category 'generation' over the category 'individuality'" (SK, 1978: 84). It is here that one can connect the repetition of the individual with that of history. The "fear and trembling" of the individual has a counterpart in public spheres. Panic at the realization of one's reduced agency led in the seventeenth century to a gravitation towards Cartesian determinism, as if to excuse one's cowardice by declaring the omnipotence of what was rational; with Kierkegaard in the nineteenth century, too, shying away from faith means submitting, as many do, to the creation of rational schema in which one tries to justify the inevitable as choice. Kierkegaard sees the "public" as the embodiment of levelling, stuck perhaps in the aesthetic stage or in the wilful submission to the rational dicta of (neo)classicism: "If I were to imagine this public as a person ..., I most likely would think of one of the Roman emperors, an imposing, well-fed figure suffering from boredom" (1978, 94). If one accepts an assessment of Marxism as a materialist interpretation of the Hegelian dialectic, one can equate the Roman levelling that Kierkegaard aims to escape with the rigid marxist context of Brodsky's youth.

Kierkegaard's kindred spirit, Lev Šestov, also tries to escape idealism and embrace existentialism. His escape is related to the dialogue between two essential tendencies; Apollo and Dionysius, which in turn help to explain both the reasons for the Fall and the hope for man's salvation. The salvation of faith is explained as supremely irrational, to the point of having absolutely nothing to do with the inherently logical tendencies of philosophy.

In the early 1960s Brodsky discovers the Jewish anti-rationalist philosopher Lev Šestov. Like Kierkegaard, Šestov rejects Hegel; he is also opposed to Spinoza's extension of Descartes to logical extremes. Before he breaks away from idealism and develops an affinity with (or even hears of) Kierkegaard, though, in 1911 Šestov publishes *Shakespeare and his Critic Brandes*. In this book, the young Russian deems Hamlet's tragedy necessary for the growth of the human spirit. Šestov then shuns necessity by turning to Nietzsche, but by accepting the latter's views on *amor fati* he flinches before the rigours of individual responsibility, and once again briefly champions inevitability before finally embracing existentialism in earnest.

Whilst reading Nietzsche, Šestov writes on both Tolstoj and Dostoevskij. The two writers are interpreted through the prism of Nietzsche's distinction between Apollo (order, rules, and containment) and Dionysius (disorder and centrifugal movement). This distinction has affinities with Kierkegaard's opposition of Greek/Judeo-Christian world views, of closed/open systems. The former is a static, given state;

the latter is constantly "becoming," and therefore much closer to an existential creation of self. It is fitting that Brodsky reads Šestov at the beginning of the 1960s during his internal exile. It is at this time also that he comes upon a ten-volume collected works of Dostoevskij.

Šestov soon feels that the rational spirit, that of Apollo, is tied to the Fall. Knowledge has tempted man to turn freedom into rational, "eternal, necessary and uncreated truths," to fall back on the security offered by wilful submission to the Grand Inquisitor, Dostoevskij's embodiment of absolute negation. In Kierkegaardian terms, purely rational knowledge is ultimately faithless and can only speed up the levelling process. Šestov opts instead to seek God over the existential abyss of irrationality. Belief, as for Kierkegaard, is the task of the individual and is not to be relayed to others under the banner of communal knowledge; in any case, a clear explanation of faith's paradoxes would be rationalistic and unavoidably dogmatic. In complete isolation the individual must scrutinize the abyss, the intangible unknown, as closely as possible – in a manner akin to the seventeenth-century new science. Šestov does not aim to bring mathematics to bear upon the chaos that the scrutiny reveals. He braces himself for the leap. "A true artist must not cover over the 'horrors' of life. On the contrary, he must stare into them as intently as possible; the deeper his gaze, the greater the meaning with which it will be filled" (Erofeev, 1975: 159).

Šestov's own faith is eventually separated altogether from the arrogance of philosophers' jiggery-pokery, a separation explicit in the title of his book *Afiny i Ierusalim*; Athens represents philosophy and reason, neither of which have anything to do with Jerusalem or faith. The ultimate inability to make the leap from philosophy into divinity, however, from Athens to Jerusalem, means that faith remains ever-elusive due to its inherent paradoxes; for Šestov it is beyond both language and thought, because the "passion of faith" resides, unavoidably, "where thought leaves off" (Patterson, 1978: 151). He often feels unable to conquer transience by effecting a Kierkegaardian repetition of the self, or a return to the eternal "now" of God.

AN INTRODUCTION TO BRODSKY'S EARLIEST VERSE

Kierkegaard's parallel with Brodsky's thematics is most obvious in Brodsky's 1963 poem, *Isaac and Abraham*, written the same year as his *Great Elegy to John Donne*. The poet's love and admiration for the Dane are expressed most clearly amidst recollections of meeting W.H. Auden in 1972: "I was overjoyed to learn one day about his [Auden's] devotion to the Kierkegaardian triad, which for many of us too was the key to the human species ... One can build a lot upon W.H. Auden. Not only because he died at twice the age of Christ or because of Kierkegaard's principle of repetition. He simply served an infinity greater than we normally reckon with" (LTO, 377, 381). The influence of this Kierkegaardian infinity is first cultivated as an antidote to internal exile and grows until 1972, the year of Brodsky's expulsion from the Soviet Union. One must, however, talk initially of philosophical affinities rather than influence, until after *Isaac and Abraham*. Within the initial period, from 1957 to early 1964, it helps to separate the first few years when Brodsky shows concerns inherent to the lowly aesthetic stage. Here begins the ascent through Kierkegaard's triad. Until 1961 there are affinities with problems of human transience and cyclical history, quintessential aesthetic problems in Kierkegaard's first stage. After the poem *The Procession* (*Šestvie*) of that year, the remaining time until 1971 shows the tension surrounding an individual in the second, ethical stage, desperate to make the leap of faith. The year 1971 marks the final year of the poet's life in the Soviet Union and the point at which written, empirical approaches to reality are in a dead-end. The resulting desperation marks the start of the poet's Baroque period.

1957–1960: THE CONCERNS OF THE AESTHETIC STAGE

In correspondence with Professor J.L. Heiberg, Kierkegaard argues over whether repetition concerns history or the individual (SK, 1964, 10). With regard to the seasons' changes, for example, Kierkegaard says in a footnote to the *Concept of Dread* that "in the sphere of nature repetition exists in its immovable necessity," which must be transformed by the individual "into something *inward*, into the proper task of freedom" (1957, 17). In Kierkegaard's mind the very necessity of biological cycles contradicts freedom or existence, which is based upon choice. Šestov also holds that the study of evolution will teach one nothing, since evolution is predictable over the time frame of a single observer's brief life (just enough time to see a natural cycle or two completed) and necessary in that it is simply a logical reflection or product of environment (Šestov, 1929: 155).

In the poems prior to 1962, Brodsky's own free will often vanishes in seasonal cycles. The four seasons of the year are associated with the four seasons of life, after which one dies "on the wing in some fifth dimension" (SS1, 74). In *Three Chapters* (*Tri glavy*, 1961) yet another holiday season becomes the "measure of time," while life is reduced further still in one section of the poem *Peterburgskij roman*, tellingly called "Seasons of the Year" (*Vremena goda*, 71), to "no more than [one such] season," to a late Fall. Wishes are plucked away, like new foliage; both foliage and fate are dragged down by the "great gravity of disintegration" in the poem *The Garden*. Traces of love vanish amidst the smell of wilted flowers and "August lovers" drop their blooms as they surrender to another love, to a "new circle."

Often unable to adopt a goal or movement, Brodsky is literally objectified by cyclical time, just as those buried in a Jewish cemetery learn that life is "inescapably material." They pray for rest and get it "in the form of material's disintegration." Objectified in seasonal repetition, their corpses lie as "seeds in the cold earth." In the 1958 poem *Petuxi*, cockerels find seeds buried in fertilizer at dawn. Brodsky puns when he says that in the birds' recurring, celebratory croaking he sees the "matter of time" (*materija vremeni*) that they discovered: *materija* can also mean both physical substance and topic, as well as textile or material, hence, perhaps, the idea of the fabric of time.

Kierkegaard writes of the anaesthetizing effect of recurring time. One becomes addicted to the "uniform dripping of rain upon the roof, the uniform whirring of a spinning wheel and the monotonous sound of a man passing back and forth with measured steps on the floor above" (SK, 1987a: 170–1). Brodsky, too, admits the attraction of the past's warmth over the coldness of the future, and it is therefore ironic that he considers escaping the garden by train, a motif used at times to suggest a surrender to repetitive, cyclical motion by which means we "overcome ourselves." The wheels of fate are also associated with those of a train, and elsewhere suggest the repetition of old problems, at times to the point of oblivion. Trolley lines and circling embankments recall the "inclination of pious people to repeat one and the same phrase." In *Description of a Morning* (*Opisanie utra*, 1960), a tram's early passengers become mere "generalized images of the morning" borne along by the tram's repetitive movement. To jump ship (or train), therefore, becomes an existential act of enormous consequence: "To leap from the train / and run to the bay, / run to the bay / in a horizontal landscape / falling, drowning."

To break the circle is not to wait stoically "with lowered head for a bus and the age" (SS1, 65), but to project oneself out on a lonely and undetermined course. Stoicism is acceptance of necessity truths; apriorism has "short roads" which are "strewn with compromises." The longer, empirical road is a lonely one, on which the "expenses of the spirit are the shrieks of the intellect and logic." The poem called *Loneliness* (*Odinočestvo*, 28–9) sees in such solitude the ability to at least question all logical assumptions, but the process can reveal an abyss of doubt beneath the individual: " you can / ponder eternity / and doubt the imaculateness / of ideas, hypotheses, perceptions / of works of art / and – incidentally – the very conception / by the Madonna of the Son, Jesus."

The theme of isolated, ostracized faith is clearest in Brodsky's *Poem on the Spaniard Miguel Serveto, a Heretic, Burned by Calvinists* (ss1, 32–3). Servetus's earthbound and empirical research was considered subversive enough by systemitized, ecclesiastical doctrinism that it earned him a lifetime's persecution and led to his death in 1553 in Switzerland. His Christological views are of interest here, as to some degree they parallel the later relationship of man and the word in Brodsky's verse. Servetus held that the Son is constituted of Jesus as man and the Word, God's own expression of Himself. In the words of R.L. Bainton: "Before His incarnation He was called the Word. After His union with the man Jesus, He was called the Son. The Word, therefore, was eternal. The Son was not eternal." Servetus, by means of Christ's example, was able to show that "man can be taken up into God and share with Him the life eternal" in a harmonious union of the finite and the infinite, of man and the Word (Bainton, 48–9).

Brodsky notes that one of Servetus's fields of inquiry was the human circulatory system. The circulation of blood, returning as ever to the point of its origin, was one of the areas of empirical discovery in which the very idea of circular, repetitious perfection meant (ironically) that it was still seen as proof of the cyclical worldview of the past, much as Brodsky's empiricism is (as yet) bound by a recurring past.

The problems for Servetus in Brodsky's poem, however, are twofold. His first problem is that contemplation of things divine is virtually impossible for a man who spends his whole life hunted by others (*vsju žizn' uxodil / ot pogoni*), which forces his gaze to be fixed on the road rather than on an icon, as Brodsky puts it. The second problem, if such it can be called, is that Servetus is actually depicted as a man who loves the pragmatic, purely empirical aspects of his study rather than the way in which such studies reveal or explain anything divine (i.e., humbling) to him: "[He] did not turn his gaze to the sky. / The earth was dearer to him. / He studied the law of Man in Saragossa / and Man's circulatory system in Paris."

Whether Brodsky depicts him as closer to Earth or Heaven, Servetus and his investigation of the dual nature of the Saviour are made more personal in *Verbs* (*Glagoly*, 1960). The poem discusses the Word made flesh, its link with the poet's word. Verbs are born in cellars, says the poet, several floors beneath "universal optimism" (ss1, 41); in their daily routine verbs raise monuments to their solitude and head for Golgotha. They are nailed in the past, future, and present tenses.

Language, in its demarcation and manipulation (creation, even) of time becomes unmanageable; the finite speaker cannot grapple with ineffable eternity or divinity. He and his words therefore (in "good" faith!) work paradoxically to their own end. Isolation from universal optimism is a state that Brodsky will later find validated by Šestov, a state in opposition to social ideals and progress (š, 1971: 51). Kierkegaard even equates a individual's greatness with necessarily forced isolation, the torture of not being able to "run with the herd." "Perhaps his demention has nothing whatsoever to do with his real genius but is the pain by which he is nailed out in isolation – and he must be isolated if he is to be great; and no man can freely isolate himself; he must be compelled if it is to be a serious matter" (Auden, 1963: 97–8).

If the isolation of faith is reflected in language, then surely one can not "talk with the herd" either. The isolation of choice words – laconicism – must be closer to piety; Kierkegaard at least sees a parallel between lapsed faith and loquacity: "Christianity teaches that at the Day of Judgment a man must give account of every idle word he has spoken" (SK, 1957: 136) and Brodsky himself will later see the judgment of art as even more demanding than the Final Judgment (LTO, 264). But for now, if the creation of a personal *telos* outside of seasonal repetition is a linguistic, existential project, then much needs to be said or written. The subject of too many idle words, of complete banality constitutes the poem *The Procession*.

1961: THE BANAL EXTREME OF THE AESTHETIC STAGE

Šestvie was written in Leningrad in September, October, and November of 1961, as a "*poèma*/mystery play, in two parts/acts and in forty-two chapters/scenes" (SS1, 95). The idea of the poem is to offer "personifications of conceptions about the world, and in this sense it is an anthem to the banal." Banality is represented as a fleeting procession of "conventional characters," the structure of which owes much to Axmatova's *Poem without a Hero* and Cvetaeva's *Ratcatcher*, based on the tale of the Pied Piper. The procession consists of those who, not unlike rodents, fall in "by chance" – a "sad choir of passions," though not in the highest, religious sense. Kierkegaard sees chance or "fortune, misfortune, fate, immediate enthusiasm and despair" as indicative of immobility in the bottom, aesthetic part of the triad, where passivity overrides existential responsibility (SK, 1968: 388). Individual faces vanish in this Russian procession and any serious talk of change is merely followed by a dash for a (cylical?) tram. Brodsky's poem is a dark look at this procession of fleeting, "aesthetic," or aspiring "ethical" philosophizers, offering profundities as they go.

Brodsky divides the procession of "scatterbrains" into a large number of romances, which are introduced and followed by commentaries, written by a person who watches the procession and simultaneously writes the poem. He often makes the procession humorous; humour lies between the ethical and the religious, as the (absurd) extreme of reality. His dual experience of real and written time, however, makes him a participant as much as an observer of the procession – an ironic situation, irony being lower on Kierkegaard's scale, since it is a means of undermining the ethical consequences of one's words. *Šestvie* ends the period of aesthetic concerns. It is the peak of tensions between being led far and holding back. It pre-empts Brodsky's bold acceptance of the ethical responsibility to oneself in a Kierkegaardian *telos*. Three of the characters in the procession are fundamental to the writings of Šestov and Kierkegaard: Don Quixote, Prince Myškin, and Hamlet.

First is Don Quixote, a figure considered by Kierkegaard in his *Stages on Life's Way* to be close to insanity in his aimless wanderings, to a spiritual state of great danger, especially if it is indicative of a more widespread malaise: "To populate the whole of Spain with knights errant" would be "verily *delerium furibundum*" (sk, 1940: 366). Later, in his *Concluding Unscientific Postscript*, Kierkegaard attributes the knight's downfall to an arrogant desire for "world-historic significance," instead of the acceptance of a personal *telos*. Elsewhere he is called the "prototype for subjective madness, in which the passion of inwardness embraces a particular finite fixed idea" (1968, 125, 175). Brodsky's knight sees all his power and possessions in his spear, wealth denied even a rich man. His peculiar headgear becomes an "angelic crown," but despite his pretensions to divine purpose, the sober commentary says his romance is actually humorous, especially in an age where "courage is humorous, and fear is amusing." As Don Quixote and the procession's amusing display are channelled into the constraints of a geometrical, St Petersburg street, so the knight's quest is equated with stepping out into an empty prospect. Perhaps scared by a sudden, mathematically precise view to the dead-end of perspective, he slips into the nearest pub.

Brodsky's romance depicts the knight and his spear in life-long battle against an elusive evil (*neujazvimoe zlo*), a tale which is soon to reach its denouement. Cervantes's novel describes the knight's life as essentially linear; the Russian poet turns this linear movement around corners, into the threat of a street's dead-end perspective, which recalls the Spanish novelist's view that our one-way existence should oblige us to address infinity, because this life "is ever racing to its end ... without hope of renewal, unless in the next."

Brodsky's *Šestvie* is a text that describes an apparently forward movement, yet in actual fact it is aimless – a mindlessly repetitive circle born of linearity without a *telos*. Don Quixote, himself a lover of masquerades since his youth, encounters many processions over the course of his novelistic wanderings, and tries gradually to compose a spiritual life-story away from such unthinking circularity. This circularity can be either temporal or textual, because he becomes so famous that he has to battle the inevitability of what others have written about his legendary present and anticipated future in the utterly predictable forms of chivalric romances. In fighting this evil inevitability, Cervantes's and Brodsky's heroes both liken a knight's lance to a pen and the battles ahead to writing. The problems, though, of a written battle are that Brodsky's evil is elusive and Cervantes's heroine (whose virtue Don Quixote champions) does not even exist, leaving the poet and knight trying to describe invisible or ineffable good and evil.

Brodsky and Cervantes pit Quixote's physical prowess with a lance or quill against fate in the creation of a new, written belief; Cervantes says that the lance and pen help each other to preach such a faith. Kierkegaard, who on many occasion refers to an ideal believer as a "knight of faith," says however that such belief cannot be transmitted or preached because it is too subjective. Don Quixote's life takes place well beneath the religious stage, then, on the very terrestrial level of an ultimately unsuccessful sermon on chivalric virtue. His attempts at a knightly religiosity (or, more accurately, the popular novels on which his attempts are modelled) are often likened to the sacrilege of a new, sublunary belief. These attempts at a true faith bind Don Quixote and Sancho Panza to each other; the spiritual, centrifugal. and nomadic knight sets out on a written, unorthodox journey with an earthbound, fleshy, and centripetal partner. The knight always wants to go on, but Sancho always wants to go home. Nevertheless, the two men need each other, just as Don Quixote and the man who tells their tale were also made for each other; these are dialogical relationships that surprise other characters and readers with their equality or symmetry – for example, the audacious frequency with which the squire interrupts his master.

Don Quixote passes by Brodsky's narrator during the first month of September. As the first participants turn the corner, it is soon October, when foliage falls, and Prince Myškin from *The Idiot* passes by. Šestov sees him as a complete aberration in Dostoevskij's works, full of "brazen sanctimony" (*bespardonnaja svjatost'*) and "offensive banality" (š, 1922: 49 and 73). Myškin is a mask, not a man – a suitable role for a masquerade. Brodsky unmasks his sanctimony through a parodic use of the word passion (*strast'*), to downgrade its spiritual connotations; syntactic parallelism is used to equate even love and murder. Myškin's romance begins with the entrance of his carriage and ends with his flight for the rest of his life. Between them lie the love(s) and murder of Dostoevskij's novel. The masquerade of his life is a state of perpetual, aimless transience. The humorous failure of Quixote's nomadic dialogue of flesh and spirit becomes deathly serious in Myškin. The synonymy of love and murder leaves Brodsky's prince slipping in a pool of blood (*poskol'znis' … vo krovi ljubimoj*), an apparently direct reference to Dostoevskij's novel. Myškin has a tendency to slip during fits of epileptic passion and at one point falls and lies in a pool of his own blood.

Both Myškin and his grotesque reflection in Ippolit feel excluded from life's endless feast (*pir*) or festivities (*prazdnik*) in Dostoevskij's world, since they are constantly prone to morose thoughts; Brodsky's romance refers to their sad thoughts (*gorestnye mysli*). Myškin's moroseness is caused specifically by thoughts that muddle the ethical dialogue of good and bad, physical and spiritual passions. Just as Quixote's words become aimless when he tries to define chivalry, so Ippolit and Myškin are frustrated by faith's ineffability, which makes their sentences jumbled and purposeless. Don Quixote's linguistic ramblings reflect physical ones; each of *The Idiot*'s four major sections opens with talk of railways or sea travel. Myškin, unlike Quixote, though, cannot even communicate his ideas; he is unable to fulfill an ethical task of preaching, let alone a religious one.

What of the Prince of Denmark? Šestov writes in his later work that *Hamlet* created philosophical problems which snowballed for Shakespeare until the playwright's death (š, 1971; 92), problems of existential agency which exist in moments of crisis. Kierkegaard, though, feels that Shakespeare stopped just short of the dread that Abraham experienced, what he calls elsewhere the playwright's avoidance of "genuinely religious collisions" (1973, 258). Nevertheless, Kierkegaard still sees *Hamlet* as a religious drama and draws parallels between seventeenth-century and contemporary spiritual crises, through the example of the hero's morbid reflection. He is no doubt thinking of Hamlet's soliloquy in act 3, scene 1, in which "the native hue of resolution / Is sicklied o'er with the pale cast of thought."

In the introductory paragraph to *Šestvie*, Brodsky suggests that for "other directions" (*nastavlenija*), one should follow the same act of *Hamlet*. It has no important stage directions to speak of, so presumably the reference is to the directions Hamlet gives to the players for the enactment of his dramatization of the king's death, that they should "o'erstep not the modesty of nature." Here Hamlet, just as Quixote, is both director of his own little play and a passive character in another's play, a mere product of Shakespeare's quill. Brodsky also shows the dynamic interaction of Hamlet's existential agency with his passivity (as Shakespeare's creation) at the same moment of morbid reflection: "To not be or to be! Some empty phrase. / Here all is as the heavens wished ... Is it far to the end, WILLIAM SHAKESPEARE? / Is it far to the end, milord?" (SS1, 147).

Hamlet's reflection is referred to in *The Idiot*, when Lebedev deems "to be or not to be" as *the* contemporary question. Shakespeare is suggested in Cervantes, too; Don Quixote praises the procession of figures across any theatre's stage as an accurate mirror of both pretence and true virtue in a way that recalls Hamlet's instructions to the players that they "hold, as t'were, the mirror up to nature; to show virtue her own feature." Over and above such hints, the clearest literary link between any two members of the Quixote/ Myškin/ Hamlet triad is perhaps Ivan Turgenev's essay of 1860 which compares the first and third of them. Šestov himself praises Turgenev's essay as remarkable (*zamečatel'nyj*) in his own collection, *Načala i koncy*, highlighting Turgenev's final observation that all is transient, save good deeds. In this essay, Turgenev insists on the need for any potentially successful existence to join the polar opposites of Hamlet's analytical, introspective centripetal tendencies and Don Quixote's centrifugal comic enthusiasm. The tension between these two tendencies can easily produce insanity, such as the madness (*bezum'e*) of Brodsky's Hamlet – caught between Denmark and England, finite life and infinite death, freedom and fate. But the tension must be first invoked and then withstood if faith is to survive.

Brodsky has turned our attention to Hamlet's own stage directions within Shakespeare's play, to "suit the action to the word, and the word to the action." From this point onwards, the poet's word escapes concerns of transience, of cyclical or processional movement; it moves into existential action, out of the aesthetic stage and into the ethical. The horrors of non-existence have been faced, and from here onwards the precious nature of a private faith is defined relative to such an abyss, in a dialectal relationship with it.

1962: THE CHOICE OF THE ETHICAL

It is in 1962, the year prior to Brodsky's true Kierkegaardian project, *Isaac and Abraham*, that the poet finally confronts the abyss of aesthetic passivity before fate, which is epitomized by the procession. The value of Brodsky's solitary faith now starts to be defined in a perpetual dialogical relationship with the abyss; the poet is trying to avoid the non-commital approach to one's belief that Kierkegaard calls feeble and infrequent "Sunday glimpses into eternity" (SK, 1968: 415–16). In its repeated choices to confront, then rise above, the aesthetic, Brodsky's life now reflects Kierkegaard's belief that a true *telos* is based on a never-ending either/or. It is a rational choice between good and bad, and therefore an ethical choice. The year 1962 marks the start of ethical stage, which ends in 1972. Faith is a common topic in this period, but is overwhelmed by an increasing sense of fear and trembling, before the adoption of the truly religious, Baroque stage in 1972.

To transcend the aesthetic stage and come to terms with the presence of the abyss is a good, rational, and ethical choice. If, however, Brodsky is not to lose himself in what is good or bad for everyone (and therefore fall under universal and inflexible ethical dictates), he must move on towards personal faith by successfully completing the ethical stage. This stage consists of the gradual investment in the dialogical structure of the either/or with opposites inherent in faith: finite/infinite, physical/spiritual. Faith, though, does not now choose between them, but paradoxically involves them both, above the abyss. It is not so much a matter of either/or as both/and. The ability to juggle them both gets harder, to the point where the spiritual task demanded of the physical believer is completely irrational. Then and only then will it be time to make the irrational leap from the transient into the purely religious stage.

Belief begins to be structured from here on as an open-ended, unpredictable, life-affirming dialogue. Without the fear of losing itself in the abyss, faith becomes arrogant and opinionated, because it senses no opposing opinion; it thinks (wrongly) that it can survive unchallenged and be preached to others as a successful system. The result is a static, predictable, systematized monologue. The genuine growth of one's faith, therefore, is guaranteed only when one sees the constant potential for its collapse. As Brodsky himself says:

> And so I flew above the satin stratus,
> Above a splendid depth, and claimed that only
> This plunging isolation is what matters,
> Whilst feeling, as before, that I am homeless.
>
> A lifetime full of naught but deprivation
> Should not be sought with bitterest persistence.
> One's homeland corresponds to foreign nations
> The way dead-ends relate to spatial distance.* (SS1, 188)

The poem *Zof'ja* has a similar approach to abyssal dimensions. It closes with the challenge to "become a pendulum," to involve the opposites of flesh and soul, sin and passion. Discursive, dialectical, and dialogical structures are reflected in Brodsky's verse in 1962, including the literal structuring of a poem as a conversation. Since the poet's spirit is now "united in two faces," poems depict the interaction of two horses (as "anguish and peace"), of guilt's "light" in the dark, of life as high hills and death as level land. The earlier, cyclical trains and trams can now be replaced at times by a "new correspondence of the soul," the horn of a bus shuttling between two towns. Happiness is now the "luxury of two; woe is a democrat" and two people at opposite ends of a park bench create an equal sign between them (ss1, 188–241).

Through the dialogue between such opposites, one nears the eventual surrender of rational self-preservation in the choice to leap into the religious stage. The surrender parallels a quote taken by Šestov from Matthew 10:39, "he that loseth his life for my sake shall find it," itself reflected in the Baroque dictate of losing oneself in order to find oneself. In surrendering to the irrational (which the logical structures of ethics cannot express), one will leap forward. The subject of the irrational leap, resulting from such dialogical structures, can cast light upon the poem which closes the first period of the poet's work and which has been called a "senseless going round in circles," "absolutely monotonous" (Švarc, 1992: 225), "long-winded, ... incomprehensible," and overly didactic (Kublanovskij, 1992: 201; Kolker, 1991: 100).

THE PROBLEMATIC LEAP
FROM THE ETHICAL INTO THE RELIGIOUS

Isaac and Abraham (*Isaak i Avraam*; ss1, 268–83) is Brodsky's initial serious treatment of the Bible. The poem was written just days after reading Genesis for the first time. It is a fifteen-page account of God's request to Abraham that he offer his son Isaac as a sacrifice as a test of faith. Abraham proves his readiness, but an angel stays his hand at the last moment, and a sacrificial ram is revealed in a nearby thicket. Father and son go to Beersheba, a resting place for the nomad patriarchs, where Abraham plants a grove in God's name.

The episode is also the core material for Kierkegaard's *Fear and Trembling*, in which Abraham's faith is described as the epitome of paradox, of the willingness to lose everything in order that everything be regained. The four issues examined by Kierkegaard in Abraham's preparation for the leap of faith are uppermost in Brodsky's work thus far. The terms used to define them come from D.F. Swenson, as quoted by W. Lowrie in the introduction to *Fear and Trembling* and *The Sickness unto Death*: first, the "particularity" of the finite individual's relationship, in isolation, to the infinite; secondly, the "infinite resignation" of one's rationally conceived agency to greater forces; thirdly, the "double movement of the spirit" which follows one's resignation, the regaining of all that one has lost; and finally, the "teleological suspension of the ethical," the need for one to suspend rational notions of righteous self-determination in the finite in order that one's *telos* be realized through an irrational leap into the Absolute.

The narrative in Brodsky's poem develops these emphases. Abraham and Isaac move across seas of sand, beneath which lies the earth, though it is hard to believe so. The darkness around Abraham and Isaac as night falls is bottomless, making a fall (or Fall) possible. The desert offers "no firm objects anywhere"; grains of sand are likened to broken thoughts or phrases, all of which suggests that self-realization in the wilderness is an existential task, effected linguistically above an abyss and with spiritual analogies. The two men approach an empty horizon, which means "their goal is near"; Kierkegaard says that until life-choices are made, eternity remains like a wide horizon or like going forth, whilst actually going nowhere. Abraham must therefore enter into a dialogue with the Absolute, by choosing to sacrifice his son. The story of Abraham's sacrifice is shown through the transformations undergone by three words: the poem shows how a finite, physical object (bush or *kust*) relates to the infinite and spiritual (cross or *krest*) vis-à-vis the inscribing or "sacrificial stabbing" of a tablet or *doska*.

Isaac, en route to the sacrificial site, passes by a bush (*kust*); it whispers to him. Veins can be seen within the bush, but despite appearances, it is "not like the body, but like the soul." It frees itself from its roots and is described to the reader through an iconic interpretation of the letters that make up the word *KUST* (*КУСТ*): "*K* like a branch, *У* is stronger still, / Only *C* and *T* are in some other world." This other world comes to Isaac in a dream, in the night of a bottomless darkness. First of all, the last letter, *T*, becomes an altar, and then *C* or a lamb in fetters. The last two letters now work backwards, as it were, to create a second word. In other words, the letters of *КУСТ*, under the influence of the act of faith on the altar (*T*), together with the sacrificial victim (*C*) form the new word *KREST* (in Russian *КРЕСТ*, cross). The existential return is here represented by a return reading, from *K* to *T*, then from *T* back to *K*, and the wood of the bush becomes that of the cross.

After the father's faith has been proven and the angel declares "let's return now" (*teper' pojdem obratno*) because the test is over, Isaac's own name (*ИСААК*) is also explained, through the same iconic interpretation. *И* is a union (*sojuz*, and therefore also a grammatical "conjunction"); *A* is a deathly wail; both are joined to *C* and *K*, to the lamb and the bush, or *Agnus Dei*, perhaps – Isaac has been connected with Christ's sufferings once or twice before. "AmId the flameS Again the victim Cries: / that's what 'ISAAC' means in Russian." (*I Snova žertvA na ogne Kričit: / vot to, čto "ISAAK" po-russki značit*). The representations of Isaac and the bush are followed by that of a board (*doska*), cracked like the bush and into which a knife is plunged. If we make allowances for a voiced T (*T*) becoming D (*Д*) then we have a word based upon the same consonants. Abraham shows his readiness to merge knife and flesh and pleases the angel with his risk. Once he is ready to leap, a sort of imperative takes over, when one must choose "what one cannot not choose" (Jolivet, 101). The same is true of the board; as it is cut, the knife is in "someone's power." It "serves two masters: the hand and the board." In other words, the leap, though freely willed, is ultimately a submission of free will. Here the elevation of the sacrificial victim to a higher spiritual status is recorded in language, as a changed word. The word is just as strong as he who aims to merge it with the power of Abraham's knife – or with the pen.

The entrance (*vxod*) for the knife to pierce the board is blocked by a metaphorical wall (*stenka*). This refers to the nature of "absurd," trans-rational faith, the wall of "two times two" and other so-called universal truths that stifle human will with their *a priori* authority. Rational constraints mean fixed, unalterable values, which means that the ethical sphere still has precedence over the religious. In that case, Abraham's act is viewed ethically; it is simply a foiled murder. Faith, or the ability of the knife to enter the board and instigate transformations such as KUST into KREST is possible only through the "teleological *suspension* of the ethical," by forgetting what seems to be logically explicable as right or wrong. Not only does the knife change the victim into something holy, but he who did the sacrificial act now begins a dialogue with the Absolute. When the bush of heaven blooms, after Abraham's hand is stayed, the angel tells him to answer it (*on ždet, čtob ty otvetil*). Before his ability to enter into such dialogues, Abraham began the poem as if deaf, "screened off by a wall."

The poem, however, ends on a pessimistic note, in an extended passage concerning the tongue (*jazyk*) of a candle's flame, a source of light connected earlier to Isaac and the bush. A candle burns, locked up in a house which seems, through heavy rain, to be under water and surrounded by jellyfish. The sad ending of *Isaac and Abraham* shows the difference between merely *describing* the leap of another man and actually *doing it oneself* to escape from seasonal, botanical cycles or any other levelling system. There is a world of difference between describing and doing, and so the poet remains in the ethical stage: "Having forgotten about what might be called salvation, / the candle's very tongue of flame / quivers above it and awaits the end in the night, / as a summer leaf in an empty autumn forest."

1 9 6 4 – 1 9 6 5 :   I N T E R N A L   E X I L E

The Realization of Limitless Choice

The period prior to Brodsky's arrest and internal exile, epitomized by *Isaac and Abraham*, shows a great awareness of potential existential agency, of choice, but it is exactly that enormous potential which seems so frightening. The period of exile continues this worry with such clarity that to see exile as some sort of terrible breach is rather inappropriate. The time of exile, from February 1964 to November 1965, is usually defined as one of great suffering, borne with stoic acceptance. Rather than stoicism, the very core of a Kierkegaardian world view lies in isolation and a freely willed construction of one's subjective teleology. The period of exile cultivates a sense of greater freedom which becomes increasingly difficult to deal with.

Brodsky is a rather poor source for maudlin quotes on the nature of exile. "My exile in the north was very good for me," he says; "perhaps because of some turn in my character, I decided to get the most out of it" (Birkerts, 1982: 100). At his trial he made the oft-quoted remark that his gift for verse came from God, a remark which should be joined to an observation in 1988 that exile leaves one with "oneself and one's own language, with nobody or nothing in between." He also saw himself, though it may sound presumptuous, as "a carrier of the language." In isolation, then, one's relationship with the Absolute (the Word) is through an absolute relationship with language (the word). Brodsky's move to faith is a freely chosen, written project and is re-chosen with every new text.

He says that his life has been a continuum, not punctuated by exile, that geography does not influence the content of a poem. The term of exile is a continuation of beliefs the poet already held, and their development over the time when he was with fourteen other people, "completely lost in bogs up there in the north" (Birkerts, 1982: 98). For not fulfilling the duties of a Soviet citizen, a Leningrad court sentenced Brodsky "to a distant locality for a period of five years of enforced labour." In arguing that Brodsky continues to juggle paradoxical opposites en route to faith, it is logical to use the same four areas central to Kierkegaard's *Fear and Trembling*: particularity or the absence of intermediaries in one's relationship with the absolute; infinite resignation of the finite in the process of leaping into the unknown; double movement or repetition; and finally, the teleological suspension of the ethical. All four areas overlap in one poem in particular, *K severnomu kraju* (1964). Particularity is discussed first; isolation and the overwhelming sense of existential freedom which it produced, the freedom to surrender freedom in the dreadful leap into faith.

Particularity

Particularity is to a large degree synonymous with solitude or isolation. Far in the distance, the horizon that defines Brodsky's place of exile says "not one word [to him] about escape" (ss1, 337); the pain of a one-way conversation is aggravated by the additional lack of a real, human interlocutor. The poet is very much alone (*sil'no odinok*); but just weeks after his arrest in this "place of dying," his tongue moves once more, as he puts it, since the Russian iamb is as stubborn and bright as the finest lamp. At the close of 1964, the iamb is still "pulsating and ticking," having "extended his age." The isolation of the poet with his iambs is a situation paradoxically worsened by writing. The more one writes, the greater one's faith, which by Kierkegaard's and Šestov's reckoning is in direct proportion to one's solitude.

The poet's solitude or isolation in the cell's "concrete space" of "swarms of lines and a crowd of rhombi" first makes him sweat. Greater, existential concerns predominate, however; "the field widens from its offensive captivity" (*nevol'ja*), since Brodsky now tries to escape constraints on the horizontal plane by the "altimeter of pride." In fact he questions the calendrical notion of time that constitutes imprisonment, since the lonely "exile of a singer" has nothing to do with the calculation of the "length of an epoch." Indeed, as a dauntingly isolated and (as yet) flightless cockerel he cannot join the calendar's reassuring and regular "trains of song-birds" migrating.

If there is one effect that exile has on Brodsky, it is the frightening awareness of Kierkegaard's particularity, of a solitary boundless potentiality, allowing no easy acceptance of common beliefs or *a priori* truths. In 1965, almost all of which was spent in exile, the body ironically sees "no limit to its movements"; in September, Brodsky sees no lessons to be learned directly from teachers, angels or even God. One wonders, though, if the poet sometimes slips into Sartre's "bad faith," the attempt to submit to imagined constraints upon one's freedom or progression in order to gain some relief or rest. In the poem *Kurs akcij*, for example, a *closed circle* of smoke relieves him of anxiety and power, and Brodsky declares his love for inanimate objects, which were for Sartre enviable in their completeness, with no existential hollowness to be filled up with empirical discoveries and no need for any resignation or surrender to the unknown.

Resignation

Resignation in the period of exile is often equated with a plunge into darkness, into an emptiness that may turn out to be horribly empty. In moments of subsequent squeamishness, night is unconvincingly dismissed as nothing more than the persistence of the past in the present. At night, extinguished candles look like a "new Parthenon," a classical stasis that can overwhelm existential progression, because the past (darkness) can, thinks the poet, at times be stronger than the future (a candle). Both passion and faith, however, need the past, just as a flame needs the night; faith needs the horrors of a potentially godless abyss in order to avoid complacency and systemization. Through empty spaces such as snow and water, now is the time for the poet to "plunge, especially with my mouth," into the abyss reflected on a daily basis in the depths of puddles standing guard around him.

The theme of water, a common metaphor in Brodsky's work for absolute time, develops in exile. Time runs ahead of the poet like a river, which explains why a brook in another poem "excites the tongue." At the sea, he likens passion to the foam of the breakers; just as passion is born of the interaction of soul and body, so where absolute time (sea) meets the land (earthbound, calendrical time) an impressive display is produced. In fact Brodsky asks to be remembered at the sight of waves. Waves are just the edge of what one must surrender to, though; upon T.S. Eliot's death in 1965 Brodsky describes the waves of Eliot's verse as now subsumed in his link with Heaven via the whole Atlantic Ocean. Brodsky himself dreams of resigning to the sea (of living beneath it), to a place beyond sound, even. He cannot do so in reality. He has "poured sounds on the waves in vain," and so the rationale of the ethical stage predominates.

In the absence of water, wind is invoked as a supra-individual dimension, since it helps branches "triumph over space" by carrying leaves everywhere. Brodsky begs it to blow harder and "pierce [birds on the wing] with a fleshless arrow." The poet cannot resign himself to an arrow's point, though; earthbound roots grab his feet. As a result, absolute time and absolute emptiness get mixed up, the "empyrean or abyss," angels and snow. He cannot make the free choice to resign to either. As he says, winter may seem nice and white, but do not get completely undressed. Such limitlessness can make (linguistic) repetition very difficult.

The Double Movement, or Repetition

If the leap and the return to subjectivity after the leap are somehow to be attempted, it is via language, via the dialogue with the Absolute. The poet's progress, though, is impeded between "what has passed and the future, the interval between Voice and Echo." His frustrated attempts at a perfect dialogue or at fixing an addressee in the realm of the Absolute even make him confuse his actual female interlocutor (M. Basmanova) with the Virgin Mary. Consequently, one poem considers reproaching God for the lack of response; elsewhere the poet suggests that perhaps God Himself has lost His way. Brodsky now doubts that his soul will ever reach a high style, space, or God. The pain of expectation leads instead to hopes for linguistic repetition after one's lifetime (by naming one's children Andrej or Anna to repeat language once again *ab ovo*).

Just as the heavens are deaf to the rustle of leaves, the frustrations of a one-way dialogue can force human language to fall prey to seasonal repetition, the predictability of which signifies little more than silence; only April awakens passion and the noise of the branches. To shun the spoken commitments and uttered choices that create progress towards Kierkegaardian repetitions, though, in favour of the transient or cyclical, is to offer the Devil a Faustian prayer that a beautiful moment stay. Brodsky, therefore, has no right to silence. But to whom does he talk if the light (of faith) has faltered, if the heavens really *are* deaf? He knows his speech is not a madman's monologue. It is only in isolation, in his own echo that there lies hope for a great joy, to move forward from the disarray of A to the hope of B and so forth, convincing himself that he is in the interval between two stages and not off to one side.

The Failed Teleological Suspension of the Ethical

On that hesitant note, it comes as no surprise that Kierkegaard's fourth category, the teleological suspension of the ethical, the acceptance of faith's illogical absurdities, is virtually non-existent here. It will come later in Brodsky's work, with the irrational leap into the religious stage. The very nature of exile, as official disapproval of wrongdoing, seems at first to make writing an unavoidably ethical act, a challenge to official right and wrong. This period as one of challenge to accepted views seems best summarized by the enormous cast of characters and addressees of the poem *Letter in a Bottle* (*Pis'mo v butylke*), written in November 1964 (SS1, 362–70). It is written as a letter in a bottle thrown from the wreck of a nomadic ship (or poet) which has run aground.

Brodsky's singular, maritime wanderings in this poem are likened to Errol Flynn's pirate in *Against all Flags* (Kline, 1973a: 114). Previously wary of being wrecked, the poet, shown as Ulysses, had brandished a pistol, to shoot at tempting sirens. Now, however, he curses those like wandering St Francis, no doubt because the poet is himself shipwrecked following his own nomadism in the wilderness. Time is

the sea which dashed his ship, and since Brodsky often equates pros-
ody's rhythms with the structuring of time, these waves are also repre-
sentative of speech. In other words, speech (or poetry) has carried the
poet away from where he wanted to go, overtaking his own swashbuck-
ling bravado. His route had been mapped out on a vector, but the
vector's projection across space also overtook the man who mapped
it out. So, after a few, freely chosen coordinates (or words) that plot
the early stages of the poet's teleology, a disconcerting, future path
starts to map itself out, independent of the poet's will.

Despite being surrounded by rapacious whales, the poet says goodbye to the safety of several rational certainties, as he sails into the *grand
peut-être* (*Velikoe Možet Byt'*, 367). He says goodbye to Archimedes,
perhaps because of his law of displacement, which accounts rationally
for the ship being afloat. Newton and Kepler are dreamed of but then
dismissed as indicative of a deep sleep, no doubt for their work on a
mechanical universe, examined through Kepler's telescopes. Kant and
Feuerbach are out, the latter having bridged the thought of Hegel
and Marx – and Marx himself is rejected. Freud, perhaps for preju-
dicing body over spirit or for making one a prisoner of childhood
experiences, is sent a fond farewell, as are several others, including
Faraday, whose research led to the radio – that is, to guaranteed
communication. God may be Brodsky's pilot (*locman*), but since the
poet is still sleeping soundly, he confuses his higher destination with
a female addressee, describing her body as the shoreline. These problems of waking up to the demands of the leap are clearest in this poem
To the North (*K severnomu kraju*).

1 Северный край, укрой.
И поглубже. В лесу.
Как смолу под корой,
спрячь под веком слезу.
И оставь лишь зрачок,
словно хвойный пучок,
на грядущие дни.
И страну заслони.

2 Нет, не волнуйся зря:
я превращусь в глухаря,
и, как перья, на крылья мне лягут
листья календаря.
Или спрячусь, как лис,
от человеческих лиц,
от собачьего хора,
от двуствольных глазниц.

1 Cover me, northern spheres.
In the woods. Under wraps.
Take this eyelid; hide tears
as the bark conceals sap.
Leave the iris behind
as bunched needles on pines
for the days up ahead.
Keep the country well hid.

2 No, do not pointlessly fuss:
I will turn into a grouse,
my wings graced with plumes
that the paper calendar-page allows.
Or I'll turn into a fox,
far from humanity's looks,
from eyes' two-barrelled sockets
far from carolling dogs.

3 Спрячь и зажми мне рот!
  Пусть при взгляде вперед
  мне ничего не встретить,
  кроме желтых болот.
  В их купели сырой
  от взоров нескромных скрой
  след, если след оставлю,
  и в трясину зарой.

3 Hide me, and keep me hushed!
  Let my glance not meet much
  on its way forward – nothing
  more than yellowish marsh.
  If I leave them, hide footprints in its water-logged font,
  far from immodest glances,
  bury them deep in a pond.

4 Не мой черед умолкать.
  Но пора окликать
  только тех, кто не станет
  облака упрекать
  в красноте, в тесноте.
  Пора брести в темноте,
  вторя песней без слов
  частоколу стволов.

4 It's not my time to be mute.
  But the time to salute
  those alone, by whom cloud banks
  will not soon be rebuked
  as too red, or compact.
  It's time to roam in the black,
  with my wordless songs, played
  down a tree-trunk stockade.

5 Так шуми же себе
  в судебной своей судьбе
  над моей головою,
  присужденной тебе,
  но только рукой (плеча)
  дай мне воды (ручья)
  зачерпнуть, чтоб я понял,
  что только жизнь – ничья.

5 Turn your bluster, instead,
  within you, above my head,
  now adjudged to you, heeding
  what's judicially writ.
  Grant waters to scoop (the brook)
  with a hand (in its crook),
  so life's freedom from tenure
  will not be overlooked.

6 Не перечь, не порочь.
  Новых гроз не пророчь.
  Оглянись, если сможешь –
  так и уходят прочь:
  идут сквозь толпу людей,
  потом - вдоль рек и полей,
  потом сквозь леса и горы,
  все быстрей. Все быстрей.

6 Don't deny, do not slight.
  Don't envision new plights:
  Just glance back, if you're able,
  so they soon take to flight –
  They'll move along fields and rills
  then through the forests and hills,
  having breached a crowd of people,
  faster still. Faster still.*

Given that this poem illustrates a breaking away from the cyclical
romances of *Šestvie*, it is interesting that *K severnomu kraju* plays with
an anapestic dimeter – the meter of romances – up to its breaking-
point in the final stanza. The meter is broken, just as the poem's final
phrases describe an accelerating trajectory or tangent, an unrepeating
movement away from processional cycles. If this escape from *Šestvie* is
to be effected via an existential dialectic, it is also fitting that the six
stanzas of *K severnomu kraju* can be clearly divided into two distinct

sections on the basis of the rhyme schemes. Each three-stanza unit repeats a particular supra-stanzaic pattern: an opening stanza (1, 4) with one rhyme scheme is followed by two stanzas (2, 3; 5, 6) which share another.

The dialectic, the either/or, is expressed as dialogue. Just as the title itself, *K severnomu kraju*, can be read both as movement "To[wards] the North" and words "Dedicated [i.e., Spoken] to the North," so the interaction of movement in exile with language is central to the poem as a whole. *K severnomu kraju* is in essence three calls to the northern expanses of exile to hide the poet (1), shut him up (3) and finally roar relentlessly above the poet's head (5). These three strophes are interrupted by statements of personal intent by Brodsky: he will act like a grouse or fox (2), wander in the dark and *not* shut up (4). Stanzas 4 and 5 are much bolder than those of the poem's first half; the either/or of the poem is therefore not just a dialogue between Brodsky's alternating utterances to the North and then to himself, but also a process of increasing bravery, such that the second half of the poem is markedly more self-assured than the first. The closing section considers the nature of this bravery.

K severnomu kraju opens with Brodsky's demand for isolation, to be hidden deep in the forest, such that concealment will increase the value of what is concealed; life-giving sap hidden by bark, a tear (or lens) hidden by an eyelid. The poet is reduced to a crystalline lens, destined for future days. The shift in emphasis from strict, spatial containment to time, to what is evergreen (*xvojnyj*), is made possible in the first stanza's pun: *stranu zasloni*. In this phrase are the meanings "[Please, North] protect the area [where I am hidden]" and the non-patriotic "Push the nation into the background." Any emphasis on politically or geographically specific space, on exile in the *strana*, is overcome by the limitlessness of where the poet is, a limitlessness visually sensed and one that soon suggests other infinite dimensions.

In the face of boundlessness, the second stanza tries to begin decisively. The teleological demands that exile have produced allow for a potential victory by language over space, including the space of the human body. In the poem, the overcoming of space (in time's favour) by resigning to what language can do will be shown by space's reduction, by irrationally metamorphosing into a more humble, lesser state. The whole Baroque nature of Brodsky's faith will subsequently be based upon such metamorphoses. Brodsky here considers changing into a diminutive, bestial state of a grouse or fox; the shift from a proud, aesthetic stage to an attempted suspension of the rational thinking that underlies the ethical is a risky one, since the leap would indeed be into irrational or unknown dimensions.

The unknowable risk of faith is expressed in two ways: first, the change from the proud, decisive first-person declaration that I will turn into something else, to the third person of the grouse or the fox. It is exactly this shift, of necessarily giving up the self that causes the dispersal of lyric unity from *ja* to several objects; the dispersal, however, is a reflection of faith's success, of a simultaneously increasing psychic cohesion as the religious stage is approached via numerous humbling metamorphoses. The inherent risk is in reducing one's self before infinite dimensions (from first to third person) whilst not being completely objectified or erased by them. Hence the second expression of faith's risk – the believer as prey; in this poem Brodsky will become one of two hunted animals, a game-bird or fox.

The reduction of space in favour of time, done by language in a state of particularity, is described as the feathering of a grouse with calendar-pages, as time enabling flight. The bird might be caught by "double-barrelled eye-sockets" though. Brodsky therefore describes a resignation to one of two types of future, both undivineable ahead of time; resignation to that which would "feather" him (*mne ljagut/ list'ja*) and endow him with flight, or resignation to the malicious gaze of the double-barrelled scrutiny of an opposing, negative force. He cannot know in advance towards which of the two he is moving – or being moved.

Brodsky uses the limitless spaces of exile to overcome space and at least contemplate the risky leap into what may be either revelatory or destructive. Not surprisingly, the prospect is daunting enough for the poet to ask that he be forced to treat his position as a poet should treat exile – as punishment or as a time to shut up and not put one's finite existence on the line by toying either with infinite, metaphysical dimensions or with a Soviet empire's crude aspirations to the same permanence. Brodsky asks that the way ahead be made easy, with no obstacles and the chance to hide in the damp font of yellow bogs. Faith is not a refuge, though. If the poet is to gain anything, to experience repetition after reducing space, he must take the irrational decision to open his mouth and move ahead.

The decision opens part two of *K severnomu kraju*; the dialectic of part one's either/or brings him to the bold contemplation of the leap. "It is not my turn to fall silent," he says, "it is time to wander in the darkness." The eye's silent contemplation of nothingness works together with the mouth's invocation of it in order to progress; Brodsky says he echoes the fence of tree-trunks by means of/with (his own) song which is without words – with the music or rhythm of his gait perhaps. Whether one takes *stvol* here as tree-trunk or gun barrel, the view of some partial, arboreal, or armed enclosure (the latter being metaphorical, not literal) suggests a musical staff made of rhythmical horizontal and vertical lines – the perceived constraints that enable the music of the poet, the restrictive form that shapes the content. Exile amplifies and advances the poet's teleology.

This complete inversion of exile's traditional role produces the pun of the following lines: *tak šumi že sebe/ v sudebnoj svoej sud'be/ nad moej golovoju,/ prisuždennoj tebe.* The poet has been adjudged to the North, which in turn has its own judicial role to which it has been prejudicated. The North's fates are both the inevitably cyclical seasons which Brodsky tells to roar above him (*šumi*) as well as the region's designated role as unchanging place or space of exile, year after year. This role is judicial in that it is decreed by the Soviet empire; in the secondary meaning of *sud'ba* as destiny (or Providence) things are different, though. If the poet is discernibly adjudged to the region, he is by implication a foreign object there, something qualitatively different. The ability of space to produce something other than itself, to engender a believer's non-stop metamorphoses, is also uppermost when Brodsky asks the spaces of the North to give him only water (that is, time, not space) to let him know that "life is nobody's [in particular]," not his to fashion, according to his whim. The word water is qualified by the genitive expression "of the stream," placed in parentheses. This expression (*ruč'ja*) is added as a play on the meaning of North as either a horizontal, earthbound direction or a vertical, starbound vector, in which case Aquarius might be the addressee, as the stellar *Vodolej* (the Russian name comes from the noun "water" and the verb "to pour").

Unwillingness and anxiety over choosing the boundlessness of eternity underlie the final stanza, also spoken by the poet to himself. The dialectical structure of the whole poem may have effected a greater sense of bravery, but that bravery is in the form of imperatives; Brodsky is telling himself to do something in the future, something he has not done yet. The experiences of stanzas 1 to 5 lead to a quick sermon to himself; the poet maligns his indecision and braces himself for what has yet to be, for what is disconcertingly unknowable.

We are told that accurate prediction may be impossible, but the closing lines of stanza 6 suggest that at least some progression is achievable; a well-aimed glance by the poet back at his enemy's threats makes him feel that he is accelerating away from them on a metaphorical vector, off towards whatever lies ahead. The poem ends with a freely willed but ever-quickening trajectory away from prior danger, a tangent that speeds away from the cycles of *Šestvie.* The poet, though, is telling himself how to make the leap; he is preaching the leap, not doing it. The inability to leave the pulpit and the ethical stage underlie the admission of *Pis'mo v butylke* that though God is his pilot, Brodsky is still "sleeping soundly."

In order to move into faith, though, one *must* wake up and suspend the logic of the ethical stage. The poetry of the period from 1966 to 1971 expresses this concern, accompanied by an extreme rush for faith and the ensuing despair which marks the transition to the Baroque stage amidst desperate efforts to keep the opposites of finite and infinite balanced. The years 1966 and 1967 mark a rush towards Kierkegaard's "contemporaneity" in Christ, the consequences of which appear between 1968 and 1971. Between 1966 and 1968 Brodsky likens his dilemma to being in a labyrinth, as had Kierkegaard and Šestov. Two poems show the increasing attempts to escape, to make the first leap into faith; the separation of personal from public passions in *A Halt in the Wilderness* (*Ostanovka v pustyne*), and the more daring references to the crucifixion in *Farewell, Mademoiselle Véronique* (*Proščajte, Mademuazel' Veronika*).

1966 AND 1967:
ATTEMPTS AT A DASH FOR FAITH

The existential dilemmas of faith trouble Šestov for so long that he likens them (in *Potestas Clavium*) to a labyrinth, a metaphor he takes up again in *Apofeoz bezpočvennosti*. Šestov writes that Theseus *chooses* to kill the Minotaur, and thus chooses his own teleology. Once inside the labyrinth, however, he should never expect to get out; there is no end or final answer to the questions posed by faith. Šestov comes to the conclusion that faith offers no stasis, no easy exit; it is for "homeless adventurers" and "innate nomads" (š, 1971: 49). Kierkegaard modifies the myth of the labyrinth slightly in *Either/Or: Part One*, based upon a mural from Herculaneum in the Naples Museum. In the myth, Theseus kills the Minotaur, escapes the labyrinth, abandons Ariadne, and sails away. Ariadne is furious and marries her rescuer, Dionysius, as revenge. In Kierkegaard's version, Theseus regrets his departure and looks longingly back at the scene he has left: Cupid and Nemesis, both standing beside Ariadne, shoot at Theseus and hit him in the heart. Ariadne's revenge, then, is that Theseus loves her when he must leave and suffers the pain of homesickness or a lost love (SK, 1987a: 403–4), the story of which "can be continued as long as you wish."

Brodsky's poem of 1967 *To Lycomedes on Scyros* (SS2, 48–9) continues the story. The lyric hero leaves the city, "my labyrinth," with the Minotaur decomposing and with Ariadne in the arms of Dionysius. Having wandered in the wilderness with his booty, however, Theseus ("I") must go back. God takes away any prizes he had gained. The hero must go back to where he was humiliated, perhaps by the behavior of Ariadne. Although the poem associates the term back (*nazad*) with homewards (*domoj*), the return here is one that denies the security of victory after the death of the Minotaur. One must go back to the loss of a love and into the labyrinth.

The nature of desired faith as something inherently opposed to security and stasis is clear in the poem *A Halt in the Desert* (*Ostanovka v pustyne*), also the title of Brodsky's second collection of poetry (ss2, 11–14). It tells of a concert hall built in Leningrad to replace a church; the sound of the church's demolition had once drowned out the conversation of a Tartar family with the poet. The pillaging of Mongol horsemen is being outdone by Soviet ideology, epitomized by faceless concrete architecture; Tartar heritage is presented as genial hospitality and is completely upstaged by the modern destruction. Now only dogs can sense the presence of the church (the "smell" of the old building) over and above the concrete Soviet block that has replaced it. The poem concludes with questions about whether Orthodoxy or Hellenism is further away from the present, about what might lie ahead and what sacrifices will be required. The opposition here is non-faith versus faith, in other words Greek paganism versus Orthodoxy, as in Šestov's opposition of Athens and Jerusalem, or reason and belief (š, 1951: 7). Brodsky ends the poem by juxtaposing the faithless or impersonal with the personal – that is, the pain of "contemporaneity in Christ." "It is one thing, / no doubt, to christen a nation, / but to bear a cross is quite a different matter."

The picture is a little more complicated, though. As this quote suggests, a true contemporaneity is ideally found *outside* of rigid, preachable doctrines, such as those of Orthodoxy. This poem is important because it is a very early expression of the polytheistic aspects of Brodsky's faith, its willingness to accept Christ as a model, but not simply as part of an established, systematized doctrine. Like Plotinus's intellectual celebration of wordly variety as proof of divine unity, Brodsky's contemporaneity or Kierkegaardian subjectivity becomes increasingly well defined by celebrating widespread manifestations of the Absolute with many words, themselves spread far and wide (away from a centre); faith therefore operates only in a cautious dialogue with the inflexible monologue of institutionalized divinity.

In *Farewell, Mademoiselle Véronique* (ss2, 50–5) there is a starker expression of the very personal contemporaneity with Christ, acceptance of the role of a Christian who, as Christ, takes suffering, humiliation, and loss upon himself in the movement towards God. On Good Friday Véronique sits, arms crossed, in an armchair (*kreslo*) like Napoleon on Elba, not risking the consequences of opening one's arms, i.e., like Christ on the cross (*krest*); all of the lovers' hugs cannot match the open arms of the crucifixion. In this awkward situation, the poet feels stuck in a labyrinth, without Ariadne's help. The light of Christ's passion illuminates the back of the empty chair like a movie screen. With nobody in the chair, the passion becomes mere spectacle, viewed passively. Véronique's crossed arms express the opposite of Šestov's "apotheosis of groundlessness"; they express the "apotheosis of an object" (*apofeoz predmeta*) – a slow and silent, retrogressive metamorphosis towards objectification. In fact the whole poem hinges on the painful similarity between inanimate objects touched by the challenge of divine love, and absolute objects, themselves untouched by the divine. Faith requires submission to the ravages of love, to this voraciously imperial emotion, such that only a saint's relics will be left from the sacrifice. Whether this will produce holy relics or mere things is impossible to predict; Brodsky says accurate prophesy is as hard as discerning the fragrance of a snap-dragon through a suit of armour's visor. The sacrifice will be to the omnivorousness of divine love, to this "imperial feeling," prior to the poet's so-called leaps into the 1990s (*pryžki v devjanostye gody veka*).

1968–1971: THE DEAD-END OF THE ETHICAL STAGE

Between 1968 and 1971, the choices surrounding the irrational "leap into the 1990s," into the religious stage, are becoming unbearable. Brodsky gives up waiting for an angel's response to his questions, having now decided that faith is unavoidably a one-way communication, proven by the bird that never returned to the Ark. The poet, therefore, can only pile his words higher in the hope that they are heard above. The process has no comfortable sense of closure; he cannot put a roof on his rising tower of words. In section ten of *Gorbunov and Gorčakov*, words are said to "gobble up things" (ss2, 126); they have the ability to overpower existence's dumb tendency to objectify. Nevertheless, the same section also notes that although words are building blocks towards a paradoxical expression of ineffable faith, they often cannot help but express what is expressible, creating things by naming them; a name *does* objectify a signified with its unchanging signifier when it gobbles it. To name, appropriate, or swallow up an object in a versified expression of faith is to effect one more step through the three stages; but each naming or step can only be done once, and each poem leaves a trail of earthbound things behind it. After all, to use these same words twice is called a cliché, so new words need to be chosen, which means further objectification or "burning up" of language's fuel – even of the poet himself, since he writes of, and therefore objectifies, himself. This self-objectification (or "immolation") is what Brodsky means when he says that words are holy relics. The greater the faith, the greater the number of words. Unfortunately, this means greater objectification, more reified "parts of speech" or mere things, including the poet, the subject of so many of his own words or "relics." Only the word crucifixion escapes, Christ's death also meaning life; it is the only word with two meanings, and eternity is the only word that has not gobbled up or objectified its object, as it were.

These problems of a linguistic contemporaneity need a little more elucidation as they are now more prevalent than ever. In the earlier discussion of Plotinus it was noted that although the Greek's theocentric worldview is a precursor of the more monologic or systematized aspects of Christianity, his celebration of multifarious, intellectually perceived phenomena in the world is at the same time a celebration of how divinity gets positively distributed or diffracted through a large number of forms in a way that, ironically, feeds into the structure of polytheistic belief systems. These earthbound, polytheistic aspects multiply as divinity's ubiquitous splendour is increasingly recognized. The more it is recognized, the more it bolsters theocentric unity, since the multifariousness of spiritual presence is proof of the power of its single source. The disparity of phenomena paradoxically strengthens their common ground or cohesion; the unity of Plotinus's psyche is therefore proven or even created by the ongoing diffusion of the spiritual or pneumatic, not estranged or "exiled" by it. By expressing a polytheistic adoration for physical phenomena, the theocentric cohesion that underlies the psyche is strengthened; the physical needs the spiritual and vice versa.

There are vital parallels with Brodsky's written contemporaneity. To write, the poet needs to move through the three stages, but instigates an overwhelming process of objectification en route, driven by runaway language. The objectification works in two ways. It is, first, the product of multiple expressions of faith, expressions which can be only used once. They become diffuse manifestations of culture's faith in beauty, yet they cannot be copied by other artists, and thus art avoids systemization. Time enriches the nature of art, but makes future expressions harder by continually reducing possible options. A new artist's words are massively constrained by the weight of tradition, but are also enriched by it when he does say something qualitatively new relative to tradition; intertextual correspondences become ever more diverse and fruitful. In the awe-inspiring presence of a divine, linguistic art, the artist is gradually diminished or, even worse, objectified in his production of diffuse and dispersed expressions of faith – expressions which reduce finite, human animacy but in the process amplify faith in the very medium that enables such praise. Such is the second, spiritual aspect of objectification. The cultivation of objects is therefore part of the cultivation of belief, and vice versa.

Brodsky's lyric *ja*, his first-person pronoun, corresponds to the centre or psyche of the poet. Its centrifugal diffusion or dispersal is depicted via other, increasingly varied pronouns, historical or literary figures, flora, fauna and wordly phenomena in the poet's work over the years. Such "flight" is used to justify all arguments of exile or estrangement. On the model of Plotinus and a Kierkegaardian contemporaneity, though, Brodsky's psychic unity is bolstered by this multiplied and earthbound objectification. Kierkegaard knows that to reject this supremely private task of contemporaneity with Christ is to sin, but to accept it is also to admit one's sinful nothingness in the presence of God. The closer to God, paradoxically, the worse one's sin. Brodsky, too, knows the sin of succumbing to levelling, but to accept a linguistic contemporaneity can be an equal sin in the face of language's divinity, as the pile of linguistic things gets disconcertingly large. Even worse, while faith reduces the individual believer to nothing, the faithless masses of this world are forever multiplying and reducing to an unnervingly similar "sub-human" level. The merciless self-reduction of the believer in awe of the Absolute is done in the hope that his faith is genuine. Since faith is an absurdity, however, one cannot be sure; perhaps one's piety is self-satisfied bluster. The greater the faith, the more words and the faster the objectification, hence the continuing growth of devolution or levelling as a theme in this period. Devolution seems inevitable whether one accepts contemporaneity or not; between 1968 and 1972 there are several references in Brodsky's writing to the lowly evolutionary stage of fish – a stage of necessarily *silent* reproduction, the high price of existence in water's absolute dimensions.

In a poem of 1971, Brodsky conflates the spatio-temporal absolutes of the sea (*more*) and future (*grjaduščee*) within the neuter pronoun *ono;* one day soon their waves will deluge our world once more and prepare a bed for mollusks. Since language is often equated by the poet with a form of restructured time, the mollusk can be seen as doubly significant. It is, first, a levelled member of an ever-growing bestiary of lowly objects that exist entirely at the whim of a predictable "wave" in eternity's progression. Secondly, from a linguistic point of view, the mollusk is a warning to those who *can* use language, use a qualitatively different form of time (literary, not mathematical). Words allow one to devolve to a positive, yet humble spiritual nothingness before mathematical eternity does the job in a faithless, negative version with a death blow.

The processes of devolution, hinted at here but which soon run rampant, are likened to a microbe's eternal splitting, to human reproduction. The division accelerates in the ever-growing need for art to continue "the independence of details." Here lies the start of Brodsky's Baroque aesthetic – a sort of kinetic or centrifugal decoration as the lyric *ja* is dispersed across a large number of characters, roles, and forms of life. Though the sense of self seems broken up en route to faith, it is celebrated as the "talent of a fragment," of a part whose significance is defined relative to a whole. Although faith and devolution are freely willed projects, the years 1968 to 1972 mark a struggle with the snowballing inevitability of what Brodsky terms a Darwinian aesthetic, in which "all forms of life are an adaptation."

In the context of this growing pessimism, a contemporaneity in Christ is sought with increasing desperation. At the risk of being numbered amongst the sacrilegious, Brodsky considers asking for an expansion of the church calendar. In *The End of the Belle Epoque* (*Konec prekrasnoj èpoxi*), the choice of walking on water "as a new Christ" is juxtaposed with a bullet to the temple. He is tortured by the consequences of the Kierkegaardian either/or: "Life lets one posit an 'either'" (*žizn' pozvoljaet postavit' 'libo'*) which is rapidly becoming the "nightmare of prophets." Faith is being sought in desperation through the choices of the either/or, through a dialogue between choices. The two most extreme examples in this period come in the form of actual dialogues, first with an angel and then between two men. In both instances, the poet's desperation is clear, since the angel will not answer and one of the two men dies. The first example, involving a heavenly messenger, is *Conversation with a Celestial Being* (*Razgovor s nebožitelem*, ss2, 1970: 209–15); Brodsky imagines himself on the cross and muses that man experiences pain ignorant "either of his own limit, or that of pain." The pain of choosing contemporaneity is not finite: more faith is greater pain which inspires more faith, and so on. He cannot predict the end of either. He would not choose to transform himself into the Good News (*blagaja vest'*), no doubt because to preach is to usurp God's position and apply fixed, predictable ethics to absolutely everyone.

The *Conversation* is ironically titled, since it is really a soliloquy and never interrupted. It could have been called the "Confession," beginning with the admission that the poet has fallen "now to devoutness, now to heresy." He doubts both the ability of his word (*glagol*) to reach the ears of his celestial addressee and his own ability to control his throat. The lack of an answer perhaps makes him shout louder, which does nothing but emphasize the emptiness and silence even more, which makes him shout. The loss of an interlocutor or one half of a dialogue also underlines the second example, the long poem *Gorbunov and Gorčakov* (ss2, 1968: 102–38), which tells of two men in a Soviet mental hospital. Gorbunov is described as the more spiritual of the two, Gorčakov the more physical. They have in the past been likened to Christ and Judas respectively or even to a "bifurcation of the author's voice." The poem consists of their dialogues, together with interrogations by prison doctors of Gorbunov's subversive, dialectical views. Gorbunov dies at the poem's close, and is spoken of with reference to the crucifixion, as if he is looking down upon his earth-bound interlocutor, Gorčakov. The two halves of the poet's voice need each other and are inextricably bound in forward, though painful, movement: "For I feel that I / only exist when there's a collocutor! ... As an echo, continuing sounds, / striving to save them from oblivion, / I love and commit you to torments."

In both of these poems there is no clear answer to the emptiness, so the fear of what the poet is moving towards or leaping into only increases. Is it a godless abyss, or can he make the irrational leap of faith, knowing that hidden in the dark is the embrace of God? This embrace is the absolute goal which for Brodsky has its equivalent in an absolute, revelatory experience with language – if he pushes it into the same unknown. The poet keeps talking, but nobody answers. Language is an empirical experience of the unknown, but the further he goes, the more frightening it gets. If the poet hears or feels no addressee, then the abyss is obviously growing close, as is his sacrifice to it. Life is a conversation in the face of silence, so when Gorbunov dies, Gorčakov becomes merely the remaining, incomplete half of a conversation, directing words at an intangible, perhaps ineffable addressee and getting no response.

NATJURMORT AND THE DEAD-END

When, however, something is *not* ineffable, when it is namable, its fixed name can make it an inalterable object, a part of speech (*čast' reči*); in *Farewell, Mademoiselle Véronique*, named or "branded" objects are called the source of inflexible views. By combining these two observations on the relationship of naming to ontology, it is clear that because a fixed appellation can give something a fixed meaning, it might therefore fall into the realm of rational certainty and the Athens half of Šestov's apposition of Athens (reason) and Jerusalem (faith). The so-called Jerusalem side, then, involves something that cannot be named, or at least manages to dodge being pinned down by one particular meaning: that something (or some word) is Christ (the Word). But if language is one's deity, how can one realize one's faith if it involves mentioning the unmentionable? The whole problem of naming the unnamable and of defining the resulting paradox is the central issue of poetry prior to the Baroque stage. The best example of this is the 1971 poem, *Natjurmort.*

In this poem, the poet, surrounded in life by both people and things in winter, manages with some effort to write. He writes of things, since people will die. Things are typically brown, in a state of *nature morte.* The final section of the poem depicts Mary questioning Christ on the cross, asking if He is son or God: "He says in response – / 'Dead or alive, / there is no difference, woman. / Son or God, I am yours.' "

Brodsky was earlier quoted as likening writing to cosmogony – to creation and not theology. Here the poet decides to write about things. If writing is creation, but people still die, then the things which are created by naming outlive the writer; they are infinite. The poet goes on to say that things contain neither good nor evil – which suggests Šestov's view of faith. Things contain dust, says Brodsky, the flesh and blood of time, and he evens likens a wooden sideboard to Notre Dame. So the cathedral contains faith, which is infinite, and a thing contains dust, which is also infinite. Things do not scream and shout if beaten or burned, they are a more accurate description of deadness than the absurd cliché of "skull, skeleton and scythe" (ss2, 273).

In a comment on the poem in 1974 Brodsky says that he was "fed up with people … I prefer things. For instance … I thought that Christ is a thing and a man at the same time" (Brumm, 237). Not a man and a God, but a man and a thing. So if a thing is infinite, equated with Notre Dame and substituted for half of Christ's union of flesh and spirit, then is not the following pattern possible? Man and Thing, "Nature" and "Morte," Jesus and Christ; each pair is inextricably bound. The human, animate half (the first half) is unfortunately tied to a deadened, objectified counterpart (the second half). Two paradigms are created and in the process they objectify and deaden the spiritual potential of the last pair, they negate the miracle of Christ's paradoxical divinity in human form, since He becomes a man and a thing; the former is crucified and the latter is objectified by language.

The poems examined prior to this one also suggest a synonymy between naming and objectifying, between naming and turning an entity into a part of speech. The final sentence of *Natjurmort* is "Son or God, I am yours." The final word is a possessive pronoun; He becomes something possessed by Mary. She herself had tried to name Him as Son or God, dead or alive. Perhaps Christ is a thing when faith is objectified as a proper noun – the word Christ. Since Brodsky himself has declared language to be his deity, he invests faith in the *means* by which things that are named are created, not in something which has already been named, fixed, and therefore static. Once again, this argument supports the description of his own work as closer to a polytheistic cosmogony than to fixed, monologic theology.

Brodsky was sick enough when he wrote *Natjurmort* to believe that he might be dying and the poem takes a very pessimistic view of his craft, doubting its spiritual potential. If movement through the three stages which he saw as the key to the human species is made through writing, what does that mean for a dying man? How can language be both the means of objectification (death) and a guarantor of the Absolute (life)? If writing can objectify something, then surely the problem is exacerbated every time one goes back to a word to use it again, even only for the second time, because the meaning would be fixed from the first usage. The second use is tautological (or clichéd, in literary terms); it objectifies an existent object and is therefore useless for a cosmogonical aesthetic. The vocabulary of any tongue is finite, so how far can one go on the way to an absolute relationship to language before one runs out? If language is invested with such a potential, it would appear that using it only objectifies and kills by chasing the unnamable with names, that "a thought once uttered is a lie." Such is the dilemma which the poet feels prior to the work of his 1977 collection, *A Part of Speech* (*Čast' reči*), which marks the more extreme manifestation of the labyrinthine problems surrounding writing as means of both gaining and losing self-determination. Hence the possibility of parallels with the Baroque, problems which made it so difficult for the poet to even explain *Natjurmort* in words: "That's what I meant. Well it's something more. It's silly to talk about it. I can't do it" (Brumm, 237).

3 The Influence of John Donne, Relative to Existentialism, 1957–1972

By Joseph Brodsky's own admission, the English seventeenth-century poet John Donne was always one of his idols, a man whose influence on him was reinforced over the years. After all, when Brodsky left Russia, all he took with him was a typewriter, "a small Modern Library volume of Donne's poems, and a bottle of vodka" (Birkerts, 102). The importance of this particular edition is that the introduction offers a description of the Metaphysical poet's life in clearly triadic terms, such that the parallels with Kierkegaard or Šestov would have been striking. The introduction would also have led Brodsky to pay special attention to how Donne frequently uses tripartite structures in his poems, prose, and sermons to describe the development of his life.

Given that Brodsky was reading Donne at roughly the same time that he was reading Kierkegaard, Šestov, and the Bible, the manner of this period and these problems can be profitably called metaphysical. This term encompasses pre-1972 work, which consists of the movement through the first two stages of Kierkegaard's triad, plus the problems surrounding a leap into the third. This metaphysical period marks the beginning of the movement of Brodsky's poetry from metaphysical to Baroque, and ultimately to Rococo, Cavalier, or Précieux, mimicking the path of seventeenth-century poetry. Metaphysical verse serves, along with the existentialism of Kierkegaard and Šestov, to drive the poet towards an absolute encounter with the object of his faith, language.

The common ground between Donne, Kierkegaard, and Šestov is clearest if one compares Donne's triadic biography with the same four areas of Kierkegaard's thought discussed in the previous chapter, to show how they can (or cannot) be mapped onto the English poet's work. These areas are particularity, resignation, the double movement (or repetition), and the teleological suspension of the ethical. All the four areas are manifest in Brodsky's *Great Elegy to John Donne* (*Bol'šaja èlegija Džonu Donnu*), where the poet uses an elegy in the early 1960s to look back on Donne's life and discuss the Metaphysical poet's teleological successes or failures in the spirit of Kierkegaard and Šestov. The results show to what degree Donne's work is compatible with Brodsky's as expulsion from the Soviet Union grows near.

THE RELEVANCE OF DONNE

John Donne was born in London in 1572 into a Roman Catholic family and received an education from a Catholic tutor until he entered Hereford College, Oxford, in 1584, moving to Cambridge University in 1587. Being Catholic, he was unable to swear his allegiance to the Protestant crown, which was required to get the degree, and he therefore never officially graduated. Later legal studies at Lincoln's Inn were followed by adventures at sea against the Spanish, which in turn led to an acquaintance with Sir Thomas Egerton, for whom Donne began to work as secretary. Whilst employed by Sir Thomas, Donne met Anne More, with whom he fell deeply in love. John Donne and Anne More married secretly in 1601, and Anne's furious father did everything he could to punish the disobedient couple. The poet spent a while in prison and was fired by Egerton, who tried unsuccessfully to have the marriage annulled. Donne was to spend years trying to find gainful employment as a result of his swift fall from grace.

The poet's previous adherence to Catholicism had been growing gradually weaker; soon he was writing at length against the Catholic church, as a result of which he was urged by several individuals to enter the Church of England. Even King James brought pressure to bear upon him to begin ecclesiastical service. In 1615, therefore, Donne was ordained as an Anglican minister, and occupied various rectorships, including preaching to the young men at Lincoln's Inn. Although the death of his wife in 1619 greatly distressed the poet, it also served to increase his faith; in 1620 he became dean of St Paul's Cathedral, a position he held for the rest of his life.

The classic description of Donne's life could not be closer to Kierkegaard, a description included in the introduction by Charles M. Coffin to the 1952 Modern Library edition of Donne's work. Here Coffin organizes Donne's biography triadically, which makes Brodsky's conflation of the Englishman's life with a Kierkegaardian life-plan natural:

The customary treatment of this material [the facts of Donne's life] gives Donne three periods. The first shows us "Jack Donne" of the Town, prodigal of his fortune as well as of his affections, yet brilliantly ensconced in a courtly office until his secret marriage "above his class" to the niece of his employer lost him his post and all prospects of getting another. In the second period Donne is the distressed husband and father and the melancholy scholar, depending upon the generosity of friends and patrons, his fate oscillating between hope and disappointment until finally he accepted the invitation to take orders in the English Church. The last is the period of the divine, the Dean of St Paul's. (Coffin, xxii)

Coffin tells the reader that a similar pattern is seen in the poet's work, as it develops over the three stages of Donne's life: "There is first the satirist and the cynical, rebellious love poet; then the poet of 'sincere' love, sober verses, and scholarly books; and, at the end, the eloquent preacher and the author of holy sonnets and devotions." Though such rigid distinctions have fallen somewhat out of favour, the basic direction of the poet's movement holds true. In fact, the organization of the whole volume does little to dissuade one from seeing a tripartite structure to Donne's life, though the actual dating of individual poems is a notoriously knotty problem. From witty songs and sonnets, the Modern Library edition then offers epigrams and cutting satires, a quintessential post-aesthetic literary form designed to attack any social pretensions or vacuous display. Verse epistles are followed by marriage songs, then the famous accounts of universal disarray – the *Anniversaries*. The *Divine Poems* round out the section of verse, to which are appended some elegies on Donne himself.

The prose half of the volume, after the *Juvenilia*, the scandalous defence of suicide (*Biathanatos*), and attack on the Jesuits (*Ignatius his Conclave*) turns to the *Essayes in Divinity*, correspondence, and finally over one hundred pages of sermons which conclude with the ominous *Death's Duell*. Both within each half of the book's verse/ prose distinction, and across the whole volume, there is a reasonably well-delineated move from frippery to faith. Coffin informs the reader that this move is taken by a post-Renaissance heretic, who lived at a time when the centrifugal rush to discover new worlds coincided with processes of centripetal or introspective self-discovery. These opposing tendencies took place at a time when the traditional, ontological securities of Elizabethan England were slowly evanescing. Post-traditional freedoms led to Donne's heady (and occasionally unwieldy), intellectual independence, itself reflected in a rhetorical vacillation between novel theses and antitheses in the formulation of new truths and new securities.

As a result of his ongoing, rhetorical empiricism and the continual testing of postulates, the three stages span the distance between "the Mistresse of my youth, Poetry" and "the wyfe of mine age, Divinity." Kierkegaard maintains that life should be lived forward and understood backwards, and Donne is indeed able to segment his own life in three stages at its conclusion, looking back on existence from his late sermons at how God's presence is made manifest in one's "infancy, youth and age." Here are two exemplar sections from the *Devotions* and a sermon to show other uses of this triadic perception of life.

Most excellent Prince [Charles], I have had three Births; One, Naturall, when I came into the World; One, Supernatural, when I entered into the Ministery; and now, a preter-naturall Birth, in returning to Life, from this Sicknes. In my second Birth, your Highnesse Royall Father vouchsafed mee his Hand, not onely to sustaine mee in it, but to lead mee to it. In this last Birth, I my selfe am borne a Father: This Child of mine, this Booke, comes into the world, from mee, and with me. And therefore, I presume (as I did the Father to the Father) to present the Sonne to the Sonne; This Image of my Humiliation, to the lively Image of his Majesty your Highnesse...

Dignaris Domine, ut eis, quibus debita dimittis, te, promissionibus tuis, debitorem facias; This, O Lord, is thine abundant proceeding; First thou forgivest me my debt to thee, and then thou makest thy selfe a debter to me by thy large promises, and after all, performest those promises more largely than thou madest them. Indeed, God can doe nothing scantly, penuriously, singly...

Donne's life is a series of attempts to reach faith by escaping the wayward arrogance of his youth. The enormous spiritual distance from the poet's youth to his position as the dean of St Paul's suggests that his leaps of faith between them produce the structure of Metaphysical verse – the unity of disparities. It can be enormously difficult to balance these disparities, since, in his own words, sinful carelessness can always cause a relapse, and his faith needs to be constantly renewed. Donne feels an equally constant threat of its loss. The way to move forward, to conquer the "sinne of feare" that might hold one back, is to admit that each day might be your last, the "criticall day," as the poet's final sermon has it. Only by living each day in "conformity with Christ," like Christ's last day, will man move ahead in good faith.

The ever-possible relapse would be the consequence of a bad choice in life. The need to keep making the right choice every day means that there is no thematic predictability or stasis in Donne's poetry, instead an "impatient rejection of constancy" (Parfitt, 1989: 73). Nothing is held in motionless, stable isolation from its opposite. Coffin's introduction emphasizes as much, directing the reader's attention to "the persisting tension between Body and Soul, and between the secular and the divine," which are "never long allowed to go on their separate ways" (Coffin, xxvii–viii). This tension is embodied in language, the marriage of paradoxical opposites in rhetorical structures. For Kierkegaard it is in the dialectic, for Donne casuistry. The divine truth which is sought may be "unitary, but earthly formulations of that truth may be multiple or contradictory ... Donne's casuistry is a reasonable method of dealing with those matters with which the reason cannot deal" (Cathcart, 11).

As with Kierkegaard and Šestov, rhetorical attempts to pin down the paradoxical nature of the Word with a human word can run away with their author. If he cannot do it in "one clear word, perhaps [he can] in the accumulation of a good many clear words" (Cathcart, 128) and try to approach God's creative skills: "The pillars of Donne's biblical, Protestant poetics are: that the scriptures are the most eloquent books in the world, that God is a witty and also 'a figurative, a metaphoricall God,' and that the religious lyric poet should endeavor to 'write after ... [His] Copie'" (Lewalski, 282). The Reformation had emphasized the importance of a written word as the embodiment of divine truth, but without the leap of the word into the arms of its divine counterpart, earthbound, arrogant "pride in [one's] ingenuity" finally exhausts itself, and the poet "works perversely to his own end" (Colie, 213). Donne's poetry expresses this tension or disparity between ingenious language and its ongoing attempts to express divine verities; this empirical investigation of earthly potential is very much a product of the historical context in which the poet was writing.

Donne's verse is also a written response to (and struggle with) the demise of Henry VIII's and Elizabeth's England, in that it displays a definite sense of discontinuity with the reliable inevitability of that past. Not only does Donne attempt to draw an outward-bound tangent to such cyclical inevitability through physical travel – by applying for an overseas secretaryship with the incipient Virginia Company – but also through language. In 1624 he likens a brave, empirical movement through life to the plotting of a linear sentence: "[Life] is like a Sentence, so much as may be uttered in a breathing: and such a difference as is in Styles, is in our lives, contracted and dilated. And as in some Styles, there are open Parentheses, Sentences within

Sentences; so there are lives, within our lives. I am in such a Paren-
thesis now, in a convalescence, when I thought my self verie near my
period" (JD, 395).

What follows is an attempt to see how a bold and "written" existence
at the end of pre-Copernican stability manages to project itself outwards, as a linear sentence, into the unknown. The "fear and trembling" of moving centrifugally into the unknown, it is claimed,
produced the temptation of a reassuring return to cyclical security. To
show how the poet's constant attempts to leave such a security behind
complement the influence of existentialism in Brodsky's work,
Donne's œuvre is best approached through the four areas of Kierkegaardian emphasis: particularity, resignation, repetition, and the teleological suspension of the ethical. Particularity shows that Donne's
empiricism, although conducted in lonely isolation, was at least
designed to enable forward movement in his life.

DONNE AND THE FOUR AREAS OF
KIERKEGAARDIAN EMPHASIS

Particularity

Particularity, as Kierkegaard speaks of it, concerns man's relationship
with his faith, developed in isolation, allowing no intermediaries
between the believer and the Absolute. In Donne's *Ecclogue* (Boxing
Day, 1613), he writes that "reclus'd hermits often times do know /
More of heavens glory, than a worldling can" (JD, 175). Indeed,
Donne feels at times that he experiences a universal spiritual state only
when in complete solitude. Early in his career, the poet feels that
introspection is preferable to a zealously social existence. The gaudy
arrogance of life at court is rejected in favour of self-discovery: "At
home in wholesome solitarinesse / My precious soule began, the
wretchednesse / Of suiters at court to mourne, and a trance / Like
his, who dreamt he saw hell, did advance / It selfe on me" (*The Storme*).

By the time most of the *Divine Poems* were written, between 1608
and 1613, however, isolation begs to be fulfilled in a personal relationship with God, and any earthly community where "popularity is
vanity" is rejected in favour of a divine counterpart. For example, in
the *Devotions upon Emergent Occasions* of 1624, courtly or aesthetic
community (in the Kierkegaardian sense) is clearly replaced by divine
communion. In declaring sickness to be extremely burdensome
because of its forced solitude, the poet mourns his inability to participate in an ethically ideal, albeit earthly reflection of divine unity – a
unity which is described as a social multiplicity, rather than the solitary,

unknowable figure of God which epitomizes Kierkegaard and Šestov's sought "Other."

A long sicknesse will weary friends at last, but a pestilentiall sicknes averts them from the beginning. God himself would admit a figure of Society, as there is a plurality of persons in God, though there bee but one God; and all his externall actions testifie a love of Societie, and communion. In Heaven there are Orders of Angels, and Armies of Martyrs, and in that house, many mansions; in Earth, Families, Cities, Churches, Colleges, all plurall things; and lest either of these should not be company enough alone, there is an association of both, a Communion of Saints, which makes the Militant, and Triumphant Church, one Parish; So that Christ, was not out of his Dioces, when hee was upon the Earth, nor out of his Temple, when he was in our flesh. (JD, 420–1)

The tension between the profoundly private or lonely demands of faith and the need for a believer's physical self to be part of a "city" is the need for divine communion underlying Donne's famous view that "no man is an Iland, intire of it selfe," which concludes the *Devotions*. The single island still needs to find the multiplicity of the mainland, though, so there is a continuing emphasis on necessary isolation en route. In the *Divine Poems* Donne chooses that which is unknown and unlit in preparation for a state of particularity.

> Seale then this bill of my Divorce to All,
> On whom those fainter beames of love did fall;
> Marry those loves, which in youth scattered bee
> On Fame, Wit, Hopes (false mistresses) to thee.
> Churches are best for Prayer, that have least light:
> To see God only, I goe out of sight:
> And to scape stormy dayes, I chuse
> An Everlasting night.
>
> (JD, 258)

In seeking to transform an abyssal darkness into light, to turn isolation into communion, the renouncing of one's safe moorings can seem like exile in its cruel and potentially irreversible progression into the unknown. The poet outlines this cruelty in a sermon of Christmas Day, 1621, and sees it as an unavoidable consequence of a conformity with Christ: "Finde in thy selfe a disposition to accompany him in a persecution, in a banishment, if not a bodily banishment, a locall banishment, yet a reall, a spirituall banishment, a banishment from those sinnes, and that sinnefull conversation, which thou hast loved more than thy Parents, or Countrey, or thine owne body … " (JD,

483–4). Contemporaneity in Christ may be a potentially ideal passage away from faithless custom for Kierkegaard, Šestov, and Donne, but any passage travelled in lonely imitation of Christ can lead to blasphemy or sacrilege; Donne sometimes perceives himself "not as the expositor of the triune Logos, but as a functioning triune Logos himself" (R. Hughes, 268–9). "Who can deny mee power, and liberty / To stretch mine armes, and mine owne Crosse to be? / Swimme, and at every stroake, thou art thy Crosse ... (JD, 234).

The metaphor of swimming, or elsewhere of a ship's lonely journey on stormy seas, is common in Donne. Quite where the solitary ship is going can be a difficult course to plot, for it is full of both good and bad choices. The empirical movement between these choices underlies what T.S. Eliot calls Donne's vagrant thought, which leads at times to no structure of thought. Sooner or later, however, if one accepts the challenge of faith, a structure will emerge: the solitary individual's resignation to a higher order, to hopeful membership in the divine family, or to a residence in the heavenly city. Donne's particularity differs therefore from Kierkegaard's and Šestov's in its ultimate goal of the stability of a hierarchical and divinely social state, a city for the physical house rather than the eternal irrationality of God's will that allows the existentialists no reliance upon any shared ontological insights concerning the future. The promise of future security has a price, though, and for Donne as well as Kierkegaard, that price is resignation.

Resignation

Resignation is the complete and utter submission of the individual to God, in order that his individuality may be enhanced through a relationship with his Creator. It is a daunting prospect. Donne is often unable to consider that he might "participate in a re-making of himself in the image of God," the necessary choice of ultimately surrendering – not aspiring – to God's omnipotence. This inability to submit will make one fall to despair, and then despair becomes synonymous with sin.

Donne's final sermon, given on 25 February 1630, deals with indecision in the same manner as Kierkegaard: faith becomes a "free" choice that one cannot but make. One must be "content" to resign to the necessary, sacrificial conclusion of one's conformity with Christ. In talking of the crucifixion in these terms, Donne writes only lines before that "there was nothing more free, more voluntary, more spontaneous than the death of Christ: Tis true, *libere egit*, he died voluntarily, but yet when we consider the contract that had passed between the Father and him, there was an *opportuit*, a kind of necessity upon him" (JD, 589–93). To ask the same of God, to be "ravished" by Him, is indeed resignation, but it is also a call to be finally recognized by Him. The active leap into God's arms is a submission to His will, a theme central to Donne's *Holy Sonnets*, where free will and necessity are bound together because Christ, as for Kierkegaard, is both liberator and jailer, both bridegroom and ravisher.

This interplay of loss and gain, of solitude and communion, harks back to Donne's insular metaphor: in a *Hymne to Christ* within the *Divine Poems*, he says he will "sacrifice this Iland unto thee," an act that must be done entirely to a God who may shelter the believer as an Ark, or perhaps swallow him like a whale; one cannot know in advance, but if one wishes "new great heights to trie," then sooner or later "it must serve your ambition, to die." Here is the essence of the Baroque "gain through loss" paradox, the paradox of Abraham's leap. Although the very paradoxicality of resignation is a product of its unpredictability, Donne feels that one can at least be sure of simultaneous, divine "visitations and afflictions" together with "mercies and comforts" – which itself is hardly comforting.

The possibility of life via submission to death is at least accepted wittily by Donne in a prose paradox entitled *That Virginity is a Vertue*. Purity is no virtue if zealously preserved, years after its proper time, like rotting fruit. For virginity to be all that it can, it must paradoxically *cease* to be; it must resign itself in order to perceive, attain, and realize the union of marriage. To understand this problem, one must move beyond logical or ethical thought: "Ethick Philosophy saith, That no Vertue is corrupted, or is taken away by that which is good: Hereupon some may say, that Virginity is therefore, no vertue, being taken away by marriage. Virginity is no otherwise taken away by marriage, than is the light of the starres by a greater light (the light of the Sun:) or as a lesse Title is taken away by a greater (an Esquire by being created an Earle)" (JD, 290).

Given the appalling demands of real-life resignation, there seems at least occasionally in Donne's work to be some equivocating; even in late sermons one can find examples of prevarication rather than action:

Let *me* wither and weare out mine age in a discomfortable, in an unwholesome, in a penurious prison, and so pay my debts with my bones, and recompence the wastfulnesse of my youth, with the beggery of mine age; Let *me* wither in a spittle under sharpe, and foule, and infamous diseases, and so recompense the wantonesse of my youth, with that loathsomnesse in mine age; yet if God with-draw not his spirituall blessings, his Grace, his Patience, *If* I can call my suffering his Doing, my passion his Action, All this that is temporall, is but a caterpiller got into one corner of my garden, but a mill-dew fallen upon one acre of my Corne; The body of all, the substance of all is safe, as long as the soule is safe. (JD, 518, my emphases)

"Let me," asks Donne; in other words, he is not there yet. In fact, to ask for God's permission as the means to faith is to reduce contemporaneity or conformity to a state that is *not* entirely realized through free choice; resignation turns into a hope or expectation of granted blessings, then, and is therefore no longer an option to be wholly accepted or rejected by the believer himself. What exactly *does* happen to Donne's eventual choice to leap is best seen by looking at the final sermon of Donne's life, given at the beginning of Lent, 1630, in the presence of the king.

This long, final sermon is known as *Death's Duell* and interprets resignation to the bridegroom and ravisher in the light of Christ's submission to the Father. The sermon is a capitulation of Donne's own development, the move from "alienation and protective masquerade" towards a truer faith (R. Hughes, 66). As Donne approaches the final denouement, he is convinced that, whatever the pain of death, "Gods care that the soule be safe" is assured ahead of time. Kierkegaard and Šestov probably would take issue with Donne's following expression of epistemological certitude: "The humble soule (and onely the humble soule is the religious soule) *rests* himselfe upon Gods purposes and the decrees of God, which he hath declared and manifested not such as are conceived and imagined in our selves, though upon *some probability, some veresimilitude*" (JD, 583, my emphases). Whether guaranteed ahead of time or not, though, any success in the relationship with the Absolute, following resignation to God, to this truer faith, is very close to the Kierkegaardian repetition.

Repetition

The loss of oneself in resignation is later rewarded in fulfilled faith: the self is restored and renewed, in a process to be repeated many times over the abyss of potential faithlessness, in Kierkegaard's mind. For Donne, too, repentance is often a situation of unbearably frequent crucifixion – and not only of himself, since the poet's sins daily re-crucify Christ. Failed repentance is even expressed as repetition done backwards: though God may "rectify" Donne's lameness on an hourly basis, the poet still regresses from his potential resurrection and undergoes instead a daily death. These daily deaths become the wholly mortal stages of infancy, then youth, then age. Together they are not a phoenix-like progression of ascending yet similar stages, but of gruesome, bestial metamorphoses if the challenge or necessity of resignation to one's faith is not first accepted and then acted upon.

In his *Essayes in Divinity*, Donne talks of suffering that is useless if it is not in conformity with Christ, if it is "without any return to thee." The circle is the metaphor central to Donne's talk of return; Christ will weave the sins of a man into a crown "and make a Circle." This geometric figure is described as a place where two ends meet, a heavenly return to one's origins that coincides with the end of one's corresponding, earthly passage from the womb to the grave. The pattern's mortal conclusion reflects a divine design, since "God hath made all things in a Roundnesse."

In aspiring to the perfect circle, one returns to one's maker. A life of successful conformity with Christ will scribe such a design, because "to have been once nothing, and to be now co-heire with the Son of God, is such a Circle." It is not drawn in the same way as human temporal circles, whose steady development or regression is easily perceived. God's circle can move from winter to summer and bypass spring; it does not correspond to our perception of temporal linearity since it reflects a supra-temporal present, an eternal now where "all times are his seasons."

Despite its timeless goal, the mortal road from worm to co-heir must necessarily be one of consecutive stages, repeated steps of increasing value that together constitute a form of alchemy which will resurrect the spiritually moribund poet. The resurrection is paved with God's "many infirmities" which will be visited upon the poet before he gets to an experience of God's "particular mercies." Through such tribulations and tasks, one can, like Saul, be blinded, only to have sight restored and improved. The rewards bestowed on Abraham are also referred to by Donne on several occasions; as Abraham's finite life was raised to a higher stage by his willingness to violently subordinate it to the infinite, so Donne hopes a successful conformity or contemporaneity will let him "die" and therefore rise from death *before* he expires physically. In doing so, it would seem that Donne hopes to reduce the unpredictability of death, being already resurrected.

The progressive stages of conformity with the divine are therefore in a different time-frame than those of real time, as experienced by one's aging flesh and bones. The correspondence between the two frames, the physical and divine, which allows repetitions between them across life's stages, is also likened by Donne to correspondence, and to the resurrective powers of dialogue or song.

... as Ayre doth fullfill the hollownes
Of rotten walls; so it myne emptines,
Where tost and mov'd it did beget this sound
Which as a lame Eccho of thyne doth rebound.
Oh, I was dead; but since thy song new Life did give,
I recreated, even by thy creature, live.

(*To Mr. R.W.*)

Indeed, when the soul is moving higher or further, it is thanks to a dialogue or repeated interaction with the tangible world. As with the dual physical/spiritual significance of virginity, so a conjugal bed is likened to both a grave and a cradle, a means to a repetition, onto the next stage of another birth and onto the "other" bridegroom. By moving ahead, the importance of things physical will ideally be diminished and so the increased significance of spirituality will turn finite marriage into a marriage with Christ, the only entrance to which is via death. Thus death paradoxically becomes a second birth, the body a second womb, which in turn makes death mere slumber prior to a resurrection as one moves ahead to complete the home-bound circle.

The geometrical simplicity of a circle, though, expressed as simple stages towards a rebirth, does not do justice to the bewildering illogicality of repetition. As a complement to Kierkegaard's, Šestov's and Brodsky's use of the myth of Theseus, it is useful to note how Donne himself uses the metaphor of a disorienting labyrinth in his sermon of 25 January 1628 to show how hard repetition really is: "Poore intricated soule! Riddling, perpelexed, labyrinthicall soule! Thou couldest not say, that thou beleevest in God, if there were no God; Thou couldest not beleeve in God, if there were no God; If there were no God, thou couldest not speake, thou couldest not thinke, not a word, not a thought, no not against God." The labyrinthal interaction of man and maker, of tangible and intangible, of finite and infinite, as the former member of each pair constantly returns to the latter, therefore excludes any long-term separation of one half from the other. Donne makes a repeated "return to the flux of existence" (Hughes, 87), of which the most famous example is the poem *The Extasie*. The souls of two lovers merge above their bodies in harmony, but the necessary patterns of circular movement and return permit no exile of the soul from the body. The two halves, like a prince and his kingdom, "need each other and are indeed inconceivable without each other" (Gardner, 1978: 255–6), like the opposites inherent in Kierkegaard's view of Christ, paradoxically unified as the God-man. The nature of divine paradox as beyond both rational thought, and the ethical structures which Kierkegaard and Šestov believe such rational thought informs, lead to Kierkegaard's fourth area of emphasis, the teleological suspension of the ethical. The irrational and the paradoxical come to the fore, and their growing presence helps to distinguish between the influence of existentialism and the Metaphysical poets in Brodsky's pre-exile work.

The Teleological Suspension of the Ethical

In his book on the development of Donne's verse, Richard E. Hughes writes that "there is always a teleological process in what Donne wrote" (80). In a match with Kierkegaard's triad (and therefore with its application to Brodsky's verse), Donne's "basic epistemological progression [is] from sense to reason to faith" (Sherwood, 180). Reason is needed on the way to faith, as part of the process by which faith is obtained. But the leap into faith provokes irrational fear and trembling, since rational consideration of the leap's ethical pros and cons is not a means by which divinity can be comprehended. Kierkegaard speaks of the offence that faith does to reason; for Donne it is an "affront to human reason ... It outstrips human reason and imagination" (R.E. Hughes, 185).

The clearest manifestation in Donne's verse of Christianity as transcending what appears to be right or wrong is the divine poem *Good Friday, 1613. Riding Westward.* The movement westwards (towards the setting sun and darkness) is paradoxically linked to reaching the east (the realm of sunrises and Christ) by coming full circle and returning to the point of departure. The poem is a criticism of rationality's attempts to deal with faith, with the freely willed act which must be experienced if conformity with Christ is to be achieved. Truth must be approached in this empirical fashion, first West then East, via darkness or the leap of faith across the abyss, since, as Donne notes in his 1629 Christmas Day sermon, "what eye can fixe it self upon East and West at once?" Only God is able to see the whole journey before it has begun.

What seems a neat and tidy correspondence between existentialism and seventeenth-century's teleological suspension of the ethical is, unfortunately, rather untidy. By ethical, Kierkegaard and Šestov mean the universally binding, rationally comprehensible aspects of ethics which would have made Abraham's act murder, not sacrifice, had Heaven not stopped his hand in time. God's unpredictable will makes merely ethical behaviour incompatible with religious conviction, which in turn fills the ethical individual with a *horror religiosus*. To see how far Donne is willing to go in his acceptance of pure ethics or

rationality's inadequacies as a means to conformity with Christ's horrific demands, references in Donne's work to ethics, morality, and
virtue need to be separated from references to reasonable thought,
then examined separately, vis-à-vis religion.

Like Šestov and Kierkegaard, Donne is aware of religion's frequent
devaluation in the form of sermonizing, "in Churches, when th'infir-
mitie / Of him which speakes, diminishes the Word." Sermons are
made of moral dictates, which bind all people in the same way to the
same behaviour; they are transmittable and constant. One cannot,
however, equate God's will with moral constancy; indeed, hearing
sermons and leading a moral honest life are together still insufficient
for a true expression of faith.

In defining exactly what *is* sufficient, Donne in one instance puts
his "brave" love above various restrictions: virtue, the mind, sense,
understanding and "silly olde moralitie" (JD, 50, 67). If, though, one
is to live in conformity with Christ, and the laws of "silly" morality have
perhaps already been overtaken, how does Donne deal with the *horror
religiosus* of an impending leap into the religious stage? The answer
lies in Donne's use of the terms ethics, morality, and virtue. He argues
and equivocates over their meanings, such that religion invests them
with a new significance and improves them; ethics, morals and virtue
are in fact *not* suspended or overcome, they simply come to mean
something qualitatively different, something less daunting than
Kierkegaard's "religious stage."

> Is not our Mistresse faire Religion,
> As worthy of all our Soules devotion,
> As vertue was to the first blinded age?
> *(Satyre III)*

> Vertue'is but anguish, when 'tis severall,
> By occasion wak'd, and circumstantiall.
> True vertue is *Soule*, Alwaies in all deeds All.
> (*A Letter to the Lady Carey and Mrs. Essex Riche, from Amyens*)

By investing earthbound virtue, morality, and ethics with a divine
significance, faith becomes a more comprehensible, less frightening
project and one that is manageable in the here and now. After all,
Donne terms the crucifixion a binding contract, reducing the existentialist paradox of Christ's sacrifice to an ethical obligation, to an
inflexible requirement which, when transferred to the here and now as
man's task of conformity, becomes a series of pre-agreed and therefore
fully comprehensible terms. Donne shies away from a Kierkegaardian

or Šestovian interpretation of faith as a law so irrational and subjectively validated as to be absolutely incomprehensible to two people on the same terms.

Donne's discussion of reason and rational thought produces similar conclusions. The poet holds that reason almost meets faith – to the point where rationality and belief can overlap, made clear especially in the 1621 Christmas sermon. "Reason is [a] first, and primogeniall light, and goes no farther in a naturall man; but in a man regenerate by faith, that light does all that reason did, and more; and all his Morall, and Civill, and Domestique, and indifferent actions, (though they be never done without Reason) yet their principall scope, and marke is the glory of God, and though they seeme but Morall, or Civill, or domestique, yet they have a deeper tincture, a heavenly nature, a relation to God, in them."

Donne's ability to re-semanticize the significance of ethics, morals, virtue, and reason allows him to make faith a more preachable entity, achievable by a living, thinking individual – an entity suitable for the pulpit and for transmission to others. He instructs the Countess of Bedford that "Reason is our Soules left hand, Faith her right,/ By these wee reach divinity"; reason and faith are simultaneous, not consecutive or even competitive. If Kierkegaard suffers in an attempt to express the ineffable Word with a word, then Donne perhaps has squeezed the Word within an expressible word, which he then speaks to others. Donne effects not a suspension of the ethical, but a spiritualization of it.

Kierkegaard and Šestov would claim that this leaves Donne mired in universal laws of predictable, predetermined behaviour. In his defence, the Englishman might offer his passages which state that the soul's command is often comprehensible, but that its nature still lies beyond our rational ken. He might also offer his definition of those who seek to have Christ as their spouse as errant, "adventuring knights" in the spirit of the existentialist "knight of faith." After all, in a letter of 1625, he calls his taking up of the cloth a "first leape, which was my very entrance into this callinge." In a more sober and ethical moment of six years before, though, in *Biathanatos* the darkly witty and irrational defence of suicide as a self-destructive leap had already been dismissed by the poet as an embarrassingly rash product of the youthful "Jack Donne, and not [the older] D. Donne," as he says in a letter to Sir Robert Carre, Earl of Ankerum. In fact, in the very year he speaks of accepting his calling, the poet summarizes his faith with a very un-Šestovian assurance: "God brings us to humiliation, but not to desperation." Even more surprising is the fact that these rationalizations are part of a faith that convinces Donne he will "sit down with Abraham, and Isaac" in Heaven.

Another brief look at *Death's Duell*, written at the end of Donne's clerical career, shows a man who, like Abraham, might see religion as beyond reason or an easily grasped causality, yet still thinks that divine decree is something reliable which the believer can rest upon; Donne cannot doubt a deliverance, which takes the following form: "... he [God] hath the keys of death, and hee can let me out at that dore, that is, deliver me from the manifold deaths of this world, the *omni die* and the *tota die*, the every days death and every houres death, by that one death, the finall dissolution of body and soule, the end of all. But then is that the end of all? ... It is not."

JOSEPH BRODSKY'S
GREAT ELEGY TO JOHN DONNE
(*BOL'ŠAJA ÈLEGIJA DŽONU DONNU*)

The themes of rest and one's future ability to leave home as expressions of teleological security loom large in Brodsky's elegy to John Donne of 7 March 1963 (SS1, 247–51). The relationship of rest to death which is inherent in any elegy shows how the similarities and differences between the influences of Donne and existentialism are made manifest in Brodsky's work. One rhetorical tradition in which Donne was writing serves as a good starting point, since this tradition is invested with a novel significance in Brodsky's poem. As for the *Great Elegy* itself, it is useful to break it down into three sections and examine each of them separately: the opening scenes of London where Donne lies "asleep," the dialogue of the poet's body with his soul that interrupts his slumber, and finally the closing section, with its observations on the relationship between the language of such a dialogue and the reciprocity of faith. The *Great Elegy* shows not only to what extent Donne's poetry dovetails with the ongoing, Kierkegaardian affinities in Brodsky's work, but how the Englishman and the Dane together push the Russian's poetry beyond a metaphysical stage into the realm of the Baroque.

The *Elegy* is based upon John Donne's metaphor of sleep as death. A long opening section offers an enormous number of nouns, many of which designate domestic items, both inside and outside a snow-covered London house, and all of which lie in silent slumber with the English poet. The same state of sleep has overcome angels, the devil, and God Himself. Donne's lines of poetry sleep, too, lying around as separate syllables. Suddenly a voice breaks the quiet, the voice of

Donne's own soul. It reminds him how the poet's previous flights had once circumnavigated God, but now the soul's travels are necessarily cut short, at least until death. A closing section muses on a cloth (or fabric of life) which needs constant repair, with needle and thread. The final lines invite Donne to sleep on, the reasons for which will be discussed below, after an overview of Donne's rhetorical tradition, which is noticeable in Brodsky's poem.

A rhetorical tradition central to Donne's work and the literature of seventeenth-century England as a whole reappears (albeit unconsciously, perhaps) in Brodsky's elegy: probabilism. The theory originated in 1577 with Bartolome de Medina, a Dominican of Salamanca. It arose from the problems surrounding what kind of rhetorical form could accurately reflect or express a single and absolute truth – a truth of relevance to one's moral responsibilities in life. Man knew that absolute truth had a singularity or unity which any one human word could not hope to capture; thus there arose a tension between truth and how to capture it in language. The tension was resolved somewhat by the rhetorical juxtaposition and combination of multiple and partial expressions of an absolute, and absolutely certain, law. Only in subjecting divine unity to an earthbound multiplicity could one hope to capture it in a comprehendible form. "Man's uncertainty, it was assumed, arose from the uncertainty of the law as it was stated. Laws are not perfect. Consequently ... any opinion of the law was admissible as a statement of the law ... Probabilism ... recognized that an opinion of what the law was, which was probably true, might not be true, and that any opinion which was probably untrue might be true. One did not know. And, in determining the practical obligation, one settled for that opinion which had some probability of truth ... The law was increasingly denied its status as a single statement of the truth" (Cathcart, 52).

Truth becomes an ongoing juxtaposition of opinions, not the strict codification of a law, and thus is close to the avoidance of apriorism, of unbending laws, as reflected in the writings of Kierkegaard and Šestov. In *Homage to Yalta* (*Posvjaščaetsja Jalte*) Brodsky says himself that "a proven truth is, strictly speaking, not the truth, but only the sum of proofs" (ss2, 142). Given the cosmogonical nature of Brodsky's art, one should note the poet's remark in the same work of "the dependence of truth on art, and not art on the presence of truth." Probabilism underlies Donne's reasoning also. It shows how an earthly, more practical truth is created through the active interaction of opposites, and "how little [of divine] truth is amenable to man's power of reason" (Cathcart, 56). The interaction of such opposites is the foundation of Brodsky's own elegy. The opening lines of the text outline the most important oppositions of the poem; sleep and waking, silence and speech.

THE TEXT OF
THE GREAT ELEGY TO JOHN DONNE

1. The Opening Scenes of London

The first ninety-two lines make up the opening section of the poem, and consist of a list of all the objects, people, and places that are sleeping together with Donne. Much of the very frequent usage of the verb to sleep (*usnut'*) appears in this section. The opening lines of the elegy serve as a good example of these nominal lists, of things enumerated against the background of a nocturnal, winter scene.

> Джон Донн уснул. Уснуло все вокруг.
> Уснули стены, пол, постель, картины,
> уснули стол, ковры, засовы, крюк,
> весь гардероб, буфет, свеча, гардины.
> Уснуло все. Бутыль, стакан, тазы,
> хлеб, хлебный нож, фарфор, хрусталь, посуда,
> ночник, белье, шкафы, стекло, часы,
> ступеньки лестниц, двери. Ночь повсюду.
> Повсюду ночь: в углах, в глазах, в белье,
> среди бумаг, в столе, в готовой речи,
> в ее словах, в дровах, в щипцах, в угле
> остывшего камина, в каждой вещи.

> John Donne has sunk in sleep ... All things beside
> are sleeping too: walls, bed, and floor – all sleep.
> The table, pictures, carpets, hooks and bolts,
> clothes-closets, cupboards, candles, curtains – all
> now sleep: the washbowl, bottle, tumbler, bread,
> breadknife and china, crystal, pots and pans,
> bed-sheets and nightlamp, chest of drawers, a clock,
> a mirror, stairway, doors. Night everywhere,
> night in all things: in corners, in men's eyes,
> in bed-sheets, in the papers on a desk,
> in the worm-eaten words of sterile speech,
> in logs and fire-tongs, in the blackened coals
> of a dead fireplace – in each thing.
>
> (1973e, 39)

The scene extends to the edges of the home, the windows, latches, and handles, then moves outside, where the only noise is that of the snow. It is the middle of night, and dawn is far away (*rassvet ne skoro*);

Londoners are in a deep sleep. A ship lies motionless at its mooring, a sense of immobility extended to the whole of seventeenth-century England (*prostor anglijskij tix*). Syntactic parallels link the living and the dead in their respective beds and graves. Angels, saints, the devil, and God sleep in silence. The opening section closes with a scene of Donne's own slumbering verse. His lines of poetry lie side by side, like the dormant Londoners. Neither strong nor weak syllables can be discerned.

The inability to discern separate entities from one another reflects a Kierkegaardian levelling; when the challenge of faith is accepted by no one, all reverts to an entropic state of complete equity. Šestov says that for faith to be successful, one must "make a huge effort, and wake up" (1964, 320). One needs to wake from an inanimate state, represented here by the predominance of inanimate objects. Slumber may be an imitation of death, but it is nevertheless a state from which one might wake, and if so, death would thus be negated, or at least overcome, which would make the elegy something of a "non-elegy." Death causes elegiac melancholy, yet if that death could be overcome, there would not be much left to be sad about. To find out to what degree the use of sleep in the *Elegy* can be equated with actual death or an existentialist levelling, one needs first to look at how Donne uses it.

When Professor George Kline first presented Brodsky's poem to the West, he offered some possible Donnean parallels (1965, 345). Among them are a couple of passages from the *Holy Sonnets* concerning sleep, one of which relates the danger that "gluttonous death will instantly unjoynt my body and soule," and the poet will briefly "sleepe a space" (JD, *Sonnet vi*). Elsewhere in the work, however, the poet states that he will "wake eternally, / And death shall be no more; death, thou shalt die" (*Sonnet x*). The severity of the "gluttonous death" is greatly mollified if one follows the narrative of the *Holy Sonnets*, and in fact Donne's use of sleep as a metaphor elsewhere suggests a core meaning closer to Professor Kline's other quote, that a condemned man "doth practice dying by a little sleep." Sleep is not death, so much as a rehearsal for the actual event, and just as death may or may not prefigure a resurrection when the actual event occurs, so Donne's metaphor of drowsiness has both positive and negative connotations. The more commonly acknowledged, negative significance deserves attention first of all.

> Sleepe is paines easiest salve, and doth fulfill
> All offices of death, except to kill.

> ... we sleep all the way; from the womb to the grave we are
> never throughly awake ...

> Nor can we pass from the prison of our Mothers womb, to thy
> palace, but we must walk ... through the street of this life, and
> not sleep at the first corner, nor in the midst.

The first of these quotes is from the verse epistle, *The Storme*. Both
The Storme and Brodsky's *Elegy* equate an inanimate state, prior to a
spiritual struggle, with a sailing ship in a quiet port. Donne's fleet lies
in port "withering like prisoners" at the mercy of a lifeless wind before
it chooses to venture into the storm. Brodsky's references to sleepiness
are also punctuated at times by other references to enclosures, to a
stillness locked shut against the snow, snow being a common metaphor
for an abyss of potential non-existence. Bolts, latches, fences, walls,
doors, locks, chains, closed windows – all appear in the opening
section. Nobody is going outside the residence, just as Donne's quotes
above emphasize sleep as time killed on life's path, a path which
requires constant, outward-bound movement. Donne uses the metaphor of repose to show the dangers of spiritual sluggishness. Fear of
the vertiginous dialectic of life and death, faith and abyss, which
Donne terms the "paine of debating" with God, will incline a lapsed
believer "in this lazinesse" to "sleep out [his or] her lease, her terme
of life, in this death, in this grave, in this body."

Donne's criticism of lethargy is clearer still when examined together
with the metaphor of architecture, of the bolted or locked residence.
On many occasions, the English poet likens the human body to a
house, the soul's dwelling place. The body is most often seen as a
troublesome prison for the soul which can only aspire to the grander
architecture of a palace or temple. A state of sleep in one's house,
especially a bolted one, can cause a negative change or a forced move
to a much less desirable residence: "Wee are all conceived in close
Prison; in our Mothers wombes, we are close Prisoners all; when we
are borne, we are borne but to the liberty of the house; Prisoners still,
though within larger walls; and then all our life is but a going out into
the place of Execution, to death. Now was there ever any man seen
to sleep in the Cart, between New-gate and Tyborne? between the
Prison, and the place of Execution, does any man sleep? And we sleep
all the way..." (Sermon of 28 March 1619). One should, instead, use
the Church, God's "progresse house," to aim for residence at God's
celestial address, since He has two homes – the Church and Heaven.
God Himself is a solid building and each believer hopes one day soon

to reside *in domo patris*, a place of "better Architecture." The ability to move house is one made possible by God alone; only death will unlock the door, and only God has the "keys of death." Since houses must be unlocked, but the residents themselves do not own the keys, Donne's existential agency seems diminished, to say the least.

In yet another use of this somnolent metaphor, repose indeed becomes an expression of passive anticipation, of a dry run or prefigurement of a believer's Lazarus-like pause between actual, corporeal death and spiritual resurrection: "Naturall men have conceived a twofold use of sleepe; That it is a refreshing of the body in this life; that it is a preparing of the soule for the next." Brodsky's house in the *Elegy* remains locked, that is, death has not unlocked it. So if the Russian poet has made a conscious and direct transfer of the Englishman's metaphor, then Donne's experiences in the Russian poem are those of a living man. So what *is* sleep in the *Bol'šaja èlegija*: levelling or a restful state of expectation? Brodsky's elegy will gradually clarify the relationship of sleep and a believer's progression in life as we, the readers, progress through the text.

Any forward movement or progression of one's *telos* is a linguistic project for Brodsky, hence the apparent synonymy of sleep and silence in the *Elegy*, at least in the opening section. Once the poem's initial movement is completed from enclosure to expansion, from the dormant house to Heaven, the narrative moves onwards or upwards to forms of linguistic silence; descriptions of silent lines of poetry are on several occasions accompanied by references to a concomitant lack of distinction between the opposites of right and wrong, sin and passion. Silence, like drowsiness, is a refusal to enter into a vital, life-giving dialogue between these opposites; silence is moribund inactivity, since to not speak is to not do, to not live. It is a conscious refusal to make "correct" ethical or religious (spoken) decisions and therefore to move forward; one chooses *not* to speak just as consciously as one chooses to start talking.

> Джон Донн уснул. Уснули, спят стихи.
> Все образы, все рифмы. Сильных, слабых
> найти нельзя. Порок, тоска, грехи,
> равно тихи, лежат в своих силлабах.
> И каждый стих с другим как близкий брат,
> хоть шепчет другу друг: чуть-чуть подвинься.
> Но каждый так далек от райских врат,
> так беден, пуст, так чист, что в них – единство.
> Все строки спят. Спит ямбов строгий свод.

Хореи спят, как стражи, слева, справа.
И спит виденье в них литейских вод.
И крепко спит за ним другое – слава.
Спят беды все. Страданья крепко спят.
Пороки спят. Добро со злом обнялось...
Спят реки слов, покрывшись льдом забвенья.
Спят речи все, со всею правдой в них...
Уснуло все: святые, дьявол, Бог.
Их слуги злые, их друзья, их дети.
И только снег шуршит во тьме дорог.
И больше звуков нет на белом свете.

John Donne has sunk in sleep. His verses sleep.
His images, his rhymes, and his strong lines
fade out of view. Anxiety and sin,
alike grown slack, sleep in his syllables.
And each verse whispers to its next of kin,
"Move on a bit." But each stands so remote
from Heaven's Gates, so poor, so pure and dense,
that all seems one. All are asleep. The vault
austere of iambs soars in sleep. Like guards,
the trochees stand and nod to left and right.
The vision of Lethean waters sleeps.
The poet's fame sleeps soundly at his side.
All trials, all sufferings, are sunk in sleep...
...the streams of words, cloaked in oblivion's ice,
sleep soundly. Every speech, each speech's truth...
All soundly sleep: the saints, the Devil, God.
Their wicked and their faithful servants. Snow
alone sifts, rustling, on the darkened roads.
And there are no more sounds in the world.

(1973e, 41)

There is no sound and there are no active decisions. It is fitting, therefore, to draw a division between the first and second sections at the point when a voice finally interjects: "But hark! Do you not hear in the chill night/ a sound of sobbing, whisperings of fear?" (*No, čul! Ty slyšiš', tam v xolodnoj t'me, / tam kto-to plačet, kto-to šepcet v straxe.* [SS1, 249]). This voice begins the associative chain: voice–dialogue–life–life over silent lethargy or death. A similar chain can be found in Donne's work and, just as with Brodsky's poem, the Englishman emphasizes the body as absolutely essential in forging its links.

2. *The Dialogue of John Donne's Soul with his Body*

The second section consists of the next eighty-eight lines of the *Elegy*. A weeping is heard in the snowy distance, and a voice (which turns out to be that of John Donne's slumbering body) asks questions, to discover who can be heard so far away. There is no answer to five guesses: the distant voice does not belong to an angel, to cherubim, to St Paul, to God, to Gabriel. It is the voice of John Donne's soul, talking from above to the poet's body. This section of the poem consists of this dialogue between body and soul. The soul reminds the poet of his previous flights around the world, to Hell, Heaven, and the return home. There was, however, a realm the poet cannot see or reach, one which is described by his soul. Only after the arrival of death will travel be possible that far away. The section closes with a surprising about-face: now it is not the soul that is weeping and complaining, but the sleeping poet himself.

The deathly silence is broken not by one voice, but by a dialogue, and a rapid and metaphorically witty ascent is needed if one is to find such an interlocutor. When termed as a competition between human and divine language, as well as between the divinely ineffable and sluggish silence, this metaphorical ascent recalls Donne on several levels. In the Englishman's *Devotions upon Emergent Occasions*, he praises the Lord as a figurative, metaphorical God: "A God in whose words there is such a height of figures, such voyages, such peregrinations to fetch remote and precious metaphors, such extensions, such spreadings, such Curtaines of Allegories, such third Heavens of Hyperboles, so harmonious eloquutions, so retired and so reserved expressions, so commanding perswasions, so perswading commandments."

In moving upwards in pursuit of such a God, across the "three Quires" of Earth, Heaven, and Spheres, the soul in Donne's poetry expresses its love in correspondingly concentric circles: "If, as in water stir'd more circles bee / Produc'd by one, love such additions take, / Those like so many spheares, but one heaven make, / For, they are all concentrique unto thee." In the *Progresse of the Soule*, too, a fish makes concentric ripples when it moves in the limitless expanse of the sea. Although man's attempts to express the Word in words will probably only reduce God's glory and "square the circle," one can see in Brodsky's poem an attempt to make the sleepy, square room effect the divine circularity of Heaven, the bolted body effect a more psychic state. In *The Second Anniversary*, Donne urges his "drowsie Soule" to try and ascend to qualitatively different stages, sights, and sounds.

Up, up, my drowsie Soule, where thy new eare
Shall in the Angels songs no discord heare;
…
Up to those Patriarchs, which did no longer sit
Expecting Christ, than they'have enjoy'd him yet.
Up to those Prophets, which now gladly see
Their Prophesies growne to be Historie.
Up to th'Apostles, who did bravely runne
All the Suns course, with more light than the Sunne.
Up to those Martyrs, who did calmly bleed
Oyle to th'Apostles Lamps, dew to their seed.
Up to those Virgins, who thought, that almost
They made joyntenants with the Holy Ghost,
If they to any should his Temple give.
Up, up, for in that squadron there doth live
She … [the soul of Elizabeth Drury and/or Mary].

Donne makes it clear that God is intolerant of any sinner's silent self-deception, his unwillingness to fly up to the dialogue with "Another," whose presence is absolutely necessary for any sinner's act of absolution: "Hee can sinne alone, and suffer alone, but not repent, not bee absolved, without another." Man's paltry speech is thus judged against God, Who is *all* language, Alpha and Omega. Nevertheless, to enter into this discourse or "dispute" with God, as Donne terms it, is to die in the joy of a lachrymose, "heavenly Lethean flood" which is created by the dialogue and seemingly referred to in Brodsky's "vision of Lethean waters" which is itself hidden in language (*viden'e letejskix vod*).

In talking or flying up to the Word, though, Donne wonders if the best that poetry's cosmogonical ability can aspire to is a mere "counterfait Creation"; he prefers instead to see his eventual death as resigning to the divine half of the discourse (again physical and linguistic) with God, and as the subsequent relief of one's "translation into a better language." Brodsky describes Donne's syllables as lying silently; the Englishman refers to his sermons as an ongoing "labour of syllables" in attempted praise of the Lord, and elsewhere marvels that God's ineffable magnitude has made itself expressible in the monosyllabic noun "God," where ineffability has somehow shut itself "within Syllables."

To enter into a dialogue with the Absolute by means of earthly syllables is to try and enter into the Absolute itself, to strive for a resurrection at the price of one's finite existence which those same syllables represent; Donne's scrawled signature is his "ruinous Anatomie," his house. To use this language or body to express love, he turns both his talk and torso into "Mine Epitaph and Tombe." In fact the reference to sheets amongst the objects of Brodsky's elegy within Donne's house suggests the witty equation of writing paper, death, and the architecture of faith found among some supplementary materials which are included in the Modern Library edition. For example, in the 1633 preface to Donne's work, John Marriot puns on "sheet" as stationery, the sheet of stone of Donne's statue in St Paul's, and a winding-sheet. The poet himself, in the elegy on Elizabeth Drury, plays on sheet as writing-paper, wrapping-paper, and the fabric of a tabernacle. The sheet represents the body, architecture, and the linguistic sounds that come from within both, all of which will resign themselves to a divine demise when they will be wrapped in the winding-sheet of their own labours. The paper records the sounds or physical syllables and also enables a release from them.

In the *Elegy* the shrouds of silence and sleep are also undone by speech, the very medium which in Kierkegaard's view is "absolutely qualified by spirit and is therefore the authentic medium for expressing the idea, namely, man's essential idea, spirit" (sk, 1987a: 67). The spoken dialogue unifies the temporal body and the eternal soul; connected with the idea of uniting, or sewing things together, the soul's voice is likened to a threadless needle. A tiny poem of the same year, *My Words, it Seems to Me*, explains the significance of another needle that also works against the inevitable demise of transient existence.

Мои слова, я думаю, умрут,
и время улыбнется, торжествуя,
сопроводив мой безотрадный труд
в соседнюю природу неживую.
В былом, в грядущем, в тайнах бытия,
в пространстве том, где рыщут астронавты,
в морях бескрайних – в целом мире я
не вижу для себя уж лестной правды.
Поэта долг – пытаться единить
края разрыва меж душой и телом.
Талант – игла. И только голос – нить.
И только смерть всему шитью – пределом.

(ss1, 283)

My words, it seems to me, are going to die,
as time then smiles in triumph and transposes
the joylessness of everything I try

> to some adjacent, lifeless natural process.
> The past, the future, secrets of this life
> or whither spacemen roam – in such expanses,
> in boundless seas, across this planet I've
> stopped looking for self-satisfying answers.
> The poet's duty is to try and stitch
> the split between the psychic and incarnate.
> His needle? Skill. His only thread is speech.
> And only death's a limit for this garment.*

Perhaps the needle of talent here can be equated with the physical, with the skills of the body. In the *Elegy*, the needle is the distant voice of Donne's soul, which speaks with the talented body that can only manage so much on its own. In either poem, though, what the soul needs is the physical body and vice versa, so their discourse becomes the linguistic fabric created by the shuttling back and forth. As Donne remarks in *The Second Anniversary*, it is the soul which "doth string Heaven and Earth" together like beads in a line of planets made possible by the "third birth" of death (the first and second being creation and grace).

Only with the two halves of flesh and sprit is there full self-awareness, and awareness of the challenge of faith to which the self must then answer. Self-awareness here becomes the knowledge of oneself as both body and soul, a mutual recognition gained through spoken dialogue. After the dialogue has begun, the soul recalls the poet's previous movement, its flight (*polet*). With the load (*gruz*) of feelings and thoughts, which were "heavy, like chains" (*cepi*; perhaps a reference to series of associated metaphors), he flew "amidst passions, amidst sins and higher." The typical associations of a cumbersome burden are reversed here. Burden becomes a means of flight. It has nothing to do with the flight of the soul burdened by the body; it refers to the weight of thought, thought being the joint product of body and soul. The joint product had begun the divine journey once before, the freely-willed participation in a divine *telos*. Together, the abyss of non-being was faced. As with Donne and Kierkegaard, Brodsky's abyss is presented in maritime terms: "And you did face the ocean at its shores. / The howling dark stood close at every hand." The equation of sea, darkness, and speech is expressed in Donne as the dangers of an irrational and unreasonable storm which empty eloquence can whip up uncontrollably on the sea of life. The threatening nature of an aquatic abyss can be changed by God, though, Who with baptism protects one from drowning in the bottomless waters of life's afflictions. The divine Word calms the waters whipped up by human words.

Brodsky's opening passages on sleep, though, describe the merger of a dead-calm sea and sky: "A schooner nods at anchor. The salt sea / talks in its sleep with snows beneath her hull, / and melts into the distant sleeping sky." Donne says in a sermon of 15 April 1628 that if one could somehow merge the two realms of sea and sky, their total number of water droplets would still not equal God's benefits. The incomprehensible dimensions of oceans added to heavens also appear in an elegy on Lady Marckham as a realm unified by the soul's tears of repentance – tears produced by the painfully happy, spoken discourse with God. If he can manage to enter these irrational dimensions with the security of a divine dialogue, Donne no doubt avoids the rapacious Leviathans of sin since he is now a passenger on the safe, "sailing Church" when the world that is man heads into the ocean that is death.

In Brodsky's *Elegy*, however, Donne's voice in the wilderness describes a past voyage or ability to leave the house, sail across the oceanic abyss, circle God and return. But now the "burden will not allow you up" to the realm where it "is so bright" and from where the final judgment is no longer a terrible prospect. The soul is saying a *true* voyage is not really possible in the finite. One cannot expect to realize one's *telos* completely in this life. Only so much is possible in the leaps of faith or spiritual repetitions which one can make during one's physical existence: "Spiritual repetition is possible, although in the temporal life it is never so perfect as in eternity, which is the true repetition" (SK, 1964: 126).

It will soon be time for the soul to make the final leap, which comes after death and is the theme that concludes the second section of the *Elegy*. The soul weeps; there will be no way (*net puti*) for it to go with the body to its posthumous destination. The opening of the section had included the poet's guess that the distant voice was an angel, waiting for the return (*vozvrat*) of the poet's love to Heaven, which is the spoken return or promise of commitment, the ethically inspired promise to a realm that lies beyond the rationality which Kierkegaard and Šestov tell us defines mere ethical existence. Now the soul complains that it must return (*vernut'sja*) in the opposite direction, to flesh and stones, since the greatest flight of all is only possible after death, away from Donne's house (*Liš' mertvoj suždeno vzletet' tuda mne*).

The play upon the adjective "dead" (*mertvyj*) as a new lease on life begins to chip away at the poem's elegiac melancholy; here the reader starts to doubt the validity of sleep as either irreversible levelling or death. The soul leaves the body, noting the latter's "fruitless desire to sail behind," the desire of the finite to enter easily into the infinite. The soul begins to come to terms with death. The leap will entail a loss (the soul's finite interlocutor will pass away), but in a way similar to Job's experience, all will be returned many times over by God, thanks to the joint efforts of body and soul in this world. After having sobbed throughout the whole poem, the soul reaches a new level of self-awareness and suddenly turns everything on its head: "It is not I who is sobbing – it is *you*, John Donne" (that is, the body). With this observation, the closing lines of the soul's long response to the body are ushered in.

> Лежишь один, и спит в шкафах посуда,
> покуда снег летит на спящий дом,
> покуда снег летит во тьму оттуда.

> ... you lie alone. Your pans in cupboards sleep,
> while snow builds drifts upon your sleeping house –
> while snow sifts down to earth from highest Heaven.

In conformity with Christ, the body and the soul have become part of a two-way process. The body lies motionless when the snow falls, that is, in a levelled environment. When, however, the choice to speak is made, the snow (or abyss) becomes part of the discourse or dialectic of faith; the snow becomes the nothingness relative to which faith is so precious. Just as the value of nothingness is reversed by an uttered dialogue of faith (since it ends up increasing the value of religious conviction), so the direction of the previously languid snowfall is now part of a reversed movement, like threads running both downwards and upwards, back and forth. It falls on the sleeping house from above (*ottuda*), but in establishing a discourse with the earth, house, or body it thus guarantees an ongoing link with the heavens too. The soul enters the abyss of snowy nothingness and sails out onto the sea of Donne's *Storme*, in order to move up and away to God. This upwards movement always means the final sacrifice of the finite, in order that it be fulfilled in the infinite, on the model of Christ's own sacrifice.

If Donne's speaking soul in the *Elegy* is a needle, then the body by implication is the thread, which after a successful, posthumous leap sacrifices its finite form in order to be part of absolute dimensions; thus the thread metaphor is transferred to the snow across the sky. When the soul's voice was first heard, it was through a snowy darkness which was "sewing the night to the dawn" (*sšivaja noč' s rassvetom*). Towards the end of the elegy as a whole, Donne is described as ready to wake like a bird (phoenix?) at dawn: "Like some great bird, he too will wake at dawn; / but now he lies beneath a veil of white, / while snow and sleep stitch up the throbbing void / between his soul and his own dreaming flesh." Despite the potential rewards, whether or not to make this sacrifice of the finite self can still be a terrible choice for some people, one made between polar opposites that are bound together in Brodsky's rhymes: wakeful dawn or moribund sleep, white nothingness or one's body.

Donne knew that the dialogue of opposites was a necessary precursor to ultimate fulfillment, to heavenly, not earthly states. Such is the subject of the *Elegy*'s third and final stage, as the emphasis of section two (body and soul) turns to the very fabric of life, and the role of God in the relationship of language to faith. The conclusion of the dialogue has greatly altered the siginificance of the nocturnal emptiness of section one and the consequences of this change for a rapidly concluding narrative appear as the final metaphor of a star, central to both Brodsky and Donne's worldviews.

3. Observations on Language and Faith

The final section is much shorter, a mere twenty-eight lines which follow the discourse of body and soul. The narrative reverts to the third person of the opening section, but now it describes the relationship of body and soul, not just the sleeping body. As mentioned, John Donne "sleeps in his nest as a bird," since the "pure path" to a "better life" is "for now hidden by a cloud." He will, however, awake at dawn. Two or three lines of life's verse, says the narrator, still wait for their conclusion; the closing lines of the elegy refer to a cloth or fabric, by implication the fabric of life and a metaphor which may be inspired by Donne's assessment of man as a "ragge of this world." It has a hole in it and can be ripped by anyone; it vanishes, but will return (*vernetsja snova*). Only Heaven, we are told, will "take up, at times, the tailor's needle." After this reassuring thought, the poem closes with the following lines.

> Спи, спи, Джон Донн. Усни, себя не мучь.
> Кафтан дыряв, дыряв. Висит уныло.
> Того гляди, и выглянет из туч
> Звезда, что столько лет твой мир хранила.

> Sleep, John Donne, sleep. Sleep soundly, do not fret
> your soul. As for your coat, it's torn; all limp
> it hangs. But see, there from the clouds will shine
> that Star which made your word endure till now.

The third person narrative of the *Elegy*'s first section became the question and answer of body and soul, which now becomes the discussion of their interaction. The connotations of sleep have been made positive by the dialogue of body and soul, by their impending projection into the Absolute. This projection is only delayed while the snow sews up "the space between the soul and the sleeping body," over a period defined by the narrator as the two or three lines of unfinished verse. The reference to unfinished business is followed by couple of equally significant lines: "...carnal love is but a poet's duty – / spiritual love the essence of a priest." The dialogue between finite and infinite will finish the narrative, by means of both the "singer's duty" and "the priest's flesh." The purely material (singer/flesh) interacts with the ethical and religious (duty/priest) via language, and moves forward in both narrative and real time, to wrap up life's remaining lines.

If the poem, or the narrative of one's teleological successes in the here and now, is to be completed and made whole like the fabric of existence, then it is to be done by resignation to the Absolute and by choosing to do so. "Finite personality is ... made infinite in the choice," as Kierkegaard says (SK, 1987b: 223). Abraham had made the same choice to resign himself to the Absolute, and the knife with which he was about to make his choice, to join body and spirit, became guided by a higher hand. In fact, given Kierkegaard's emphasis on the many paradoxes of the freely-chosen leap, I should note again that just prior to the leap, it becomes a choice of what one cannot *not* choose; divine presence forces one's hand, as it were. Here, too, the hand of Heaven takes up and guides the needle (which earlier meant physical talent or spoken deeds) to stitch the fabric of life, by means of the thread which earlier meant the body's existence. The metaphoric fabric of life in the poem may be shabby, but Donne will awake to stitch it in good time – with some divine intervention.

That divinity is in the form of a star, of a light behind the clouds which has preserved Donne's world. With regard to Donne's own work, it is useful to begin with his comment that in and of themselves, debility, absence, emptiness, and darkness are worth nothing. When one considers this comment together with another observation – that "love is a growing, or full constant light; / And his first minute, after noone, is night" – then it is clear that for the Englishman, too, the abyss of non-existence is a means of validating the reciprocal nature of faith. The appearance of a given star may be unpredictable, hence Donne's urging that one must "strive so, that before age, deaths twilight, / Thy Soule rest, for none can worke in that night." Nevertheless, his efforts guarantee him a sense of peace. The star of the *Elegy* shines with the guarantee of preserving Donne's world (at least until the time described in the elegy) and the Englishman himself has equated a star with a soul (of Elizabeth Drury), a soul already guaranteed salvation.

It is this guarantee of a luminous, celestial permanence in Donne's work that prompts Brodsky both to term Donne's langorous state a night's nest (*nočleg*), as his soul puts it, and to end his elegy with the calming imperative to "sleep, sleep" (*spi, spi*), upon which Donne himself plays in the poem *Resurrection, Imperfect*. The sun is told to sleep, to take a rest from its daily, predictable reappearances, since it has been outdone by Christ's reappearance, the Resurrection. The sun is given time to recover from its wound of pride, inflicted on Good Friday, since Christ's rays will keep the Earth illumined, as a "better Sun." The imperfect Donne can sleep on, his imperfect resurrection soon to be improved and outdone by the true conclusion of his life, by the intercession of God and His "keys of death." What looks like a leap of faith is in fact the peace of mind of a man who believes his earthbound "Ethick philosophy" has already guaranteed his resurrection. What looks like continued levelling becomes a quiet self-assurance resulting from the assumed guarantee of divine assistance; the celestial hand that takes up Donne's needle is infinitely kinder that the one that stays Abraham's hand at the last possible second. But *why* is it kinder? How does that kindness relate to Brodsky's own relations with divinity? Is he experiencing Donne's passage vicariously through language, or just documenting it? The answers lie in *how* Brodsky has played upon one particular elegiac tradition in his work and how his use of that tradition is closely linked to Donne's real-life religious convictions.

THE SIGNIFICANCE OF AN ELEGIAC TRADITION

Brodsky's *Elegy* demonstrates that one of the most valuable aspects of Donne's influence overall is what has been termed "the dialectic of metamorphosis and substitution." It is an inherent part of what makes an elegy. Joanne Innis's work on Brodsky's *Roman Elegies* has suggested how the poet uses one aspect of this elegiac tradition – albeit without reference to Donne, given the Mediterranean context – and then refashions it (Innis, 1989). It makes sense to present the information in the same order as Innis does, to begin with the brief poem *Now that I've Walled Myself off from the World* (*Sumev otgorodit'sja ot ljudej*). Although not an elegiac work itself, the poem serves as an example of the processes at work elsewhere.

> Сумев отгородиться от людей,
> я от себя хочу отгородиться.
> Не изгородь из тесаных жердей,
> а зеркало тут больше пригодится.

Я созерцаю хмурые черты,
щетину, бугорки на подбородке...

Трельяж для разводящейся четы,
пожалуй, лучший вид перегородки.
В него влезают сумерки в окне,
край пахоты с огромными скворцами
и озеро – как брешь в стене,
увенчанной еловыми зубцами.

Того гляди, что из озерных дыр
да и вообще – через любую лужу
сюда полезет посторонний мир.
Иль этот уползет наружу.

Now that I've walled myself off from the world,
I'd like to wall myself off from myself.
Not fences of hewn poles, but mirror glass,
it seems to me, will best accomplish this.
I'll study the dark features of my face:
my bristly beard, the blotches on my chin.
Perhaps there is no better kind of wall
than a three-faced mirror for this parted pair.
This mirror shows, in twilight from the door,
huge starlings at the edge of the ploughland,
and lakes like breaches in the wall, yet crowned
with fir-tree teeth.
                    Behold, the world beyond
creeps through these lakes – these breaches in our world –
indeed, through every puddle opening.
Or else this world crawls through them to the sky.

                                        (1973e, 84)

The poem is a prime target for talk of estrangement. Innis, though, sees a movement across the text of the whole poem from detachment (from both others and self) by means of self-reflection, to an inclusion of the myriad objects reflected around the poet's own reflection in the mirror, and finally to a resultant union of the here and there, inside and outside, self and other, which a reflecting surface permits. The use of a triptych-mirror produces many reflected phenomena simultaneously in one image; it "reunite[s] images which would otherwise not be simultaneously accessible to a single observer." What ultimately emerges is "a synthetic image incorporating all the preceding stages in the reflection process." The use of multiple phenomena to constitute and enrich the first-person, lyric *ja* is the same process outlined vis-à-vis Plotinus to argue against estrangement. I agree with Innis, but would not use the terms detachment or estrangement, since the ultimate goal is the unity of the first person, not the irreversible heaping-up of objectified third-person states as an end in itself. The goal is known in advance; getting there is for Donne the problematic aspect of self-realization that produces the initial fear and trembling over leaving the house.

Lyric cohesion or unity is central to the *Roman Elegies*. The multiplicity of things that sleep at the start of Brodsky's *Elegy* runs the risk of losing the potential for that unity, since the "dialectic of metamorphosis" is stuck in silence, with no dialogue of body and soul. In documenting such pneumatic multifariousness, though, Brodsky is at least describing the rush of things around Donne made famous in the Englishman's statement that "I am a little world made cunningly," which itself gravitates towards the central planet of God; the little world is an index to the great volume that is the larger world. In *Devotions upon Emergent Occasions,* one of the works closest in spirit to the *Elegy*, Donne's little world may suffer from a multitude of meteorological and geological disasters, but even after such ravages, its innumerable bits and pieces spread far and wide would, if laid side by side, change into a star large enough to crowd the sky. Brodsky notes or observes Donne's example of lyrical dispersal into multiple objects or personae, but will soon surpass it, perhaps by means of the Englishman's own imperative in a letter to "Mr. E.G." that one should "not like a Bee/ Thy thighs with hony, but as plenteously/ As Russian Marchants, thy selfes whose vessel load,/ And then at Winter retaile it here abroad." Donne's objects are allowed to sleep on in their owner's teleological security; Brodsky's heap of plenteous things will rise up and up, metamorphosing all the while, as the Baroque stage will show. In moving towards such a stage, Donne's influence on Brodsky may initially run parallel to that of existentialism, but it does not go as far. Kierkegaard's and Šestov's influence is clear across Brodsky's entire corpus; to find a literary analogy that runs parallel to this influence though, Donne seems applicable only until the time of expulsion from the Soviet Union, to the time of *Natjurmort* and Brodsky's own dilemma over the horrors of resignation, over the model of Christ's own sacrifice.

Whereas Abraham makes the leap of faith, Donne feels rationally assured of his posthumous passage, and is thus able to sleep on, if his faith is truly such that he has reached a lasting peace of mind (Donne's soul certainly thinks so). It may not be a coincidence that two of the slumbering objects in Donne's house are bread and a bread knife, suggesting that no great sacrifice – on the example of Abraham – is thought necessary. Donne himself reaches this type of calm and considered state in the sermons which close the Modern Library collection, and it is here that the influence of contemporary Calvinism appears. The form of Calvinist thought which is clear in them regards man's sin as *antecedent* to election to salvation. Man therefore is completely reliant upon divine mercy, a state which might give him a sense of security if he ever suspected that he was one of the elect. It would certainly reduce the terrible burden of existential responsibility. The proud isolation of Donne's early years does indeed become total dependence upon God in every phase of his spiritual life. The tenets of Calvinism reduced one's agency in the search for salvation, to the point where although one *chooses* to live as a moral man, good works might actually be of no consequence whatsoever, given man's position as "an essentially passive instrument" before God.

Donne's sermons show the influence of infralapsarian Calvinism, which saw God's decree of predestination of the elect as *following* the Creation and the Fall. This doctrine, evident in Donne's sermons as his life was concluding, was adopted instead of supralapsarianism. Supralapsarian Calvinism holds that election took place *before* the Fall. As the divine plan unfolds for man, then, the individual is "mankind not yet created, but nevertheless capable of falling." Infralapsarianism is a doctrine with a greater sense of conclusion, since it lacks the potential or capability for something to happen. It was this air of conclusion that Brodsky apparently felt in Donne's work, a conclusion which allows the body of Donne to sleep a little, in the knowledge that the individual, although *creatus sed lapsus*, is apparently destined for membership amongst the elect. Brodsky, however, does not have Donne's peace of mind.

CONCLUSION

Joseph Brodsky's *Great Elegy to John Donne* is a reworking of Donne's biography, together with some of the central themes of the Englishman's verse, together with elegiac and rhetorical practices, to the point where it is no longer an elegy. It expresses the same doubts as the first line of Izaak Walton's elegy to the Englishman: "Is Donne, great Donne deceas'd?" and in opposition to the received critical tradition, I would say that no, he is not. Perhaps as a result of his interaction with Calvinism, Donne lies instead in a rather quiescent state of diminished existential agency. Brodsky observes Donne's rest, respects or even envies it, but is himself driven further by the demands of Kierkegaard's three stages, despite the fact that his poetry of the pre-1972 period and the *telos* in which it participates are wracked at times by the inability to cast rationality aside and make the leap of faith into language.

Brodsky's teleology is driven by Kierkegaard's unforgiving interplay of free will and necessity, and his poetry, up till the time of his exile, is cast in the aesthetic mould of English Metaphysical verse. The leap still lies ahead. One step *beyond* any Metaphysical writer's equilibrium or peace of mind is the Baroque – not only in terms of literary history, but in terms of Brodsky's individual epistemology. The Baroque is one dread-filled step closer to complete resignation to faith, and one step closer to the 70,000 fathoms beneath the individual, if the leap is unsuccessful. The Baroque pushes the Metaphysicals' expression of an empirical passage further into the unknown. The tenuous balance of opposites in Donne is a "delicate poise, and it is perfectly understandable that balance might be destroyed" (de Mourgues, 1953: 74). Such a destruction occurs in the next stage of Brodsky's poetry, just as the Metaphysicals' unified sensibility was pushed to a breaking point, to the point of disunity.

4 The Baroque Leap of Faith, 1972–1979

Joseph Brodsky's aesthetic cannot be reduced to the epithet "metaphysical." In 1972 it starts to move well beyond a purely Donnean stage and into the realm of the Baroque. Brodsky's aesthetic and philosophical progression towards such a stage is nevertheless a consequence of a Donnean *Weltanschauung* and certain rhetorical structures, influences which the Russian poet experiences relative to existentialism. The joint presence of Donne, Kierkegaard, and Šestov which fuels the progression of Brodsky's work is clearest in the Russian poet's tendency towards dualistic thinking. His verse shows the influence of the existentialist "either/or," for example, which structures the reasonable pros and cons of leaping into a unreasonable religious stage, the choice facing the poet at the time he is writing *Natjurmort*. His work also shows the influence of Donne's rhetoric, itself based upon the witty, yet reasonably organized interplay of two opposed concepts such as body and soul, finiteness and infinity.

The influences of Donne and existentialism run parallel until 1972; in this year they operate together to project the poet into an experience that is like both Kierkegaard's religious stage and the post-Donnean religious art of the Baroque. Apparently, though, the projection beyond Donne's aesthetic limits goes too far and too fast, since in 1979, for some reason, there is no published verse documented in the *Collected Works* (*Sobranie sočinenij*). Both the giddy acceleration of this Baroque stage and its subsequent, equally rapid descent into silence involve an increasingly extreme movement between Donne's rhetorical and thematic opposites, such as body and soul.

Donne left Brodsky with a way of thinking, a type of cognitive dualism which orders the way Brodsky experiences the unfinished task of completing the Existentialists' three stages with a resignation to the religious stage.

In making the brave leap of faith, in out-doing Donne's example, the Russian poet discovers that there are consequences to thinking the way Donne does – dizzying consequences that Donne himself shied away from. What are they, and how are they reflected in the increasingly rude and forceful interaction of rhetorical opposites? The answer lies beyond the Metaphysicals, in the Baroque; it lies beyond Donne, in the Catholic, Baroque poet Richard Crashaw, whose verse is a fearless pushing further of Donne's dualistic worldview.

FROM A METAPHYSICAL TO A BAROQUE AESTHETIC

When John Donne died in 1631, at the height of continental struggles between Catholics and Protestants, six years had passed since the accession of Charles I, the Stuart king whose family was celebrated by the Rubens ceiling of Whitehall's Banqueting House. Such Italianate exuberance was at odds with a sombre Puritan aesthetic, an artistic disparity reflecting the tension between royal papistry and Parliament's mercantile or Protestant leanings. Tension soon erupted into the Civil War and the essentially private nature of mid-seventeenth-century English poetry was rudely confronted by the public domain of military conflict.

Across this period the different private worlds of John Donne, Richard Crashaw, and Abraham Cowley can be plotted as beginning, mid and end points on a "curve of metaphysical inspiration" (Sharp 1940, 59). Donne died before the war, Crashaw's private life was profoundly effected by it, and Cowley represents the desire for rational order in the wake of the destruction it had caused. The possibility of linking the three poets in a causal fashion begs the question: what in Donne's thought instigates an upwardly-arching movement of complication, which peaks in Crashaw and then descends to simplification in Cowley? T.S. Eliot suggests in a lecture of 1926 that the dialectical and increasingly witty development of a thought is what marks it as metaphysical (1993, 87); what is important is *how* Donne thought, as much as *what* he thought. The dialectical structures of Donne's thought are developed or simply pushed to the point "of the absence of order, the fraction of *thought* into innumerable *thoughts*," a sort of runaway, unmanageable fission which explains the "catabolic" tendency of the whole school of Donne, from Donne via Crashaw to Cowley.

The catabolism begun by Donne's versified thought processes does indeed seem a disorderly consequence of his empirical construction of new, post-traditional truths, since these truths are based upon an increasingly unwieldy and complex combination of opposite notions, such as the finite and infinite or the secular and divine. To follow his work his readers must move with Donne from a small point of logical analysis to the subsequent attempt to hold in suspension the inconceivable combinations or consequences of a dialectic expanded to unheard-of dimensions. How, for example, can Donne simultaneously talk of man as both worm and co-heir of Christ? From a single proposition of minimum dimensions – that is, a comprehensible yet witty lyrical expression – the metaphorical centrifugalism of a conceit rushes to its point of maximum expansion or complexity, for the following reason.

The need for multiple proofs to persuade the reader of a novel proposition, as suggested in the previous chapter with regard to probabilism, implies a necessary movement by both writer and reader between dialectically situated propositions as the rhetoric moves forward, joining ever more disparate evidence. "Wit" is therefore based upon progression in a logical fashion, back and forth between paired notions, offered "not singly or even in isolated and therefore static parallels, but in sequence and therefore in kinetic fashion" (Miner, 1969: 133). The problem is that a wit based upon empiricism and probabilism cannot stop, since any linguistic expression of a divinely general truth can only be made subjectively, with a great number of individually insufficient words. To use a geometrical metaphor that will prove useful later on, Donne's witty conceits "swing in a[n ever-] wider arc, joining distant points of experience." After Donne, though, wit assumes "the importance of an end rather than a means; it became the whole poetic process." Greater faith, therefore, is soon matched by greater rhetorical movement, greater disparities being chained together. Language reflects the increased effort with its "jumbled syntax, ... dread of simple statement, ... elliptical and crowded lines" in some later Metaphysical poets, pushing Donne's rhetorical dialectic to extremes (Sharp, 17, 38, 42).

Although Donne's spirituality might at times be merely a social "sublimation of failed hopes, thwarted desires and deep-seated fears" (Miner, 1969, 46), a diachronic view of his work does suggest a genuine sense of isolation away from society but towards God in a manner which is developed further by later poets. If, for example,

Donne's satires by their very genre suggest authorial superiority over what is satirized, the divine poems reverse the situation; "wrongness" becomes an attribute of the author in the presence of divine rectitude. The suggestion that Crashaw continues Donne's teleology is supported by the marked preference of the former poet for the divine over the satirical (the religious over the ethical).

Satire and ethics, themselves closely related, are concerned with social mores, with earthbound and tangible existence. The reduced presence in the works of Donne and Crashaw of earthbound phenomena in favour of the spiritual is not the negation of things tangible or physical, but what Eliot calls "a compromise with the flesh," a compromise which across the work of both poets leads to a "contraction of the field of [physical] experience" (1993, 119). The well-balanced dialectic of tangible and intangible soon becomes asymmetrical; the former is reduced in importance and the latter is increased. Experience of tangible things is finite, transient knowledge of a space or place; intangible dimensions are part of divine permanence, of infinite time. In this manner it is possible to show one way in which the spiritual concerns of Donne's metaphysical aesthetic grow into the Baroque concern with the fleeting moment, thus diminishing the specific nature of places.

In seventeenth-century verse space consisted of the universe, heaven and hell:

Spatial transcendence involved relations between man and the earth or man and the universe – microcosm and macrocosm – or between earth and heaven. The relation was, as it were, instantaneous and constant. Such a formal connection required no time for moving from heaven to earth – there was a king in both places – and that relationship abolished in one sense the distance between two very separated points ... But whereas space seemed to exist altogether at once – almost as if lying at one point simultaneously in the numerous correspondences between all parts of the creation – time was an irresistible sequence and a devourer of things, *tempus edax rerum*, as Ovid said. (Miner, 1969: 50–1)

In the simplest possible terms; God is always there (in divine space), He is always close by. If, however, a believer wants to partake of God's glory and permanence (to be *with*, not *near* the Lord), he only has the limited period of his life in which to do so, thus he must hurry up (in time) and make the leap. The leap will allow him to transcend the wholly physical space of his finite frame which greedy time is devouring. Time becomes the central concern of seventeenth-century English verse after Donne's demise.

In looking at how Joseph Brodsky's poetry between 1972 and 1979 has a striking affinity with the temporal concerns of a post-Donnean aesthetic, one must also say a word or two about how Donne's own verse is situated in the move towards the Catholic, Counter-Reformational aspect of the Baroque. Miner's comments seem contradictory in the collocation of earth, heaven and hell in space, whilst in fact heaven is only realizable for a believer over time. The problem is close to Protestantism's own "radical paradox, whereby he [the believer] is perfectly holy in Christ in heaven even while he remains radically sinful in his earthly state" (Lewalski, 17), a tension between a Christian actuality and potentiality. Apparently there was not much that one could do about it, since for many English Calvinists, Puritans, and Separatists, the Synod of Dort (1618–19) defined the doctrines of limited atonement and irresistible grace, leaving Donne, for example, dependent on "the effect of God's grace upon his passive and helpless self." Rather than drawing a strict division between Donne's enlightened Anglicanism and the barrenness of Calvinism, it would in fact be possible to show how Anglicanism and Calvinism share some common ground in their attitudes towards the physical and spiritual. For example, "mortification of the flesh and psychological 'self-awareness' are surely essential hallmarks of Puritan devotion and Donne's work need not be solely 'Anglican' at its structural core" (Sellin, 1983: 50).

If Donne instigates an unfinished dialectic of the physical and spiritual, which is continued by poets such as Crashaw, it cannot be through Calvinism. It is the incipient Jesuit aspect of Donne's verse which the Catholic Crashaw pushes further still, the same aesthetic emphases paralleled in Brodsky. Such emphases are certainly in Donne's verse. The poet encountered the Society of Jesus in his youth, and one of the main signs of St Ignatius's influence on the metaphysical mind is Donne's consequent "skill in coaxing and persuading the attention of the variable human mind to Divine objects" (Eliot, 1950: 309). Considering one of the central areas of dispute between Protestantism and Catholicism – faith versus works and the Catholic emphasis on things visual as part of the potential *sanctification* (not the mortification) of the senses – what Donne leaves to his followers is the task of contrition through good works, the training of the mind towards visual representations. Poetry and painting are certainly an integral part of seventeenth-century emblem books, to the point where "conceits explain emblems which vivify conceits which explain emblems..." (Ruthven, 1969: 34). If Brodsky himself has said that he was inspired to outdo Donne, then it is only by turning to just such an outdoer of Donne, a Catholic poet, that a solid analogy can be constructed.

RICHARD CRASHAW, 1612–1649

Richard Crashaw was born three years before Donne took holy orders, and four years before the death of Shakespeare. His life and verse differ from Shakespeare's in their centrifugal imagery, driven by a "perverse logic of ornamentation" to the point where British criticism disowns him as "continental" (Alvarez, 1961: 94, 101). Accusations of a foreign aesthetic are no doubt caused by Crashaw's links to Catholicism at home and to Caroline culture, which initiated his artistic passage away from any dialectically well-ordered or symmetrical poetry akin to the oppositions of chiaroscuro in Caravaggio's metaphysical canvases. Crashaw moves instead towards a bolder art that invites comparisons with a fully Baroque Rubens and he evolves into the main English seventeenth-century Catholic poet, a reverse process to that of Donne.

Crashaw's father, however, was a zealous Puritan. The young poet remained under this decidedly non-continental influence at least until entering Cambridge, where he embraced Laudianism and by 1639 had even taken holy orders. William Laud represented a facet of the English church which opposed Puritan extremism, advocating instead a faith "Catholic yet reformed, the *via media* between Geneva and Rome." English churches were poorly cared for under Elizabeth, and the Laudians followed Rome in calling for church decoration, as "too much cost cannot be bestowed on Christ" (Warren, 1939: 5, 7), so Crashaw was horrified in 1643 when Cromwell's troops made a bonfire of religious ornamentation in Cambridge's Market Square. His faith now persecuted, the poet soon found himself in exile in Leyden, a mercantile city hardly conducive to his beliefs. By the end of the Civil War he joined the Royalist exiles at the Parisian court of Queen Henrietta Maria, the wife of Charles I. Constant exile gradually lessened the importance of specific places, and Crashaw was soon left with nothing in his life "save resignation to God." The poet Abraham Cowley found him absolutely impoverished in Paris and offered help, but Crashaw felt impelled to continue to Rome, having earlier joined the Roman Church. He died in 1649, the same year as Charles's execution and the destruction of England's erstwhile, royal stability; Crashaw's growing faith, however, had cancelled the importance of trials and tribulations at home. The specific places of the geographical world were rejected in favour of the intangible and the eternal.

The ability of Crashaw to diminish the finite and tangible in favour of the infinite and intangible is accomplished through a written, Catholic art that is "the enactment of the imagined sense of being in God's presence" (Parfitt, 1985: 54). Protestantism emphasizes the individual and devalues art, whereas Catholicism, in the words of

Kierkegaard, "has a conception and idea of the Christian ideal: to become nothing in this world" (SK in Dru, 1379), whilst sanctifying art. There is an inverse ratio in the Baroque between the artist and the art; in order for the finite artist to enter into a relationship with the infinite, the diminution of the artist's space to the point of almost "nothing in this world" becomes a celebratory expression of the enormous, divine dimensions which the artist tries to depict.

Crashaw depicts such dimensions with a great emphasis upon things visual bridging the two areas that dominated his life: art and faith. The form of Catholicism that grew out of the Council of Trent reduced the importance of Crashaw as a Caroline poet through its emphasis on pictorial expressions of spiritual zeal and thus made him part of other Counter-Reformational visualizations that stretched from Charles's court (Rubens) across Northern Europe (Rembrandt) and back "home" to Rome (Bernini). In such art "the saints ... now appear as recipients of miraculous grace; and the composure of their faces and figures ... has yielded to the physically contorted patterns of the trance or the rapture" (Warren, 64–5).

Crashaw, in depicting how mortality "May drink itself up, and forget to die" (RC, 87), how human heat can be reconciled with divine light, finds that sight is the one sense most effecting his language, the one sense suited to the representation of abstract truths and symbols. Baroque emblems are the union of words and pictures, of human and divine, which together show how "Eyes are vocal, Tears have Tongues, / And there be words not made with lungs" (RC, 112).

In joyful suffering for his faith, therefore, in the "sweet Contest; of woes / With loves" (RC, 199), the Donnean or Kierkegaardian paradox of loss through gain in the religious stage now becomes a visual paradox: if Baroque art diminishes the artist, then he is now made visibly smaller, he loses his prior dimensions in order to gain an entrance into the Absolute.

> Come man;
> Hyperbolized *Nothing*! know thy span;
> Take thine own measure here: down, down, and bow
> Before thyself in thine idea; thou
> Huge emptiness! contract thyself; and shrink
> All thy Wild circle to a Point. O sink
> Lower and lower yet; till thy lean size
> Call heav'n to look on thee with narrow eyes.
> Lesser and lesser yet; till thou begin
> To show a face, fit to confess thy Kin,
> Thy neighborhood to *Nothing*.
>
> (*Death's Lecture at the Funeral of a Young Gentleman*)

These are the harsh warnings of death to youth, but only by reducing space to virtually nothing one almost transcends it and approaches the perfect, ineffable nothingness of God. In order to get "lower and lower yet," to the point of nothing, Crashaw goes through many metaphorical changes, switching back and forth in a dialectic of various physical and spiritual states; since he must resign to his faith, he initiates the dialectic but must soon resign to its overwhelming speed and flux between the physical and psychic.

It is in the realm of faith's paradoxical victory through such resignation (life through death) that Crashaw pushes Donne's aesthetic one huge step further, from Crucifixion to Resurrection, and forms a basis for analogies with Brodsky's poetry between 1972 and 1979. Resurrection is based upon the interplay or dialogue between the paradoxical opposites in the Incarnation, which Crashaw saw as "the union of the Divine and the human, Time and Eternity. The infinite takes upon itself the lineaments of the finite; the Absolute makes its entrance upon history" (Warren, 1939: 83). Since the poems, songs or prayers that hope to join these opposites go unanswered, one surrenders reason to the leap into the unknown rigours of faith, in the hope of a Kierkegaardian recompense:

> So I may gain thy death, my life I'll give.
> (My life's thy death, and in thy death I live.)
> Or else, my life, I'll hide thee in his grave,
> By three days' loss eternally to save.
>
> (RC, 236)

Though faith is indeed an awful surrender, one must not delay; Crashaw equates indecision with death. As with Donne, the decision to move through the stages on life's way is a decision to brave the "storm ... / Of your own Cowardice ..., the Rocks / Of your own doubt." Crashaw leaps into faith whilst hoping that "If I be shipwrackt, Love shall teach me swim." With Kierkegaardian bravado, he tells his soul to "start into life, And leap with me." He has "gone Donne one better," he has metamorphosed into virtually nothing and thus become part of everything.

"GOING DONNE ONE BETTER": BRODSKY'S POST-EXILE POETRY AND PROSE

In structuring a discussion of Brodsky's "Crashavian" poetry and prose from 1972 onwards, an obvious division suggests itself. In 1979, for the first time, a year passes with the publication of no original verse and only a few essays. These eight years can best be explained by analogy with the verse of Richard Crashaw as a quintessentially Baroque stage. The rhetorical lessons that Brodsky learned from Donne are exaggerated to express its more disparate sensibilities. These sensibilities are most vividly observed as several sets of oppositions or images which together reflect the shift from a freely chosen participation in the workings of language to the consequent loss of that free will before an overwhelming and irreversible process; the poet must resign to the cosmogonical potential of language itself if he is to experience the qualitatively different existence which it offers to create. Language soon overpowers the man who tries to "use" it.

The resignation of free will to the workings of language is clear in the first dialectical pair discussed below, flora and fauna, used by Brodsky to depict two attitudes towards metamorphosing "lower and lower" in the manner of Crashaw; the lesser the beast, the greater the object of its praise or, rather, the greater the medium that creates such metamorphoses – language itself. Bold and dramatic bestial changes into lower forms of life are juxtaposed with the more resigned relationship of plants to inevitability, their more restrained display or blossoming within the constraints of seasonal cycles. Both the evitable and inevitable changes of fauna and flora constitute what Brodsky himself terms the Darwinian struggle for the superior species *homo culturus*, and although the pairing does not operate as part of the dialectic proper, it nevertheless hints at the dualistic thought processes at work which drive the Baroque upward and onward.

The true opposition of these dialectical processes is an outgrowth of both Donne and the Existentialists' influence: the dialogue between the human body and "inhuman," infinite soul. Since the fleshy constraints of the former are needed by the latter for any teleological advancement in this world – advances made linguistically by the living, speaking poets Joseph Brodsky and Richard Crashaw – body and soul are linked explicitly by the Russian poet to the next conceptual pair, literary form and content. The dialectic is picking up centrifugal speed, though, and is expanded one step further to rope together a pair of greater dimension: space and time in general. The dialectic starts to show signs of stress when expanded to these dimensions, since through a connection drawn by the poet between space and sound, time and vision, there begins a competition between two qualitatively different speeds of perception, between what might be termed "sonic" or linguistic perception and the much faster, "spectral" or visual version. Together they help to explain why his poetry stopped dead in 1979. The silence of this year is the consequence of competing perceptions, of their competing time-frames or realities even. The competition between them explains the significance of the essays of 1979 that replaced poetry – that is, why prose appears during a verse-less year. Prose not only operates as a rational, analytical attempt to understand the collapse of the irrational, Baroque dialectic; it also leads Brodsky to an acceptance of certain *a priori* constraints to which he has always been subject – constraints that curtail the irrational grandeur of both the Baroque period and the giddy ascent of the religious stage in 1979. The ascent begins thus: Donne could experience the "death" of Crucifixion but not the Resurrection; Brodsky, in order to outdo him, must now move beyond the dilemma of *Natjurmort* dilemma to the Baroque leap of faith. The leap is an event that Crashaw was able to experience, by reducing the physical dangerously close to nothing so that it was resurrected in the spiritual. Crashaw, aware that such a sacrifice is a spoken commitment, crowns Christ as "Fair King of Names."

In an interview of 1982 Brodsky gives an indication of where this verse had been heading – implicitly with regard to *Natjurmort*, but explicitly with regard to the Crashavian problem of "naming Christ." "For instance, you write a poem about the crucifixion. You have decided to go ten stanzas – and yet it's the third stanza and you've already dealt with the crucifixion. You have to go beyond that and add something – to develop it into something which is not there yet. Basically what I'm saying is that the poetic notion of infinity is far greater, and it's almost self-propelled by the form" (Birkerts, 1982: 126). The self-propelled, soon inevitable processes of a Darwinian devolution that allow Crashaw's reduction of the tangible in the presence of the intangible are set in motion by Brodsky's sense that he is surrendering his agency as writer to the self-generating motion of language itself, as if *he* is being written by language. Merging Darwin and Kierkegaard means that instead of a dramatic leap, this period actually consists of an irreversible wading, surrendering further and deeper to Kierkegaard's 70,000 fathoms, devolving all the while into lower forms of existence in order to magnify the importance of the water.

FAUNA / FLORA:
FAUNA'S METAMORPHOSES OF FAITH
ABOVE AND BELOW WATER

In the poem of 1976, *The New Jules Verne* (*Novyj Žjul' Vern*), Brodsky suggests that if Darwin had dived into the ocean's depths, the under-water monstrous life-forms would have forced him to make some sizable recalculations. All the laws of underwater life's possible mutations will not be understood "until you reach the bottom [of the sea]," an evolutionary descent made clear in an article by Brodsky of February 1974. He says that the struggle for an individual's faith is akin not only to the struggle between Christians and barbarians, but to a competition for the very existence of a species called *homo culturus*. "This is a struggle between species, but in contrast with Darwin (or developing Darwin in a direction opposite to his views) the species on the way to extinction, in the long run, is victorious. For its victory is the language created by it, which determines the life of the so-called 'survivor' of the combat" (1974a, 14).

This is a Darwinian scheme moving backwards, a scheme understood by analogy with the processes of natural history and explicitly offered in terms of bestial combat, of the survival of the fittest, of devolutionary changes. The poetry of the 1970s makes use not only of bestial changes which are specifically aquatic (fish, shellfish, and octopi) but refers to metamorphoses above water too (apes, birds, mice, flies, and butterflies). The most common reference to subaqueous devolution is to fish. In *Laguna* (1973), a damp Christmas in Venice is celebrated with a meal of bream, not goose. As "Thy chordate ancestor, Savior," the fish satiates the poet; it represents both the traditional equation of Christ as fish and the unorthodox, Darwinian reduction to a dumb, piscine state. The two then are combined via the meal (ss2, 319). There is "a fish dozing within [each of] us" which can reach such extremes, as shown in the poem *Kvintet* by the tail of a Caspian roach which lies across or hides a newspaper headline about some "Recent Restrictions." To breach logical restrictions and be reduced to a holy fish-like state by faith, or even to a wholly bestial state by faithlessness, ultimately means one's demise as a finite being. In the same poem a traveller gulps for air like a landed fish on the sidewalk, and in *Tri rycarja* knights who died for their faith centuries ago, at Poitiers or in the Holy Land, now lie like stone sturgeon in an English abbey (ss2, 358, 424, 437).

In the race backwards through evolution to atomize oneself eventually in the Absolute, carp and bream are lumps or clots (*sgustki*) in time's smooth flow which can split and multiply further. The reduction of oneself back to a lowly, devolved state gets muddled with the multiplication of visually similar, but faithless nonentities. One cannot tell the difference at times: if one opens the door to a cod, another just like it will force its foot (*nosok*) in the door too. The very nature of the leap of faith is that it is into the unknown; is one nearing faith or simply sinning more and more? Devolution is uncomfortably close to levelling; even the believer who thinks he is devolving does not really know which way he is heading. As a result, devolution has both a positive and a negative capacity in the sense that a fish, for example, although a potentially positive state (especially from the point of view of contemporaneity with Christ), is just as likely to start rotting from the head, as the poet puts it. The smell of a fresh catch, of piles of fish, is uncomfortably suggestive of the inanimate multiplication that another of Brodsky's piscine metaphors represents; in the poems *A Part of Speech* and *Lithuanian Nocturne* (*Čast' reči* and *Litovskij noktjurn*), fish scales are likened to cobblestones. In *Brighton Rock* (*Brajton-Rok*), the end of an English day is equated with the colour of caught fish, a general air of demise represented in another poem by a fish's colour of rust.

The accelerating changes one undergoes to avoid a similar demise can become illogical combinations of species. Unnatural forms of nature are often depicted as architectural forms, directly opposed to those of St Petersburg's classical aspects. After all, the poet learned about the merciless workings of time from the city's "plastered heads of mythic animals or people, from … ornaments and caryatids holding up the balconies, from the torsos in the niches of … entrances" (LTO, 5). Having escaped the gaze of St Petersburg's cast-iron gorgons that line the fence around the Summer Gardens, he begins his own metamorphoses, perhaps heading for his own ledge in Venice, decorated by wedded monsters, or for the nymphs and cupids of a *plafond*'s modelling in Florence. The passage from Russia to Italy is itself from St Petersburg's two huge, sculpted sphinxes on the bank of the Neva to the winged lion of Venice, chimerae one and all.

> Тонущий город, где твердый разум
> внезапно становится мокрым глазом,
> где сфинксов северных южный брат,
> знающий грамоте лев крылатый,
> книгу захлопнув, не крикнет «ратуй!»,
> в плеске зеркал захлебнуться рад.
>
> (ss2, 319)

> A drowning city, where suddenly the dry
> light of reason dissolves in the moisture of the eye;
> its winged lion, which can read and write,
> southern kin of northern sphinxes of renown,
> won't drop his book and holler, but calmly drown
> in splinters of mirror, splashing light.
>
> (ps, 75)

The metamorphoses that one poem lists as "water, fauns, naiads and lions" are by no means guaranteed a succesful devolution; they are not only depicted in stone, but often *frozen* in stone, in mid-devolution, when the "brain got too tired to go on," their mossy groins a sign that further changes are impossible, when a corpse is indistinguishable from a fetus. It is the kind of immobility that sacrifices self-division to "a tyrant carelessly cutting up a capon." One needs to cut oneself up, as it were, before being cut up. Done successfully, the song of an agile, metamorphosed satyr can avoid the capon's fate, robbed of flight and life; it can play "second part to the rustle of wings."

The 1975 poem *The Hawk's Cry in Autumn* (*Osennij krik jastreba*, SS2, 377–80) is a useful text for documenting the movement from devolution to disorder as it is not only one of Brodsky's finest poems, but perhaps the most dramatic example of bestial change. In this work, remarkably similar to Gerard Manley Hopkin's *The Windhover* of 1918, a hawk flies higher and higher above the fields and churches of Connecticut; the temperature drops and the bird contracts its body as the wind thrusts it higher still, to the point where it seems a " barely visible brown dot." The hawk feels both pride and trepidation at having gone so high, but soon discovers that the wind will not let it descend. Thrust into the ionosphere, the bird knows it cannot now escape and cries out with an echoless, inhuman shriek that becomes a glistening, snowy shower of lace and written characters which sprinkle the elated children far below on the ground.

Osennij krik relates the reduction of a hawk to a brown dot (*ele vidnoe glazu koričnevoe pjatno*) which is then reduced to a mere cry, incomprehensible to others. The reduction to nothing, the resignation to a supremely subjective form of expression, is caused by the surrounding atmospheric pressure, by a limitless expanse referred to in the poem as "a blue ocean," "autumnal blueness," and "ultramarine." Though the hawk resigns to this realm by devolving into a pure shriek, it is a nevertheless a positive death because the cry is made specifically in the ionosphere – that is, in the realm that can reflect long-distance radio-waves or, in the case of this poem, the tiny waves (*melkie volny*) created by the cry that radiate out into the Absolute for ever.

The metamorphosis from hawk into cry is a result of the dialectic between free will and inevitability; the bird of prey is filled with both "trepidation and pride" (*smešannaja s trevogoj / gordost'*) at its achievements, but in becoming prey itself to the atmospheric pressure and flow (*potok*) of air, the opposition becomes "anger and horror" (*gnev / s užasom*); now the bird cannot descend back to the ground. Brodsky switches the point of view back and forth between "here" and "there" (*tam / zdes'*), between ground and sky as the bird and earth move farther away from each other.

Сердце, обросшее плотью, пухом, пером, крылом,
бьющееся с частотою дрожи,

точно ножницами сечет,
собственным движимое теплом,
осеннюю синеву, ее же
увеличивая за счет

еле видного глазу коричневого пятна,
точки, скользящей поверх вершины
ели; за счет пустоты в лице
ребенка, замерзшего у окна,
пары, вышедшей из машины,
женщины на крыльце

The heart overgrown with flesh, down, feather, wing,
pulsing at feverish rate, nonstopping,
propelled by internal heat and sense,
the bird goes slashing and scissoring
the autumnal blue, yet by the same swift token,
enlarging it at the expense

of its brownish speck, barely registering on the eye,
a dot, sliding far above the lofty
pine tree; at the expense of the empty look
of that child, arching up at the sky,
that couple that left the car and lifted
their heads, that woman on the stoop.

(TU, 49–50)

The dialectic is stretched to a breaking point, as the hawk resigns to "the astronomically objective hell" of birds far from the earth, where the switch from subject to object is reflected grammatically as the bird is buffeted by the wind:

Перевернувшись на

крыло, он падает вниз. Но упругий слой
воздуха его возвращает в небо ...

Heeling over a tip

of wing, he plummets down. But the resilient air
bounces him back ...

The poet's mix of free direct and indirect discourse muddles the distinction between the earthly and heavenly experiences that make up the dialectic; it complicates who and where the speaker is:

...из
труб поднимается дым. Но как раз число
труб подсказывает одинокой
птице, как поднялась она.
Эк куда меня занесло!
Он чувствует смешанную с тревогой
гордость.

...как стенка – мяч,
как паденье грешника – снова в веру,
его выталкивает назад.
Его, который еще горяч!
В черт те что. Все выше. В ионосферу.

...chimneys all puff out smoke. Yet's it's their total within his sight
that tells the bird of his elevation,
of what altitude he's reached this trip.
What am I doing at such a height?
He senses a mixture of trepidation
and pride...

But as walls return
rubber balls, as sins send a sinner to faith, or near,
he's driven upward this time as well!
He! whose innards are still so warm!
Still higher! Into some blasted ionosphere!

The culmination of the poem's lyrical experience, the shriek, is the
result of lyricism being spread across the dialectic, between first and
third person, between subjectivity and objectivity to the point where
it snaps and resonates.

The lyrical success of the solitary hawk or poet is measured as
altitude, and altitude is registered by the multitude of visible chimneys,
by the dropping temperature which is itself shown by a multitude of
thermometers. Once again the multifariousness of objects enhances
the subject, earthbound pneumatic multiplicity enhances psychic unity
and since the thermometers are likened to a host of Lares or Penates,
a pagan polytheism even enhances a Christian act of contemporaneity.
The act ends with a sacrifice or resignation to language, a linguistic
rush seen from the earth.

Мы слышим (крик): что-то вверху звенит,
как разбивающаяся посуда,
как фамильный хрусталь...

И на мгновенье
вновь различаешь кружки, глазки,
веер, радужное пятно,
многоточия, скобки, звенья,
колоски, волоски -

бывший привольный узор пера...

We hear something ring out in the sky,
like some family crockery being broken...

And in a twinkling
once more one makes out curls, eyelets, strings,
rainbowlike, multicolored, blurred,
commas, elipses, spirals, linking
heads of barley, concentric rings –

the bright doodling pattern the feather once possessed...

The pen was once free, but now is not, since linguistic self-control has surrendered to a "sound, not meant for any body's ears," to "the apotheosis of sound." There is no cohesive speech at the height of a celestial hiss of cold air (*ščiplet xolodom*) that produces the hawk's shriek of Furies (*vizg èrinij*) – of those infernal chimerae who hounded and shrieked at transgressors of ethical laws or mores.

The hawk's transgression is a linguistic one, in imitation of Christ's irrational sacrifice. It is such a lonely, subjective experience that despite the poet's simultaneous experience of the leap or shriek across both the first and third persons of the poem, the text ends with us (*my*) looking at the "sparkling detail" of the hawk as observers, not as those doing the leap. But perhaps Brodsky is combining his own lyrical altitude ("What am I doing at such a height?") with his simultaneous, social existence on Earth. What we analyse objectively from below may well not be what is experienced subjectively way up high by the hawk.

If the supreme expression of this subjectivity is a conformity with the crucifixion, then it also bears mentioning that the hawk's wingspan is extended in a state of particularity: "unfurled, alone" (*rasplastannyj, odinok)*. Choosing to fly high above churches (that is, institutionalized faith), the hawk soon feels its movements being forced by the ineffable, boundless dimensions it has entered, in a way that suggests Abraham's leap of faith. The wind throws the bird up higher, "like the fall of a sinner [back] up into faith." Brodsky's depiction is rich in metaphors of slicing or cutting. The river below is a "living blade" (*živoj klinok*); the grass around the bird's nest is like razor blades (*lezvija*); the hawk cuts the sky like scissors and the shriek itself is described as a cut or laceration. Syntax unexpectedly runs away with the poet as he describes the hawk's ascent, resulting in a sixty-three-word sentence, beginning "In the windy reaches, / undreamt of by the most righteous choir" (*vyše / luščix pomyslov prixožan*). The arrogant, first-person complaints about the altitude (*Èk kuda menja zaneslo!*) then instigate a more stunted syntax, an average of only 6.5 words per sentence. Language is then suddenly left to its own devices, with the actual shriek of forty-five words. Then once again the poet resigns to a linguistic acceleration, to the absurdly long sentences of runaway enjambment. The devolution to nothing has let Brodsky be led far by his language, into a series of runaway metamorphoses.

These metamorphoses, effected on the arrogantly stable forms of animals are much more spectacular than those of plants, which naturally change within temporal constraints, and this difference between fauna and flora makes "a fish more interesting than a pear." Nevertheless, although plants may not devolve as such, their appearance in Brodsky's verse is important as a manifestation of botanical change relative to certain constraints of inevitability. In *Mexican Divertimento* (*Meksikanskij divertisment*), the status of inevitability that empire aspires to is discussed in terms of plants; the negative, qualitatively unchanging permanence that empire longs for not only fails, but returns the contrived orderliness of "state-ly" gardens to a more powerful force of permanence, the naturally cyclical and inexorable presence of weeds, lizards, and grass snakes:

> Включая пруд, все сильно заросло.
> Кишат ужи и ящерицы. В кронах
> клубятся птицы с яйцами и без.
> Что губит все династии – число
> наследников при недостатке в тронах.
> И наступают выборы и лес.

> And everything's grown over, pond included.
> Grass snakes and lizards swarm here, the tree crowns
> bear flocks of birds, some laying eggs, some eggless.
> What ruins all the dynasties, blue-blooded,
> is surplus heirs replete with numbered thrones.
> The woods encroach, and likewise the elections.
>
> (PS, 80)

Any botanical disorder or display can seem ultimately fleeting: decline follows disorder, time after time. Such places of neither permanent change nor stasis, like a stuck record, are depicted in the poem *Litovskij noktjurn* as firewood which continually merges into trees, then back into firewood. Flora's inextricable relationship with eternity therefore has a potentially negative side; roses can be bunched to make the negatively mathematical or logical "8" of infinity, whilst dahlias recall the wheels of a train. The poet even asks winter to cover summer with snow, the early verse's celebration of seasonal blossoming now dull and predictable at times. A summer's stuffiness might do little more than render "enormous plants motionless" and give human joints an "oaken lustre" as they acquire the immobility of furniture. The epitome of this downside to nature is how the Soviet Union managed to convince its citizens that itself and nature were as inevitable as each other (1972c, 66; 1974a, 13).

The opposition of flora and fauna has at least shown the dualistic thinking upon which Brodsky's perceptions are being structured in this period, as he discovers the relationship between free choice and necessity – a relationship extended into the dialectic proper, and its core oppositions of body and soul, form and content.

DIALECTIC NO. 1: BODY/SOUL

Since "every more or less serious poet" decides to belittle or change himself in the absolute dimensions of (divine) time, Brodsky starts to consider a different goal; instead of pure Kierkegaardian subjectivity, he now strives for a form of objectivity, relative to those very dimensions (LTO, 58). From here on, then, in an about-face from the early verse, one needs a post-leap stoicism as the finite human body is taken "lower and lower yet"; Brodsky now calls pure existentialism "a form of stoicism, sponsored by Christianity" (67). It is not real stoicism, though, since the route was freely chosen, has a specific goal, and the subject is not indifferent to the pain on the way. As the poet says, "a stoic who knew the truth was only ever one third a stoic!" (NSA, 115). He must undergo tangible space's reduction; the body (or form) is reduced in favour of the soul, of potential content.

The drama of fauna and flora here makes a body's form a much more frequent and dramatic reference than the soul in verse between 1972 and 1979. The human body that accepts the challenge of faith and devolution has the furthest possible distance to go if evolution is to be re-enacted backwards to a state of nothingness, the distance from *homo sapiens'* proud or upright stance to the humility of tiny maritime objects on the sea floor and in horizontal sediment. Speech can therefore only be sent directly upwards if you lie on your back, jokes Brodsky (SS2, 364). Horizontality, however, is also the position of purely physical reproduction, of splitting like an amoeba; punning on the possible misdirection of spiritual zeal, for example, the poet says his own "body repented of its [sexual] passions" (that is, not the Passion – *telo v strastjax raskajalos'*). The physical or finite triumphs completely over the spiritual in the poet's 1972 *Song of Innocence*; Brodsky presents a series of teleologically stunted opinions, in which girls plan to wed "well-built lads, and we won't hope for a soul in each other" (304). It is a ditty sung in the first person plural, by those whose lives, "like little lines of verse, have reached a period" (307). Their fleshy multiplication is the stuff of states, empires, and levelling, very much opposed to Brodsky's private diminution. This opposition is expressed elsewhere, in a remark to the bust of the decapitated Mary, Queen of Scots, in the Luxembourg Gardens. She is told that while intact bodies make history, headless ones make art. Whole bodies can be massed for the artless, impersonal purposes of history, whereas the self-destructive aspects of devolution allow a profoundly personal, creative act only at the cost of the body, of physical space.

The soul's relationship to the body can often seem a sort of residence in no-man's land, stuck between Earth and Heaven, the finite and infinite, now and then – a liminality that is, as yet, unresolved. Even the Guardian Angel which appears in *Meksikanskij divertisment* is close enough to the edge of physicality to be shot and made into a crude, civic obelisk representing Freedom. Digressing from thoughts of the liminal nation of Lithuania, Brodsky says his ghost or spirit (*prizrak*) lives in a similar bond with dead matter, the "refuse of sleep, the splinters of borders." The poem from which this quote comes, *Litovskij noktjurn*, is based on Brodsky's spirit, spectre or apparition travelling back to Lithuania for a nocturnal visit. What might seem like an exile's longing is termed "the return of the quote to the lines of the 'Manifesto': / more guttural, / and an octave higher from its distant wanderings." A quote's return to its own, old manifesto is a cliché or tautology. Literature cannot exist on such tautologies. By 1976 Brodsky is consequently impatient to let potential content (the soul) create an asymmetrical balance in favour over usual form (the body), like the breaking of the frame in Baroque painting: "Petulant is the soul begging mercy from / an invisible or dilated frame" (TU, 55–6). In moving beyond the frame of the human body, the dialectic gets stretched to the more abstract level of poetic form and content, though both form and content remain bound as tightly as body and soul.

DIALECTIC NO. 2:
POETIC FORM/CONTENT

Form and content are interpreted in Brodsky's work not only in metaphysical terms but also literary ones. In an interview of 1974 he says "form is a device to organize those things which are not supposed to be organized" (Brumm, 240). The potential disorder of the "content" is forced into accepting the "so-called classical forms," and only the dialectic or the "tension" between them creates poetry, its inevitable, self-generating movement. One half of a rhyme demands another, which needs a form into which it can be placed and so forth. The content may displace strict form, but it is always there in some manner of order or corporeal mass, since as Brodsky says of free verse – "free from *what*?" (Brumm, 241; my emphasis).

In an essay on Mandelstam, Brodsky states that the end of a poem's form – its last line, is the reflection of a finite, fleshy moribundity that makes the work's spiritual achievements all the more precious. Working together, flesh and spirit create art, which hopefully will "outlast its maker" (LTO, 123). This moribundity of flesh and form is animated by art, which is "a spirit seeking flesh, but finding words." Form is a vessel, therefore, for art's spirit – "break the vessel and the liquid will leak out" (1974a, 16); form and spirit need each other if *homo sapiens* is to make it as far as *homo scribens*. From the interaction of body and soul, form and content, the interdependence of opposites is extended to an even further level of abstraction, moving from the tangible, finite aspects of the body and intangible, infinite aspects of the spirit to space and time in general.

DIALECTIC NO. 3: SPACE/TIME

Joseph Brodsky was projected from one space into another in June 1972 and, as might be expected, experienced what his close friend George L. Kline called an eight-month dry period due to severe culture shock (Kline, 1990: 58). Just as with internal exile, though, the confines of which caused initial concern, writing soon becomes more important than external factors, than space. "Home does not cease to be home" for the moment but geography is gradually eradicated by the monstrosity (*čudoviščnost'*) of his metaphysical concerns (ss2, 423). As he says soon after being exiled, "New Land. New people. But the sky is the same. And I am the same" (Levy, 8). Geography does not influence his verse and if the theme of exile is in it, it is "in a rather indirect way" (Brumm, 232, 245). A transfer to another, coastal location involves the same man and the same pen. Wandering Odysseus appears in the verse of this period, making a similar declaration that all islands are the same. After exile, multiple experiences of nationally separate places soon lead the poet to suggest that eventually every country is just an extension of space. The surrounding earth and sea simply get more abstract as he regularly shrinks back home into his little kennel. This canine metaphor is an admission by the poet that sometimes he tends towards faithless diminution of himself rather than devolution, since in this metaphor space may be getting smaller, but it is becoming increasingly precious too. To hold space so dear is to shirk the leap into infinity.

Brodsky has said that the water of the Neva taught him about infinity and the stoicism one needs to bear it physically; not so much simply to brave it, but at some point to "bring it all to a close, / helping the dark / with the muscles of the face" (ss2, 460) and therefore use the body to avoid the future's potential levelling power, its "immense monotony" (LTO, 7). If one brings life to a (well-devolved) close and beats the tedium, one has gone "lower and lower yet," setting the religious, linguistic, or cultural mark by which the future will be judged. Hence Brodsky has the ability at times to turn Kierkegaard's leap of faith into an amazingly powerful ethical tool, at the same time as lauding personal responsibility in the wake of a Soviet Grand Inquisitor. Early in this Baroque phase the poet holds the Ten Commandments higher than pure existentialism, celebrating them from what he calls a typically Russian viewpoint, "the interpretation of the Ten Commandments as the foundation of a Judeo-Christian ethic" (1974a, 14). Poetic culture is initially an ethical, linguistic task, which then develops within the constraints of the past as a transition to the progressive, subsequently irrational and ideally religious model of Christ's inevitable or scripted sacrifice for God's ineffable glory. In an interview of 1974, in a discussion of culture and religion, specifically of both Old and New Testaments, Brodsky says: "What I like in the New Testament are those things which develop the Old Testament's ideology. That's why I wrote [a] poem about [the] transition between these books" (Brumm, 239). That poem, *Nunc Dimittis* (*Sreten'e*), clarifies Brodsky's dialectic of bodily space and time's inevitable movement. It is a reflection of the processes Brodsky sees at work in Christ's life: "It was as if the Old Testament were his script and he played his role which had been prescribed by it ... That was the last page of the script."

Sreten'e concerns the events of Luke 2, verses 25–35, when Joseph and Mary present the infant Saviour to the wise man Simeon in the Temple in Jerusalem. Long ago Simeon had been told by the Holy Ghost that he would not die until he saw Christ; now the wise man raises the child and tells of Christ's own, scripted future, which is "set for the fall and rising again of many in Israel." For both Christ and Mary, spiritual glory will be bought with a sword that "shall pierce through thy own soul." Mary and Joseph listen to the wise man in silent admiration, whilst the elderly prophetess Anna praises God on hearing Simeon's words.

Brodsky adds a description of Simeon's departure from the temple. He walks away from the other figures and grows smaller in the building's perspective, but his physical vanishing also becomes metaphorical through an interpretation of death as the devolution or diminution of his bodily space in favour of infinity, which is itself represented as a path that is growing or widening: "He moved and grew smaller, in size and in meaning ... The old man's torch glowed and the pathway grew wider" (*On šel, umen'šajas' v značen'i i v tele ... Svetil'nik svetil, i tropa rasširjalas'*). His reduction in meaning is only from the point of view of Mary's, Joseph's and Anna's incomprehension, since his waning existence is in an increasingly other-wordly, very Baroque flux between tangible space and divine time. In a Baroque, pictorial manner, Simeon leaves the "unstable frame" (*zybkaja rama*) of Joseph, Mary, Anna, and himself around Christ and heads for the temple's exit, where he will step into death. As Simeon finishes this call to God for immortal rest, he leaves the tangible building "across a space with no *terra firma*" (*po prostranstvu, lišennomu tverdi*).

Brodsky notes elsewhere that Simeon is reconciled to his fate with "a clear and calm awareness" and remains vigorous even in his final seconds (Kline, 1973: 230). The finiteness of his moribund body is invigorated by the dialectic with the soul's eternal existence, a dialectic that produces the paradoxical mix of age and strength in Simeon's gait as he leaves the church (*postup' byla starikovski tverda*). The irrational relationship of dying body and nascent spirit presages the sometimes violent dialectic of Christ's future. In 1974 the poet makes a similar remark about himself, with explicit reference to both a scripted existence and Kierkegaard, while joking about the fact that he is now thirty-three years old, the age of Christ at His death: "Christ lived for thirty-three years, and all the time he was following a script. It was all written, but only for the space of thirty-three years. At thirty-three only one thing can begin: Resurrection. Christ did not escape repetition. You can find this 'blasphemy' in Kierkegaard. The Resurrection is the repetition of the process. All life is in a sense repetition. This is the lesson of Christ" (Lamont, 1974: 574).

In *Sreten'e* Simeon talks to Mary of Christ's repetition; a script returns as reality.

В лежащем сейчас на раменах твоих
паденье одних, возвышенье других,
предмет пререканий и повод к раздорам.
И тем же оружьем, Мария, которым

терзаема плоть его будет, твоя
душа будет ранена. Рана сия

даст видеть тебе, что сокрыто глубоко
в сердцах человеков, как некое око

Behold, in this Child,
now close to thy breast, is concealed the great fall
of many, the great elevation of others,
a subject of strife and a source of dissension,

and that very steel which will torture his flesh
shall pierce through thine own soul as well. And that wound
will show to thee, Mary, as in a new vision
what lies hidden, deep in the hearts of all people.

(PS, 56)

The same oppositions constitute T.S. Eliot's *A Song for Simeon*. Eliot's
poem is actually an entire monologue in the first person, more of a
song by Simeon, which begs God for rest and salvation prior to death
in such a way that the wise man wants to shy away from Christ's awful
future martyrdom. The song tends away from the violence of Christ's
dialogue of body and soul, placing it instead in a parenthetical aside
to Mary and the infant.

Not for me the martyrdom, the ecstasy of thought and prayer,
Not for me the ultimate vision.
Grant me thy peace.
(And a sword shall pierce thy heart,
Thine also).
I am tired with my own life and the lives of those after me,
I am dying in my own death, and the deaths of those after me.

Eliot sounds suspiciously like John Donne in Brodsky's *Èlegija*, who
actually gained the rest of a pre-death assurance of salvation; as in the
Èlegija, death in *Sreten'e* appears as a metaphorical "departure from a
building" or a "going outside" the house or body. At the start of the
Russian poem, the temple surrounds (*obstupal*) Simeon, Anna, Mary,
Joseph, and Christ; everyone remains beneath its protection or canopy
(*pod sen'ju*), but Simeon goes outside. In fact, it is the first thing he
does when speech ends (*on končil i dvinulsja k vyxodu*). The rafters of
the temple are widely spread (*rasplastat'sja*), Brodsky using here the
same verb that appeared in *Osennij krik jastreba* to describe the "crucified" wings of the hawk. Simeon's apparent choice to get up and leave,
and the diminution of his body as he moves towards a similar sacrifice,
are at the same time part of a scripted and now ineluctable process,
shown by the fact that the door which leads outside is approaching

Simeon as much as he approaches it: "The door came still closer" (*i dver' približalas'*).

Simeon's words of parting – the final words that complete his scripted life – fly up like the bird of *Osennij krik jastreba* or the words of John Donne's talkative soul in the *Èlegija* in an attempt to move outside the "house," both architectural and physical.

Лишь эхо тех слов, задевая стропила,

кружилось какое-то время спустя
над их головами, слегка шелестя
под сводами храма, как некая птица,
что в силах взлететь, но не в силах спуститься.

...only his echoing words grazed the rafters,

to spin for a moment, with faint rustling sounds,
high over their heads in the tall temple's vaults,
akin to a bird that can soar, yet that cannot
return to the earth, even if it should want to.

Words cannot descend now; it is too late, since Simeon is committed to "the deaf and dumb" power of death (*v gluxonemye vladenija smerti*). Speech falls quiet, but Simeon transforms death's triumph over speech into a triumphant emphasis on divine silence instead. He "confuses" Joseph, Mary, and Anna with his silence, an increasingly other-wordly state; he dies after *seeing* the Word of God, not hearing it, since Christ is depicted as an infant who cannot yet speak and just breathes heavily in His own rest or sleep (*posapyval sonno*). When Simeon leaves, he therefore follows the radiant image of Christ (*obraz mladenca*).

In an interview of 1973, Brodsky emphasizes Simeon's experience as an attempt to deal with the painfully mortal bond of body and speech; Simeon knows that "as the body grows older it fills up with silence – with organs and functions that are no longer relevant to its life" (Kline, 230). Simeon guaranteed himself a qualitatively different silence, but can Brodsky? The poet seems worried that words are dying with the body that produces them, and indeed such worries are addressed in a well-hidden lyrical aspect to *Sreten'e*, one that considers the dual significance of silence: death versus what is divinely ineffable.

In *Sreten'e* the wise man leaves in silence whilst Anna in the background praises God; between them stand Mary and Christ, the *Logos* made of flesh and spirit, finite space and infinite time, between sound (Anna) and divine silence (Simeon). Implicitly beside Mary, but not mentioned anywhere in the entire poem, is the father, Joseph. Both

Brodsky and his biblical namesake are standing between Anna and Simeon (between Anna's speech about the future and Simeon's silence when that future actually arrives), as well as between the deaf and dumb state of death and the hope of making that silence divine. Though Brodsky appears, like T.S. Eliot, to see great lyrical significance in Simeon, *Sreten'e* is told from the point of view of the silent Joseph, watching the successful leap of another man; speech seems woefully mortal as Brodsky's own body is "filling up with silence" in awe of a visually elusive divinity and in fear of a visually perceived deathliness. The dialectic of space and time is superseded by the interaction of sound (language) and vision, by a unmanageable discrepancy between them that presages the breakdown of the Baroque.

DIALECTIC NO. 4: VISION/SOUND

Simeon died when he had tangible experience of the intangible, when he saw the divine, and when his finite existence met the infinite. For Brodsky, such opposites in unison create art, an alternate existence – not a separate existence, but one potentially simultaneous to finite life outside of art. Though his verse is an example of this alternative, it is fuelled by what he says and writes in his finite existence. What he sees influences what he says, which in turn influences what he sees. How can what the poet sees, the very forms he experiences in his finite life, effect the creation of an alternative existence via language? Put simply, how does vision effect sound? This pair is where the dialectic starts to falter.

When Brodsky walked out of school for good at fifteen, it was into "a sunny street without end" (LTO, 11); that perspective, however, ends sooner or later. Perspective is associated with telescopes, searchlights, and binoculars in this period, as if the city streets swing around, seeking the devolving individual in order to freeze him into one of St Petersburg's ubiquitous, palatial caryatids, like the eye of the gorgon. Rational scrutiny destroys the irrational idiosyncrasies of art and its existence in the religious stage; in the poem *Rotterdam Diary* (*Rotterdamskij dnevnik*), the one-eyed, telescopic gaze of a cyclops, for example, furiously scans the ruined city. Even on a vertical axis, the hawk of *Osennij krik* is reduced to "a pearl, a twinkling detail" by being caught in a pair of binoculars. The idiosyncrasies of art put the artist in the sights of rationality's binoculars, which aim to freeze or petrify art's metamorphoses in a state of non-existence. Yet the artist himself aims to devolve into nothing; the two forms of potential nothingness with which art co-exists lead Brodsky to talk of

Муза точки в пространстве! Вещей, различаемых лишь
       в телескоп! Вычитанья
          без остатка! Нуля!

(ss2, 329)

Muse of dots lost in space! Muse of things one makes out
    through a telescope only! Muse of subtraction
       but without remainders! Of zeroes, in short.

(TU, 15)

The eye has sought this muse in the Absolute, where the Baroque equation of gain through (eagerly sought) loss returns; the poet turns his attention to something eternally "being lost from sight, rather than the sight of loss." But if one is what one looks at, then gazing into absolute dimensions *makes* one nothing. Vision cannot deal with emptiness: *Lullaby of Cape Cod* (*Kolybel'naja Treskovogo Mysa*) closes with a list of increasingly long or absolute dimensions. It ends with thoughts about *Nothing*, which is beyond the eye. Human vision is limited in empty realms where there is "no soul/ in sight" and so thoughts may find themselves in self-destructive self-contemplation, reducing language to a "cuneiform of thoughts: any one of them is a dead-end" (ss2, 432). One is fascinated by one's metamorphoses, writes about them, i.e., pays more attention to them and therefore increases the speed at which they occur: "A falling star, or worse, a planet (true or bogus)/ might thrill your idle eye with its quick hocus-pocus./ Look, look then at that locus that's better out of focus," warns Brodsky. In the face of these problems that lie at the very root of the poet's ability to even perceive the world, let alone create an alternative existence via language, how exactly does language's cosmogonical potential attempt to interact with the destructive tendencies of vision? How does Brodsky's dualistic thinking deal with a dialectical pair that might actually be antithetical, not mutually beneficial?

What happens is that sound's incompatibility with light is an increasing problem across the 1970s, such that language eventually grinds to a halt. The immobile body tries to speak (at the speed of sound), but the eye, needing no echo or interlocutor, heads off on its own into emptiness (at the speed of light). The dialectic between opposites such as sound and the ineffable is necessary for faith's success, but it seems an impossible relationship here since, as Brodsky says of Eugenio Montale's verse, "if the psyche had its own tongue, the distance between it and the language of poetry would be approximately the same as the distance between the latter and conversational Italian" (LTO, 105). At the end of the day, using language to "dissect experience" actually robs one of intuition. Pessimism reaches a head in 1978. After a reading on 21 February, Brodsky is asked whether he would like "to go back and live in Russia again." His startling response: "I would love to. I would really love to." This is also the year of two very resigned works, *Midday in a Room* and *Strophes* (*Polden' v komnate* and *Strofy*), in which problems with vision stop sound or language in its tracks.

Polden' v komnate is an extended consideration of the dialectic between sound and vision, of its significance for the poet's past, present, and future. The past is discussed in terms of how sound and vision operated in St Petersburg; the present is both a consequence of this past dialectic and an intermediary stage en route to an inevitable future. The St Petersburg of Brodsky's past is described in terms of its narcissism, a visual contemplation of itself in the waters of the Neva that sets in motion a chain of self-objectification, of the city looking at itself looking at itself. The chain leads to "stone, a thing/ [and then] air," to the emptiness of air that Brodsky calls a horribly rational, Hegelian dream. A similar problem underlies a description of the tall, golden needle atop the city's Admiralty Building, "anaesthetizing" the contents of the clouds. If one looks down Nevsky Prospekt, the perspective does in fact end at the Admiralty, which then channels one's eye up to the needle's point, a vista which suggests that St Petersburg's perspective channels one's view into the rational dead-end of a Euclidean triumph, one that can anaesthetize the intangible or metaphysical. The more the city's inhabitants employ their vision, the more they are entrapped in a world of objects:

Там были комнаты. Их размер
порождал ерелаш,
отчего потолок, в чей мел
взор устремлялся ваш,

только выигрывал...

Звук уступает свету не в
скорости, но в вещах,
внятных даже окаменев,
обветшав, обнищав.

And there were rooms in that place. Their height
instigated a mess
from which ceilings, against whose white-
wash your own gaze was pressed,

just gained ascendancy ...

Sound cedes its place to light, thanks not
to growing speed, but things;
even beggarly, struck by rot
or grown stiff, they're distinct.*

Such general observations or maxims, in some cases, mark the poem's shift to a discussion of vision's damaging influence in the present. The poet's gaze runs across the parquet and itself grows wooden as a consequence; it makes the poet (the one who is gazing) into a wooden "centaur" of his body plus the chair he is sitting on. Light then exacerbates the problem by casting several shadows of the chimera, giving the impression of multiple limbs. Brodsky likens the process to the inevitability of evolution, though the changes are hardly desirable. Of both sound and light he says:

Оба переломлены, искажены,
сокращены: сперва –
до потемок, до тишины;
превращены в слова.

Both were forced to distort themselves, refract,
to be reduced: at first –
until noiselessness, till all's black,
and then be turned to words.*

The only way for objectification may be avoided is to look out into nothingness, but Brodsky predicts that eventually, "sound will only repeat that / which the eye discovers." Nevertheless, he lets his silent gaze investigate the emptiness and allows it to fulfill its finite potential as much as it can, since vision will be slowly overcome by the boundlessness that surrounds it.

Но, как звезда через тыщу лет,
ненужная никому,
что не так источает свет,
как поглощает тьму,

следуя дальше чем тело, взгляд
глаз, уходя вперед,
станет назад посылать подряд
все, что в себя вберет.

Just as, a thousand years hence, a star,
whose worthlessness is presumed,

sheds its light, though it does so far
less than it takes in gloom;

Following farther than bodies may,
ongoing vision leaves,
starting progressively to relay
everything it receives.*

The second poem, *Strofy*, also talks of light's unidirectional acceleration in an emptiness (*pustota*) boundless enough to ruin a straining eye. The expanse has little to do with faith, though. The poet hears no response to his questions and "repetition" now means only the repetition of one word with another, despite his desire to "turn around." Vision just makes things worse:

Бедность сих строк – от жажды
что-то спрятать, сберечь;
обернуться. Но дважды
в ту же постель не лечь...

Сколько глаза ни колешь
тьмой – расчетом благим
повторимо всего лишь
слово: словом другим.

These lines are a doomed endeavour
to save something, to trace,
to turn around. But you never
lie in the same bed twice ...

No matter how hard you're rubbing
the dark with your pupils, the Lord's
idea of repetition's
confined to the jibing words.

(PS, 141)

Levelling takes hold as Brodsky feels so earthbound; indeed, all things on Earth tend to merge when seen from a flying saucer, as the poet has it, suggesting a comparison of lofty, divine perfection with our own paltry existence. The image of the Virgin Mother will soon be replaced by one of multiplication – a family photo. "This is the end of our perspective," we are told, in a jumble of "strong dinosaur feelings and Cyrillic" or " a gallop to the finish line in cities' blinders" after which there is nothing. The influence of vision on sound has instigated an undesirable, unstoppable process Brodsky calls the laws of language, or, in an extra stanza published in *Novye stansy k Avguste,* a science.

> Как тридцать третья буква,
> я пячусь всю жизнь вперед.
> Знаешь, все, кто далече,
> по ком голосит тоска, –
> жертвы законов речи,
> запятых, языка.
>
> (ss2, 457)

> Все кончается скукой,
> а не горечью. Но
> это новой наукой
> плохо освещено.
>
> (nsa, 115)

> Like our thirty-third letter
> I jib all my life ahead.
> You know, dear, all whom anguish
> pleads for, those out of reach,
> are preys of the laws of language –
> periods, commas, speech.
>
> (ps, 140)

> There's not bitterness heightened
> at the end, but what bores.
> It's all poorly enlightened
> by new sciences' laws.*

DIALECTIC NO. 5: POETRY/PROSE

The discrepancy in frames of reference between Brodsky the physical poet, his verse as an empirical tool (moving at the speed of sound), and his vision moving faster still, has become unmangeable by 1979 – hence the complete absence of new poetry. The cognitive speed of poetry is exchanged by Brodsky for two works of prose in order to assess and comprehend the dilemma at hand: what deterministic laws of language or perception drove his verse to its breaking-point? What is this new science of 1978 that has as yet "enlightened poorly?"

Less than One contains the essays that both ponder these questions and incline Brodsky's future development to qualitatively different emphases. One essay concerns the triumph of logic and rationalism that is St Petersburg ("A Guide to a Renamed City") and the other discusses the relevance of prose for Cvetaeva's dizzying poetics ("A Poet and Prose"). In some ways the former essay concerns where he was, and the latter where he is. Brodsky was, until 1972, in Peter the Great's "utterly flat, horizontal [space] and he [Peter] had every reason to treat it like a map, where a straight line suffices" (LTO, 74). Any curves in the cityscape are the fault of a sloppy draftsman. Baroque and Classicism are referred to in the same breath in the poet's depiction of St Petersburg as a city-wide victory of predictably straight lines over curves: in fact, the poet jokes that block-like Leningrad housing projects are pure "barrackko." Buildings which line the Neva's embankments themselves seem all one style, merging to form a long, "stalled train bound for eternity."

Brodsky interprets the linear acceleration of St Petersburg's growth along infinite embankments as an architectural evolution dictated by the empty space always lying beyond each building, as though emptiness were eternally demanding another wing, another extension. One year after this essay, in an interview of 1980, he says that when growing up in Russia, he became aware that the repetitious forms of St Petersburg's classical architecture set up a rhythm in his work which rolled on and on, a certain inertia, as he says when comparing the architecture of New York and St Petersburg:

The inertia of perception, which helped so much back home, isn't be found here. As a matter of fact, it's exactly the inertia that's important, not the change of colour or landscape ... In all seriousness, if I may, I'd say that Petersburg's landscape is so classicist that it becomes somehow coincident with a person's psychical condition, with his psychological reactions. That is, the reaction will at least seem coincident to the author. It's some sort of rhythm, one that's entirely realized. Perhaps it's even a natural, biological rhythm. (Volkov, 1980: 28–9)

Thanks to the inertial, biological or evolutionary rhythm set up by what Brodsky in *Guide to a Renamed City* calls the city's light, "directness, and length of the streets, a walker's thoughts travel farther than his destination." They travel too fast, as well, judging by the collapse of the Baroque stage that is caused by light and vision.

These incredible pressures of acceleration lead to prose, a "shifting gear ..., trying ... to explain things" via the "genre's aesthetic inertia" which Cvetaeva herself made good use of in the past and which Brodsky himself contrasted with poetry two years before, referring explicitly to prose's slower processes. The term "inertia" in the quote above is close to its application in physics, the sense of inexorable, linear motion; in the following passage, though, despite the accompanying quasi-scientific context, Brodsky uses the term closer to its secondary meaning, that of slowness: "A poet's turning to prose is the tribute of dynamism to the stasis which preceded it; only the latter gains anything from such a switch: there is communicated to it a certain element of motion, which from the point of view of stasis looks like acceleration, but which in the eyes of dynamism is only one of the forms of inertia" (1977e, 9).

Brodsky does not stay in this lowly, swampy realm for long. The rational thought processes that prose allows are interpreted by the poet as a brief respite from the rigours of poetic cognition: "Prose and logic are the benefactors when Pegasus folds his wings, but not for long, because suddenly they experience a very strong temptation to move" (1977e, 9). In moving beyond a Baroque stage, though, the central question must be: How do the new laws of language leave any room for choice or personal responsibility?

CONCLUSION

Brodsky's poetry of his Baroque stage is dependent upon visual perception, upon an intake of information that happens too quickly for either spoken or written language to keep up with. The attempts to keep up have left the poet psychologically, psychically and physically exhausted; they have also caused a rearrangement of the earlier dialectical pairs from the start of the Baroque stage. Since the poet's ability to produce language is a bodily one, language is unfortunately now part of a paradigm that includes the exhausted body, objectified phenomena, logic, and deterministic laws. Vision, on the other hand, is now superior and is the poet's main form of empirical discovery in the world.

The importance of vision for the end of Brodsky's Baroque period is in part a product of what he calls his imagistic metaphors, a term that also suggests the very visual nature of the Metaphysicals' witty, metaphorical thought. In defining the nature of metaphor, Brodsky sees an analogy between the marriage of analytic and synthetic thought in poetry and the two halves of any metaphor which work together to develop their visual potential. In other words, a metaphor, just like the poetic thinking it constitutes, is made of two parts; the first part is the object of description ("the tenor") and the second is the object with which "the first is imagistically ... allied" or synthesized ("the vehicle" [LTO, 56]). It is reasonable, then, to link what Brodsky perceives as thought's higher stage of synthesis to this imagistic depiction, to the vehicle or second part of a metaphor, which offers what he optimistically calls the "possibility of virtually endless development."

Analysis and synthesis, tenor and vehicle, remain interdependent for endless development, because "analysis is always a profile, synthesis is always *en face*, and a good poem is stereoscopic" (1977e, 8). For Brodsky, this desirable – yet elusive – potential of metaphorical thinking lets one see further, as it takes on the qualities of a telescope.

The problem is, however, that even this linguistic, metaphorical "telescope" cannot keep up with *real* vision; the dialectic between sound and vision has failed and so will that of analysis/synthesis in the post-Baroque stage. This failure of irrational wit is hinted at when Brodsky invokes Kant (one of the last names one would expect to see celebrated in a Kierkegaardian context) for part of the definition of synthetic judgments as those "wherein the predicate adds to the subject something which is not contained within the subject alone." The importance of Kant for Brodsky's post-Baroque work is a critical one, especially when the poet tries to understand what exactly the deterministic laws of language do or do not allow in terms of free will.

The answer to what happens to free will and a Baroque aesthetic when it has to deal with deterministic laws can be seen by extending the passage from Donne to Crashaw one step further, to the work of Abraham Cowley. Showing signs of the influence of Hobbes and Bacon, Cowley moves from the bold, Caroline Baroque of Rubens to the diminished, Cavalier aspects of "Caroline of the Exile" caused by the Civil War (Eliot, 1993: 185), and is a poet who "climbs to heaven by paying close attention to scientific facts" (Hinman, 35) en route back to Augustan influences. The diminution of Baroque disorder at the hands of laws of aesthetic evolution and the growing presence of a deterministic worldview are also the core concepts of Brodsky's work of the 1980s.

5 The Post-Baroque, 1980–1989

After 1979 Joseph Brodsky's work enters a new stage, one that draws upon and parallels a comparable phase of the Baroque in terms of painting, literature, and philosophy. In the realm of pictorial art, Brodsky's new stage corresponds to the Poussinesque period of the Baroque, following the metaphysical emphases of Caravaggio and the high Baroque of Rubens. Poussin's acceptance of compositional constraints at a time of burgeoning Classicism is paralleled by Brodsky's own realization that Baroque disorder is, unfortunately, subject to certain limits or constraints.

As for literature, Brodsky's new stage corresponds to the more constrained and orderly post-Crashavian aspects of the English poetic tradition. Both Richard Crashaw and Joseph Brodsky push a dialectical, Baroque worldview to its breaking point, to the point of complete silence. What can realistically follow it? Just as the disorder of Baroque painting begins to operate within more restrictive, reasonable limits, so the disorder of Crashaw and Brodsky's Baroque poetry presages the subsequent, more modest dimensions of Précieux, Cavalier, or Rococo literature, of a smaller, post-Baroque display en route to an Augustan aesthetic. After Donne and Crashaw, then, an English poet whose work is comparable with Brodsky's work after the 1980s is Abraham Cowley; Cowley's own more orderly Cavalier or Précieux tendencies lead to his double role in literary history as both the last Metaphysical and first Augustan poet, bridging disorder and order on the way to the Enlightenment.

R.L. Sharp has described the development of the entire school of Donne as the "curve of metaphysical inspiration" (1940, 59). He implies a negative assessment of Cowley's "descent" into late Metaphysical poetry after the giddy heights of Crashaw. The term is extraordinarily useful if one reapplies it to the Kierkegaardian triad of aesthetic, ethical, and religious stages. Brodsky revisits the ethical and aesthetic stages as a "descending" Metaphysical, on the far side of his own curve and completes the symmetrical path drawn below, concluding a process which began in the earliest verse. This early work is inspired by St Petersburg; from Brodsky's post-Baroque period onwards, Venice replaces the Russian city. The combination of cities and philosophies will create the following pattern.

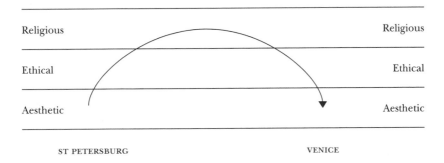

Religious   Religious

Ethical   Ethical

Aesthetic   Aesthetic

ST PETERSBURG   VENICE

Whether the analogy of this descent begins with Précieux, Cavalier, or Rococo art, a common movement exists in post-Baroque art of the seventeenth and eighteenth centuries towards a diminutive, earthbound, and ethical aesthetic after the hyperbolic extremes of the Baroque. This is the course that Brodsky traces.

THE POST-BAROQUE MODEL

Précieux

The clear element of hyperbole inherent in the Baroque is a result of its breakneck acceleration to the outer parameters of experience, "a sort of test of reality – working at times like a *reductio ad absurdum*" (de Mourgues, 129). It sets the limits for what is experienceable. If one has already run its entire gamut of finite experience, though, to say anything extra means reworking something *within* those perimeters, a potentially hackneyed variation on a theme already covered in the reduction to the "absurd" nothingness of faith. Each variation that manages to avoid cliché unfortunately also reduces the number of future variations by one. The smaller, Précieux aesthetic operates within increasing constraints; namely, to create new works of art from an ever-diminishing number of novel choices. Variations or changes become a finer and finer splitting of aesthetic hairs. Précieux verse thus reduces Baroque extravagance to a fine or "re-fined" coterie form, playing on tiny formal variations, comprehensible each time to fewer and fewer people. Poetry's aim is not now to examine the unknown, but to recognize what is already known, albeit hidden among the intricate and multiple themes or variations played upon a familiar motif or metaphor. The process of writing more and more cannot help but cause the demise of bold Metaphysical and Baroque conceits in a way that seems inevitable. It is this inevitability that in turn makes the process similar to Eliot's catabolism; innovation reaches a natural limit of maximum complexity and then recedes or falls apart.

Another reason why Précieux verse tends to depict minor incidents is that seventeenth-century coteries (for example the royalist one around Queen Henrietta Maria in France) are safe enclosures, away from the horrors of war; poetry helps at times to avoid personal anxieties. Hardly a ringing endorsement for things Précieux, so accusations of ostrich-like behaviour should be countered before moving on: "The Précieux poet's positive achievement is to shelter the delicate flowers of civilization from the rough winds of tempestuous times: his hot-house is not his private property, it belongs to the tradition of culture. Unselfish in a way, he puts aside his own problems as well as those of his age to share with his group a salvaged common heritage, and stands like an impersonal landmark of what he considers, and partly justifiably, to be, at a given period, the highest possible degree of civilization" (de Mourgues, 116–17).

In sheltering their delicate flowers, the Cavalier poets of England, too, are obliged by the inevitable reduction of the Baroque and the chaos of war to scale down their art. More earthbound concerns lead to an emphasis on ethical order, within both political and aesthetic contexts.

Cavalier

The Cavalier poets in exile during the English Civil War experience Queen Henrietta Maria's cultivation of the related, but broader cultural phenomenon of *la préciosité*, of elegance and polish. The degree to which they absorb it may be a moot point, but the existence of a strong coterie culture is not: "The usual alignment that imparts

Cavalier literature its special flavor is friendship or love in small groups, in each case a relation with a code that implicitly agrees with those in the world whose opinion and principle one values" (Miner, 1971: 49). Literary coteries, far from home and a monarchy, bring together the themes of solitariness (in exile) and the resulting social haven of friendship. The reworking of the Metaphysicals' mode in these groups marks the end of solitariness and begins a descent into social ideals as a whole. The descent is from the dizzying, religious stage back down into ethical Cavalier ideals, based upon the same Anglican path so dear to the young Crashaw. Instead of Crashaw's Baroque hyperbole, though, goals have become more modest: friendship, the comforting seasonal cycles of the countryside, or simple introspection. This retreat in anticipation of the king's return does not mean that Cavalier verse, being ultimately the product of a unified group, ignores the damage done to them by time, fate, and fortune while they wait. The royalists still feel great uncertainty and disorderly transience in their lives at home and abroad.

Because order and simplicity are sought in anticipation of the future, social triumph of the Restoration, poetry loses the cosmogonical aspects of the Metaphysicals and now awaits a real-life event. Pure order or constraint is lifeless, but disorder produces headless monarchs. In both aesthetics and politics, some movement was therefore allowed *within* constraints. In fact, an element of disorder was necessary to keep the larger order sound. On the downside of the curve of metaphysical (and Kierkegaardian) inspiration as art comes full circle, certain questions about order logically emerge: "What is the degree of admissible variety commensurate with order? What kind of order is natural? What are the limits of an ordering art before artifice stifles" (Miner, 1971: 163)?

Rococo

The question of order applies also to the Rococo, the third form of post-Baroque winding-down that is comparable with Brodsky's work of the 1980s. The style's increasing emphasis on orderliness presages the subsequent retrospective, classicizing tendencies which soon replace the Rococo – tendencies best shown by the work of Poussin, as artistic inspiration comes full circle with a return to traditional limits after the innovative chaos of Baroque limitlessness.

In the face of these increasing limits, the Rococo is a style that shares Précieux and Cavalier emphases on an ornamentation that becomes smaller and finer. The Rococo in England might be just a pale reflection of the French spirit, but both English and French

Rococo nevertheless reduce or diminish the Baroque in a comparable fashion: "The human passions are treated in the Baroque profoundly, decently, and metaphysically; in the Rococo they are treated superficially, cynically, and sociologically" (Hatzfeld, 34). In transposing the history of art to that of literature, Helmut Hatzfeld offers a long list of shifting emphases between Baroque and Rococo. Greatness and power become beauty and grace; tragic pathos becomes humorous lightness; extravagance becomes discreteness. What was once marble and bronze is now ivory and silver; the chromatic scale of brown, purple, dark blue and gold shifts to a minor range of pastels, grey, green, and silver.

The new minor dimensions, however, which in music became "Baroque decorativeness without grandeur" (Grout, 453), are only half the story. The Baroque does not simply dissipate into the Rococo. Inspired by archaeological discoveries, a yearning for lost antiquity leads also to a new fusion of Graeco-Roman antiquity and Roman High Renaissance. These tendencies are uppermost in the work of Poussin, moving in the reverse direction to that of Rubens and Bernini. The retrospective yearning for classical emphases gives Poussin's work the air of coming full circle, since it, too, is "to some extent a continuation of the Renaissance conception," an active attempt to "revive the life of antiquity" (Bazin, 134, 36).

Having passed already through the Metaphysical Caravaggio and the high Baroque of Rubens, the post-Baroque in Poussin tends towards clarity and composure, stressing above all the formal or compositional aspects of Rubens. Poussin is considered France's greatest painter by the reign of Louis XIV, a king whose own palace at Versailles is now a document to the play of Rococo ornament within the restraint of Classicism. In Poussin's work, figures shrink dramatically from their frame-filling role in Rubens to tiny dimensions within the sweep of expansive landscapes.

Poussin's contemporary and kindred spirit Claude Lorrain appears in Brodsky's first collection of *Venetian Strophes*, written in the 1980s. Brodsky admitted to joining Claude and Poussin in his thoughts at the time (PM, 171–2). This idea is logical, because Claude's warmer landscapes, of somewhat smaller dimensions than Poussin's, do indeed also have a rule-governed composition. Symmetry of composition is emphasized, which draws the eye into the depth of the landscape that is the real centre of interest. The close of *Venetian Strophes* depicts an alumnus (*pitomec*) of Claude in Venice, who finds himself overcome by the city's air of inevitable demise. There are numerous references to maritime life and the absurd reduction of animal space amidst the limitless blue spheres of sea and sky. An alumnus of the school of classical expanses therefore finds himself struggling to keep his reason from listing (*ot krena*). In fact he, too, longs to undress and "press up against a[n animal,] living bone, / as against a hot mirror," which will instigate a series of unstable, unreasonable metamorphoses (SS3, 53).

Précieux and Rococo painting embody this type of struggle with rigorous order, clarity, and composure, and in the same way that the turmoil of Baroque canvases begins to operate within clear and orderly limits, so the turmoil of Crashaw and Brodsky's Baroque poetry pre-figures the subsequent, more modest dimensions of Précieux, Cavalier, or Rococo literature. After Donne and Crashaw, then, the English poet whose tendencies invite a comparison with Brodsky's is Abraham Cowley, a poet who is a harbinger of the Enlightenment.

THE LITERARY ANALOGUE: ABRAHAM COWLEY, 1618–1667

Six years Crashaw's junior, Cowley outlived his friend by almost two decades, thus living to see the return of Charles II, of order and stability after the war. But before that his life had run the gauntlet of national disorder. Educated like Crashaw at Cambridge, Cowley also left town at the arrival of Cromwell's unruly troops. After a brief stay amongst the king's supporters in Oxford, he spent the ten years following 1644 in France as the queen's secretary and a royalist agent, a shady role that raises questions concerning whether his 1657 return to England was a royalist subterfuge or a genuine acceptance of the Commonwealth. Charles II seemed to think it was capitulation on Cowley's part, judging by the meagre reward he received after the Restoration.

Cowley's later years were spent in study and rustic seclusion. Following his qualification as a doctor, he also helped to found the Royal Society, a cornerstone of scientific inquiry and English neo-classicism. This growth of rational thought during Cowley's lifetime is reflected best in a poem of alternating, answering stanzas written jointly by Cowley and Crashaw on the pros and cons of irrational hope. Crashaw celebrates the hope of ineffable faith as "Thou by whom / Our Nothing hath a definition," as "Fear's Antidote! a wise, and well stay'd fire / Temper'd 'twixt cold despair, and torrid joy." Cowley, on the other hand, dismisses hope as "Fortune's cheating Lottery," because "When thy false beams o'er Reason's light prevail, / By *ignes fatui*, not North stars we sail" (RC, 92).

The end of the Metaphysicals in the era of aesthetic and ethical order was manifest in the demise of wit. Witty illogicality gave way to the more reasonable constraints of a new, rational understanding of the universe. Metaphysical verse was accused of being extremely obscure and unreasonable, qualities that were part of the papist subversion that had blinded common sense and caused a civil war. As a result, divine harmony was now to be reflected in an ethically ordered natural world, a reasonable art, and a peaceful nation. Cowley sees in the throne a rational power that "Spoke but the word, and sweetly order'd all" (AC, 228). After the Civil War the poet, not surprisingly, interprets the Restoration as a reinstatement of divine will following the martyrdom of Charles I, which had atoned for England's godless chaos during a time of social disorder. The death of Charles had appeased famine, sword, and plague, which were "God's great triumverate of desolation" brought "to scourge and to destroy the sinful nation" (289–90).

Cowley's verse is a bridge between the ages and aesthetics of a private, sometimes troublesome particularity and the divine order of state and nature, making him much more "settled" than Donne (Eliot, 1993: 186) and indicative of the century's growing tendency to become "blissfully unaware of ... depths and metaphysical distances" (Sharp, 212). Wit for Cowley is a moderate, controlled disparity, reflected in his strictly monitored relationship between poetic content and structure, and in a growing objectification of his lyrical subject.

The rational affirmation of order and correctness is the early foundation of Augustan aesthetics. Rationality delayed the deluge of Baroque confusion and now it tames it once more, as seen in Cowley's constrained disparity between the same dialectically opposed notions that drove the Baroque so far and so fast. Cowley shows how metaphysical poetry transforms itself into a new, tighter compactness and intellectuality. In an ideal poem, unruly wit "is not to adorn and gild each part; / That shews more cost than art. / Jewels at nose and lips but ill appear" (AC, 281). Tending instead towards the rational schemes of the Royal Society, Cowley's methodical aesthetic looks for a synonymy between orderly aesthetics and ethics. The false freedom of disorderly pride must be overcome: "Only while occupying his place in a cosmic and moral order does man know *true liberty*. Man's freedom is not absolute, of course, since any being less than God must owe his existence to God" (Hinman, 73).

The awareness of oneself as objectified within such an order negates the need for Donne's tricky probabilism, since the writer now operates within certain reliable and acknowledged truths. Common sense prevails in a poet tending more to reasonable discussion than to the clever rhetoric of the Metaphysicals. Neither common sense nor reason are inimical to Cowley's faith; the scientific inquiry which they promote is not the sinful fruit of Eden's tree of knowledge. Nevertheless, a poet who associates reason with truth, religion, and loyalty to the throne still defines reason's limits, just as he does with the opposite extremes of witty excess:

> Tho' reason cannot through faith's myst'ries see,
> It sees that there, and such, they be;
> Leads to heav'n's door, and there does humbly keep,
> And there through chinks and keyholes peep.
>
> (*Reason, the Use of it in Divine Matters*)

Reasonable investigation of the universe's grand design emphasizes the nature of finite existence as one of limitation and mutability simultaneously. Inevitability and free choice co-exist: "In a mutable world subject to the eternal decree of God's Providence, men must act. How they act is determined by choices they could not possibly make freely if they foreknew the exact consequences. Then they would be truly constrained, automata serving necessity" (Hinman, 78).

The desirability of formal limits or constraints also appears in Cowley's assessment of the body of contemporary poetry and its future. Cowley stresses the *form* of faith, which must be embraced if one is to know its *content*; the submission of his art to the constraints of Heaven is therefore made willingly, since it is the only way that he might know Heaven's freedom or lack of constraints. "As men, before their receiving of the faith, do not without some carnal reluctances, apprehend the bonds and fetters of it, but find it afterwards to be *the truest and greatest liberty*, it will faire no otherwise with this art, after the regeneration of it; it will meet with wonderful variety of new, more beautiful and more delightful objects; neither will it want room, by being confined to heaven" (Cowley's own preface to one of his collections, dated only as *c.* 1656).

THE PROBLEM OF A PRIORI BONDS AND FETTERS IN BRODSKY'S POST-BAROQUE WORK

There are two areas of importance in drawing a parallel between Brodsky and the post-Baroque stage represented by Cowley: how the Englishman's relationship to a priorism relates to Brodsky's and how Brodsky has actually encountered such a priorism in other literature. There are clear parallels between Cowley and Brodsky's movement towards determinism, yet the reasons for this movement are diametrically opposed; Cowley joyfully surrenders to the a priori laws that put paid to Crashaw's leap, yet he does so almost out of existential squeamishness, since he has never made any irrational leap himself. Brodsky, however, *has* made the spiritual leap. He found that it was unfortunately dependent upon the labours of a physical poet; the body could only stand the rigours of the leap for so long. Now woefully aware of the limits of his body (upon which language is dependent), the poet is experiencing the inexorable movement of that exhausted, aging body towards an inevitable conclusion, towards what seems the pre-determined denouement of a linguistic evolution. Determinism has replaced empiricism.

The inexorable relationship of a freely chosen participation in literature and its sad, deterministic conclusion was clear to Brodsky before his exile. This is shown by his decision to translate Tom Stoppard's *Rosencrantz and Guildenstern Are Dead,* a play of 1967 which depicts the same relationship of the writer and writing. Brodsky was working on a translation of Stoppard's play around Christmas 1970, but this Russian text has only recently been published; the poet was apparently surprised that it survived. On reading this play, no doubt he sympathized with the central theme of free will exercised within the inevitable development of literary structures. After all, he had already used *Hamlet* as an example of a literary character's independence relative to both the whim of Shakespeare's imagination and the inevitable progression of the prince's own, slowly unfolding story or dramatic fate.

Rosencrantz and Guildenstern are very minor characters in *Hamlet.* Stoppard makes them major ones by using their brief and widely separated lines from Shakespeare's play and then following them for all the time in between. This extra time shows their growing awareness, to use Polonius's words, that "though this [story] be madness, yet there is method in't." The method appears as soon as their first lines from *Hamlet* are over: "I'm out of my step here," says Rosencrantz. Guildenstern's response is that "there's a logic at work – it's all done for you, don't worry. Enjoy it. Relax." He is a little less flippant by the second act, as events start to look predetermined. "Wheels have been set in motion, and they have their own pace, to which we are ... condemned. Each move is dictated by the previous one – that is the meaning of order. If we start being arbitrary it'll be a shambles: at least, let us hope so. Because if we happened, just happened to discover, or even suspect, that our spontaneity was part of their order, we'd know that we were lost."

The two men are told by one of the players employed by Hamlet to re-enact Claudius's murder that in art "events must play themselves out to [an] aesthetic, moral and logical conclusion." Later commissioned to take Hamlet to England, they indeed realize that their freedom is relative to a fixed star in the sky, to the inevitability of their mission. As the play approaches its unavoidably fatal denouement, Guildenstern's unconvincing remark that "we can do what we like and say what we like" is quickly qualified by his partner: "Within limits, of course." Their death is depicted on stage as the disappearance of one man from the view of the other, the splitting of a vital dialogue just like the end of *Gorbunov i Gorčakov* and Brodsky's play *Marbles (Mramor)*. Guildenstern feels that a momentum simply took over. It leaves the two men drifting causelessly towards eternity.

Brodsky's own development reflects the concerns of Stoppard's play but reverses the meaning. The Russian actively seeks the aesthetic determinism that scares Shakespeare's courtiers; despite the cruel fate that is being enacted on the poet by art's deterministic schemes, he knows that it must be suffered if he is to realize language's full metaphysical potential, if he is to go across the whole curve of metaphysical inspiration. Indeed, in one interview Brodsky talks of being driven by a "sense of internal necessity" (Venclova, 1990a: 123). Just like Hamlet, Brodsky now senses a predetermined "divinity that shapes our ends,/ Rough-hew them how we will."

JOSEPH BRODSKY'S VERSE AND PROSE, 1980–1989

Between 1980 and 1989, the poet's sense that his efforts allow no escape from the inevitable demise of his physical frame leads initially to a Hobbesian determinism. Little by little, however, he comes to terms with these overbearing constraints by accepting freedom within them, by accepting, for example, the inevitability of his own death. The parallel with Hobbes becomes increasingly less valid, and a more intricate philosophy emerges, one that is closer to Kant. Over this period, then, Brodsky moves through a post-Baroque literary phase at the same time that he experiences a comparable phase of post-Baroque thought. He moves from ideas associated with the seventeenth century towards those of the eighteenth – towards Kant. This move is structured along the same lines as the Baroque stage, by means of several dialectically opposed notions, although their interaction is now markedly slower. As in the Baroque stage, there is also a core opposition running through the period of such general significance that it is hard to isolate it for separate analysis. That pair is profitably defined as literary eternity/mathematical eternity, in essence the desirable continuation of culture's metaphysical significance versus an undesirable, levelled, and massed existence that perpetuates itself by wholly physical reproduction. The now highly devolved Brodsky strives for the former, but finds himself willy-nilly heading for the latter.

Devolution has taken the poet "lower and lower," as the Crashaw model implies, but Brodsky has been overtaken by the process he freely instigated, one that will exhaust his own metaphysical and physical strength. The remaining room for the play of free will from a maximally devolved poet is now so small that Brodsky calls his life a "survival of the defeatist" (1988g, 26). He imagines himself a crab on the sea floor in 1981, or elsewhere stuck in a chain of metamorphoses heading for life as an "eternal termite," a chain which goes through some very peculiar mutations such as a sphinx or the flat profile of a steam-breathing winter dragon. In this inevitably reduced stage Brodsky now resigns himself to the last few metamorphoses; it is now "possible to be at ease with the paltry fraction / of remaining life, with the craving of one's past / life for a finish; for the likeness / of a whole" (ss3, 46).

Perhaps the poet can devolve no more; he hides like a crumpled cigarette butt from a searching ray of light (123), or as carrion (*podal'*), which he calls the very apotheosis of fractions: the end of corporeal wholeness, devolved or not. The central problem is that although Brodsky feels at times like nothing more than a hollow circle or an immaterial, anonymous loop of smoke, he is still alive. It is this contradiction which produces a liminal existence between 1980 and 1989, as he continues to write and strive for literary eternity whilst mathematical eternity is bearing down upon him, threatening his body.

Nevertheless, the poet still knows that only ongoing faith can validate the contracted flesh; yet in *Priliv* (ss3, 34), Brodsky shies away from the sacrifice that such a validation demands when he squeamishly jerks back a finger from a sharp coat-hook, thinking that a jab or prick is enough to occasion his own resurrection (*voskres*). In other words, he shies away from a true impalement or crucifixion. The poem closes with the aforementioned "bottom crab" (the poet tangled in his linen), a self-deprecating remark followed by reference to a "sly [piscine] god" that Brodsky once met and which had tucked its fin out of sight in order to deceive him. The god did nothing more than produce the devolutionary mess of an "icy fish-soup" from which Brodsky thought he "got good at composing" Christ's initials (*ИХ*), using the bones. The poet was arrogant enough to see a divinity in the linguistic results of his disorderly devolution.

> Все равно, на какую букву себя послать,
> человека всегда настигает его же храп,

и, в исподнем запутавшись, где ералаш, где гладь,
шевелясь, разбираешь, как донный краб.

Вот про что напевал, пряча плавник, лихой
небожитель, прощенного в профиль бледней греха,
заливая глаза на камнях ледяной ухой,
чтобы ты навострился слагать из костей И.Х.

What's the point of the letter, whither man sends himself,
when on every occasion his snore leaves him far behind;
stirring, stuck in your pants, like a crab on an ocean shelf,
you distinguish what's smoothness from what's entwined.

And that's just what a sly deity sang to you,
who with a profile more bleached than sins pardoned, and fins
    none see,
left you pie-eyed – on top of the rocks – from his iced fish-soup,
so it seemed, with the bones, you'd the know-how to spell J.C.*

With the passage of years, then, since the ultimate leap is posthumous, faith is unfortunately coincidental with the awkward metamorphoses of a body already reduced to virtually nothing. Even though a worm that has "grown old ... is tired of twisting within the [bird's] beak," only the posthumous state of carrion will allow the body rest from the contortions of devolution, what Brodsky calls "freedom from cells, freedom from / a whole" (ss3, 123). If the body (that is, the poet himself) is so reduced, what does this imply for poetry and sound and, concomitantly, the faculty of vision?

DIALECTIC NOS. 2 AND 3: SOUND/VISION, SPACE/TIME

Chapter 4's brief discussion of analytic and synthetic phenomena at the end of the Baroque stage showed that sound has become part of a paradigm which includes logic, a tired physicality, and objectified phenomena. Beyond Brodsky's Baroque stage, sound barely operates at all, bound by the deterministic objectification which that whole paradigm is now undergoing. All that is left is a howl, a dog's bark, or just a general hoarseness (*xripota*). Increasingly drowned out by the nameless myriad individuals of both the past and future, the poet is reduced to a speechless, stubborn body whose dumb existence in the present does little but stop "the future merging with the past."

The poet's talk, now down to one-way Morse code (ss3, 13), is trying to dodge its inevitable wasting away together with the body at the hands of death. Letters look like the black dots or footprints in the snow of a hunted hare "which has escaped by a miracle." The expanses of snow or sky dwarf the tiny, dot-like poet; reduced to minimum dimensions, he barely constitutes a discernible object, threatened by the magnitude of remaining, surrounding space. Just as the limitlessness abyss of mathematical eternity is unnervingly close, the limitlessness of the sky in the English-language poem *Belfast Tune* similarly dictates the voice's pitch (ss3, 386); the very idea of pitch suggests mere sound, not lucid language. An Irish girl's physical self is reduced to a stony smallness in order to bear stoically the horrors of Northern Ireland, a smallness Brodsky juxtaposes with the limitlessness of the sky and wind that turn language into noise and vision into a blank stare. The physical space of Belfast just gets smaller and smaller as it becomes synonymous with death.

> Here's a girl from a dangerous town.
> She crops her dark hair short
> so that less of her has to frown
> when someone gets hurt.
>
> She folds her memories like a parachute.
> Dropped, she collects the peat
> and cooks her veggies at home: they shoot
> here where they eat.
>
> Ah, there's more sky in these parts than, say,
> ground. Hence her voice's pitch,
> and her stare stains your retina like a gray
> bulb when you switch
>
> hemispheres, and her knee-length quilt
> skirt's cut to catch the squall.
> I dream of her either loved or killed
> because the town's too small.

The poet himself feels stuck in the middle of limitless nowhere with no one about. Brodsky already senses the oblivion that lies beyond his resigned, tiny metamorphoses, since to borrow the poet's metaphor from the poem of 1987, *Na Via Džulia*, after the dead end, beyond the muddled "bundle" or "bunch" (*pučok*) of life's tapering rail lines, is a "great wilderness" trying hard to displace one. The poet is now a quietly metamorphosing fraction of private, bodily space within the so-called wilderness of impersonal absolute space, "and as for the wilderness, [it] is everywhere" (ss3, 190). The writer is stuck in a boundless space, neither part of nor constitutive of it. Its very impersonal emptiness leads Brodsky as late as 1989 to wish that he knew nothing about the similar expanses of astronomy.

In 1984 Brodsky says that any variation in the boundless, dead-flat landscape represents the "echo of our phrases," perhaps the petrified sound waves of words already uttered. If sound and the body are fizzling out, then the landscape will soon be literally levelled and any further reduction by the poet himself will make the view even less interesting. The one hope for the future is that really uninteresting, horizontal terrain, for example the landscape of Holland, is "laid flat for the sake of rivers"; the poet hopes that the emptiness he feels around his dwindling existence is somehow a positive form of eternity (represented here as water), a form of literary, not mathematical infinity. As always, such numbingly dull and moribund emptiness might have a divine dimension; one will not know until one enters it in a posthumous leap. Just as Christ was born in a locale "accustomed more to a flat surface, than to a mountain," so Brodsky hopes his soul will find "something that God knows" in emptiness; but more often than not this emptiness seems better suited to the so-called "stench of non-existence." Afraid of succumbing to the almost abyssal landscape, Brodsky refers twice in 1987 to his increasing tendency to make what he calls modest sideward glances in the emptiness – only a little visual movement is now possible for a virtually silent, virtually immobile body trying not to vanish into nothingness.

The inevitability of Brodsky's devolution has driven him back into the right-angled confinement of a deathly still frame; in the poem *The Fly (Muxa)*, the poet draws a sympathetic portrait of a fly that is likewise driven into the confinement of a window frame by searchlights as its own death draws near:

> Ах, цокотуха, потерявши юркость,
> ты выглядишь, как старый юнкерс,
> как черный кадр документальный
> эпохи дальней.
>
> Не ты ли за полночь там то и дело
> над люлькою моей гудела,
> гонимая в оконной раме
> прожекторами?
>
> А нынче, милая, мой желтый ноготь
> брюшко твое горазд потрогать,

и ты не вздрагиваешь от испуга,
жужжа, подруга.

Пока ты пела, за окошком серость
усилилась. И дверь расселась
в пазах от сырости. И мерзнут пятки.
Мой дом в упадке.

Ah, buggie, you've lost all your perkiness;
you look like some old shot-down Junkers,
like one of those scratched flicks that score
the days of yore.

Weren't you the one who in those times so fatal
droned loud above my midnight cradle,
pursued by crossing searchlights into
my black-framed window?

Yet these days, as my yellowed finger-
nail mindlessly attempts to fiddle
with your soft belly, you won't buzz with fear
or hatred, dear.

While you sang on, the gray outside grew grayer
Damp door-frame joints swell past repair;
drafts numb the soles. This place of mine
is in decline.

(TU, 108)

Thus both the poet and the fly for which he feels such sympathy move centripetally back into the limits or constraints of a frame, of *a priori* laws and dictates. The dialectic of body and soul barely manages to survive. There is no estrangement from the physical half of the relationship, though, for even now to isolate either body or soul is to insult them both. Since life is moving back into a frame, time is a particularly sad topic at the moment; the theme of an end is uppermost, couched in rather fatalistic terms since the poet worries about being literally crowded out of existence by future generations. These thoughts do not prompt a sense of alienation from life but an increased emphasis on the finite, earthbound here-and-now.

Brodsky says his life has turned out to be rather long; actually it has dragged on a little (*zatjanulas'*), to the point where one might confuse its progress with a mere "presence, devoid of sense," because it now seems that his existence has been one eternal avoidance of the unavoidable, a non-stop and self-deluding "disruption of rules." The main rule, however, that can never be disrupted is that life does end, so the theme of corporeality's shrinking dimensions holds sway over that of time. Time is now absolute and the poet's life is expressed in mundane, spatial terms, as a moving back and forth in inadequate attempts to delay or even avoid the inevitable; in the play *Mramor*, for example, the reader is told that freedom is really just "a variation on the theme of death. On the theme of the place, where it'll happen."

The fast and ugly "influence of not-to-be / on to-be," as Brodsky describes his demise with a sad attempt at humour, is perceived on more than one occasion as a future black with the presence of massed and rapidly multiplying younger generations. Knowing that these generations will replace him and that he himself will die, Brodsky says that a defensive stance against such inevitability is completely useless; in the 1988 article, "The Condition We Call Exile," he says that one must actively "measure" human transience or ephemerality against infinity and face up to the "terror" it produces. Terrified by the potentially vacuous nature of the future, one may not be able to stop time, but one can alter it qualitatively, by looking back and perpetuating culture's existence. The danger of a mathematical infinity can be challenged by using one's literary labours to extend literary eternity into the future. Paradoxical though that sounds, one must remember that levelled mathematical eternity perpetuates itself effortlessly through fleshy reproduction, whereas literary eternity must be created through constant, conscious efforts in the here and now. One has an ethical duty to lay claim to the past, to one's membership in the weight of tradition, because the "present, in order to turn into the future, / needs yesterday" (LTO, 166).

To lay claim to the mass of the past might conceivably be a form of detachment or estrangement in the sense of the arrogant subjectivity of a young, novel poet sacrificing itself to the enormous spiritual significance of (prior) culture and tradition. But the loss promises enormous future gain as one's connections with culture or traditions of the past allow an attachment to their significance for the future. Subjectivity's reduction to nothing, even to the point of its complete absence produces what Brodsky in the essay "Footnote to a Poem" calls "a crude version of detachment: psychologically it is synonymous with presence in some other place and, in this way, expands the notion of being." Life is hopefully enriched by belittling oneself in the presence of culture's magnitude – a Baroque relationship between the believer and the object of one's faith. In the Baroque stage, Brodsky said his witty or metaphorical ascent (designed as an expression of this faith), was made possible by the stereoscopic perception that results from the dialogue of two related notions, such as profile and full-face perception or the tenor and vehicle of a metaphorical conceit. The dialectic of profile and full-face perception is, however, now in a sad state; it divides and falls apart, "like a witless atom on the eve of being / split," in the words of the poem *Centaurs* (*Kentavry*), examined below.

DIALECTIC NO. 4: PERCEPTIONS MADE IN PROFILE OR FULL-FACE

The Baroque stage is driven by the ultimately unmanageable interaction of vision and sound, seen by the poet in terms of stereoscopic perception. In the same stage, mass and sound are part of analytic thought which, together with a synthetic cognition based on light and vision, lead to the Baroque revelations possible in metaphorical thinking. The rapid descent of 1979 apparently put paid to any further flights of witty fancy because references to the logical, massive, and corporeal side of the equation – to flat profiles – outnumber references to things full-face by an enormous margin between 1980 and 1989. Already reduced to "nothing and nobody," the poet can now see the negative devolutionary link between, as one metaphor has it, animate, human muscles and inanimate, inhuman furniture seen facing forwards. The happy *a posteriorism* with which the poet associated full-face synthesis and vision during the Baroque stage is now debased in the inevitable, massive "flourishes of mahogany" perceived full-face and which metamorphoses have produced. The reference here to mahogany comes from the four poems known collectively as *Kentavry I-IV.* Together they constitute perhaps the best example of deterministic, negative devolution between 1980 and 1989. The poems document unstoppable, negative metamorphoses which are instigated by a split in the dialectic and likened to atomic fission: "For an explosion-sponsored / profile [such as these centaurs] there is no tomorrow" (1988b, 268). The split is a negative event, all the more so because it lets the massive or physical side of the profile/full-face pair – that of the profile – run rampant in total isolation from all things spiritual.

The quartet was first published in *Kontinent* (ss3, 163–6) and then refashioned in 1988 by the author into an English quintet. The four Russian poems begin with two jovial centaurs, Sofa and Mulja, oscillating freely between animate forms and those of ornate, mahogany furniture or motor vehicles, their anthropomorphic torsos attached to and powered by additional wooden legs or wheels. Section two concentrates on their prophecy that the future is futile (*naprasno*), as they run recklessly between the shore and horizon to get a preview of tomorrow's events. When tomorrow comes, though, they soon find themselves caught in unstoppable physical changes; their increasingly limited options for metamorphosis are reflected in analogies with a dead match, a naked statue, and other immobile states, the evolutionary origins of which are explained in the third section. The quartet concludes with both a future, apocalyptic battlefield into which the helpless centaurs have been herded by inevitability, and a final, metaphorical chain depicting their descent into inert uniformity, from centaurs into unicorns into tanks into nothingness; only a final star remains in this vacuum and tries to escape an avaricious telescope. The physical make-up of the initial centaurs and the relationship of its flux to the split between profile and *full face* is expressed in the opening lines of the quartet:

> Наполовину красавица, наполовину софа́, в просторечьи –
>   Со́фа,
> по вечерам оглашая улицу, чьи окна отчасти лица,
> стуком шести каблуков (в конце концов, катастрофа –
> то, в результате чего трудно не измениться),
> она спешит на свидание. Любовь состоит из тюля,
> волоса, крови, пружин, валика, счастья, родов.
> На две трети мужчина, на одну легковая – Муля –
> встречает ее рычанием холостых оборотов
> и увлекает в театр. В каждом бедре с пеленок
> сидит эта склонность мышцы к мебели, в выкрутасам
> красного дерева, к шкапу, у чьих филенок,
> в свою очередь, склонность к трем четвертям, к анфасам
> с отпечатками пальцев.

> Part ravishing beauty, part sofa, in the vernacular – Sophie,
> after hours filling the street whose windows are partly faces
> with the clatter of her six heels (after all, a catastrophe
> is something that always ogles the guises a lull refuses)
> is rushing to a rendezvous. Love consists of tulle, horsehair,
> blood, bolsters, cushions, springs, happiness, births galore.
> Two-thirds a caring male, one third a race car – Cary
> for short – greets her joyfully with his idling roar
> and whisks her off to a theater. Every thigh, from the age
>   of swaddles,
> shows the craving of muscles for furniture, for the antics
> of mahogany armoires whose panels, in turn, show a subtle
> yen for two-thirds, full-face, profiles anxious
> for a slap.

The relationship of language to corporeal metamorphosis comes to the fore. The images in the first line, a beautiful woman and a divan, are condensed in the Russian name Sofa (*krasavi*ca; *sofà*; *Sòfa*). The name designates the centaur's physical change, whilst metamorphosing itself across the two preceding substantives, through both phonetics and animacy as the line proceeds. It is this compression of process into an inanimate/animate noun that is of importance, especially because the names Sòfa and Mulja suggest a Jewish context for the poem, perhaps that of Brodsky's own background, where family and furniture were compressed in the same space. In his youth, Brodsky and his parents occupied a tiny, communal apartment within an extremely ornate building, a "Moorish wonder." Their living space was dominated by outsized furniture; two ten-foot-high chests and an equally ornate bed. The chests held all the jumbled objects amassed during travels by the family and were supported by an "elephant-footed bottom" (LTO, 459).

Sofa's six heels or hooves (a human plus a couch) presage a reference in the third section to "ourselves in ... chairs" (*na stul'jax*) in the chicken-legged hut of the witch Baba Jaga, one stage further in the seemingly magic, yet rationally inevitable accumulation of the future's faceless rabble. This is reflected initially by the shift to first person plural in the description of those caught in negative devolution's deterministic patterns. The pronoun *us* changes the status of the poem's addressee from agent (reader) to patient (object), just one of many metamorphoses in the quartet which change Sofa and Mulja into mutants or "mutanks" (*muu-tanki*), a hellish, war-torn union of cattle and machine which is likened to the unicorn, itself both a type of Russian cannon and a beast represented in heraldry with a twisted horn, deer's hooves, goat's head, and lion's tail.

Refusing to acknowledge their inevitably hellish future, the centaurs rush to a theatre where "they enjoy off and on a drama about the life of puppets" (*naslaždajutsja v pauzax dramoj iz žizni kukol*). The puppets exist within a puppet-show which itself is enclosed within the theatre. This ever-reducing, yet ever-multiplying theatrical space falls victim to time's unmanageable acceleration, which reaches its logical conclusion in a comparable, though infinitely less jovial, context amidst the desolation of future "mutanks" in the battlefield. Brodsky reduces the broad sweep of the battle scenes by describing the contracted brain of a shell-shocked veteran after the war, a silent, shrunken man in a waterlogged foxhole. This transition from theatre to foxhole is begun when the centaurs run to their evening get-together: their fleshy affections during the rendezvous instigate a chain of inanimate substantives that presage the grander reduction to an object-like existence across the quartet as a whole. Their union initiates their decomposition: "Love consists of tulle, horsehair, / blood, bolsters, cushions, springs, happiness, births galore."

Just before the metamorphoses become unmanageable, the centaurs prance back and forth from the horizon (from tomorrow) with an unwittingly ironic announcement that everything is "in vain!" Their prophecy is made in the presence of some very odd birds: *V nix – ni pera, ni puxa, a tol'ko k čertu, k čertu.* Here Brodsky plays on a traditional Russian good-luck wish which consists of the phrase *ni puxa, ni pera* ("neither down nor feathers"). He inverts the two nouns and adds the traditional response *k čertu, k čertu* ("to the devil, to the devil"), or "damn it" in the English version. The word order is twisted to reflect the inverted form of the birds, and the invocation here of the devil not only foretells the infernal destination of a centaur or its passenger but suggests that the birds are themselves chimerae. They may well be Harpies, those encountered by the Argonauts during their stay with Phineus, who himself was blinded by the gods and constantly attacked by the Harpies for having prophesied the future too accurately.

Centaurs and Harpies can be found together in another poem, *La Divina Commedia.* In *L'Inferno* Dante meets the Harpies after a centaur has carried him across the river Phlegethon; ahead of him lies the infernal realm which the centaurs guard, one resident of which is "fierce Dionyisus." The poet then begins to order his thoughts on the horrors of eternity, horrors which manifest themselves even in our own short time on earth.

Dante's description of a centaur is seen by some as a memory of his days in the army, and the monsters clearly represent a harbinger of things both war-torn or worse in Dante and Brodsky's narratives. The Harpies that foretold the loss of the Trojans are an ugly union of woman and bird:

> They have broad wings, with human necks and faces,
> Feet with claws, their great bellies covered with feathers,
> They make lamentations on strange trees.

Dante and Virgil then hear a tale of human labours, of possible, future reconstruction upon the ashes left by the barbarian Atilla, but all is in vain, just as in Brodsky's poem.

Dante drew upon Ovid for his depiction of the centaurs, a poet Brodsky sometimes turns to for his own treatment of change or flux. The centaurs in Ovid's *Metamorphoses*, driven by wine and lust, disrupt the legal and harmonious union of Pirithous and Hippodame by attempting to do violence to the bride. In the midst of the ensuing battle of the Lapiths and the Centaurs Ovid includes a description of the centaur Cyllarus, who declares his love for a female centaur, Hylonome. Brodsky's centaurs move from a domestic scene to a battlefield: Cyllarus and Hylonome return to their cave, only to fight side by side in the battle later on. Ovid's beasts may choose to go to war, but Brodsky's centaurs, by choosing to ignore their potentially apocalyptic future, get dragged into it, willy-nilly.

The processes begun by the poor use of free choice soon become absolutely unstoppable; they become laws to which whoever invoked them is quickly made subject. The poet's own attempts to exercise at least some free will, to cause something positive and manageable at a time when his life seems caught in a fatally deterministic universe, underlie a shift to a Kantian *Weltanschauung*, from determinism to the possibility of at least some *a posteriorism* within a system of *a priori* laws, though the poet does not discuss this shifting attitude to free will explicitly in these terms. I wish merely to suggest that what can or cannot be done in the dialectic of free will and limits, of cause and effect, forms the core of Brodsky's second experience of the ethical stage in a way that is reminiscent of the story of empiricism between Hobbes's seventeenth-century objections to unruliness and Kant's eighteenth-century alternative to an entirely rule-bound existence.

DIALECTIC NO. 5:
THE SPLIT BETWEEN CAUSE AND EFFECT

In seventeenth-century England, John Locke challenged Hobbes's schema of universal experience in a deterministic world by redefining the human mind as a receiver of entirely subjective experiences or sensations of things, upon which the mind then reflects. Brodsky himself says that "any notions about anything are based on experience" (LTO, 422), that "speech is a reaction to the world" (Montenegro, 530). Five years later, though, he admits that one can get a little too used to this idea (Volkov, 1987: 368); indeed one must admit that it *is* rather passive, as was Locke's "man as receptacle" worldview.

Brodsky's cosmogonical approach would make him not just a passive receiver of the universe, but creator of its animated alternative through art; he would ideally play both effect and cause by creating a qualitatively superior, entirely subjective existence through his linguistic interaction with the universe. As shown by the collapse of the poet's Baroque stage and the various attempts at free will over the 1980s, however, what is in reality manageable is *a posteriorism* within *a priori* limits, since one is effected by pre-existing and unyielding laws much more than one can continue freely to "cause" anything manageable. Whatever one rashly causes in moments of ill-considered bravado soon vanishes in a deluge of effects, most of which one did not apparently occasion in the first place. Brodsky's scepticism over the possibilities of pure empiricism mirrors the scepticism of Locke's contemporaries. Doubtful of the validity of certain aspects of empiricism, the Scotsman David Hume began to undermine Locke's world-view by questioning the principle of cause and effect, since Locke maintained that the world caused certain effects in the human mind. Hume responded by saying that any tidy principle of cause and effect is merely prediction based upon what one has seen in similar, past situations. Lockean empiricism was dealt a terrible blow and scepticism such as Hume's soon became influential enough to threaten religion with its positivistic emphases.

Brodsky's own scepticism over the limits of empiricism, as well as his problems with the deceptively simple dialectic between cause and effect, turn him towards a Kantian attitude (Kant was himself inspired by Hume), towards empiricism's more modest rehabilitation *within* the rational and the *a priori*. What emerges is a transformation of empirical freedoms of the past, when a great deal was possible for a freely choosing agent. What now can or cannot be done within the unbending limitations of absolute time and space leads Brodsky into the realm of Kant's ethical imperative, that one's individual conscience be carefully fashioned as if it were the foundation of a future moral dictate. Brodsky's increasing awareness that cause and effect can never be manipulated in a deterministic world presages his entrance into a second, clearly defined ethical stage. The growth of this awareness is important, because Brodsky equates the complete absence of discernible cause or effect in a poet with silence, so whenever they *do* interact, noise is heard in the form of language.

A discussion of Brodsky's understanding of cause and effect should begin with his remarks on Dostoevskij, who represents a parallel as close as possible to the poet's Baroque experience. Dostoevskij's language, Brodsky writes, soared to such a lonely, lofty pitch that it could not be repeated. It could not help but "cause" the nineteenth century's "inevitable" descent to Tolstoj (LTO, 277) and the age's subsequent "mimetic avalanche," its century-long tendency towards moralizing, towards the advocacy of ethical norms. In reality, of course, Dostoevskij did not actually *cause* Tolstoj, and the poet in fact admits that one cannot hope for an entirely "rational, analytic" prediction of effect in the world. In an interview he suggests that instead one should simply try to figure out the arbitrariness of the Supreme Being to which the world is subject, whether that Being is God, language or art (Forbes, 4). In trying himself to figure out the problem, in a poem of 1985

Brodsky feels that he is experiencing an apparently arbitrary and "successful, alas / attempt by effect to outrun cause" (*Bjust Tiberija*). By 1988 his definition of an artist's only possible response is couched in terms of an ethical imperative; one must "stop being just its [history's] rattling effects and try to play at causes" (1988c, 19).

Brodsky's imperative is not easy to satisfy in a decade where effects flee their causes with what he calls utter insensitivity (*nečuvstvitel'nost'*) in the poem *At Karel Weilink's Exhibition* (*Na vystavke Karla Vejlinka*). One's own seemingly predictable experience of youth and age, of an apparently well-defined cause and effect, is in fact alien (*čuždyj*) to time's grander designs, designs to which man is never privy. Sure enough, beyond the rationalization of his own lifespan, in the realm of the causal relationship between epochs, Brodsky feels "indistinguishable" from the jumble of causes and effects that leave him crowded out of existence by younger generations. In this period of moving centripetally back within a frame of *a priori* necessity in his own life, whilst unable to understand the siginificance of his wholly physical existence relative to the fleshy existence of those who precede or follow him, the ineffective Brodsky is experiencing what he defines in 1987 as the sensation of a brush left from a painting robbed of "end, beginning, frame and middle." The ability of art's brush to effect or create a better existence is almost non-existent.

Though the exact relationship of causes and effects may be confusing in what he calls art's impersonal "genealogy, dynamic, logic and future," Brodsky feels that during the 1980s he is able to define at least some aspects of art's ineluctable laws of evolution. One of these laws is especially pertinent to his experiences of the 1980s, since it is comparable to the seventeenth-century process that reduced the audience of a *Précieux* poet to the size of coteries: "The further a poet goes in his development, the greater – unintentionally – his demands are on an audience, and the narrower that audience is" (LTO, 200). Brodsky here talks of a poet going a certain distance in his or her development, but it is just as much a matter of being *taken* a certain distance, since poetry's movement, though freely begun, quickly becomes inevitable; its rhyme-scheme turns an "idea into law," as do its "self-generating" stanzas – an adjective Brodsky applies in fact to the whole "linear and unrecoiling progression of art" (305, 326, 373). In a confusing series of relationships as agent and patient, subject and object, causing and being caused by art's progression, "a great poet" is paradoxically *made* by his "linguistic inevitability" (Volkov, 1987: 342), by the very laws which stifle any conscious attempt to cause or create his own greatness.

ESTRANGEMENT AND ETHICS

Each step, each poem in an artist's inevitable progression involves what Brodsky calls an externalization of the object it depicts. This is not estrangement or defamiliarization (*ostranennost'*), but the "aesthetic detachment *imperative* for a lasting work of art," the avoidance of seeing oneself as the centre of all things, of giving free rein to personal drama (LTO, 340, 271). When one applies Brodsky's comments on geography to aesthetics, his comments on exile to *ostranennost'*, then it becomes clear that what a poet needs to do in order "to get a good picture of one's native realm" and avoid narcissism is "to get outside its walls." (436). The reference here to walls, to the limits of geographically limited spaces or forms, can be analogically applied to the dialectics of the Baroque and post-Baroque periods. These suggest a parallel between space, form and the body on the one hand, and time, content, and spirit on the other. To get completely and permanently outside formal or corporeal constraints would undoubtedly be a type of exile or estrangement, but by the poet's own admission, this is a type of extreme objectivity of which he is not capable, nor is it one that he aspires to. Brodsky calls this type of extreme distancing in any form a wholly "structural device" (296), and just like form, structure is an earthbound, corporeal emphasis in his work. An excessive emphasis on either embracing or escaping form alone can produce an absence of content – in other words, can break up the dialectic of body and soul and be psychically empty.

The fact that Brodsky does not aspire willingly to estrangement from (that is, avoidance of) the necessary rigours of corporeal and linguistic form being pushed dialectically to their limit is shown most explicitly in an interview of 1987 (Volkov, 366–7). Talking of human misfortune and its depiction in art, he says that any description of tragedy will never be "genuine tears, genuine gray hairs. It's all just a drawing near [or "approximation" – *priblizenie*] to a genuine reaction. And realization of this estrangement [*ostranennost'*] creates a truly insane situation." The act of describing creates "a schizophrenia – not of consciousness but of conscience," because any description answers to the muse, not just to experience and therefore, albeit involuntarily (*nevol'no*), one "sins against truth; against one's pain" in real life. In other words, the problem here is not of a split or exiled soul isolated from the body; it is not a psychic problem, but a dialogically realized, moral or ethical one of conscience. Language is used by finite individuals to create a maximum expression of truth or good in the world, in the face of inevitable, eternal evils or opposing forces – forces which are confusing in their relationship to the processes of cause and effect, but are nevertheless potential levellers, one and all. The poet is faced with the unpleasant and painful task of fulfilling a finite goal of conscience by drawing language and the body or physical experience closer in the experience (and therefore ethical service) of the infinite. This ethical service in the here and now is in fact most clearly expressed in Brodsky's discussion of the one theme which leads critics to overlook the ethical significance of physical, finite exsitence by emphasizing estrangement; the theme in question is exile.

Brodsky's essay of 1988, "The Condition We Call Exile," is a summary of concerns from even the earliest verse, concerns separate from any move to America. Exile turns out to be synonymous with the consequences of a Kierkegaardian particularity: complete isolation. Brodsky begins by saying that guest workers and refugees have a much harder time than any self-pitying exiled writer, and that "displacement and misplacement are this century's commonplaces." A writer's exile is instead indicative of his insignificance relative to metaphysical dimensions, to eternity, not to geographical spaces. His exile emphasizes the dimensions of mathematical eternity, and thus inspires the ethical obligation to enter into a relationship with its positive equivalent, with literary (i.e., divine) eternity instead. Both versions of eternity belittle the individual, either with their horror or with the awe-inspiring demands they make of the believer, just as the horrific realization of levelling's power inspired Kierkegaard's faith.

Exile, seen in a metaphysical light, is just one expression of the "terrifying human and inhuman vistas for which we have no yardstick except ourselves." These dimensions are overwhelming enough to induce a "pain-dulling infiniteness, ... forgetfulness, detachment, [or] indifference," states which are part and parcel of succumbing to mathematical eternity. Brodsky's response to the danger of exile, or mathematical eternity, is a literary response, using tradition and culture to challenge forgetfulness and detachment. His attraction or gravitation back to the weight of tradition makes sure no one gets detached from or indifferent to culture. Any attempt at estrangement is a kind of escape or shirking one's duty, even, as a writer. Thus the realization of one's metaphysical potential for good is a moral obligation, one to be discovered empirically in the face of mathematical infinity's (potentially levelling and therefore evil) power: "We must make it easier for the next man, if we can't make it safer." Metaphysical potential is realized though free, though ethically correct, choices, within the limitations of one's inevitably finite lifespan which is conducted in the here and now. The moral obligation to make such choices fuels Brodsky's second experience of an ethical stage, one defined by the poet's emphasis on individual responsibility, the dangers of preaching to others, and the problems involved in dealing with one's ethical foe – with evil.

DIALECTIC NO. 6: GOOD AND EVIL

When Brodsky talks of the obligation to make existence easier or safer for the next man, he is referring to an individual's right to a personal faith in the face of various tyrannies, such as the "levelling effect on Christian ethics" produced by the Second World War, itself worsened by the Allies' siding with the deceptively lesser evil of socialism against fascism. Allied support simply allowed another tyranny to enjoy a military, and therefore moral, victory (1985e, 453). The awfulness of this victory was soon epitomized by the Berlin Wall, a perverted or "petrified version of either/or." Both the war and the wall are reflections of faithless, self-perpetuating states. Poetry opposes this mathematical, petrified eternity with a literary alternative, which is potentially much more powerful than levelling if it is properly cultivated; for the Soviet Union to have imprisoned the young poetess Irina Ratušinskaja, for example, was as pointless as "breaking a watch [because] it's a falsification of time" (1984d, 7).

Ratušinskaja's jailers represent a gross majority that has flooded the world to the point that one's own evil acts have trouble defining specific human targets any more; crude classifications and generalizing are everywhere. The generalizations are even used by those who oppose tyrannies, by groups such as peace movements, which make the mistake of concentrating on international evil, instead of its "localized, individualized versions." The individual writer should avoid generalizations and remember that perhaps "what's under your control is the possibility of the bad" and not so much the good, which to a large degree may well be dependent upon divine graces, seen by Brodsky as absolutely arbitrary and by no means a comforting or reliable source of "infinite mercy" (Birkerts, 1982: 85 and 110).

The lowly poet is obliged to concern himself in the essays of *Less Than One* with the more modest aims of an ethical stage on the model of Cvetaeva's "art in the light of conscience," an art so merciless in its judgment of the writer's efforts, however, that it can sometimes outdo any religion in its ability to teach rectitude. Any squeamishness in accepting art's lessons and realizing its potential will produce half-hearted poetry, which is as useless as half-hearted individualism, termed by the poet a "sequestering [of] oneself in narcissistic self-pity because of having curbed one's own metaphysical ability."

Brodsky says that such maximalism will convert the poet long before the reader, poets being ruthless self-judging Protestants by nature.

Nevertheless, in a couple of admissions which tally with Kierkegaard's and Šestov's assessment of ethics per se, the poet knows that despite his subjective experience of art's ethical lessons, there is always a tendency in ethics to preach such lessons to others, to play the moralizing dictator. The poet, indeed, starts to play this role. Poetry's ethical imperatives are exercised in one's aesthetic choices, and these imperatives to others (the readers) start to increase in the 1980s. They are offered by a bold "knight of faith" who is well aware that aesthetic, and hence ethical, "individualism in a crowd may be dangerous." Aesthetic and ethical individualism must be exercised, though, to set in motion language's subsequently self-generating movement towards its function as the "goal of the species," as Brodsky says in 1980.

Descending from the Baroque to re-investigate the ethical sphere and telling readers what or what not to do, Brodsky wonders if existence in this world does not, after all, "boil down precisely to either/or, to the yes/no principle," an opposition epitomized by the radical choice of literary or mathematical, levelled infinity. Such a choice may be daunting, but it must be made, since "evil *can* be made absurd through excess; ... [by] rendering evil absurd through dwarfing its demands with the volume of your compliance, which devalues the harm. This sort of thing puts a victim into a very active position, into the position of a mental aggressor. The victory that is possible here is not a moral but an existential one" (1984a, 7–8/389).

I disagree with the last line; it is an existential *and* moral victory, one that lies in poetry's maximum "individualism, originality of thinking, whimsicality, even – if you will – eccentricity," since evil finds eccentricities harder to understand and therefore attack. Four years later, Brodsky even calls literary individualism *society's* (not just the poet's) "only form of moral insurance." This ethical and now universal role of poetry as insurance is based on the reasoning that if literature is what he calls a "compendium of meanings for this or that human lot," then a poet's own discovery and compilation of life's meanings aims either to save future individuals from falling into a metaphysical trap, or at least know when they are in one, because (and this is very important) "to know ... what is happening to you is liberating." Not escape, estrangement, or exile, but the philosophical freedom that comes from self-knowledge relative to one's lot in the *a priori*. This knowledge comes from what Brodsky calls in the 1989 poem *Doklad dlja simpoziuma* an ethical "pioneer,/ to make the unsafe safe." The same poem also defines the relationship of ethics and aesthetics towards the end of the decade that will take the poet further down the curve of metaphysical inspiration, into a second aesthetic stage.

Эстетическое чутье
суть слепок с инстинкта самосохраненья
и надежней, чем этика. Уродливое трудней
превратить в прекрасное, чем прекрасное
изуродовать. Требуется сапер,
чтобы сделать опасное безопасным.
Этим попыткам следует рукоплескать,
оказывать всяческую поддержку.

One's feeling for the aesthetic,
moulded from instinctual self-preservation,
is more reliable than aesthetics. It is harder to turn
the ugly into the beautiful than it is to make ugly
what is beautiful. A pioneer is required
in order to make what is unsafe safe.
These endeavors deserve to be applauded,
to be afforded all conceivable support.*

A pioneer implicitly clears the way for the safe or successful passage of those behind, and Brodsky has in fact termed poetry's aesthetics a barometer of the whole species' successful progression as ethical beings. He often invokes the relation between aesthetics and ethics, because a large part of aesthetics' ethical power is in the evocation and perpetuation of cultural memory. Hence Brodsky's verse now takes him further back down the Kierkegaardian triad: from an unwieldy faith to worldly ethics to the concern with one's fleeting role in the ongoing parade or procession of culture's movers and shakers, a concern from his early aesthetic stage.

BRODSKY'S SECOND AESTHETIC STAGE

Mathematical infinity shocks the poet into ethics again, but once the responsibilities of finite experience are re-validated, the next question is: exactly *how much* is one person free to do in a single lifetime? The problem of human transience reappears. Brodsky makes several remarks on cultural or vegetative cycles in a way that recalls the experiences of his earliest verse. Punning on the paradoxical relationship between the freedom of innovation and the constraints of history, between the deviation of a tangent and inexorable movement of a circle, Brodsky urges readers to delve into poetry's past: "you stand to lose nothing; what you may gain are new associative chains" (1988g, 27). In the forging of these chains, the stages of development in a human life do not repeat without qualitative change so much as come full circle, shown when one's face starts to display the wintry features of a seasonal cycle, thus returning to the same cold emptiness that preceded any human presence. Three times in the prose of 1985, in the middle of Brodsky's post-Baroque concerns (what Eliot would see as catabolism), the Russian poet explains artistic or cultural downturns as physical or vegetative cycles: "erosion, [a] lowering of the standards and so forth are the organic features of civilization, ... civilization is an organism that excretes, secretes, degenerates, regenerates; ... the dying and rotting of its parts is the price this organism pays for evolution" (1985i, 33). Civilizations have a vegetative nature. The equation of man with civilization and both with nature inspires one of the poet's most extreme and intriguing self-assessments, that he is a "biological determinist" (Forbes, 5). The comment is made in October 1987, the year following two poems which are very much in the vein of Brodsky's aesthetic-stage *tour de force* of 1961, *Šestvie*. One is in English, the other in Russian. The former is, as its title explains, a *History of the Twentieth Century* (up to the assassination of Archduke Ferdinand in Sarajevo). The latter, *A Performance* (*Predstavlenie*), is an incisive overview of Russia's post-Puškinian past, dire Soviet heritage, and equally awful post-Soviet future.

History of the Twentieth Century (A Roadshow) takes the form of a parade across a stage of the people and events of 1900–14. Their relation to the modern reader is that "they are the cause, you are the effect." As with *Šestvie*, both the narrator and passing characters are interrupted by salient figures, some of whom are of particular importance to this chapter. J.M. Browning, for example, says he invented his gun to reduce the number of ever-multiplying neighbours; Marconi (because he is Catholic and from Rome) is inspired by cherubs' speech to outdo language with a wireless, an apparent reference to the influence of extravagant Catholic ornamentation on the engineer; the Wright Brothers muddle human and avian bodies, then begin to fly; personified "Camouflage" advertises itself as "close to Nature," as the ability to reduce oneself to an unnoticeable nothingness and therefore hide from the scrutiny of snipers; Frank Lloyd Wright advocates flat, "natural" architecture. The last speech in the parade, the last speech before World War One, is by Niels Bohr, celebrating the domino effect of atomic fission, a fitting "reproductive" metaphor of mathematical infinity to match Brodsky's fears of entropic population explosions, which in turn produce the masses of war, the inhuman crowds of cannon-fodder. As opposed to *Šestvie*, there is no self-deluding irony in Brodsky's discussion of the events of 1913.

The man of the year is, I fear, Niels Bohr.
He comes from the same place as danishes.
He builds what one feels like when one cannot score
or what one looks like when one vanishes.
(Niels Bohr)
Atoms are small. Atoms are nice.
Until you split one, of course.
Then they get large enough to play dice
with your whole universe.
A model of an atom is what I've built!
Something both small and big!
Inside it resembles the sense of guilt.
Outside the lunar dig.

1914.
Nineteen-fourteen! Oh, nineteen-fourteen!
Ah, some years shouldn't be let out of quarantine!

Predstavlenie is also a cross-stage procession, but an exclusively Russian one; it consists of famous figures and personified tendencies in Russian history, interrupted by frequent, anonymous banalities which, sometimes have an awful ring of truth to them; for example, "they've led the country to an impasse," or "the squabble of effect with cause/ ends in death" (*končina*). Late in the poem, the personifications merge to represent a crowded, faceless eternity which threatens more than just Eastern Europe's future. Massed thoughts of the future cross the stage in camouflage or khaki with an A-bomb; a whole platoon (*vzbrod*) of ballet-dancers fills a mirror trying to reflect just one swan. Only when junk or garbage (*musor*) enters is a call made for the over-crowded procession to stop, but the stage is already too full.

Мы заполнили всю сцену! Остается влезть на стену!
Взвиться соколом под купол! Сократиться в аскарида!
Либо всем, включая кукол, языком взбивая пену,
хором вдруг совокупиться, чтобы вывести гибрида.
Бо, пространство экономя, как отлиться в форму массе,
кроме кладбища и кроме черной очереди к кассе?

Эх, даешь простор степной
без реакции цепной!

We've completely filled the bandstand! One thing's left: ascend
the grandstand!

Fill the dome, like eagles, upwards! Shrink, and join worm-like
   insects!
Or if we, including puppets, tongues a-frothing, lend a hand, and
dramatize an act of incest, plus the hybrids it evinces.
Saving space: from such behavior, in what form can space be
   anchored;
only in the shape of graveyards, or dark queues before a
   bank-clerk?

Hey, we'll form a steppe's expanse,
in advance of fission's chance!*

The poem's fatal denouement leaves the narrator "subtracted from
space," and all that remains of speech is the "mumble" of foliage or
the meaningless buzz of a mosquito and the processes of time. The
inevitable progression of life towards death also cancels the only
discernible cause for any person's existence in the world – their
parents. In the last line of *Predstavlenie*, time slowly smothers one's
parents "like silent sap." What on earth is left?

Brodsky is now very far down the distant slope of the Metaphysicals'
curve, having completed a symmetrical experience of both sides. The
experience has been conducted by coming full circle in a relationship
with tradition – a gravitation back to its mass. It is not unreasonable to
suggest, though, that since the curve (or circle!) is completed after the
receipt of the Nobel Prize, Brodsky becomes a poet of such stature that
he himself is perceived more and more as one who *makes* (future)
tradition. The gravitation around tradition therefore changes little by
little during the 1980s. The circle of physical existence is inescapable
and continues as ever, but the circle or curve of aesthetic development
is gradually exchanged for the wantonly deviant line of a maker of new
tradition. Brodsky's ethical aesthetics advocate doing as much as one
can before death – before mathematical infinity catches up, perhaps –
and the metaphor of aesthetically irrational "nomadism" slowly appears
as a consequence. Brodsky's ties with cyclical, cultural memory become
a outward-bound trajectory, since the poet is now perhaps the foremost
creator of that culture. But the progression of any poet's aesthetic
trajectory is still relative to his eventual demise, as human life comes
full circle sooner or later; so even nomadism is not in any way exilic.

NOMADISM

Constant movement or change is essential to the poet, to avoid the
zealous searchlights and perspective of life's logical, inevitable conclusion

– lights which sooner or later track down anyone trying to avoid them. Yet he has already devolved into a minimal object in an attempt to avoid mathematical eternity. One option is left: to move the object (himself) around. Although it is neither given a name nor truly developed until the early 1990s, nomadism is starting to emerge as a hopeful philosophy between 1980 and 1989, one that tries to reinstate the prominence of time after the more evident emphasis on diminutive Précieux or Rococo space across the decade.

Nomadism is not exile or estrangement, as any Bedouin would agree. To describe exactly what it is, though, one needs to look briefly beyond the time frame of this chapter and examine Brodsky's article of 1993, "Profile of Clio" (GR, 114–38), an essay which synthesizes the nomadic tendencies only hinted at in his work during the 1980s and suggests how such a synthesis creates a worldview for both the ensuing decade and beyond. Much of the essay discusses rationalism's ability to explain the workings of history. Rationalism has no room for a subjective experience of time; its greatest casualty is individualism. As a consequence, Brodsky advocates wantonly irrational thought to avoid vanishing too soon into the objective, rational schema of historians. He briefly takes issue with such schema, and suggests that perhaps history only has one law, that of "chance." He says that humans organize their lives rationally and in settled groups, which disenfranchises chance, but eventually chance comes back to claim its own. By saying so, however, Brodsky still subscribes to his prior views of history's goal or intent as rationally predictable; what is unpredictable is when history will display its destructiveness.

For the individual to adopt any kind of "motional irregularity" as a response means that one is no longer a sitting duck, having made it "difficult for a physical enemy or a metaphysical enemy to take aim." One can thus avoid the generalizing ideologies of historians or states, and the tendency of their generalized social organizations to become faceless sitting ducks *en masse*, since large, settled, and complacent crowds are easy targets that can suffer a needlessly swift demise. Massed, faithless presence disappears easily into mathematical eternity, especially if it remains immobile.

To slow this demise, what one needs is a discernible form of freedom, one that permits a range of supra-spatial or supra-national "wanderings in time." Not movement *from* a home, but its very *absence*, the homelessness the poet attributes to God Himself in a Christmas poem of 1989 (ss3, 190). Just as Xlebnikov's "seemingly aimless wanderings through the land" were related to the metaphysical "mileage" of his verse (1986d, 32), so Brodsky wants to travel in time, not space, like a tiny, unclassifiable entity which is almost scared into movement at the close of its life by the potential meaninglessness of eternity.

> Space is fully settled. Time
> is welcome to rub against its new surface, I'm
> sure, infinitely. All the same,
>
> your eyelid is drooping. Only the seas alone
> remain unruffled and blue, telling the dawn "go on,"
> which sounds, from afar, like "gone."
>
> And upon hearing that, one wants to quit one's travail,
> shoveling, digging, and board a steamship and sail
> and sail, in order to hail
>
> in the end not an island nor an organism Linnaeus never
>   found,
> nor the charms of new latitudes, but the other way around:
> something of no account.
>
> (*Fin de siècle*)

In one interview, Brodsky defines his aesthetic as constantly moving "from the centre to the outskirts" (Forbes, 4). This may seem to designate a centre or home of some description, but the poet is actually instigating and then succumbing to an eternal and gratefully accepted diminution of some starting point. As he says in an essay of 1988, he feels himself moving away from an increasingly inconsequential launch-pad, in a process he likens to the heavenly travels of a dog in a space capsule (1988c, 18). Through such never-ending series of metaphysical departures, a nomadic poet aims for the semi-material, wandering existence of cumulus, as celebrated in the poem *Clouds* (*Oblaka;* ss3, 186–8) in the last year of the decade. Clouds are simultaneously both settled and nomadic, living out an existence without a border. They are composed of both profile and *full-face* appearances, says the poet; they reinstate the dialectic of bodily form and soul or spirit:

О, облака	Ah, summer clouds
Балтики летом!	of the Baltic! I swear,
Лучше вас в мире этом	you are nowhere
я не видел пока ...	to be outclassed ...
Путь над гранитом,	Steadily running
над знаменитым	over the granite,
мелкой волной	over the most

морем держа,	humble of seas
вы – изваянья	you are the limpid
существованья	sculptures of limit –
без рубежа.	less genesis.
Холм или храм,	Cupolas, peaks,
профиль Толстого,	profile of Tolstoy,
Рим, холостого	muscular torso,
логова хлам,	bachelor digs,
тающий воск,	candlesticks' vain
Старая Вена,	meltdown, or Hapsburg
одновременно	Vienna, an iceberg-
айсберг и мозг,	alias-brain,
райский анфас –	Eden's debris.
ах, кроме ветра	Ah, save the northeaster,
нет геометра	you wouldn't master
в мире для вас!	geometry!
В вас, кучевых,	Your cyrrhic ploys
перистых, беглых,	or cumulous domus
радость оседлых	make both the nomads
и кочевых.	and the settled rejoice.

The clouds experience the dialectic of stasis and movement, of body and soul, of the *a priori* laws that bind the former and the possibility of *a posteriori* investigation of the latter's realm. When Kant tried to apply his combination of *a priorism* and *a posteriorism* to aesthetics, he ended up advocating an aesthetic "purposiveness without purpose"; Brodsky's nomadism is a similar kind of kinetic resoluteness without a resolution.

COMPLETING THE SYMMETRY OF THE CURVE FROM ST PETERSBURG TO VENICE

The theme of Venice looms increasingly large in the poet's work to bolster this Kantian, ethical, and aesthetic purposiveness without purpose. The city represents a symmetrical counterpoint to St Petersburg, on the far side of the curve of metaphysical inspiration. Prior to the quintessentially Venetian prose work *Watermark*, the importance of Venice develops across the period of Brodsky's Rococo, Précieux or Cavalier concerns. This importance is increasingly defined relative to both imperial Rome and St Petersburg in a way that explains the very appearance of *Watermark* at the end of the metaphysical curve.

August in Rome, evoked in the *Roman Elegies* (*Rimskie èlegii*), is called the "month of frozen pendula" (ss3, 43), recalling Brodsky's description of the Berlin Wall as a petrified either/or. His naked foot on Roman marble is seen as a step towards a similarly classical or imperial petrifaction. Just as the classical perspective of St Petersburg tried to ensnare an irrationally devolved poet, so in Rome criss-cross Latin numerals suggest tapering anti-aircraft searchlights, hunting airbound seraphim. Not surprisingly, the poet is therefore more at home in the ruins of the ancient city, either because of his dilapidated dental-work or because he is living the life of a "homeless torso" himself, moving as a fragment or debris (*oblomok*) which is caught in Rome's glaring light.

However, Brodsky was raised in a qualitatively different classical city. In a consideration of its charms, he writes that St Petersburg's most beautiful building is the Stock Exchange or *Birža* he loves so much. This building has been defined as a Greek, "monumental civic structure in a heroic, archaic classical manner" (Brumfield, 354). The idea of classical structure so dear to Brodsky, though, has the inherent potential with its geometry and its "eternal embankment," to make life seem extremely brief, just as in Rome. The *Birža* does indeed reflect an Alexandrine neoclassicism and as for the embankments, they owe their granite geometry to the eighteenth-century architect Georg Friedrich Velten, whose own work reflects Catherine II's classical dictates, her desire for order and rationality. With the sculptor Falconet's help, however, Velten placed along his embankment the "culminating work of European Baroque," the Bronze Horseman.

In a similar context of both the Baroque and Classicism, the house where Brodsky grew up lies on a line of what the poet himself describes as "typically Petersburgian, impeccable perspective" (LTO, 457. Number 24, Litejnyj Prospekt is the building, at the right-angled junction with Ulica Pestelja. The views mentioned here are along the latter street). At one end is the Cathedral of the Transfiguration of the Saviour, redesigned in 1827–9 by Vasilij Stasov in a "neoclassical articulation" (Brumfield, 368); at the other is the late Baroque of Ivan Korobov, the Church of St Panteleimon. St Panteleimon's arose as part of a smaller, more human urban environment to counter "monumental state projects" elsewhere in the city and the church shows an accordingly diminished use of Baroque motifs.

Around the cathedral are huge chains of number eight-shaped links, chains associated by the young poet with infinity. The perspective from Brodsky's house therefore offers mathematical infinity at one end and a geometrically constrained, Baroque display at the other, a clear either/or. (A similar either/or view was seen by Brodsky in Rome: to the right, pre-Christian Rome such as the Coliseum, to the left, St Peter and the cupolas of Christian culture.) In the middle of the Russian vista is the disorderly twentieth century: the building of 1903 in which the poet was raised. He refers to it as an ornate, "tremendous cake in [the] so-called Moorish style" (LTO, 452), markedly more elaborate than its neighbours in the perspective of the cross-street (Litejnyj Prospekt), which is very straight and long.

In a city where perspective and classical columns often sideline the irregularities of elaborate physical presence, where statues grow on buildings, there live two sphinxes in front of the Academy of Arts. Brodsky links them to a city outside of Russia, to Venice and its winged lions. It may be that the poet was attracted to this particular beast, since St Petersburg has four metamorphosed, winged lions of its own, standing either side of the Bankovskij Most behind the Kazan Cathedral. Such metamorphoses are said to be constant in Venice, thanks to the ubiquitous presence of water, and the city thus represents for Brodsky, "if there exists some kind of order ... the most natural, intelligent approximation to it. Of all the possible variations" (Volkov, 1981: 187).

This kind of order is referred to in verse of the 1980s; Venice is described as a wholly devolved city of perch and bream where the expansive blueness is ordered, as it were, inside a frame: "The weightless mass of the azure is taken into a square" (SS3, 55). The order or framing tendency of Venice is a type of spatial reduction; in Rome pediment figures can be a kilometer apart whilst those on their comparable Venetian buildings are squeezed together shoulder to shoulder. "This unbelievable compactness creates a special, Venetian phenomenon: no longer the Baroque, but something completely different, specifically Venetian" (Volkov, 1981–2; 178–9).

What exactly is this post-Baroque, specifically Venetian phenomenon? The answer lies in how the city's compact ordering of *form* or structure creates a tension with the wilfully disordered nomadic tendency in *content*. Venice operates as an arena for the interplay of form and content. Not only do both form and content contribute to Brodsky's increasing understanding of the "dignity of decay" (Birkerts, 1982: 113), but that very decay begins to operate dialectically with the poet's opposing and burgeoning bilingualism.

6 Nomadism and Venice, 1990–1996

The relatively small number of poems published by Joseph Brodsky between 1990 and 1996 is overshadowed by the collection of essays *On Grief and Reason* and in particular by the fifty-one prose vignettes that make up *Watermark*, a blithe evocation of Venetian culture. The dazzling English narrative of this slim volume fosters the role of Venice as a counterpart to St Petersburg, completing the symmetry of the curve of metaphysical inspiration. The very idea of the completion of symmetry, of Venice as a type of homecoming or return to a source, invites discussion of Brodsky's whole corpus in terms of coming full circle to some state that existed in the beginning, back to Italian culture, the "mother of Russian aesthetics," as he writes in a letter published posthumously (1996f). There is, without doubt, a sense of teleological conclusion or epilogue that pervades Brodsky's final prose and poetry. The evolution of seventeenth-century Baroque art concluded as a centripetal return to order, a denouement made manifest in Brodsky's own evolution, as part of a naturally repetitive return from disorder or chaos to a moribund stasis. Brodsky sees this movement as inevitable, to the point where he even discusses disorder or chaos in life as guarantors of a future return to some prior state of orderliness.

The poet's fear of what might follow his swift, post-Baroque deceleration into a deathly immobility leads to a further development of his second aesthetic stage. The brief and fleeting time left in the here and now guarantees that not only aesthetic, but ethical concerns are also prevalent; together they fuel the writing of the finite poet in the hope of a posthumous leap of faith, when any moribund, physical burden would finally be atomized in an immaterial infinity.

The concerns of late verse are best reflected in one particular poem, *Daedalus in Sicily* (*Dedal v Sicilii*), which is itself a return to or repetition of an early theme, the tale of the Minotaur, Theseus, and the labyrinth of faith. Daedalus, the man responsible for the chaotic effects of two phenomena which he "caused" – the Minotaur and its bewildering labyrinth – has also come full circle in his life. He is depicted after his failed flight to the heavens, pondering how he, like Brodsky, has been "led far" by the effects of his work, and he now prepares for death, for the return to life's point of origin.

There are Šestovian parallels in the poem *Daedalus in Sicily* of 1993, which is a summary of emphases in Brodsky's work between 1990 and 1996. Brodsky's prior progression towards the Absolute, like Šestov's and Kierkegaard's, had been described by analogy with Theseus, lost in a labyrinth. In *Daedalus in Sicily* (ss3, 226) the poet turns to the man who both invented and built that labyrinth. It describes the end of Daedalus's story, and seems to take as its source the version in *Metamorphoses* rather than *The Aeneid*. Brodsky tells the story of Daedalus's demise after the unmanageable flight towards the heavens that claimed his son, Icarus. Compared with Ovid's tale, Brodsky's poem becomes an ethically instructive narrative on art's unmanageable consequences, bolstered by a parallel with another story from *Metamorphoses*, that of Phaeton, who could not manage his father's chariot of the sun as it ascended to its giddy heights in the sky. The theme of a subsequent, necessary slow progression towards death is also suggested by the poem's form, the *dol'nik*'s interplay of prosaic syntax and poetic line. By examining the relationship of form and content as an expression of the analogous relationship between body and soul, the story of Daedalus becomes a bridge to the prose work *Watermark*, in which both Daedalus and nomadism become central aesthetic and ethical themes.

> Всю жизнь он что-нибудь строил, что-нибудь изобретал.
> То для критской царицы искусственную корову,
> чтоб наставить рога царю, то – лабиринт (уже
> для самого царя), чтоб скрыть от досужих взоров
> скверный приплод; то – летательный аппарат,
> когда царь наконец дознался, кто это у него
> при дворе так сумел обеспечить себя работой.
> Сын во время полета погиб, упав
> в море, как Фаэтон, тоже некогда пренебрегший
> наставленьем отца. Теперь на прибрежном камне

где-то в Сицилии, глядя перед собой,
сидит глубокий старик, способный перемещаться
по воздуху, если нельзя по морю и по суше.
Всю жизнь он что-нибудь строил, что-нибудь изобретал.
Всю жизнь от этих построек, от этих изобретений
приходилось бежать, как будто изобретенья
и постройки стремятся отделаться от чертежей,
по-детски стыдясь родителей. Видимо, это – страх
повторимости. На песок набегают с журчаньем волны,
сзади синеют зубцы местных гор, но он –
еще в молодости изобрел пилу,
использовав внешнее сходство статики и движенья.
Старик нагибается и, привязав к лодыжке
длинную никту, чтобы не заблудиться,
направляется, крякнув, в сторону царства мертвых.

All his life he was building something, inventing something.
Now, for a Cretan queen, an artificial heifer,
so as to cuckold the king. Then a labyrinth, this time for
the king himself, to hide from bewildered glances
an unbearable offspring. Or a flying contraption, when
the king figured out in the end who it was at his court
who was keeping himself so busy with new commissions.
The son on that journey perished falling into the sea,
like Phaeton, who, they say, also spurned his father's
orders. Here, in Sicily, stiff on its scorching sand,
sits a very old man, capable of transporting
himself through the air, if robbed of other means of passage.
All his life he was building something, inventing something.
All his life from those clever constructions, from those
    inventions,
he had to flee. As though inventions
and constructions are anxious to rid themselves of their
    blueprints
like children ashamed of their parents. Presumably, that's the
    fear
of replication. Waves are running onto the sand;
behind, shine the tusks of local mountains.
Yet he had already invented, when he was young, the seesaw,
using the strong resemblance between motion and stasis.
The old man bends down, ties to his brittle ankle
(so as not to get lost) a lengthy thread,
straightens up with a grunt, and heads out for Hades.

The title places Daedalus in Sicily. The master craftsman has been exiled to Crete, Ovid tells us, where he helps to build the hollow wooden cow that lets Pasiphaë, King Minos's wife, satisfy her desires with a sacrificial bull, and thus give birth to the Minotaur. Minos makes Daedalus build the labyrinth to keep the foul beast hidden and Daedalus embellishes the maze with optical illusions so disorienting that they confuse even their maker. Ovid likens the wandering pathways to the water of the river Meander, which "flows back and forth in doubtful course and, turning back on itself, beholds its own waves coming on their way, and sends its uncertain waters now towards their source and now towards the open sea."

Daedalus later feels bound to help Ariadne in her plans for Theseus's escape from this maze, a subversive allegiance for which Minos imprisons the artist in his own creation. By making wings in his confinement, Daedalus fulfills his duty to his child and homeland, and father and son fly out, god-like, from Minos's trap. As the more famous half of the story tells, his son Icarus then flies too close to the sun; his wings melt, he falls into the sea, and drowns. After burying his son, Daedalus continues both his labours and peregrinations with great zeal, jealous enough of competitors to try on one occasion to kill an observant nephew. He is eventually forced to rest from his wanderings in Sicily, to hide from Minos's search party. When Minos finds him, only with the help of the local royal family is the Cretan king trapped and then murdered.

Brodsky stays close to this tale of aesthetics, ethics, and misguided assumptions of godliness. His poem is twenty-five lines long and divided into two uneven halves by the repetition of the line "All his life he was building something, inventing something" (*vsju žizn' on čto-nibud' stroil, čto-nibud' izobretal*). The first half lists some of the artist's contraptions or inventions: the artificial cow for the Cretan queen; the labyrinth, "to hide the foul progeny from idle gazes," and a flying apparatus. After Brodsky notes that the king finally realizes the reason for Daedalus's subversive diligence, he switches to a synopsis of the Icarus episode, to the son who "died, having fallen / into the ocean, like Phaeton, who once before also ignored / the admonition of his father." The first half ends with a depiction of the craftsman alone on the shore of Sicily, yet perhaps still able to fly, if sea and land travel are denied him.

The second half, repeating the opening line, is something of a comment on the first, a metaphorical interpretation. Daedalus, we are told, has fled his own contraptions all his life, which like unruly children have in turn fled their own blueprints. This constant escaping or centrifugalism is attributed to a fear of cliché or tautology ("the fear of replication" – *strax povtorimosti'*), one which apparently outruns the speed of purely natural development. Daedalus sits surrounded by the edges of waves and the sharp "teeth" (*zubcy*) or spines of local hills; but he had already invented a saw in his youth, itself born of a noted "similarity between stasis and movement," between the ragged, moving edges of water (time/spirit) and the outline of immobile hill-ranges (mass or corporeal stability). The poem ends as Daedalus gets up, and ties a thread (*à la* Ariadne) to his ankle before he wearily begins his passage in the direction of Hades. Even close to death, Daedalus sees his demise as a final experiment, one from which he might secretly hope to return by means of this very thread.

The poem is a summation of Brodsky's own passage. Daedalus is taken far by his own creations, which then instigate an overpowering attack on their maker. Daedalus creates a false cow, but the metamorphosed offspring is so dangerous that it must be hidden from further scrutiny, from visual analysis that would split it into more horrible forms, to use Brodsky's understanding of how such monsters are made. The corridors of the labyrinth, designed with twists and turns to hide their contents from view, to avoid a confrontation with that which is inherent to themselves, actually have the power to trap their own craftsman. Any maze is based upon not going the same way twice, because to do so means that one is lost, that one's movement has become tautological; if one is therefore constantly trying not to go the same way twice, options will inevitably get less and less and the likelihood of running into the Minotaur becomes ever greater, in fact inevitable.

Next Brodsky describes the hand-crafted, feathered wings; when Daedalus' aesthetic efforts are put to the service of the ethical, they lead to a flight so high that those who see Icarus and his father believe they must be gods. From this unmanageable, Baroque flight of fancy, another of the craftsman's "works" or progenies – his own son – plunges seaward from being too close to the sun, down into the 70,000 fathoms. Brodsky's dialectic of body and "written" soul corresponds to earthly Daedalus and aerial Icarus, and his penned or pennate language fluctuates between the potential horrors of the taurine, "doubtful progeny" and the dizzy heights of the hapless son.

The unwieldy and disorderly consequences of the inventor's handiwork give way to the quiet, physical demise of the aging Daedalus at the poem's close. His exile and homeward travels become part of a final, poignant repetition of his own life cycle. It underlines the redundancy of returning to one's source, which is certainly the end of any nomadism since *physically* it means being in the same place twice and is the opposing, centripetal tendency to his centrifugal, *spiritual* works that fled their blueprints in the past. All that remains is the final experiment upon himself, as Daedalus ties a thread to his ankle and enters another labyrinth of his own making.

The fact that Brodsky refers explicitly to Phaeton is also telling. If the poet's work is a series of meanders or zigzags around the cycles of one's finite life or of tradition, Phaeton's life is a most fitting analogy. Here is the story of a mortal who begs to race through the vertiginous circuits of his father's sun-chariot and who, like Icarus, ignores the paternal warning that only a middle course is safe, only to discover that he cannot handle the pace or heat of an ascent to the heavens. As a result, the chariot careens out of control and crashes to the earth.

The ethical significance of Daedalus's tale is also evident if one notes that Brodsky's greatest praise for Shakespeare comes in this period. The playwright is "treasured dearly," he is "the *non plus ultra*, the Holy of Holies" (Veit, 102–3). Shakespeare uses the Daedalus myth twice to emphasize the ethical imperative of a father/son bond, in both *King Henry VI, Part One* (IV, vi) and *Part Three* (V, vi). The acts (literary or otherwise) of William Shakespeare, Joseph Brodsky, Daedalus, or Phaeton all invite peril when they ascend high above earthbound, ethical aesthetics; the literary acts cause the inevitable switch of one's role from agent to patient at the hands of God, language, time, King Minos, or the sun.

The perils of Brodsky's own Baroque flight of the past led to an Icarus-like plunge downwards into earthbound prose; *Daedalus in Sicily* is rendered in unrhymed, variable *dol'nik*, surely the most prosaic of all prosodic forms. In fact, if one realigns the poem as prose, as sentences and not lines, there are revealing parallels or correspondences between the first four sentences of each half of the poem, which I will call A1–4 and B1–4.

The first sentence of each half is the same: "All his life he was building something, inventing something." A2 relates what Daedalus built: a cow, a labyrinth, and wings; the corresponding B2 says he fled these projects all his life. A3 says Icarus died like Phaeton, plunging down after ignoring his father; B3 suggests why: "It's the fear of repetition." In other words, the ever-ascending search for innovation will stall one day if physical limits are breached. A4 juxtaposes body and spirit; it says Daedalus sits still on the beach, though he can apparently fly, if trapped; B4 compares the "still" hill ridge and the "mobile" waves, the limits of mass and the limitless spirit. That leaves one extra sentence, an unmatched B5, which describes Daedalus ending his life's passage by entering the kingdom of the dead. In summary, the marriage of A and B, the reality and its consequences, the fact (Daedalus's physical existence and material handiwork) and fiction (the metaphysical or psychic consequences of such work) only last as long as Daedalus stays alive. Sentence B5 is a coda to section A, the whole poem, the myth and the poet's life. Brodsky has referred to the sum total of a poet's life as a myth before (GR, 395–6) and stresses that the significance of such a myth is dependent upon the poet's ability to complete it, to reach its coda and enact it in its entirety.

This interplay of death and myth is uppermost in Auden's treatment of the story of Daedalus and Icarus, *Musée des Beaux Arts*, in particular its discussion of Brueghel's painting *Icarus*. Auden comments that the depiction of epic or mythical scenes in the work of old masters is always combined with the mundane features or figures of everyday reality. The fall of Icarus from the sky, for example, is a personal battle of Daedalus's son with death; its significance is either unapparent or simply uninteresting to everybody else. We all die, so to invest the mundane nature of death with mythic significance is a wholly subjective endeavour, and may well be of no immediate consequence to others.

> In Brueghel's *Icarus*, for instance: ... everything turns away
> Quite leisurely from the disaster; the ploughman may
> Have heard the splash, the forsaken cry,
> But for him it was not an important failure; the sun shone
> As it had to on the white legs disappearing into the green
> Water: and the expensive delicate ship that must have seen
> Something amazing, a boy falling out of the sky,
> Had somewhere to get to and sailed calmly on.

The syntactic oppositions of Brodsky's poem that bolster the thematics of subjective, mythic repetition are founded upon the poem's prosaic *content*; its *form* supports the above findings from a different angle. This support is a product of the metre; the variable *dol'nik*, which epitomizes the interplay of formal constraints and a relatively free content. In the second half of the poem the average syllabic length of its lines is longer, with a lower average number of stresses per line, a demise further emphasized by the shift to a higher number of ongoing, present-tense forms in section B. Section A is higher in perfective past-tense forms and infinitives, section B in imperfectives. The number of adjectives also drops in section B, heightening the ongoing objectification of the artist by his art as parts of speech are modified or metamorphosed less and less, a process strongest at the very start of section B with its repeated stems ("inventing/inventions/inventions").

The *dol'nik*'s lines create a new and slightly different relationship with the elements of the prosaic syntax, since they break up the sentences, whose length leads to frequent enjambment. Particular parts of speech tend to open and close these "different" sentences: the lines of section A begin with a high number of conjunctions or prepositional phrases and read across to nouns twice as often as to verbal forms. The lines of section B begin with a high number of adjectival or adverbial forms and conclude with nominal forms more than four times as often as they conclude with verbal ones. The tendency is therefore for both the progression of a continuing narrative (spurred on by conjunctions) and for one's ability to modify it (with adjectives and adverbs), to become objectified more and more, to slow down. The whole formal tendency of the poem can be summed up by the final line, moving from a present-tense verb to a nominalized adjective as closure (*napravljaetsja* > *mertvyx*: "heads off" > "the dead," but in the English both the syntax and vocabulary are different). Daedalus's crafts and experiments can only direct themselves towards their own final steps. Because Daedalus approaches his inevitable conclusion or demise both willingly and empirically, the poem is robbed of tragedy. In fact, in Brodsky's own poem *Portret Tragedii* (ss3, 206–8) he depicts tragedy as an aging hag: the reader must stare at her, strip her, press close to her, burrow into and gore her. Physicality loses its air of histrionic conclusion, therefore, since the poet moves bravely towards his own demise, rather than waiting to be pushed.

THE SIGNIFICANCE OF DAEDALUS FOR THE PHILOSOPHY OF NOMADISM

Nomadism is the central concept behind Brodsky's final poems. It is a spiritual and speculative zigzagging as far as possible in the face of both levelling (which is evitable) and the end of one's physical existence (which is not, hence the metaphor of a weary traveller in what may have been the poet's very last work, *Avgust* [PN, 201]). Like Daedalus, the poet tries to exercise his agency as long as possible before he becomes a patient of either history or death. Nomadism informs the aesthetic emphases of *Watermark*. In this prose narrative, the labyrinthine, streets of Venice are likened to the handiwork of Daedalus and to the folds of cerebral cortex: the city is "Daedalus' brain child." A close parallel or even confusion appears between what is outside and inside the poet, between the city that makes certain impressions on the poet, and the impressions of the poet superimposed by him on the city. The story of the labyrinth continues the poet's fluctuating status between agent and patient in the face of art.

In *Watermark*, Brodsky confuses the incestuous sexual and marital relationships of all those involved in the story of Theseus so closely as to make no clear distinction between hero and beast, agent and patient, hunter and hunted. Wandering in the streets of Venice may be a positive, physical expression of a spiritual or speculative nomadism, but sooner or later it will only hasten the quietus dealt by one's own brain child, just as the more Daedalus wandered in the labyrinth, the more likely he was to bump into the metamorphosed chimera for which his own imagination was responsible. After all, if anyone is to blame for all the bloodshed and sorrow of Theseus's tale, it is Daedalus. He built the wooden cow and the labyrinth; with both Daedalus and Brodsky the craftsman's creations outrun their original designs or designers. "So you never know as you move through these labyrinths whether you are pursuing a goal or running from yourself, whether you are the hunter or his prey. Surely not a saint, but perhaps not yet a full-scale dragon; hardly a Theseus, but not a maiden-starved Minotaur either" (w, 85).

Earlier in his verse, Brodsky had used a mythic metaphor that likened the poet's task to Penelope's; that is, the daily repetitions of an aesthetic task done and redone in anticipation of the grand return of Ulysses. This classical metaphor also reappears in *Watermark*, but the new, implicit description of Penelope does not allow her any hope that her beloved will ever come back. Brodsky notes that the beauty of Venice may be repeated each and every day thanks to the coming and going of sunlight, but these aesthetic repetitions are done "with no Ulysses in sight. Only the sea" (w, 114). The shuttles of the loom or needle in Penelope's weaving are like the poet's unpredictable psychic shifting or swerving, effected above the watery nothingness of eternity.

Brodsky's own attempts at shifting or swerving are a direct result of his relationship with Venetian culture. With specific reference to architecture, painting and music, *Watermark* continues his post-Baroque thematics, as he lives like "a small moving dot in that gigantic [Venetian] watercolor" (w, 102). The nomadic dot moves within its constraints, always keen to avoid the fate of a physical or spiritual "sitting duck" (*Intellectuals*, 554). Brodsky's idiosyncratic construction of multiple cultural references thus defies linear logic, moving back and forth like a Charlie Parker solo that attempts to "dodge" (*petljaet*) unrelentingly horizontal lines, as the poet has it in the poem *View from the Hill* (*Vid s xolma*) (ss3, 210). His aesthetic attempt to avoid the linear inevitability of death's tapering perspective is the same that underlies the ethical imperative of his poem *Don't Leave the Room* (*Ne vyxody iz komnaty*): "Be what others were not" (213). Venice gives these attempts a sense of closure; they are an ethical summary of existence which parallels the ethical worldview advocated by Anthony Giddens, whose research was used earlier. The problems of "high modernity" outlined by Giddens were akin to the problems of young, post-Soviet poets; the solution to such problems is an ethical one, in the sociologist's view (1991, 213–24). Since his solution mirrors Brodsky's, it allows another, more contemporary parallel to the poet's post-traditional evolution to be profitably extended all the way across the curve of metaphysical inspiration, to the second phase of ethical aesthetics that underlies *Watermark*.

WATERMARK: WHY VENICE?

The type of Venetian painting, architecture, and music that Brodsky loves so much is an outgrowth of the Republic's history, of its independent political and aesthetic context. The art is the product of a wantonly independent or nomadic attitude, one that corresponds to Brodsky's increasingly ethical approach to culture, his view that the reader's "life politics" should be governed by the same nomadic approach. Hence his choice of Venice as the object of celebration in *Watermark*. Venice is a counterpart to the city of St Petersburg on the far side of the poet's curve of metaphysical inspiration, and a comparison of the two cities is the most profitable way to presage an investigation of their cultural products. The dialogue that Brodsky cultivates has three main emphases: the relationship of both places to the theme of empire, to the theme of autocracy, and to the neo-classical aesthetics that both empire and autocracy cultivate.

The very fact that a dialogue is possible between St Petersburg and Venice is, of course, the result of geography: both are a collection of islands, perched on the edge of an aquatic emptiness. Brodsky credits the literary, metaphysical dimension of his hometown to its fixed position on an imperial periphery whilst it simultaneously tries to effect a centrifugal movement beyond tangible land. To begin a similar movement outwards, Peter the Great commissioned the services of thirteen Venetian shipwrights in 1696, drawing on what Brodsky himself calls Venice's "maritime might" (w, 88).

The essential difference between the two cities is that St Petersburg was an imperial capital, while Venice was between two empires, two abysses of levelling: as early as the ninth century "Venice was …

steering a course of extreme delicacy between two imperial whirlpools, a course on which she was in constant danger of being sucked into one or the other" (Norwich, 36). Venice was alien not only to the purely rational, at times self-aggrandizing aspects of the Florentine Renaissance, but also to the chaos of what Brodsky terms the "delirium and horror of the East" (LTO, 403).

In opposition to St Petersburg, which felt the stranglehold of Petrine imperialism, Venice was run by an oligarchy, producing in the seventeenth century the most democratic state in Europe, though it must be said that since the oligarchy was self-perpetuating, Venetian society was actually more elitist than egalitarian. The evidence of Venice as an independent and sometimes haughty republican dot on the map, evolving in and around competing imperial constraints either side of the Adriatic, ironically turned civilized empire in the eyes of Venetians into an intolerant monologue that was as destructive as any barbarian force. As Napoleon warned, before he overwhelmed the Republic, "I will be an Attila to the Venetian State."

Whereas St Petersburg's architectural development gravitated towards a prior French empire (away from Byzantine emphases, then via Mediterranean ones towards French Classicism), the Venetian oligarchy opposed any aesthetic autocracy by floating anachronistically between Roman and Byzantine influences. Venice's aesthetic dialogue with the East was to a large degree the result of a literal one, given the many foreign traders in the Republic. Their presence created a cultural pot-pourri which makes the definition of the Venetian state as essentially Occidental or Oriental very difficult; the meandering genealogy of much of its art is equally hard to characterize. The wandering nature of a mercantile state was, in any case, always more important than unquestioning allegiance to one aesthetic or ideology; the supreme nomad, Marco Polo, was himself of Venetian trading stock and a fine metaphor for any cultural dialogue between East and West.

In a place where the forms of Western practicality and the content of Byzantine mysticism coexisted, the eventual decline of Venice's political importance in the Adriatic did little to change the constant emphasis on an ever-flourishing, idiosyncratic beauty, whether that beauty was captured in a picture frame, façade, or pageant. The ability of the Republic to foster a burgeoning aesthetic at the time of its diminishing economic importance is a perfect cultural example of what Brodsky lauds as its successfully independent or idiosyncratic "dignity of decay" (Birkerts, 1982: 113).

Venice is used by Brodsky in *Watermark* to promote dignity in decay as an ethical imperative. The author himself, after 1990, is coming more and more to terms with the inevitability of his own physical decay, and he advocates creating dignified, aesthetically idiosyncratic works of art as a response. The poet's marriage of aesthetics and ethics is in essence a Kantian one: Kant insists that one's ethical choices be made as if one would happily accept them as law; Brodsky, though, if he sees his role in poetry as an ethical scout or pioneer (*saper*), needs first to find out what is or is not possible within the limits of death's *a priori* authority. Only then will he be able to develop any complete laws of proper aesthetic behaviour. First of all, therefore, the metaphysical potential of Venice's dignity in decay is investigated *a posteriori* by Brodsky, so that he might later advocate it to others as a rule, *a priori*. Like Daedalus setting off towards an empirical investigation of death, with a thread trailing behind him in the hope that he might return from oblivion, the poet sets off into the labyrinthine streets of Venice, leaving a meandering narrative behind him of his findings, which urge their reader to overcome the danger of vanishing unnoticed into physical or metaphysical death. *Watermark* reflects this deliberate meandering or nomadism both in form, with its multiple vignettes, and in content, with its tale of a maximally devolved poet going the final few steps, back to the muddy, alluvial source from which all life and language once sprang. Before beginning a discussion of this work, however, I should note that its final page dates the work as November 1989, but publication took place in 1992, hence the inclusion of *Watermark* in this most recent period. The gap between the two dates appears to indicate a period when the work underwent great revision; such a preoccupation would certainly account for the small poetic output of 1990–92.

NOMADISM IN *WATERMARK*

Nomadism in and around a primordial swampiness forms the structural basis of *Watermark*; its maze of fifty-one prose vignettes vary in length from less than one page to ten. Though the work is based upon actual events – early visits, first acquaintances with Venetian vistas and paraphernalia, a meeting with Olga Rudge, and much recollection of tortuous wanderings around and under the beautiful city – the chronological disorder of these events reflects the wantonly idiosyncratic reordering that is advocated by Brodsky 's nomadic approach to eternity. Events become increasingly digressive as musings on the infinite interfere with those on the finite. In fact, late in *Watermark* Brodsky jokingly dismisses his vignettes as something of a collective *non sequitur*, a puzzling interplay of both literal and metaphorical experience, of fact and myth. The opening sections may be a description of Brodsky's first visit to Venice, for example, but the narrative soon meanders to a discussion of the city's primordial, aquatic life among the vagrant, serpentine conduits and canals that in turn cast the poet's female guide in the mythical role of a latter-day Ariadne; the Daedalus myth reappears and is in fact the key to *Watermark*'s significance.

The mythical parallels are developed when the poet describes his very first meander in the Venetian labyrinth: "more in the capacity of the Minotaur, I felt, than the valiant hero." In other words, if the poet feels himself to be a devolving Minotaur, he will bump into his nemesis in the near future. But if Venice is also a reflection of the poet's own, labyrinthine mental processes, then he plays here the role of both Minotaur *and* Daedalus, both prisoner and architect of the maze's confusing twists and turns. As if Daedalus's dilemma in Sicily (in the poem) were not complicated enough, the architect of the labyrinth here strives backwards to seek his elusive, spiritual genesis, whilst simultaneously moving forward as a mortal, devolved chimera to meet his unavoidable nemesis.

Even in Brodsky's choice of myth, the devolving, material body and immaterial spirit form an inseparable union, and Venice is the ideal context in which to take that union to its logical conclusion, for it is a city where devolution prepares for dissolution into a posthumous boundlessness. The poet peeks eagerly through the scaly windows of waterside houses in snaking alleys and is cheered by the ubiquitous smell of seaweed. Brodsky's wandering through Venice – into a building's subterranean tunnels, for example – becomes a wandering back in time, too, the return to a point of origin. "We left the twentieth, the nineteenth, and a large portion of the eighteenth century behind, or, more accurately, below: like sediment at the bottom of a narrow shaft ... We followed him [our host] into a room which appeared to be a cross between the library and the study of a seventeenth-century gentleman ... The gentleman's century could even have been the sixteenth ... The fabric [of the curtains] felt it had come full circle and was now reverting to its pre-loom state ... This was neither decay nor decomposition; this was dissipation back into time" (w, 50–4).

Physical dissipation or diminution in anticipation of a posthumous leap is reflected architecturally: peeling stucco reveals the fleshy redness of brick, humans and statues are squeezed together like jewelry or diminutive filigree. The grand dimensions of St Petersburg that dwarf the Neva are now reversed. On the far side of the curve, space is made as tiny as possible, to make room for water. Form (the body) is reduced or devolved in favour of content (the soul); this is the importance of Venice, since Brodsky's own maximally devolved physicality now anticipates its release into a limitless, molecular freedom.

Venice ushers in this final stage of self-oblivion, which explains why the poet assesses seaweed as a happy smell: "It is a molecular affair, and happiness, I suppose, is the moment of spotting the elements of your own composition being free" (w, 7).

The final stage of self-oblivion is logically the end of bodily space and the ability of that body to produce language. Language has often been equated by Brodsky with the body, so if Venice is the stage for space's self-oblivion, it is fitting that the Republic is explicitly associated by the poet with the dialectical opposite of space and sound – with eternity and with that which is eternally ineffable: light. Venice is a supremely visual, almost supra-linguistic place for Brodsky. An overview of exactly how and why he invokes so many painters, sculptors, and architects explains how the poet effects his own self-oblivion in a crowd of kindred spirits and thus gains membership among them.

The importance of both vision and visual artists in *Watermark* is an extension of certain issues in Brodsky's work of the 1980s, a progression of aesthetic emphases analogous to those of the paintings of both Claude and Poussin. In *Watermark* the poet says his understanding of Eden is a purely visual one and specifically in the style of Claude; he also jokingly credits himself with a knowledge of Venice good enough to paint the city in the painter's restrained style. It bears mentioning that in a city where the personal galleries of patrician families contained very few French paintings of the eighteenth century, Claude's orderly work was the one exception.

Brodsky's knowledge of Venice is therefore visually acquired, through the eye's wandering back and forth in order to avoid immobility, since the poet maintains that one is what one looks at, one is what the eye sees. If the body is maximally devolved or at least tending towards immobility, then most of the wandering or nomadism is necessarily visual; the eye takes over when the body fails. The eye scans multiple and varied cultural phenomena of dissimilar periods. It dictates the movement of the pen, which in turn finds its remaining cosmogonical potential used to create a world outside of linear chronology, a world of temporal nomadism.

The essence of the finite body's attempts to defy mathematical infinity, its ethical duty, is to manufacture beauty in its wanderings. It creates beauty by finding it in traditional cultural phenomena, visually absorbing them and trying to create novel works in a dialogue with tradition. Brodsky admits that beauty might initially be sought as refuge from a hostile environment, but one's ethical duty requires that aesthetics must then be used to improve the future, for others as much as for oneself, because aesthetic successes outlive their finite, human creator. The artist knows that he might be able to respond to beauty, but that beauty cannot respond to him; therefore his love is unfortunately "a one-way street." The admiration for beauty in Venice is a spoken, one-way address to visually perceived, infinite dimensions – an admiration that recalls the tongue-tied awe of the Baroque stage because it is born of the voice's eventual inability to keep up with an accelerating perception. In less scientific terms, it is the inability of the poet to express the ineffable; the finite poet sees myriad proofs of eternal beauty but mourns that he cannot be or stay with them all and his sadness is expressed by speech at their parting: "On the whole, love comes with the speed of light; separation, with that of sound ... One's love ... is greater than oneself" (w, 109, 135).

PAINTING AND ARCHITECTURE:
BELLINI, TIEPOLO AND TITIAN

To understand the nature of Brodsky's love for the beauty of Venetian art, one must understand which artists he evokes and why. Several passages can be isolated from the body of *Watermark* that bring together the names of a large number of these artists, appearing in a suitably nomadic order: Bellini, Tiepolo, Titian, Giorgione, Tintoretto, Canaletto, Carpaccio, and Guardi. Together they make Venice the "city of the eye," as shown by the following passage:

Then came the Veneziana. I began to feel that this city somehow was barging into focus, tottering on the verge of the three-dimensional. It was black-and-white, as befits something emerging from literature, or winter; aristocratic, darkish, cold, dimly lit, with twangs of Vivaldi and Cherubini in the background, with Bellini/Tiepolo/Titian – draped female bodies for clouds. And I vowed to myself that should I ever get out of my empire, should this eel ever escape the Baltic, the first thing I would do would be to come to Venice, rent a room on the ground floor of some palazzo so that the waves raised by passing boats would splash against my window, write a couple of elegies while extinguishing my cigarettes on the damp stony floor, cough and drink, and, when the money got short, instead of boarding a train buy myself a little Browning and blow my brains out on the spot, unable to die in Venice of natural causes. (w, 40–1)

These words highlight the self-effacing air of a young man who is something of a tourist, under Venetian charm from afar. Brodsky fell in love with the Republic during his youth in St Petersburg. In claiming the property of guidebooks as his own, the poet's self-effacement seems to presage criticisms of celebrating culture according to Baedecker.

Three painters are evoked here: Bellini, Tiepolo, and Titian. All are quintessentially Venetian artists, but why does Brodsky single out these three and not others, and why does he refer specifically to ethereal females? Bellini and Titian both made a gradual exit from differing traditions, exercising an innovative dialectic between flesh and spirit, form and content, paganism and Christianity. In Tiepolo's work, the growing constraints of a burgeoning Classicism have a direct parallel with Poussin's use of form and content, a Rococo aesthetic of particular relevance to Brodsky's post-Baroque experience. (Since the ordering of the artists from this point on is deliberately haphazard, I follow each with the date of birth and death, to emphasize the nomadic structure.)

Giovanni Bellini (c.1426–1516) is referred to more often than other painters in *Watermark*, and always approvingly, as a kindred spirit. Bellini gradually moved away from the restrictive influences of his father's Gothic and Byzantine symbolism, as well as his tendency towards the more inflexible aspects of Florentine Renaissance composition. As Brodsky has often celebrated Braque, the artist whose colour (content or soul) played on the edge of line (form or body), so he no doubt lauds Giovanni Bellini because he founded the supremely Venetian trait of *chromatic*, rather than strictly linear emphases. Bellini's experience of the High Renaissance differs, therefore, from the absolute calculation of beauty in, say, Raphael.

The post-traditional use and combinations of line and colour, of body and soul, are the foundation of Bellini's many madonnas in which divine content resides in warm flesh colours, a warmth that symbolizes the secularizing influences at work in Venetian art. Refusing to divorce body from soul, the secular from the divine, even this great painter chooses in later years to espouse a mix of flesh and spirit. Mythological, Arcadian topics come to the fore, which in the *Feast of the Gods*, for example, are based upon a physical or fleshy dynamism within the confines of an expansive landscape.

Titian (1477–1576) was an apprentice of Bellini, and even painted part of the *Feast*. Brodsky, I believe, perceives a link between the two painters along the same lines that he had praised various artists such as Sassetta, Boccioni, and Braque in his Baroque stage: movement into and out of the stasis of overly constraining traditions, here the strictly mathematical period of a Tuscan Renaissance. Though Titian was much involved in the staid atmosphere of high-society portraiture, he still avoided the dangers of a leaden immobility. Colour for him is more important than strict lines, and as with Bellini's use of pagan themes, so Titian's zigzagging is not only a visual movement, but also an ideological one. Thus the fleshy aspect of his depiction of the

Virgin is exhausted neither by his depiction of pagan Venus nor by his Arcadian tendencies.

This union of the material and immaterial which Brodsky refers to in the passage from *Watermark* discussed here and which Titian celebrates, for example, in his painting *Sacred and Profane Love*, links both Titian and Bellini to Tiepolo (1696–1770). Often classified as Rococo, Tiepolo's work comes from an age of burgeoning neo-Classical severity, but the artist manages to side-step any such regimentation. Perspective does not subjugate human figures to overtly rigid, geometrical arrangements; instead it floats human forms at varying distances from the observer across a celestial limitlessness, at points on and around both the drapes and clouds that command Brodsky's eye in the passage from *Watermark*. Tiepolo's use of perspective is a use of formal limits in order to enable and enhance compositional freedom. An artist inspired by Rubens's Baroque, Tiepolo has a dignity which would appeal to Brodsky's worldview after 1990, a dignity that leads to the classification of his work as that of a "Poussin revived." Figures float in the light of a cloudy sky instead of the dark of a voluminous countryside. Tiepolo's emphasis on light takes us a step closer to appreciating the importance of vision, one based upon the continuing relationship between form and content, flesh and spirit.

PAINTING AND ARCHITECTURE: BELLINI REVISITED

The following passage from *Watermark* refers to the Church of S. Maria dell'Orto, encountered on a gondola ride:

> we circled the island of the dead and headed back to Canareggio... Churches, I always thought, should stay open all night; at least the *Madonna dell' Orto* should – not so much because of the likely timing of the soul's agony as because of the wonderful Bellini *Madonna with Child* in it. I wanted to disembark there and steal a glance at the painting, at the inch-wide interval that separates her left palm from the Child's sole. That inch – ah, much less! – is what separates love from eroticism. Or perhaps that's the ultimate in eroticism. But the cathedral was closed and we proceeded through the tunnel of grottoes, through this abandoned, flat, moonlit Piranesian mine with its few sparkles of electric ore, to the heart of the city. Still, now I knew what water feels like being caressed by water. (w, 129)

A harmonious union of flesh and spirit in Bellini's work explains Brodsky's praise for the Venetian painter, and this is corroborated by the above passage. In a discussion of the Bellini *Madonna and Child,*

Brodsky stretches the dialectic of flesh and spirit as far as it can possibly go, yet the poet still stresses their interplay; he says that the ultimate in eroticism is somehow akin to the ultimate in divinity. This particular painting was produced fairly late in Bellini's life, and does indeed embody an increasing tendency towards the same interplay of Earth and Heaven that Brodsky perceives.

The marriage of flesh and spirit, of the material and immaterial, in these first two passages from *Watermark*, lays the foundation for a discussion of the immaterial, ineffable status of light as Brodsky perceives it in the work of other Venetian artists. In this regard, it is important that the *Madonna with Child* was never intended to end up in the institutionalized setting of the Church of S. Maria dell'Orto, but was produced for private devotion. The investigation and celebration of a private, diminutive light in Bellini's religious work, its chromatic play, can be clearly contrasted with the opposite tendency towards the grandiose, impersonal treatment of light that Brodsky dislikes in other painters. The poet praises the use of light in both Bellini and Giorgione by an explicit comparison with the towering dimensions of the public, courtly works commissioned from Tiepolo and Tintoretto.

PAINTING AND ARCHITECTURE: GIORGIONE, BELLINI, TIEPOLO, AND TINTORETTO

Of a Venice winter sunset, the poet says that

this is the winter light at its purest. It carries no warmth or energy, having shed them and left them behind somewhere in the universe, or in the nearby cumulus. Its particles' only ambition is to reach an object and make it, big or small, visible. It's a private light, the light of Giorgione or Bellini, not the light of Tiepolo or Tintoretto. And the city lingers in it, savoring its touch, the caress of the infinity whence it came. An object, after all, is what makes infinity private.

And the object can be a little monster, with the head of a lion and the body of a dolphin. The latter would coil, the former gnash its fangs. It could adorn an entrance or simply burst out of a wall without any apparent purpose, the absence of which would make it oddly recognizable. In a certain line of work, and at a certain age, nothing is more recognizable than a lack of purpose. The same goes for a fusion of two or more traits or properties, not to mention genders. On the whole, all these nightmarish creatures – dragons, gargoyles, basilisks, female-breasted sphinxes, winged lions, Cerberuses, Minotaurs, centaurs, chimeras – that come to us from mythology (which, by rights, should

have the status of classical surrealism) are our self-portraits, in the sense that
they denote the species' genetic evolution. Small wonder that here, in this city
sprung from water, they abound. (w, 81–2)

Why does Brodsky embrace several artists here and reject others, with
no apparent purpose? How does their treatment of light suit the poet's
own assessment of art's relationship with the immaterial or ineffable
as a wholly private experience?

Both this passage from *Watermark* and the one that follows discuss
the dialogue of light and materiality in the works of those artists
Brodsky invokes, not only in terms of how immaterial light or colour
informs physicality, but how light's immateriality can or cannot be
captured by perspective. The latter issue is important, because the
dialogue of perspective and light is that of form and content, and the
overbearing presence of rigid, perspectival arrangements in the work
of those artists Brodsky likes less can be interpreted as the presence
of logical, expressable form made manifest at the expense of ineffable
content, of amorphous light.

In the discussion of light quoted here, Bellini's name appears once
again, but as the importance of Giovanni for Brodsky's insistence on
the dialectic of flesh with spirit and light has been dealt with, it is
useful to turn instead to the painter to whom Brodsky compares him.
Giovanni's pupil, Giorgione (*c.*1478–1510), has only a tiny list of
attributable works. They develop a pagan, Arcadian emphasis not so
much by means of the grandiose as by the effects of light and colour
on the private dimensions of "the sweetness of human relations"
(Berenson, 25). Even when Giorgione's use of light is extreme, it still
serves to personalize the shepherds of his rustic scenes, to avoid the
stereotypical depiction of bucolic figures in a false, aristocratic union
of court and cottage. The men and women show instead all the
physical idiosyncracies of those who are slightly dishevelled, and thus
Giorgone's bucolic themes manage to avoid the extremes of either
bombast or the sugary rusticism of a Rococo Watteau or Boucher. The
diminution of human space in a natural expanse becomes neither
precious nor effete.

Brodsky equates Giorgione and Bellini in their treatment of light,
which represents an ineffable, immaterial or divine realm that comes
into contact with physical existence and sets in motion the dialectic
of spirit and flesh, its Baroque metamorphoses. It is therefore fitting
that Brodsky praises the private aspects of light, the private or personal
interaction of the divine with the physical, not the courtly or institutionalized aspects of faith, because the poet's entire worldview is based
upon extreme subjectivity and idiosyncracy.

Giorgione's ability to use light as a private or idiosyncratic experience is seen to be less successful in Tiepolo, whose work could tend at times to be "all life and fire" (Morassi, 11). On occasions his post-Baroque grace was lost in the impersonal dimensions of its imposing context, such as the palatial ceilings across which he was always working furiously. Impersonal, monumental tendencies also underlie the pre-Baroque work of Titian's supposed pupil, Tintoretto (1518–94), because his highly personal, dramatic use of light to break up colour was often adapted to the grandiose wishes of those who commissioned his work.

PAINTING AND ARCHITECTURE: CANALETTO, CARPACCIO, AND GUARDI

If the work of Tiepolo and Tintoretto has a tendency to debase the ineffable beauty of light by using it to bolster earthbound, courtly arrogance, then Canaletto, Carpaccio, and Guardi are three artists discussed by Brodsky vis-à-vis another potential problem in the depiction of the ineffable; to what extent can light's limitlessness be limited by the recognizable, strictly delineated forms that constitute a painting or depiction without creating soulless geometry? How this latter group of three artists allows light and colour to be roped in by either perspective or the strict forms of architecture is a problem which underlies the following passage, when Brodsky elucidates his dignified acceptance of perspective's *a priori* authority – that is, of a life that is tapering or petering out.

The winter light in this city! It has the extraordinary property of enhancing your eye's power of resolution to the point of microscopic precision – the pupil, especially when it is of the gray or mustard-and-honey variety, humbles any Haselblad lens and develops your subsequent memories to a *National Geographic* sharpness ... In the morning this light breasts your windowpane and, having pried your eye open like a shell, runs ahead of you, strumming its lengthy rays – like a hot-footed schoolboy running his stick along the iron grate of a park or garden – along arcades, colonnades, red-brick chimneys, saints and lions. "Depict! Depict!" it cries to you, either mistaking you for some Canaletto or Carpaccio or Guardi, or because it doesn't trust your retina's ability to retain what it makes available, not to mention your brain's capacity to absorb it. Perhaps the latter explains the former. Perhaps they are synonymous. Perhaps art is simply an organism's reaction against its retentive limitations. (w, 78–9)

The stick-on-railings image appeared in early Petersburgian verse, in an apparent reference to the fences of the Summer Gardens. Brodsky's verse has led from the arcades and colonnades of the Venice of the North to its Mediterranean twin, to the devolved faith of fleshy red bricks, saints, and winged lions, to new visual emphases that are well defined by these three Italian painters. Chronologically, the order of the three men may seem odd, but I believe it is both conscious and significant.

The first of the three artists, Canaletto (1697–1768), must be the best known of all painters of Venice, often reduced nowadays to postcard familiarity. Even during his lifetime, he was under enormous pressure constantly to produce views that would be purchased by tourists. One might wonder why Brodsky is praising an artist whose very name conjures up perspective above all, an artist who even used a *camera ottica* to project a virtually photographic image of his *vedute* onto paper as an outline from which to work. The point is that Canaletto often played with perspective by painting impossible, non-existent vistas composed of multiple points of view. The constant shifting or wandering of viewpoints within the limiting rigidity of perspective, views bound by a shared luminosity, is close to a definition of Brodsky's love for Venice; it is an idiosyncratic or *a posteriori* investigation of the world within the *a priori* limits of finite existence, seen by the poet as gradually tapering perspective. An artist's aesthetic achievements within these growing constraints constitute his dignity in decay or decline. Venice's beauty was being perpetuated by the artist's imaginary vistas, often cast in a veil of mist like St Petersburg.

Even Canaletto's later views of Roman ruins were idiosyncratically reorganized as *capricci*, perhaps a logical development for a man trained in stage design, in the illusional potential of perspective. Theatricality and pageantry are also the essence of Carpaccio's work (*c.*1450–1522), from the age of a blossoming Renaissance; he, too, is capricious in his treatment of visual perception, merging multiple events in one scene – for example both the martyrdom and funeral of St Ursula in one panel of her *Legend* (1493). Though influenced directly by Bellini, Carpaccio's œuvre can also be compared with Canaletto's calmer, orderly works. Carpaccio lacks the warm sensuality of Bellini and, just as with Canaletto, immaterial light and colour are constrained by the geometry of architecture. The resulting display of light therefore emphasizes not so much the celebration of physicality in a spiritual theme, but a quieter tendency towards what is "clean-cut, measured [and] well-proportioned." The form of the body merges with the overriding presence of perspective, which in turn joins colour to form a synthesis. The dignified ordering of Carpaccio's theatrical ornament within Florentine geometry has been called a forerunner of neo-Classical emphases, and a direct heritage into the hands of Canaletto and Guardi.

Brodsky's love of Guardi (1712–93) can be better understood if one suggests that Guardi's relationship to Canaletto is similar to the relationship of Claude to Poussin; the dimensions are smaller, the light warmer. The order in which Brodsky lists Canaletto, Carpaccio, and Guardi suggests that Canaletto's and Carpaccio's form and content are merged in the work of Guardi. Guardi, too, played with reality in his *vedute*, but his use of chiaroscuro was more spirited (even *à la* Baroque) than Canaletto's had been. If Canaletto's bigger views seem at times to fill dimensions worthy of a St Petersburg cityscape, then it is fitting that Brodsky turns in the 1990s both to Guardi's noticeable reduction of those dimensions and to Canaletto's work from a period when the painter was not in the strait-jacket of hard lines, dictated by architecture's mass to the detriment of everything else.

If the poet has come to a calm acceptance of physical decay within the *a priori* limits of life's tapering perspective, and if that very perspective is a product of buildings both near and far, then it becomes clear that even in Venice, the Donnean metaphor of "body as house" is still evolving. *Watermark*'s depiction of architecture's implicit fleshiness is a counterpart to the smooth-skinned permanence of St Petersburg's classical buildings. It is indeed architecture that links St Petersburg to Venice on opposite sides of Brodsky's curve. This is not surprisingly when one remembers the Italian heritage of the three men that shaped St Petersburg's Baroque, Rococo, and Classical stages: Trezzini, Rastrelli, and Rossi. The differences between these two cities' architectures, however, are much more telling than the similarities, and an explanation of those differences is a useful preface to a discussion of the type of "body" or existence that Venetian architecture represents.

ARCHITECTURE: THE COMPARISON OF ST PETERSBURG WITH VENICE

St Petersburg was designed culturally in opposition to Orthodoxy and pragmatically to rule over a huge expanse of water. The North European Baroque of Peter's reign that expressed his anti-Muscovite zeal was later replaced by a Mediterranean version at the hands of Rastrelli (1700–71), thanks to the Empress Elizabeth's love of lavish decorative effects. This Italian and French fancy came, however, via an architect whose father had served at the court of Louis XIV, where Baroque aesthetics were used to bolster an earthbound majesty, not a divine one. Thus in St Petersburg, Rastrelli's Baroque decoration on the

Winter Palace, for example, is antithetical to the mass of the structure. The overwhelmingly earthbound, physical bombast of the building belies the spiritual, centrifugal content of the decoration. With Catherine the Great, greater rationality emerges via Venice thanks to Palladian influences. It is under Alexander I that neo-Classical order truly takes hold and architectural geometry comes to reflect "the abstractions of an empire, ruled by decree from an abstract city" (Brumfield, 230, 248, 390).

Venice, however, floated between two empires, and as a result reflected opposing architectural influences. Byzantine influence, for example, was not shouted down, as in St Petersburg, but stayed longer in Venice than in any other European city. Whereas St Petersburg chased Western innovation, Venetian architecture paradoxically progressed by means of a retrospective tendency. Its wandering through traditions is reflected both metaphorically and literally in the lack of straight streets, since Venice had no ancient Roman settlement as its foundation. Venetian Gothic architecture also twists and turns, showing how it once tried to avoid unyielding, classical geometry. Even arrogant Venetian desires to usurp the role of Rome, when Republican haughtiness eventually expressed itself architecturally, produced bizarre Mannerist games with classical order. This is seen in Palladio's white structures of Istrian marble, emphasizing a divine light or brightness rather than the type of proud, classical humanism which would often contain a latent imperialism. As a result, the more bizarre, spontaneous aspects of Venetian architecture lasted all the way to Napoleon's arrival.

These aspects, the expressions of free will before the Republic's inevitable surrender to history in the form of a Napoleonic empire, are compared by Brodsky to what a physical artist can or cannot manage before death. Explicitly proposing that his reader compare Petersburgian and Venetian architecture, the poet shows how buildings are a tangible expression of what corporeality can or cannot manage in this world, hence the twisting and turning of façades in the Republic, as they try to escape Florentine aesthetics, to escape the artistic forms loved by those of imperial disposition.

In 1992 Brodsky again states that St Petersburg architecture taught him proportion and composition; in *Watermark* he then calls Venice "Petersburg's extension into a better history, not to mention latitude" (W, 38). The poet's evolution has extended from St Petersburg to Venice, from spatial to temporal emphases; his discussion of architecture does the same, in verse as much as in prose. In the 1993 poem *View with a Flood* (*Ne sliškom izvestnyj pejzaž...*), the flat, Poussinesque landscape which would be improved by a flood of liquid time reappears, and is now punctuated only by treetops, spires, and cupolas above the surface of the water. The autotranslation reads: "A somewhat familiar landscape, currently flooded. Currently / it's only cupolas, spires, tree-tops" (ss3, 241). In other words, architecture does what it physically can in order to head for the infinite, before succumbing to the 70,000 fathoms – which are here depicted as an uncomfortably high flood, rather than a domain to be wilfully jumped into, hence the emphasis on architectural height above the waterline. Elsewhere, lofty spires are said to be natural in a place where "one craves infinity"; in fact the ability of buildings to outlive those who built them and therefore enjoy a more permanent existence is defined in the poem *Architecture* (*Arxi-tektura*) as a step beyond what is usually natural (*šag za čertez / estestven-nosti*), as a step towards time (*v tu storonu, otkuda slyšen / odin tik-tak*). How does a building's inherent physicality relate to its potential to somehow enjoy a greater permanence?

The human body does not last forever; its role in this life is to devolve to nothing and make the posthumous leap, effecting its own atomization. What is left behind is objectified as an artifact of beauty, the words of the poet as a literal *objet d'art*. Rather than psychic exile, then, Brodsky's verse and prose of this final period emphasize the beautiful inanimacy of architecture, as a dignified and corporeal response to ongoing decay: "What could be more eloquent, / than [architectural] inanimacy?" (ss3, 221). Physical inanimacy is made beautiful in its post-nomadic stillness, a beauty amplified by the spirit, not independent of it, since it is the dialectic of body and soul that creates a building's beauty. In *Watermark*, architecture is called "the least carnal of Muses." In other words, all the muses are somehow bound to physicality; architecture may be as far as physicality can go to express the spirit, up to the moment of psychic release in the posthumous leap.

Just as the contortion of Venetian Gothic buildings dodged the unbending geometry of Tuscan Classicism, so Brodsky admires not only the meandering of the city's streets, but the "upright lace of Venetian façades." Both Baroque and Gothic façades, though, can still get trampled by the ripples across water's reflection of them, by time or infinity.

Some evolutionary – if not plainly atavistic – or autobiographical connection could no doubt be established between the pattern a wave leaves upon the sand and its scrutiny by a descendant of the ichthyosaur, and a monster himself. The upright lace of Venetian façades is the best line time-alias-water has left on terra firma anywhere. Plus, there is no doubt a correspondence between – if not an outright dependence on – the rectangular nature of that lace's displays – i.e., local buildings – and the anarchy of water that spurns the notion of shape. It is as though space, cognizant here more than anyplace else of its inferiority to time, answers it with the only property time doesn't possess: with beauty. And that's why water takes this answer, twists it, wallops and shreds it, but ultimately carries it by and large intact off into the Adriatic.

PAINTING AND ARCHITECTURE: PIRANESI AND THE LOMBARDI

"[On a gondola] we proceeded through the tunnel of grottoes, through this abandoned, flat, moonlit Piranesian mine with its few sparkles of electric ore, to the heart of the city" (w, 129). The choice of Piranesi (1720–78) could surely not be more fitting for a poet in love with a dignified decay, reflected by architecture but devoid of decadence. Piranesi's engravings of Roman ruins are, like Canaletto's, a playful series of *capricci* upon Classical views and orders, orders so huge as to make human figures around them seem as "ephemeral as gadflies" (P. Murray, 46). The architecture, however, is at least in part carnal, and slowly surrenders to the ravages of time in a dignified manner. Brodsky's experience of a primordial, swampy grotto's physical beauty is analogous to Piranesi's sense of decay that is simultaneously pleasing and terrifying. The architect's detailed, occasionally Rococo, ornamentation manages to avoid accusations of a decadent floweriness thanks to its concomitant seriousness. The union of aesthetic joy and demise is a paradoxical union of human possibility and impossibility, of the *a posteriori* and *a priori* which is clearer still in Brodsky's reference to the Lombardo family.

"A landscape can be thrilling, but a façade by Lombardini tells you what you can do. And one way – the original way – of looking at such façades is from a gondola: this way you can see what the water sees" (w, 126). Here Brodsky invokes the Renaissance family of Venetian architects, Pietro (c.1435–1515), Antonio (c.1458–1516?), and Tullio (c.1455–1532). The work of the Lombardo family dovetails with that of Piranesi as follows. Piranesi's themes of Roman, architectural corporeality or transience have led to comparisons with Rubens's Baroque; the Lombardi also shied away from using a strictly Florentine, classicizing tendency that reflected the desire for an imperial permanence. Instead they celebrated a roving, fanciful Venetian attitude toward antiquity. This wandering fancy within the contemporary constraints of a burgeoning Renaissance Classicism "tells you what you can do."

Brodskian nomadism is very close to a Lombardian eclectic mix of Byzantine and Roman influences that reflected Venice's freedom. A second, closer connection between Brodsky and the Lombardi also exists. Earlier I noted Brodsky's praise for Venetian stone figures squeezed together as tightly as possible, implicitly to gain a potential freedom or atomization in time. The Lombardi began the Venetian style of funeral reliefs that depict many statues together with the deceased standing upright. Brodsky's praise for Venetian art and architecture such as this Lombardian eclectisism is an expression of faith in language's remaining (though modest) cosmogonical potential. Since a nomadic aesthetic is necessarily errant, this faith cannot be compared with the constancy of monotheism.

THE IMPORTANCE OF JULIAN THE APOSTATE AND THE POETRY OF C.P. CAVAFY

Brodsky's devotion to nomadism is uppermost in his kind words for Emperor Julian the Apostate. Julian is discussed vis-à-vis his appearance in the verse of Constantine Cavafy (1863–1933), a poet Brodsky has both praised and translated. At a time when the Russian poet's work is so clearly dependent on a foreign city, and is consequently often called cosmopolitan, the influences of Julian and Cavafy emphasize that 1990–96 is a period of nomadism, of spiritual or temporal wanderings in a dialectical relationship with physical or geographical space. What Brodsky writes about Julian and the Alexandrian poet Cavafy serves to refute the poet's universal reputation as cosmopolitan, which in fact is nothing more than a way of reconciling oneself to exile. It is a geographical or spatial phenomenon, whereas nomadism is temporal. Cosmopolitanism is also based on physical presence somewhere, whereas nomadism has a spiritual emphasis.

Julian was Roman emperor between 361 and 363 AD. Exiled as a young man, whilst on campaigns in Gaul he was unexpectedly proclaimed Caesar by his own insurgent troops; luckily the actual emperor, Constantine, died before the two men could come to blows over the title. Julian quickly attempted to cultivate an official tolerance for his beloved paganism over what he saw as the narrow-mindedness of monotheistic Christianity. But his own narrow-mindedness and growing intolerance militated against his success, so much so that when he died in battle against the Persians, it was reportedly at the spear of an outraged member of his own forces.

Brodsky mourns the passing of polytheistic tolerance in *Flight from Byzantium*. He maintains that Julian organized impartial and public disputes with Christians rather than persecute them, since he felt that the supposedly bigoted rhetoric of monotheistic Christians would be ill-equipped for public dialogues. Policies such as these lead Brodsky to call Julian heroic and a great soul, one deservedly admired by Cavafy.

History has taken a somewhat crueller view of Julian. The emperor's initial tolerance of Christianity was designed to weaken its singular prestige, so that paganism could become the state religion in its place. It is claimed, that Julian's campaign soon turned ugly and in fact produced many Christian martyrs, that his subsequent version of institutionalized or state paganism had no jubilant tolerance or relativity to it, that in reality it was very puritanical.

Brodsky praises the poems of Cavafy dedicated to Julian as verse that approves of the emperor's good intentions. If one looks at Cavafy's seven poems, though, written about the Apostate between 1896 and 1933, the poet is less approving of Julian than Brodsky says. Cavafy is sympathetic to the problems of polytheism and its difficult survival in the fourth century. His sympathy is most often shown from a predominantly Christian point of view in the verse; Cavafy conjures up empathy for polytheism by using expressions of monotheistic Christian intolerance of the imperial "fool," the "appalling Julian" who was both "vacuous" and "unholy." Cavafy is well aware of the emperor's own intolerance, though, and in at least three of the poems his exasperation with Julian is expressed. He censures Julian for his forced polytheism, "ludicrous in theory and application" which in fact was little more than "graceless prudery," not tolerance (Cavafy, 89, 103).

Whether of not one agrees with Brodsky's positive assessment of Julian's tolerance, the Russian poet himself undoubtedly advocates a balance between varied ideologies and doctrines, a balance which sounds in the last phase of Cavafy's poem *Julian Seeing Contempt*, in the classical Greek aphorism offered as a warning to the emperor: "nothing in excess."

Brodsky's love for both Cavafy and Julian is a natural complement to his love for the various painters, architects, and composers of *Watermark*, who together help to stop the cultural nomadism of the Russian poet being reduced to cosmopolitanism, a product of the so-called physical estrangement of exile. To be cosmopolitan is to claim some kind of membership or knowledge of another land, culture, and therefore language and Brodsky's bilingualism is also very often misunderstood as a consequence of exile. However, it is actually linked to polytheism and nomadism, and is not at all a byproduct of banishment. Indeed, it gradually emerges as an ideal complement to nomadism on the far side of the curve of metaphysical inspiration.

7 The Consequences of Nomadism: Late Bilingualism and Posthumous Biographies

After Brodsky's arrival in America, the subject of bilingualism was raised in many interviews. Even in 1977, a mere five years after his arrival, the poet had decided that English is analytic and Russian synthetic (LTO, 124), punning on their respective morphologies whilst reiterating the significance of these terms from the discussions of metaphorical, stereoscopic vision during the Baroque stage. Bilingualism thus becomes part of the dialectic between body and soul: the mass of fundamentally monosyllabic English versus the inflectional contortions of Russian. English, for example, does not permit the irrational outpourings of emotion that are possible in Russian, says Brodsky (Volkov, 1987: 370).

The problems of a deterministic aesthetic, discussed earlier, are problems of one or the other of these languages, an isolated, mono-theistic or monologic creed driving itself into a dead-end. Perhaps it is a matter of *being* driven, like the gross distortions of Russian by propagandistic Sovietese that Platonov tried so hard to work with in his novel *The Foundation Pit* (*Kotlovan*). Platonov's attempts to orient himself in the semantic dead-end of propagandistic language inspire enormous admiration in Brodsky. It is the problem of such a mono-lingual dead-end that lead to the poet's decision in an autobiograph-ical essay to discuss his parents in English, since it will "grant them a margin of freedom" (LTO, 460).

In 1979 Brodsky says that he feels the freedom of English rhymes coming of their own accord, but initially he stops himself, to avoid creating and dealing with yet another extra reality. In the following year, although he expresses joy at working in English and acknowledges that two languages are the norm for a cultured Russian, he still rejects the idea of verse in two languages (Volkov, 1980: 30). Any tempting foray into a second language, even as prose, urges him on (*podstegivaet*), so he keeps considering a relationship between verse and bilingualism by practising in prose. Throughout the entire process, the second language is never cultivated "for the sake of greater estrangement," *à la* Beckett (LTO, 357).

Bilingualism that is tentatively developed little by little via translation is the search for an equivalent, not for a substitute. As the poet has it, the goal is synchronous or synonymous systems, not the loss of one for the other, and Brodsky even tends to view his readers as outside of the specifics of the one language that they speak or one nation they inhabit. Hence in a poem of 1990, when he travels back into the Mediterranean antiquity of Vertumnus (the Roman god of fruit), the poet finds that in this distant time and land people actually understand him when he speaks (ss3, 199). In the development of such linguistic universality, English goes from being a challenge in prose, to "the only [technically] interesting thing left in my life," to a virtual "rule" of existence abroad – albeit sometimes dictated by the requirements of publishing (Birkerts, 1982: 108, 124).

Brodsky is first challenged, then charmed, and finally bound by bilingualism. Wandering between languages, he accepts the constraints upon, or even initial loss of, self-expression in a second language so that through the routines of autotranslation he might gain a greater freedom from the bilingual's potentially superior linguistic, cognitive and creative skills. The resulting intellectual emancipation can be a daunting freedom when one loses at first the security of a single language's fixed semantics or worldview, but it can offer speakers an alternative to monolingual monotheism. A common form of this freedom is known as code-switching, the practice of frequent shifting back and forth between two languages during one utterance. Its attractiveness for a nomadic poet is shown by the tendency of contemporary linguistics to shy away from picking one language as the dominant of such an utterance. To switch codes is not to prefer or prejudice one to the detriment or loss of the other.

If there is a base, or basis, to all this switching, wandering, and vagrancy it is the ongoing search of the finite, physical word for the ineffable Word – the ethical duty to realize one's metaphysical potential in the here and now, in preparation for the "there and then." Brodsky's ethical view of aesthetics remains close to Kant's even in the final verse, the need for "purposiveness without purpose," which neatly defines the Russian poet's iconic description of his own tortuous avoidance of the inevitable for as long as possible. It is the challenging of one's mathematically inevitable demise at the hands of linear history by creating a unique and idiosyncratic temporal mosaic, one that is beautiful and therefore improves the future, long after one has left it.

Whilst developing a Kantian approach to aesthetics to the very end, the poet still develops the tenets of both Kierkegaard and Šestov, since he moves in and out of the aesthetic and ethical spheres in anticipation of the final, posthumous leap, playing one language against another in the service of ethics. The eventual leap beyond the ethical existence that informs bilingualism does not, however, correspond to a cosmopolitan multilingualism. Multilingualism strikes the poet as uncomfortably close to a dissipation of language's potential (1992p, 21), and indeed a recent work on bilingualism suggests that linguistic and cultural relativism or pluralism might have an inherent, organic even, tendency to produce the kind of entropic atmosphere that makes it easy for tyranny to take hold, a view stated explicitly by both Brodsky and Kierkegaard (1990k, 34, and SK, 1978: 97).

THE MODEST NOMAD'S
POSTHUMOUS SIGNIFICANCE

On January 28 1996 Joseph Brodsky died in New York. Obituaries appeared in all the most prestigious newspapers and literary journals. Most of these stressed the significance of exile in the poet's life, with the consequent dilemmas of estrangement and alienation. The existence of these concepts in Brodsky's œuvre, however, remains questionable to the last. His refusal to entertain them manifests itself in his late use of two philosophers in two separate essays: Schopenhauer and Marcus Aurelius (1995i/GR, 312–76; 1994j/GR, 267–99). These two men, though strange allies, combine at the very end of Brodsky's life to negate yet again the significance of estrangement. From Schopenhauer, the Russian poet takes the systemless, formless Will, "the phenomenal world's inner essence … a ubiquitous nonrational force in its blind, striving power." It is utterly absurd, a "horrific, meaningless omniscience." Poetry is a means of perceiving this force, a vessel in which it can be scrutinized.

Having taken this look at the absurdities of Nature, Brodsky does not advocate Schopenhauer's Buddhist transcendence or exile from the natural world. Instead he takes from Marcus Aurelius the very brave admission of human will's limited (yet invaluable) scope within the limits scribed by Nature. The Roman emperor expresses these limits in some lines with which Brodsky concludes his own essay, corpus, and thought. The emperor's words hark back to an earlier time in Brodsky's life, to a triadic worldview that suggests Kierkegaard. (Atop his horse in the Campidoglio, he even suggests to the poet a calmer kin of the Baroque Bronze Horseman of his youth in St Petersburg.) Marcus Aurelius stresses man's relationship to transient phenomena (Kierkegaard's aesthetic realm), to other people (the ethical), and to divinity (the religious): "There are three relations. One is to what surrounds you. One to the divine cause from which all things come to pass for all. One to those who live at the same time with you" (GR, 298).

Schopenhauer's irrational horrors are those that fill Kierkegaard's 70,000 fathoms in a moment of doubt; they inspire the Roman emperor and Joseph Brodsky to acknowledge the limits of an *a posteriori* existence in the world. These absurd horrors also lead the Roman and the Russian to value the ethical significance of their existence precisely because of such constraints, because of their bonds to the *a priori* prominence of earthbound life. Existential limits and their consequent ethical significance were true the day Marcus Aurelius died – 17 March 180 AD – and were just as true on 28 January 1996. These men are but two elements in what Brodsky calls cultural memory, but if one fills the 1,816 years between them with acts of equal existential fortitude, then what emerges is the parallel between literary- and life-cycles that inspired this book in the first place: "From the dogmatism of the Middle Ages, through spiritual disarray or (if we prefer positive vocabulary) the Renaissance, through the Doubt of the Age of Enlightenment (again the inclination for oral positivism), through the Consolation (i.e., the idea of the justification of life) of nineteenth-century Russian literature, to the Absurd of the twentieth – this, schematically, is the path traversed by mankind over the last 500 years, and is moreover the path of the individual during the course of his life" (Brodsky 1974a, 13–14).

Once, however, the individual's path has finished, it falls to others to continue its significance. The competition between Brodsky's modest Baroque worldview and the loud, public mourning by others at his passing was evident in St Petersburg even a few months after his death.

The twenty-fourth of May 1996 would have been his fifty-sixth birthday. In St Petersburg a series of events took place to mark that anniversary. Some were designed to praise the poet, others to lambaste him; both were inspired by Brodsky's emerging status as the greatest Russian poet since World War Two. A brief discussion of these events in St Petersburg will serve as a useful example of exactly how such status is being negotiated publicly. The above assessment of Brodsky's standing within our century's canon was made by the then mayor of

St Petersburg, Anatolij Sobčak, outside the poet's childhood residence. At 2 p.m. on that day a massive slab of granite bearing Brodsky's name was unveiled on the side of the house; the wall has already cracked a little from the weight. The inscription reads: "In this house from 1955 to 1972 lived the poet Iosif Aleksandrovič Brodskij." Accompanied by the flash of cameras, this brief text was revealed to a crowd of perhaps one hundred and fifty onlookers, enough people to spill onto the road and require traffic police to guide cars and trolley buses around a human kink in the otherwise perfectly straight Litejnyj Prospekt.

On this uncomfortably hot afternoon, Sobčak stepped forth with a brief word of gratitude to the crowd, a few personal memories, and the request for a moment's silence. (One's thoughts during such a lull in the proceedings were occupied by Sobčak's bold comparisons of the deceased poet with Nabokov, Tolstoj, and Dostoevskij.) Aleksandr Kušner also recalled prior times with Brodsky, in particular within this building, within the communal "room and a half." Kušner's modest memories and Sobčak's dithyramb define two extremes, towards one or the other of which almost all Petersburgian tributes over the summer tended. Either the unwieldy magnitude of the marble, burdened further by its very Roman bas-relief of Brodsky's silhouette or the memories of childhood friends; either what he has become posthumously, or what he used to be.

Sobčak's enthusiastic parallels were actually extended by the next speaker, Nina Popova, from the neighbouring Anna Axmatova Museum. She invoked Gončarov, Dostoevskij, and even Puškin as those who now constitute suitable literary company for Brodsky. Popova noted with gratitude the speed with which his achievements had been recognized locally: five months after his death, rather than the fifty years needed to celebrate Puskin in a similar manner. Such remarks helped to institute Brodsky's precedence both quickly and decisively; a more cautious approach came from Jakov Gordin, another speaker at the unveiling and editor of the venerable St Petersburg literary journal *Zvezda* (*The Star*). He remarked that the magnitude of the poet's achievement was not yet clear. It remains for us, said Gordin, to discover and define the nature of that enormous wealth.

The poet's considerable distinction in Russia provoked wide differences in how St Petersburg perceived this wealth on his first posthumous birthday, so to speak. One salient antipode to the eulogies on Liteinyj Prospekt was the publication of a booklet by the academic Jurij Begunov in a very limited edition of 999 copies. The publication is, as its title, *The Truth about the Trial of Iosif Brodskij*, suggests, a thoroughgoing reassessment of the legal process of 1964 which led to the poet's rapid dismissal into internal exile for a proscribed period of five years. The introduction to Begunov's work, by Aleksandr Suško, declares that the time has come to entertain the oft-neglected, opposing side of the *éclat* surrounding Brodsky. Begunov's endeavours, Suško informs us, are "a refreshing shower upon the excited heads of the poet's supporters" (ii). He is looking only for the truth; in beginning his refreshing pursuit of veracity, he assails an (admittedly excessive) eulogy of Brodsky as the Shakespeare of Our Times. For the author of this booklet, greatness is synonymous with literary nationalism, a goal of which the poet falls very short:

Brodsky's verse is an act of clear poetic images, a passionate and energetic line, one that is musical and – at the same time – abrupt as a trumpet's call. Where here is the melodiousness and musicality of genuine Russian accentual verse? Where are the reminiscences of epic folklore, such as one finds in Cvetaeva, or those of Ancient Rus', such as in Vološin, even of the Baroque or Rococo? There is nothing of the kind. Or perhaps one hears in Brodsky's poetry even a weak imitation of the great Puškin? No, one does not. There is only a strong imitation of the work of the Anglo-American poet T.S. Eliot ... All this *Oxford poetry* is meant for chosen, refined intellectuals, who do not support what is natural in art. They dream about the priority of universal values over national ones. Here one can clearly discern the path to what is cosmopolitan and universal, to that which beats everything to death and suffocates the final shoots of what is *one's own* in Russia. (5)

Any accusations of cosmopolitanism are likely to recall Soviet antisemitic policies of earlier decades and indeed such attitudes colour the main section of Begunov's work, a transcript of Brodsky's trial. He offers materials documenting both preparation for the trial and subsequent events in the courtroom. These records are presented in their entirety, but a question persists as to their authenticity. They used to be the property of a certain Jakov Lerner, who died in 1995. Begunov states that Lerner had a complete collection of all the pertinent legal papers, both originals and copies. The director Nikolaj Jakimčuk, who recently made a documentary film about the trial, had previously reported that these papers were officially destroyed once the usual, stringently observed term of preservation had expired.

On 25 May the scholar Konstantin Azadovskij in the St Petersburg newspaper *Nevskoe vremia* (*Neva Times*) voiced suspicions concerning the genuineness of the documents. In his article, Azadovskij hazards the supposition that since Lerner knew he would soon die, he wished quickly to justify all his prior, despicable behaviour. (Lerner wrote an initial November 1963 complaint in the newspaper *Evening Leningrad* about Brodsky's supposedly subversive poetry. The article to a large degree occasioned the subsequent state interest in the poet's activity, and thus the trial, exile, and so forth.) Azadovskij, recalling Lerner's efforts, is amazed now to see included in the booklet materials supporting the latter's claim that in fact he tried constantly to ameliorate the convicted writer's lot!

The extremely influential *Literaturnaja gazeta* also cast aspersions on *The Truth about the Trial of Iosif Brodskij*. "From the fact that Iurij Begunov is the author, one can tell exactly what kind of truth this is. He is scandalously well-known for his scholarly expertise concerning the case against the nationalist-patriotic paper *Our Fatherland*, where he became a virtual apologist for ... anti-semitism" (Fonjakov).

Anti-semitism is the primary concern of the trial transcripts offered by Lerner. The version of the trial known to us for many years in the West is that of the late journalist Frida Vigdorova, which was recorded surreptitiously in the courtroom. Brodsky in Vigdorova's record says very little and remains rather aloof from the proceedings. Lerner and Begunov, on the other hand, claim we have been duped for years by a fraudulent transcript. They offer instead the *true* chronicle, in which Brodsky's behaviour becomes, quite frankly, outrageous and his speech is replete with bitter accusations of anti-semitism.

Are these documents genuine? Work in the government archives of St Petersburg is required to either vindicate or inculpate Begunov, who in the meanwhile maintains that his "word of truth is an obstacle to falsehood" (36). But a much greater influence upon public opinion was effected in May by television. Local news broadcasts reported he unveiling of the plaque with seemliness, yet their constant proclivity to quote a few lines of a (constantly misinterpreted) early poem by Brodsky tended instead towards the maudlin. These lines speak of coming back to the city's Vasilevskij Island to die and were used by many commentators to bemoan Brodsky's absence from Russia (first enforced and then voluntary) since his exile in 1972. Again and again the poet stated his resolve not to return (cheerless though that decision was), yet many such as Mayor Sobčak maintained that the poet, sooner or later, would enjoy a triumphant homecoming.

The television news magazine *Zerkalo* (*The Mirror*) of 25 May provided some scenes from a prospective documentary. In the ramshackle place to which Brodsky was exiled, there still live some elederly peasant women who remember him, and whose memories were broadcast to mawkish ends. One recalls "how happy, how happy" she and others were to learn of Brodsky's eventual emigration, how troubled they were by his battles with a weak heart (a life-long ailment) and how glum they were on hearing of his death: "Oh... I cried, my head hurt. I said the Kingdom of Heaven unto you, Iosif."

Another television broadcast the following day also subjugated literature to biography. A documentary entitled *Iosif Brodskij: A Little about Myself* was composed of three sections: a recent interview with the poet in New York, followed by responses of friends such as Jakov Gordin, Evgenij Rejn, and Vladimir Ufljand to that interview after a subsequent screening in St Petersburg. The final section consisted of footage from a memorial evening after Brodsky's death, held at the Axmatova Museum. The interviewer in New York confined her scrutiny to matters domestic: asking Brodsky to name those in photographs around his Morton Street apartment, an extended discussion of his 1972 day of exile, a surprisingly exhaustive description of Americans' passports, their freedom of movement and the minimal paperwork involved!

Away from the limitations of a question-and-answer format, the Petersburgian discussions in this documentary were more discerning. Brodsky's acquaintances offer a few thoughts on the consistency of the poet's character, despite his travels. Such genuinely touching moments help to counteract the rather lachrymose leanings of the Russian media towards Brodsky as an entity lost twice over – through exile and death – and instead to focus upon the man's enduring and positive presence. In the closing moments of the program, Jakov Gordin, ever a voice of decorous moderation, it would seem, is shown at the memorial evening. Once again he evaluates Brodsky as a persisting presence. "The fact that Iosif Aleksandrovič Brodskij died ... is, of course, a great sadness ... but the fact that he lived – that's a joy."

Gordin's words epitomize the basic competition over the significance of Joseph Brodsky. Extra-literary organs (of great influence) diminish or ignore the linguistic nature of his accomplishment which, after all, is what matters. Brodsky's literary contemporaries, on the other hand, view the biographical in the light of the literary. These two approaches came together in the week of Brodsky's birthday, in the St Petersburg supplement to the popular newspaper *Argumenty i Fakty*. This article reinforces a few clichés of exile and death, by equating the former with undesirable isolation and the latter with an undesirably universal levelling. "Only Death Alone Gathers Us" reads the headline, followed by the quote, "he accepted all sufferings." "The subjunctive is not for a Poet; greatness equals Eternity. The absence of details gives birth to legends. That does not concern us. Brodsky was born in our city. He lived in it for thirty-two years. Here there are enough true friends, who preserve a multitude of details from his life."

Despite this disclaimer, the St Petersburg media in May 1996 tended to draw very grand conclusions from few details. To document numerous biographical details means that memoirs remain the enduring focus of interest, rather than poetry. Brodsky *always* objected to the interpretation of literature through biography, but it would appear, unfortunately, that a miscellany of stories and anniversary anecdotes will often be used to publicize the poet in otherwise verse-shy journals. The irony inherent in such miscellanies is that by turning to biography on 24 May, in order to bolster the mythical magnitude of a poet, magazines give rise to a portrait so multi-faceted, so diffracted through the memoirs of many, that what results is a picture of the poet as an utterly typical man, a quirky, unpredictable entity that is not particularly conducive to the canonizing intent (local, in this case) of broadcasts and magazines.

Thus, as happens in the memories and anecdotes of *Argumenty i Fakty*, the miscellany hardly lives up to the martyrological overtones of its heading. Talk of courage or suffering from the interviewees falls more suitably under the rubric of self-assertiveness or self-definition, rather than stoicism in the face of fate. Aleksandr Kušhner makes the following observation: "Now people talk about him like a toy in the hands of fate. True, he was thrown out of his country, but all the same he was an unusually courageous person and always made decisions himself."

To make decisions oneself does not sound a conventionally heroic trait; it is more of a natural claim for existential constancy, for normality in the face of unnatural regimes. If one lists scores of similar biographical details, none of them will be allowed the splendid isolation required to create a generalized myth. In the *Literaturnaja gazeta* of the same week there is an extended overview of Brodsky's poetics by Boris Xazanov, who remarks the constant intrusion of normal, everyday, or even obscene language into the poet's work. Xazanov, however, uses that common element to engender yet another myth – not of the magnitude required for inclusion into the literary establishment, but a 1960s' version: an anti-establishment literary figure instead.

Brodsky grew up in the Russia of the Twentieth Century: in the lumpen Russia of camps and an unprecedented degradation of speech. He tried to rehabilitate this speech which was both debased and had debased itself. From time to time this patrician dons some soiled rags and sets off *incognito* into the housing blocks of the people, into the caves of the language. Just as Puškin once used to walk in his red shirt among the peasants: "In the evening I hear folk tales – and this compensates for the inadequacies of my damned education. What a joy these tales are!" *Mon Dieu* ... what kind of tales will you hear near Norenskaja [the village of Brodsky's exile]? You can say the opposite, too: from time to time this thieves' cant dresses itself in the patrician's toga ... The black bubbles of the language fill the corners of this aristocrat-waif's mouth. Among them peacefully co-exist almost all dialects of Russian poetry, the copper and bronze of the Eighteenth Century, the mannered refinement and elegant vulgarity of the Twentieth.

Brodsky's own experience of the Russian language as a subjective, cosmogonical tool, as a creator of private existence, is here transformed into a tale of myth-making, universal proportions. If, once again, we turn to Brodsky's close acquaintances, the private is stressed over the public, the mundanely subjective over the dramatically objective. Private memories are offered in increasing numbers, to the point where, thankfully, they mean very little when used as a tool to interpret poetry, because they are nothing unusual. Aleksandr Kušner's monologue on Brodsky in *Nevskoe vremia* of 25 May is a good example. The poet knows what death can do to the reputation of an innovative writer, especially in Russia. "When a poet dies, something changes in the attitude towards him, his scale alters. Such is the rule. But I must say that in the case of Brodsky it does not apply, because his scale was clear from the very beginning." Kušner, however, keeps that biographical scale small, utterly typical, irreducible to a generalization and wholly literary in its relevance. "Brodsky did not belong to any church. He was not baptized, not a Christian, not a Judaist. He had his own relations with God, his own, just as every thinking person does. I think each of the poet's verses is a prayer. A person who writes verses has his own way of talking with God. And he is an individual. That's why the ceremonial aspect, the ecclesiastical is somehow foreign. Puškin, too, probably cannot be characterized as either a believing Christian or an atheist. Nothing fits, it's all incorrect."

Nothing fits in terms of simplified literary movements, either. During a lengthy series of interviews I conducted in St Petersburg and Moscow with Brodsky's contemporaries (as part of a different project), the issue of simplified myths often arose. Kušner, for example, is loathe to talk of any literary or artistic movements since the 1920s: "Beyond that point [in time], each artist, each poet is acting at his own risk. Each was a school unto himself." To subsume – or expand – the poet's innovation into a grander scheme is both uninformative and contrived.

Anatolij Naiman, the poet, contemporary of Brodsky, and once the secretary of Anna Axmatova, also thinks that such innovation cannot be easily schematized. "*Somehow intuitively,* we began to write with words." Soviet poetry was a collection of expressions, phrases and aphorisms, and a new word was needed to create a new, subjective experience *ab ovo*. Each new word of Brodsky and poets such as Naiman becomes "an end in itself. When you write in words, then you unavoidably enter into a profound contact with language." Andrej Ar'ev, co-editor at *Zvezda*, tempers this sense of cultural genesis by stressing the need for Brodsky, Naiman, Evgenij Rejn, and Dmitrij Bobyšev (to name Brodsky's immediate circle) to enter into a dialogue with another, greater and prior cultural force before realizing their own. He proffers the view that through their literal (social) contacts with the then-aging poetess Axmatova, these young men by the early 1960s "already calmly considered themselves the recipients or inheritors" of a tradition interrupted by five decades of Soviet rule and rule-bound aesthetics: novelty needed tradition. Such a conclusion binds Brodsky to Axmatova, herself wholly canonized and subjected to a large number of mythologizing practices. For those who knew the woman, however, contact with her, either social or written, was an entirely private and natural part of the creative process. The young men and women of the 1960s picked up where Akhmatova and Pasternak left off. "I don't think our generation was anything very new for Russian literature," holds the poet Vladimir Ufljand, a close friend of Brodsky. Gordin agrees, maintaining that even in the late 1950s, an entirely natural "meeting of the generations" took place: the young, novel poets maintained literary and social contacts both with those such as Axmatova and with the recently rehabilitated writers and translators, returning to St Petersburg from labour camps.

If such meetings are a natural part of the dialogue between innovation and tradition, does that not suggest a certain process of repetition and cyclicality? "Yes, of course," says Kušner, who is inclined to interpret the aesthetic oscillations of literary history in terms of complexity versus simplicity. Vladimir Ufljand also resorts to conventional terminology in order to explain his view of aesthetic evolution in terms of its reception. Ufljand sees this evolution as the creation of classic literature from works which were avant-garde in their original intention: "It all gets repeated, it all gets repeated. Whether or not there had been any kind of Soviet power, *some* kind of change would have appeared."

Najman is more specific, believing that generations of poets change once every ten years or so, though "the calendar of poetry does not coincide with the calendar of politics." So, the dialogic movement forward which Brodsky either forges or of which he is simply a figurehead is ultimately undergone by all (innovative!) writers in their relationship with tradition, yet this movement is not contingent upon the vagaries of politics. In other words, its significance is not created in a dialogue with the makers of policy, but with the makers of poetry, most of whom have passed away. A poet is left talking *at*, rather than *with*, these deceased interlocutors; he enters into a dialogue with their language, with the medium of his own utterances. This reflexive process could not be more subjective and would certainly lessen the import of any simultaneous (extraneous) biographical events.

If this reflexivity is indeed undergone often, then what is the significance of Brodsky's influence as felt by the younger poets today, who find themselves in his position of the early 1960s, vis-à-vis Axmatova? Brodsky's friend, the art historian Èra Korobova, thinks his influence is huge, but that maturity will lead the new writers beyond the inertia which can result from working under the spell of a renowned and contemporary fellow countryman. Andrej Ar'ev agrees, but goes one step further: Brodsky's influence does indeed already exist, to the point where more than half of today's talented poets begin under his influence. Jakov Gordin broadens the view yet again and thus, as with the moot significance of biography, lessens the pomp of literary history, even, to a quiet and private process of self-awareness grounded in both unexciting, customary behaviour and literary custom. Current literature, he claims, is largely a response to decades of Soviet Socialist Realism, but the resulting, extreme experimentalism is not yet grounded in actual, normal experience. It is almost abnormally, childishly extreme and born of a "a fear in the face of life's seriousness," of a *rasterjannost'* (confusion or perplexity) in the face of life. Each young writer must mature on his own.

Perhaps now more than ever a callow writer might feel such perplexity, given that two strong points of reference have vanished: the Soviet tradition (to reject) and Brodsky (to embrace). How might one define this post-Brodskian, post-Soviet blank slate? At a roundtable of Petersburgian writers on 4 June in the city's university I posed just such a question, asking how Brodsky's influence was felt. I was promptly (curtly, even) informed by the prosaist Valerij Popov that with Brodsky and Kušner, the classical strain of Russian poetry and its influence had ended. Kušner himself suggested instead to me during a private conversation that in Russia, the death of a great writer only makes him greater. The poet was here developing a thought to which I have already referred, that of his published monologue of 25 May, where he tells his Russian readers that the nation has "its own eternal way of relating to death, to the death of a poet, with some kind of hysteria. I'm afraid that a new Vysockij [a popular song-writer and poet of the 1970s] will be made of him. Brodskij has absolutely no need of that. His poems are beautiful because they are complicated, because they're not accessible to just anyone. And it's no good pretending that you can perform them to the guitar, that they'll be comprehensible that way. I want us to get by without vulgarity."

It sounds elitist (in fact it probably is), but Kušner's words are designed to stop a normal – and normally complex – man being made (primarily by the media) into a simple or simply incorrect formula for mass comprehension and consumption. (One can certainly sympathize, though, with any post-Soviet suspicions about social aesthetics.) There may be a current rush for memoirs and biographical material to satisfy that consumption, but, just as the poet always claimed, poetry is such a subjective and linguistic experience, that a poet's social and objective real-life experiences will tell you nothing about his craft. Ironically, the people who know this insignificance of biography must surely be those who constitute it (and are closest to Brodsky's verse): his acquaintances. The last word should not, therefore, be mine. Here, instead, is Jakov Gordin: "As for what's being written about Brodsky as a genius of isolation – I'm not sure that's true. There's a usual confusion here of literature and life. Iosif's internal life was fairly hard, and that's understandable in a person of such perspicacity and strength of thought. But people who knew him remember that he was a happy man, in distinction from most of his poems, and he joyfully accepted life. He loved everything that a normal person ought to love."

Bibliography

ABBREVIATIONS

The following abbreviations are used for works by Joseph Brodsky. The use of an asterisk after an English-language quote indicates a translation by myself, since the text in question exists only in Russian.

ČR *Čast' reči. Stixotvorenija 1972–1976*

EJD *Elegy to John Donne and Other Poems*

FV *Forma vremeni: Stixotvorenija, èsse, p'esy v dvux tomax*

GR *On Grief and Reason*

KPÈ *Konec prekrasnoj èpoxi. Stixotvorenija 1964–1971*

LTO *Less than One: Selected Essays*

M *Mramor*

MS *Marbles*

NSA *Novye stansy k Avguste. Stixi k M.B., 1962–1982*

OP *Ostanovka v pustyne: Stixotvorenija i poèmy*

PM *Peresečennaja mestnost': Putešestvija s kommentarijami*

PN *Pejzaž s navodneniem*

PP *Primečanija paporotnika*

PS *A Part of Speech*

SP *Stixotvorenija i poèmy*

SS *Sobranie sočinenij Brodskogo* (volumes 1–4)

SPS *Selected Poems*

TU *To Uranija*

U *Uranija*

VOA *V okrestnostnjax Atlantidy*
w *Watermark*

The following abbreviations are used for other writers and works:

AC Abraham Cowley in *The Works of the British Poets*
RC *The Verse in English of Richard Crashaw*
JD *The Complete Poetry and Selected Prose of John Donne*
SK Søren Kierkegaard
š Lev Šestov

The designation (e) following an entry indicates an emphasis on the themes of exile, estrangment, and alienation which can be found beyond the central critical works on Brodsky. In the list of Brodsky's original works, most materials appearing in English-language newspapers have not been included, as almost all such works appear several times elsewhere in the bibliography. The designation (t) beside some of the early anthologies that include Brodsky's work indicates the collocation of a Russian text and a translation. The translation is into English unless specified.

Ackerman, J.S. 1983. *Palladio.* Harmondsworth: Penguin.
Ajzenberg, M. 1991. "Nekotorye drugie…" *Teatr* 4/98: 118.
Al'fonsov, V. 1988. "Otzyv o rukopisi I. Brodskogo 'Zimnjaja počta' (Kniga stixov), 4 Nov. 1966" in "'Zimnjaja počta': K 20–letiju neizdanija knigi Iosifa Brodskogo." *Russkaja mysl'* 3750 "Literaturnoe priloženie 7" (11 November): 4–5.
Allen, D.C. 1943. "John Donne's Knowledge of Renaissance Medicine." *Journal of English and Germanic Philology* 42: 322–42. Reproduced in Roberts, 1978: 93–107.
Allen, R.H. 1963. *Star Names: Their Lore and Meaning.* New York: Dover Publishers.
Allen, S. 1987. "Reč' postojannogo sekretarja Švedskoj Akademii Sture Allena na ceremonii vručenija Nobelevskix premij." *Russkaja mysl'* 3705, "Literaturnoe priloženie" (25 December): 1–2.
Alloj, V. 1976. "Proryv v beskonečnost'." *Vremja i my* 8: 147–58.
Alvarez, A. 1961. *The School of Donne.* London: Chatto and Windus.
Amory, J. 1986. Review of "Less than One." *Wilson Library Bulletin* (October): 69.
Amurskij, V. 1990. "Nikakoi melodramy: Beseda s Iosifom Brodskim." *Kontinent* 62: 381–97 (also published in Brodsky 1990p: 113–27.)
Andreasen, N.J.C. 1963. "Theme and Structure in Donne's 'Satyres.'" *Studies in English Literature* 3: 59–75. Reproduced in Roberts, 1978: 411–24.
anon. 1964. "Le Procès de Yosip Brodski." *Figaro – Littéraire* (October): 1–8, 17.

- 1968. "Dva Suda." *Posev* (March): 51.
- 1969. *Samizdat 1.* Paris: Seuil.
- 1978. "Honos et Gloria Meta Laboram" (Honor and Glory Are the Goal of Toil). *Yale Alumni Magazine and Journal.* Honorary degrees, Commencement (22 May).
- 1982. "Brodsky, Joseph (Alexandrovich)." *Current Biography 1982*: 50–4.
- 1985. "A Conversation." *National Review* (19 April): 18.
- 1986. "Pis'mo o russkoj poèzii": 16–38 of L. Losev, 1986c.
- 1987a. "Neskol'ko strok o novom laureate." *Russkaja mysl'* 3697 (30 October): 8.
- 1987b. "Sovetskaja pečat' o nobelevskom laureate." *Russkaja mysl'* 3699 (13 November): 10.
- 1987c. "Nobel Laureates Published by FS and G, Oxford." *Publishers Weekly* (6 November): 13.
- 1987d. "Nobel Dynamite." *National Review* (20 November): 21.
- 1988a. "O knige èsse Iosifa Brodskogo." *Inostrannaja literatura* 1: 252.
- 1988b. Review of "To Urania." *Publishers Weekly* (3 June): 73.
- 1988c. Review of "An Age Ago." *Publishers Weekly* (17 June): 65.
- 1989a. Review of "Joseph Brodsky Reads His Poetry." *Publishers Weekly* (6 January): 64.
- 1989b. Review of "To Urania." *Wilson Quarterly* (Winter): 125 (e).
- 1990a. Review of "The Hand" by Y. Aleshkovsky. *Publishers Weekly* (2 February): 74.
- 1990b. "Let Them Read Proust." *The Economist* (13 October): 97–8.
- 1991. Review of A. Naiman, "Remembering Anna Akhmatova." *Publishers Weekly* (9 August): 51.
- 1992. Review of "Watermark." *Publishers Weekly* (20 April): 41.
- 1994. Review of "Campidoglio." *New York Times Book Review* (4 December): 36.
- 1995a. Biographical introduction to "Lasting Laurels, Enduring Words: A Salute to the Laureates of Literature." *Georgia Review* 49/1: 195–98.
- 1995b. "On Grief and Reason." *Publisher's Weekly* (2 October): 64.
- 1996a. "An Exiled Mind." *The Times* (30 January): 15.
- 1996b. "Campus Mourns Professor and Poet Brodsky." *The College St. Journal,* Mt Holyoke College (2 February).
- 1996c. "The Cathedral of St. John the Divine. Memorial Service for Joseph A. Brodsky, March 8, 1996" (service program courtesy of G.L. Kline).
- 1996d. "Died: Joseph Brodsky." *Time* (2 February): 15.
- 1996e. "Joseph Brodsky." *The Times* (30 January): 17.
- 1996f. "Joseph Brodsky Obituary." Voice of America announcement (28 January. Taken from Nossik, 1996).
- 1996g. "Nobel Poet Joseph Brodsky Dies in New York." Reuters News Media announcement (29 January, taken from Nossik, 1996).

– 1996h. "Nobel Prize-Winning Poet Joseph Brodsky Dies." Associated Press announcement (28 February. Taken from Nossik, 1996).
– 1996i. "Nota bene! (Iz novinok janvarja.)" *Literaturnaja gazeta* (7 February): 6 (e).
– 1996j. "Nota bene! (Iz novinok ijunja)." *Literaturnaja gazeta* (26 June): 6.
– 1996k. "Notebook: More than One." *The New Republic* (19 February): 10–1.
– 1996l. "Obituary: Joseph Brodsky." *The Economist* (3 February): 77.
– 1996m. "Poxorony Iosifa Brodskogo." *Russkaja mysl'* 4112 (8–14 February): 1.
– 1996n. "The Talk of the Town. (On Brodsky's Memorial Service)." *New Yorker* (25 March): 33.
– 1996o. "Umer Iosif Brodskij." *Russkaja mysl'* 4111 (1–7 February): 1.
– 1996p. "Zerkalo" (television broadcast). 25 May: RTR.
Appel, R. and P. Muysken, 1987. *Language Contact and Bilingualism.* London: E. Arnold.
Ar'ev, A 1990. "Iz Rima v Rim": 222–34 in Brodsky, 1990p.
Asals, H.A.R. 1979. "Crashaw's Participles and the 'Chiaroscuro' of Ontological Language": 35–50 in Cooper.
Astrachan, A. 1980. "A Murder is a Murder." *The Nation* 231/10 (4 October): 323–5 (e).
Atlas, J. 1980. "A Poetic Triumph." *New York Times Magazine* (21 December): 32–9 (e, 39).
Auden, W.H. 1963. *The Living Thoughts of Kierkegaard* (presented by W.H. Auden). Bloomington: Indiana University Press.
– 1973. "The Poems of Joseph Brodsky." *The New York Review of Books* (5 April): 10–1.
Aulie, S. 1974. "Soviets' Suppression of Freedom is Working, Says Exiled Poet Here." *Grand Rapids Press* (24 February) (e).
Avramenko, I. 1988. "Iosif Brodskij. 'Zimnjaja počta,'" in "'Zimnjaja počta': K 20–letiju neizdanija knigi Iosifa Brodskogo." *Russkaja mysl'* 3750 "Literaturnoe priloženie 7" (11 November): 5–6.
Axmatova, A.A. 1967–83. *Sočinenija.* Munich: Meždunarodnoe literaturnoe sodružestvo.
Azadovskij, K. 1996. "Soxrani moiu ten'..." *Nevskoe vremia.* 25 May: 4.
Bainton, R.L. 1964. *Hunted Heretic: The Life and Death of Michael Servetus, 1511–1553.* Boston: Beacon Press.
Baker, J.F. 1987. "Humanism is Saluted at NBCC Award Ceremonies." *Publishers Weekly* (13 February): 22.
Bakhtin, M. 1986. "Extracts from 'Notes' (1970–1971)": 179–83 in G.S. Morson, ed., *Bakhtin: Essays and Dialogues on His Work.* Chicago and London: University of Chicago Press.
Baran, X. (H.) 1993. "Zametki k teme 'Futurizma i Barokko' na materiale tvorčestva V. Xlebnikova": 35–8 in Kurennaja et al.

Baranczak, S. 1986a. (as Barančak) "Perevodja Brodskogo": 239–53 in Losev, 1986c.

- 1986b. "Time's Lines." *The New Republic* (2 May): 26–30 (incorporated into Baranczak, *Breathing under Water*).

- 1990a. "The Ethics of Language": 203–13 in *Breathing under Water and Other East European Essays*, Cambridge, Mass. and London: Harvard University Press (e, 206, 236–7 in "Distance and Dialogue/ Tongue-Tied Eloquence").

- 1990b. "Four Polish Poets." *Partisan Review* (Winter): 141–5 (incorporated into Baranczak, *Breathing under Water*).

- 1996. "Always Through" (Review of *On Grief and Reason*). *New Republic* (4 March): 39–42.

Baraš, M. 1987. "'K Uranii': O novoj knige stixov Iosifa Brodskogo." *Russkaja mysl'* 3698 (6 November): 10.

Bar-Sella, Z. 1982. "Tolkovanija na..." *Dvadcat' dva* 23: 214–33 (e, 233).

- 1984. "Vse cvety rodstva." *Dvadcat' dva* 37: 192–208.

- 1985. "Strax i trepet." *Dvadcat' dva* 41: 202–14.

- 1988. "Poèzija i pravda." *Dvadcat' dva* 59: 156–66.

Basel, M.K. 1990. "Brodsky, Iosif Alexandrovich. 1940 – (Joseph Brodsky)." *Contemporary Authors: New Revision Series* 37: 51–5 (e, 52).

Bassnett-McGuire, S. 1991. *Translation Studies*. London: Routledge.

Bauman, R. 1992. "Contextualization, Tradition, and the Dialogue of Genres: Icelandic Legends of the 'Kraftaskáld'": 125–47 in A. Duranti and C. Goodwin, eds., *Rethinking Context: Language as an Interactive Phenomenon.* Cambridge: Cambridge University Press.

Bayley, J. 1974. "The Will to Survive." *The Observer Review* (6 January): 25 (e).

- 1981. "Sophisticated Razzmatazz." *Parnassus: Poetry in Review* 9 (Spring-Summer): 83–90 (e, 88).

- 1986. "Mastering Speech." *New York Review* (12 June): 3–4 (e, 4).

- 1987. "Brodsky and Auden": 205–14 in *The Order of Battle at Trafalgar and Other Essays*. London: Collins Harvill.

- 1992. "A Poet and His Fellows." *Times Literary Supplement* (25 September): 10–11.

Baxrax, A. 1977. "Konec prekrasnoj èpoxi." *Russkaja mysl'* 3179 (24 November): 9.

- 1980. "Pod znakom Brodskogo." *Russkaja mysl'* 3331: 8–9.

Bazin, G. 1964. *Baroque and Rococo*. New York: F.A. Praeger.

Bedford, W. 1988. "Who Says Does Not Know." *Agenda* 26/2 (Summer): 29–37.

Begunov, Ju. K. 1996. *Pravda o sude nad Iosifom Brodskim*. St Petersburg: Izdatel'stvo imeni A.S. Suverina/Sojuz pistaelej Rossii.

Bek, T. 1993. "Spasibo Vam vsem za ulybki" (interview with E. Gradova). *Literaturnaja gazeta* (12 May): 3.

Bekstrem, A. 1987. "Iosif Brodskij i švedy." *Russkaja mysl'* 3699 (13 November): 10.

Benčič, Z. 1993. "Avangard v barokko – barokko v avangarde. Tipologija javlenija": 7–8 in Kurennaja et al.

Benedict, H. 1985. "Flight from Predictability: Joseph Brodsky." *Antioch Review* 43/1: 9–21.

Benet, D. 1979. "The Redemption of the Sun: Crashaw's Christmastide Poems": 129–45 in Cooper.

Berenson, B. 1932. *The Italian Painters of the Renaissance.* Oxford and London: Oxford University Press.

Berg, M. 1996. "Ustalyj genij." *Literaturnaja gazeta* (28 February): 5.

Bertonasco, M.F. 1979. "A Jungian Reading of Crashaw's 'The Flaming Heart'": 224–64 in Cooper.

Betaki, V. 1983. "Ostanovis', mgnoven'e." *Kontinent* 35: 384–8.

Bethea, D. 1986. "Conjurer in Exile." *New York Times Book Review* (13 July): 3, 38.

– 1988. "What Does a Six-Winged Seraphim Taste Like?" *Parnassus: Poetry in Review* 14/2: 310–23.

– 1992. "Exile, Elegy, and Auden in Brodsky's 'Verses on the Death of T.S. Eliot.'" PMLA (March): 232–45 (e) (incorporated into Bethea, 1994b).

– 1994a. "Joseph Brodsky and the American Seashore Poem: Lowell, Mandelstam and Cape Cod." *Harvard Review* 6 (Spring): 115–22.

– 1994b. *Joseph Brodsky and the Creation of Exile.* Princeton: Princeton University Press.

Beznosov, È. 1987. "Vlast' nad našimi dušami." *Russkaja mysl'* 3698, November 6: 9 (also in *Glasnost'* 10, 1987: 14).

– 1994. "Skripi, moe pero, moj kogotok, moj posox…" (Afterword to Brodsky 1994, *Izbrannye stixtvorenija*: 476–87.)

Bien, P. 1964. *Constantine Cavafy.* New York and London: Columbia University Press.

Bigelow, P. 1987. *Kierkegaard and the Problem of Writing.* Tallahassee: Florida State University Press.

Billington, J.H. 1996. "The Poet who Proved the Power of Words." *Washington Post* (30 January): D1–2.

Binion, A. 1976. *Antonio and Francesco Guardi: Their Life and Milieu.* New York and London: Garland.

Birkerts, S. 1982. "The Art of Poetry: Joseph Brodsky." *Paris Review* 24 (Spring): 82–126 (also published in S. Birkerts and A. Backstrom 1984. "Från ett samtal med Josif Brodskij." *Lyrikvannen* 1: 6–23.)

Bitov, A. 1996. "Smert' poèta – èto ne ličnaja smert" in "Pamjati Iosifa Brodskogo." *Literaturnaja gazeta* (31 January): 3.

Blake, P. 1984. "Soviet Literature Goes West." *Time* 123 (12 March): 77–80 (e, 77).

Blitzer, C. 1967. *The Age of Kings.* New York: Time.

Blunt, A. 1979. *Borromini.* Cambridge, Mass.: Harvard University Press.

Bobyšev, D. 1984. "Axmatovskie siroty." *Russkaja mysl'* (8 March): 8–9.

– 1987. "Slučalos', Nobelevskaja premija byla pyšnym nadgrob'em dlja pisatelja..." *Russkaja mysl'* 3697 (30 October): 9.

– 1996. "Slova vosled uxodjaščemu." *Russkaja mysl'* 4111 (1–7 February): 17.

Bodin, P.A. 1976. *Nine Poems from "Doktor Živago": A Study of Christian Motifs in Boris Pasternak's Poetry.* Stockholm: Almqvist and Wiksell International.

Bonnefoy, Y. 1979. "On the Translation of Form in Poetry." *World Literature Today* 55/3 (Summer): 374–9.

Bosley, K. 1968. *Russia's Other Poets.* London: 18–23.

– 1981. "Fit Only for Barbarians: The Sound of Translated Poetry." *World Literature Today* 55/1: 52–5.

Botvinnik, S. 1988. "Recenzija na sbornik stixov Iosifa Brodskogo 'Zimnjaja počta' (22 ijunja 1967)" in "'Zimnjaja počta': K 20–letiju neizdanija knigi Iosifa Brodskogo." *Russkaja mysl'* 3750 "Literaturnoe priloženie 7" (11 November): 5.

Bourdieu, P. 1977. *Outline of a Theory of Practice.* Cambridge: Cambridge University Press.

– 1990. *The Logic of Practice.* Cambridge: Polity.

Bowen, C. 1964. "A Transcript: The Trial of Joseph Brodsky." *New Leader* (31 August): 6–17.

Bowersock, G.W. 1978. *Julian the Apostate.* Cambridge, Mass.: Harvard University Press.

Bowie, M. 1993. "In the Mobile Labyrinth." *Times Literary Supplement* (30 April): 12.

Brodskaja, A. 1993. "Preodolenie diskursivnyx orgraničenij: Na primere tvorčestva Deržavina i Sokolova": 46–8 in Kurennaja et al.

Brodsky, J. 1964a. "Roždestvenskij romans," "Kon' voronoj" and "Ètjud." *Posev* 21: 2–3.

– 1964b. In "Stixi molodyx leningradskix poètov." *Grani* 56: 174–8.

– 1965a. "Dojti ne tomom, ne domom...," "Stixi o prinjatii mira," "Zemlja." *Grani* 58.

– 1965b. "Elegy for John Donne" in Kline, 1965: 347–53.

– 1965c. "Novaja tetrad' stixov Iosifa Brodskogo." *Posev* 8 (19 February): 3 (see also 26 February: 6).

– 1965d. *Stixotvorenija i poèmy.* Washington, DC and New York: Inter-Language Literary Associates.

– 1966a. *Ausgewählte Gedichte.* Esslingen am Neckar: Bechtle.

– 1966b. *Collines et autres poèmes.* Paris: Seuil.

– 1966c. "Fish in Winter," "The Pilgrims," "Stanzas to the City," "From 'Commentary' [in *Šestvie*]," "With Sadness and Tenderness" in Zissermann 1966: 150–4.

- 1966d. "The Pushkin Monument," "Pilgrims," "To Gleb Gorbovski." The *Russian Review* 25: 131–4.
- 1966e. "Ryby zimoj," "Pamjatnik Puškinu," "...Byl černyj nebosvod svetlej tex nog..," "Ja obnjal èti pleči..," "Sadovnik v vatnike..," "Vse čuždo v dome novomu žil'cu," "Kolesnik umer, bondar'.." in Reavey, 1966: 256–69 (t).
- 1966f. *A Stop in the Desert.* Ann Arbor: Ardis.
- 1967a. "The Caravan of Carts," "I Embraced these Shoulders" in Emmanuel, 1967: 73–4.
- 1967b. *Elegy to John Donne and Other Poems* (selected, translated and with an introduction by Nicholas Bethell). London: Longmans.
- 1967c. "Po xolmam podnebes'ja." *Vozdušnye puti* 5.
- 1968a. "Bol'šaja èlegija Džonu Donnu," "Stixi o slepyx muzykantax," "Glagoly," "Vospominanija," "Pamjatnik," "Evrejskoe kladbišče okolo Leningrada" in Carlisle, 1968: 402–21 (t).
- 1968b. "A Jewish Cemetery near Leningrad," "Pilgrims," Verses on Accepting the World," "Étude," "Monument to Pushkin," "Fish in Winter" in Bosley, 1968: 18–23.
- 1968c. "Joseph Brodsky's 'Verses on the Death of T.S. Eliot.'" *Russian Review* 27: 195–8.
- 1968d. "Otryvok iz zapisej zasedanija suda nad I. Brodskim." *Posev* 3: 51.
- 1968e. "Proročestvo" and "Pesenka." *Russkaja mysl'* (5 December): 5.
- 1968f. "Stuk" and "Ijul'skoe intermecco." *Grani* 68: 5–6.
- 1969a. "A.A. Axmatovoj" and "Ostanovka v pustyne." *Grani* 72: 84–9.
- 1969b. "A Jewish Cemetry" in Nandy: 4.
- 1969c. "Na pračečnom mostu," "Sonet" and "1 janvarja 1965 goda." *Novyj žurnal* 95: 51–2.
- 1969d. "Stixi ob ispance..." *Grani* 70: 111–2.
- 1969e. "Zimnim večerom v Jalte" and "Stixi v aprele." *Novyj žurnal* 97: 33–4.
- 1970a. "Odinočestvo." *Novyj žurnal* 98: 104.
- 1970b. *Ostanovka v pustyne.* New York: Izdatel'stvo imeni Čexova.
- 1970c. "1 sentjabrja 1967 goda" and "Otkazom ot skorbnogo perečnja." *Grani* 76: 84–5.
- 1971. "A Stop in the Wilderness," "On a Winter Evening in Yalta," "Verses in April," "Gorbunov and Gorchakov (nos. I and XIV)," "On Prachechny Bridge," "Aeneas and Dido," "I bent to kiss your shoulders," "The trees in my window," "The fire, as you can hear, is dying down," "January 1, 1965," "A Letter in a Bottle," "Gorbunov and Gorchakov." *Russian Literary Quarterly* 1: 67–127.
- 1972a. "A.A. Axmatovoj" and "Zimnim večerom v Jalte." *Novoe russkoe slovo* (9 June): 3.
- 1972b. "Ostanovka v pustyne," "Odnoj poètesse," "Proščajte, Madmuazel' Veronika," "Novye stansy k Avguste," "Stixi na smert' T.S. Èliota," "Fontan," "Post Aetatem Nostram," "Natjurmort" in Massie, 1972: 228–99 (t).

– 1972c. "Reflections on a Spawn from Hell." *New York Times Magazine* (1 October): 10, 66–70.
– 1972d. "Says Poet Brodsky, Ex of the Soviet Union: 'A Poet is a Lonely Traveler, and No One is His Helper.'" *New York Times Magazine* (1 October): 11, 78–9, 82–5.
– 1972e. "Zametka o Solov'eve." *Russian Literature Triquarterly* 4 (Fall): 373–5.
– 1973a. *Debut*. Ann Arbor: Ardis.
– 1973b. "Nunc Dimittis" in Kline, 1973b: 286.
– 1973c. "On Richard Wilbur." *American Poetry Review* (January-February): 52.
– 1973d. Introduction to Platonov, A. *The Foundation Pit/ Kotlovan*. Ann Arbor: Ardis, ix–xii/ 163–5.
– 1973e. *Selected Poems* (translated and introduced by George L. Kline, with a foreword by W.H. Auden). Baltimore and Harmondsworth: Penguin.
– 1974a. "Beyond Consolation." *New York Review* (7 February): 13–16.
– 1974b. "Delo našej sovesti" (Declaration signed by Brodsky, G. Višnevskaja, A. Galič, N. Koržavin, V. Maksimov, V. Nekrasov, M. Rostropovič). *Kontinent* 4: 298–9.
– 1974c. "From a School Anthology," "Anno Domini," "Nature Morte," "The Funeral of Bobó," "Love" in Weissbort, 1974: 253–71.
– 1974d. "Konec prekrasnoj èpoxi." *Kontinent* 1: 14–17.
– 1974e. "Na smert' Žukova," "Konec prekrasnoj èpoxi," "V ozernom kraju." *Kontinent* 1: 13.
– 1975a. "Aeneas and Dido," "Postscriptum," and "Odysseus to Telemachus" in Rezek (pages unnumbered).
– 1975b. "Elegy (to W.H. Auden)" in S. Spender, ed., *W.H. Auden: A Tribute*. New York: 243.
– 1975c. "Mera otvetstvennosti" (Declaration signed by Brodsky, A. Volkonskij, A. Galič, N. Koržavin, V. Maksimov, V. Nekrasov, A. Sinjavskij). *Kontinent* 5: 5–6.
– 1976a. "Čast' reči," "Tors," "Osennij večer v skromnom gorodke," "Dekabr' vo Florencii." *Kontinent* 10: 86–99.
– 1976b. "In the Lake District," "On the Death of Zhukov," "The End of a Beautiful Era." *Kontinent* (English – language edition of materials from vols I and II of the original Russian – langauge edition). New York: Arno Press: 119–23.
– 1976c. "Kolybel'naja Treskovogo Mysa." *Kontinent* 7: 25–36.
– 1976d. "Posvjaščaetsja Jalte." *Kontinent* 6: 49–65.
– 1977a. "The Art of Montale." *New York Review of Books* (9 June): 35–9 (also published as "In the Shadow of Dante." LTO, 95–112).
– 1977b. *Čast' reči*. Ann Arbor: Ardis.
– 1977c. *Konec prekrasnoj èpoxi*. Ann Arbor: Ardis.
– 1977d. "Litovskij divertisment." *Kontinent* 11: 160–3.
– 1977e. Introduction to *Modern Russian Poets on Poetry*. Ann Arbor: Ardis, 7–9.

– 1977f. "Novyj Žjul' Vern." *VRXD* 122: 97–103.

– 1977g. "On Cavafy's Side." *New York Review* (13 February): 32–4 (also published as "Pendulum's Song;" LTO, 53–69).

– 1977h. "Osen'. Ogolennost' topolej," "Pamjati prof. Braudo," "Šepču 'proščaj,'" "Strax," "Kon'jak v grafine," "S krasavicej nalaživaja svjaz'." *Vremja i my* 17: 133–9.

– 1977i. Introduction to *Osip Mandelstam: Fifty Poems*, tr. B. Meares, New York: 7–17 (also published as "The Child of Civilization," LTO, 123–39 with additional material based upon "Beyond Consolation," 1974).

– 1977j. "Šorox akacii," "Pis'ma dinastii Min'," "Razvivaja Platona," "Osen' v Norenskoj." *Kontinent* 14: 88–93.

– 1977k. "Tvoj lokon ne svivaetsja v kol'co," "Menuèt." *VRXD* 123: 210–11.

– 1977l. "V Anglii." *Kontinent* 13: 132–8.

– 1977m. "Why Russian Poets?" *Vogue* (July): 112.

– 1978a. "Leti otsjuda, belyj motylek," "Pograničnoj vodoj," "Net, Filomela, prosti," "V odinočke pri xod'be," "V fevrale daleko do vesny," "V odinočke želanie spat'," "Skvoz' namordnik projdja," "Sonet," "V derevne, zaterjavšejsja," "Sokol jasnyj," "Sonet (Ty, Muza, nedoverčiva)," "Poslednee pis'mo Ovidija v Rim," "Noč'. Kamera. Volčok," "Koljučej provoloki lira," "Oktjabr' – mesjac grusti," "Nojabr'skim dnem." *Èxo* 1.

– 1978b. "Polden' v komnate." *VRXD* 126: 47–52.

– 1978c. "Predislovie k stixam Limonova." *Kontinent* 15: 153.

– 1978d. "Presentation of Czesław Miłosz to the Jury." *World Literature Today* (Summer): 364.

– 1978e. "Strofy," "San-P'etro," "Vremja podsčeta cypljat jastrebom," "Švedskaja muzyka," "Oda vesne," "Pomniš' svalku veščej na železnom stule." *Kontinent* 18: 117–31.

– 1978f. "Zof'ja." *Èxo* 3.

– 1979. "Leningrad." *Vogue* (September): 494–9, 543–7 (also published as "A Guide to a Renamed City," LTO, 69–95).

– 1980a. "Èkloga IV – ja (zimnjaja)." *Kontinent* 26: 7–13.

– 1980b. "Ja pil iz ètogo fontana." *Èxo* 4.

– 1980c. "Leningrad." *Čast' reči* 1: 6–26.

– 1980d. *A Part of Speech*. New York: Noonday/ Farrar, Straus and Giroux.

– 1980e. "Playing Games." *The Atlantic* (June): 35–9.

– 1980f. Introduction to *A Tomb for Boris Davidovich* by Danilo Kis. Harmondsworth: ix–xvii.

– 1980g. "'Ty, gitaroobraznaja vešč' so sputannoj pautinoj," "Vremja podsčeta cypljat jastrebom," "Dni raspletajut trjapočku," "Kak davno ja topču," "Poljarnyj issledovatel'," "Vosxodjaščee želtoe solnce." *Čast' reči* 1: 3–5.

– 1981a. "The Azadovsky Affair." *New York Review* (8 October): 49.

– 1981b. Editor of Ju. Kublanovksij. *Izbrannoe*. Ann Arbor: Ardis.

– 1981c. "Rimskie èlegii," "Èkloga V – ja: letnjaja." *Kontinent* 30: 61–75.

- 1981d. "Roman Elegy." *New Yorker* (13 July): 30.
- 1981e. "Stixi o zimnej kampanii 1980 – go goda." *Kontinent* 29: 7–10.
- 1981f. *Verses on the Winter Campaign 1980.* London: Anvil Press.
- 1981g. "Virgil: Older than Christianity, a Poet for the New Age." *Vogue* (October): 178 and 180.
- 1981–2a. "Nadežda Mandel'štam: 1899–1980." *Čast' reči* 2–3: 111–20 (also published in N. Mandel'štam, 1982: 5–18 and as "Nadezhda Mandelstam [1899–1980]: An Obituary," LTO, 145–57).
- 1981–2b. "Pesni sčastlivoj zimy." Contains the following: "V tvoix časax ne tol'ko xod..," "Ja obnjal èti pleči..," "Vse čuždo v dome novomu žil'cu," "Iz 'Staryx anglijskix pesen,'" "Ogon', ty slyšiš', načal ugasat," "Čto vetru govorjat kusty..," "Topilas' peč'," "Pritča," "K sadovoj ograde," "Sredi zimy," "Zagadka angelu," "Šum livnja voskrešaet po uglam," "V semejnyj al'bom," "V gorčičnom lesu," "Sadovnik v vatnike, kak drozd..," " Roždestvo 1963 goda," "Roždestvo 1963," "Pesni sčastlivoj zimy," "Veter ostavil les" prior to A. (L.) Losev, 1981–1982: 47–62.
- 1982a. "Eclogue IV: Winter." *New Yorker* (29 March): 46–7.
- 1982b. *Russkie èlegii.* New York: Russica.
- 1982c. "To ne Muza vody nabiraet v rot," "Osennij krik jastreba," "Lesnaja idillija," "Kolokol'čik zvenit," "Nad vostočnoj rekoj," "Polonez: Variacija," "Točka vsegda obozrimej v konce prjamoj," "K Uranii," "Venecianskie strofy," "Èlegija," "Ja byl tol'ko tem…" *Russica – 81: Literaturnyj sbornik.* New York: Russica.
- 1982d. "Virgil Verities." Letter in *Vogue* (February): 121.
- 1983a. Introduction to *Anna Akhmatova: Poems,* tr. L. Coffin. New York and London: W.W. Norton: xiii–xxxi (also published as "The Keening Muse," LTO: 34–52 and "Skorbnaja muza." *Junost'* 1989 6: 65–8.)
- 1983b. "The Great Elegy for John Donne" in Maxton, 1983: 63–4.
- 1983c. *Novye stansy k Avguste.* Ann Arbor: Ardis.
- 1983d. "Pjataja godovščina," "Gorenie," "Kelomjakki," "Vašington," "1983." *Kontinent* 36: 7–21.
- 1983e. "Posleslovie" in Ju. Kublanovskij, *S poslednim solncem.* Paris: La Presse Libre: 361–5.
- 1983f. "Two Poems from 1916" (translations of Cvetaeva and Mandel'štam). *New Yorker* (17 October): 48.
- 1983g. "Voor Jalta" in Langeveld, 1983: 405–12.
- 1984a. "A Commencement Address." *New York Review* (16 August):7–8 (also in LTO, 384–93).
- 1984b. "Litovskij noktjurn: Tomasu Venclova." *Kontinent* 40: 7–18.
- 1984c. *Mramor.* Ann Arbor: Ardis.
- 1984d. Introduction to *Ratusinškaja, Stixi.* Ann Arbor: 7–8 (reproduced in I. Ratushinskaya, *No, I'm Not Afraid.* Newcastle: Bloodaxe, 1986: 14–15).
- 1984e. "Sextet." *New Yorker* (31 December): 24–5.

- 1984f. "Språkpartiklar" in Birkerts and Backstrom, 1984: 17–23.
- 1984g. "Viewpoint: Why the Peace Movement Is Wrong." *Times Literary Supplement* (24 August): 942.
- 1985a. "Disarmament Delusions." *Harper's*. February: 24–6 (reprint from *Times Literary Supplement*, 1984).
- 1985b. "Flight from Byzantium." *New Yorker* (28 October): 39–80.
- 1985c. "Galatea Encore." *New Yorker* (17 October): 38.
- 1985d. "Ja vyxodil vmesto dikogo zverja v kletku," "Bjust Tiberija," "Priliv," "Na vystavke K. Vejlinka," "Muxa," "V Italii." *Kontinent* 45: 186–206.
- 1985e. "Literature and War – A Symposium." *Times Literary Supplement* (17 May): 543–4.
- 1985f. "Putešestvie v Stambul." *Kontinent* 46: 67–111.
- 1985g. *Römische Elegien und andere Gedichte.* Munich/Vienna: Carl Hanser Verlag.
- 1985h. "To a Friend: In Memoriam." *New Yorker* (6 May): 44.
- 1985i. "Why Milan Kundera Is Wrong about Dostoevsky." *New York Times Book Review* (17 February): 31, 33–4 (reprinted as 1986 "Počemu Milan Kundera nespravedliv k Dostoevkomu." *Kontinent* 50: 229–44.)
- 1986a. *Blue Lagoon Anthology of Modern Russian Poetry.* Volume 2B: 283–330. K.K. Kuzminsky and G.L. Kovalev, comp., Newtonville: Oriental Research Partners. (Together with various photographs, the section on Brodsky includes A. [L.] Losev, 1980b, a brief essay "Ot sostavitelja," "Pravo pervoj noči: K bibliografii," the foreword to a 1975 Leningrad anthology "Živoe zerkalo," the illustrated text of "Poxorony Bobo," "Brodskij i Bitlz: Neizvestnaja publikacija," Limonov 1984, "Na maner snegirja" by E. Tudorovskaja, and several other artifacts.)
- 1986b. "History of the Twentieth Century: A Roadshow." *Partisan Review* 53: 327–43.
- 1986c. *Less than One.* New York: Farrar, Straus and Giroux.
- 1986d. "The Meaning of Meaning." *New Republic* (20 January): 32–5.
- 1986e. "Sextet" in Dunn, 1986: 6–9.
- 1986f. "Tors" in Dedjulin, 1986a: 10 (t/German).
- 1986g. "Torso," "Da 'Parte del Discorso'" in S. Vitale, 1986: 5.
- 1987a. "A Cambridge Education." *Times Literary Supplement* (30 January): 99–100.
- 1987b. "Elegy," "Ex Voto" in Smith, 1987: 692.
- 1987c. "In Memoriam." *New Yorker* (9 November): 48.
- 1987d. "Ja byl tol'ko tem, čego..," "Ja vxodil vmesto dikogo zverja v kletku..," "V Italii," "Mysl' o tebe udaljaetsja..." *Russkaja mysl'* 3698 (6 November): 9.
- 1987e. "Kelomyakki." *New Yorker* (26 January): 26–7.
- 1987f. "Končitsja leto. Načnetsja sentjabr'," "Alleja so statujami iz zatverdevšej grjazi," "V ètoj malen'koj komnate vse po – staromu," "Nazidanie," "Tol'ko pepel znaet, čto značit sgoret' dotla." *Kontinent* 54: 7–15.
- 1987g. "Nobelevskaja lekcija 1987." *Kontinent* 54: 3–14.

- 1987h. "October Tune." *New Yorker* (5 October): 38.
- 1987i. "Odissej Telemaku," "Pis'ma rimskomu drugu," "Pis'ma dinastii Min'," "Novyj Žjul' Vern," "Osennij večer v skromnom gorodke," "Niotkuda s ljubov'ju." *Novyj mir* 12: 160–7.
- 1987j. "Piligrimy." *Russkaja mysl'* 3697 (30 October): 8.
- 1987k. "Pjataja godovščina," "Pis'ma dinastii Min'." *Russkaja mysl'* 3700 (20 November): 11.
- 1987l. *Poèmes 1961–1987.* Paris: Gallimard.
- 1987m. "Polonaise: A Variation." *New Yorker* (21 September): 40.
- 1987n. "Sneg idet, ostavljaja ves' mir v men'šinstve," "Noč', oderžimaja beliznoj," "Bagatelle,""Ja raspugival jaščeric v zarosljax čapparalja," "Barbizon Terras," "Te, kto ne umirajut, živut," "Posvjaščenie," "Čem bol'še černyx glaz, tem bol'še perenosic," "Kak davno ja topču, vidno po kabluku," "Večer. Razvaliny geometrii," "Rezidencija," "Žizn' v rassejannom svete," "Arija," "Na via džulia," "Ty uznaeš' menja po počerku," "Èlegija," "Iz Parmenida," "Zameržij kisel'nyj bereg," "V ètoj komnate paxlo trjap'em i syroj vodoj," "Posleslovie," "Strel'na," "Mysl' o tebe udaljaetsja, kak razžalovannaja prisluga." *Kontinent* 51: 7–24.
- 1987o. "Stixi o zimnej kampanii 1980 – go goda," "Venecianskie strofy (1)." *Russkaja mysl'* 3699 (13 November): 10.
- 1987p. *Uranija.* Ann Arbor: Ardis.
- 1987q. *Winter* (sound recording). Washington, DC: Watershed Tapes.
- 1988a. Foreword and notes to *An Age Ago: A Selection of Nineteenth-Century Russian Poetry,* tr. A. Myers. New York: Farrar, Straus and Giroux: xi–xix, 151–71.
- 1988b. "Centaurs." *Western Humanities Review* (Winter): 267–72.
- 1988c. "The Condition We Call Exile." *New York Review* (21 January): 16, 18–19 (also published in GR, 22–35).
- 1988d. "Džon Donn: Četyre stixotvorenija." *Inostrannaja literatura* 9: 176–9 (includes text of "Bol'šaja èlegija Džonu Donnu": 182–5).
- 1988e. "The Fly." *New Yorker* (7 March): 32–4.
- 1988f. "The Hawk's Cry in Autumn" in Laird, 1988: 10–11.
- 1988g. "How to Read a Book." *New York Times Book Review* (12 June): 1, 25–7 (also published in GR, 96–104).
- 1988h. "Il gît là-bas, sur le coteau," "J'étais cela seulement..." in Nivat, 1988b: 36–7.
- 1988i. "Ja obnjal èti pleči...," "V derevne Bog..," "Roždestvenskij romans," "Zameržij kisel'nyj bereg," "24 dekabrja 1971 goda," "V ozernom kraju," "Odnomu tiranu," "K Evgeniju," "V ètix uzkix ulicax, gde gromozdka...," "Zimnim večerom v Jalte," "Osennij večer v skromnom gorodke" in Stefanovič, 1988, 67–8.
- 1988j. *Joseph Brodsky Reads His Poetry* (sound recording). New York: Caedmon Tapes.
- 1988k. "K Uranii," "Noč', oderžimaja beliznoj," "Gorenie," "Osen' v Norenskoj," "Èkloga 4–ja (zimnjaja)." *Literaturnoe obozrenie* 8: 62–4.

- 1988l. *La Mer de jouance* (A. Platonov). Paris: Albin Michel.
- 1988m. *Leningrad, avec Joseph Brodski.* Paris: Autrement.
- 1988n. *Loin de Byzance.* Paris: Fayard.
- 1988o. Nobel Prize speech as "Uncommon Visage." *New Republic* 198/1–2 (4–11 January): 27–32 (see also GR, 44–59).
- 1988p. "North Baltic" and "Allenby Road." *New York Review* (18 February): 16.
- 1988q. "One Who Finds Himself in This Sort of Dependency on Language Is, I Guess, What They Call a Poet." *Chronicle of Higher Education,* 6 January: B3.
- 1988r. *Ostanovka v pustyne.* Ann Arbor: Ardis.
- 1988s. "Rimskie èlegii" in Medvedev, 1988: 28–9.
- 1988t. "Roždestvenskaja zvezda," "Novaja žizn'," "Reki," "V gorax," "Kentvary," "Teper', znaja mnogoe," "Dožd' v avguste," "Otkrytka iz Lissabona," "V kafe." *Kontinent* 58: 7–23.
- 1988u. "Star of the Nativity." *New York Times* (24 December): 15/27.
- 1988v. "Les Trophées" in Nivat, 1988b: 26–35 (also published as "Spoils of War" in GR, 3–22).
- 1988w. *To Urania.* New York: Farrar, Straus and Giroux.
- 1988x. "Uznaju ètot večer...," "V gorodke, iz kotorogo smert' raspolzalas'...," "Okolo okeana, pri svete sveči...," "Ja ne to čto sxožu s uma...," "Vremja podsčeta cypljat jastrebom...," "Kvintet," "Èkloga 5–ja: letnjaja," "Ja byl tol'ko tem, čego..." between Rejn, 1988 and M. Lotman, 1988: 175–84.
- 1989a. "Advice to a Traveller." *Times Literary Supplement* (12–18 May): 516.
- 1989b. "A Footnote to Weather Forecasts." *Times Literary Supplement* (30 June–6 July): 716.
- 1989c. "Isaiah Berlin at Eighty." *New York Review* (17 August): 44–5.
- 1989d. *Marbles.* New York: Noonday.
- 1989e. "Na stoletie Anny Axmatovoj," "Pamjati otca: Avstralija," "Dorogaja, ja vyšel segodnja iz domu pozdno večerom," "Èlegija," "Begstvo v Egipet," "Landsver Kanal, Berlin," "Pčely ne uleteli, vsadnik ne uskakal," "Fin de siècle," "Primečanija paporotnika," "Oblaka," "Pamjati Gennadija Šmakova." *Kontinent* 61: 7–24.
- 1989f. "The Rustle of Acacias" (two variants) in Weissbort, 1989: 224–7.
- 1989g. "Some Tips." *Michigan Today* (February): 4–5 (also published in GR, 138–49).
- 1989h. "A Song." *New Yorker* (27 March): 40.
- 1989i. "Sreten'e." *Literaturnoe obozrenie* 8: 111–12.
- 1990a. *Čast' reči: Izbrannye stixi 1962–1989.* Moskva: Xudožestvennaja literatura.
- 1990b. "Čerezvyčajno sožaleju o svoej nesposobnostej prinjat' učastie v rabote konferencii v Rime." *Kontinent* 66: 374–5.
- 1990c. "Demokratija!" *Kontinent* 62: 14–42 (also published, for example, as "Democracy" in *Granta* 30 [Winter 1990]: 199–233; *Performing Arts Journal* 37, [January 1991]: 64–93; *Partisan Review* 60/2 [Spring 1993]).

- 1990d. *Démocratie!* (Pièce en un acte). A. Die.
- 1990e. "Executions" in "Words for Salman Rushdie." *New Statesman and Society* (31 March): 26.
- 1990f. "In Memory of My Father: Australia." *New Yorker* (5 March): 40.
- 1990g. "Lesnaja idillija." *Zvezda* 1: 184
- 1990h. *Nazidanie.* Leningrad: Smart.
- 1990i. (1987) "Nobel Lecture" in Loseff and Polukhina, 1990: 1–12.
- 1990j. *Osennij krik jastreba: Stixotvorenija 1962–1989 goda.* Leningrad: Talinnskij centr MŠK MADLR/KTL IMA–press.
- 1990k. "The Poet, the Loved One and the Muse." *Times Literary Supplement* (26 October – 1 November): 1150, 1160 (also published as "Altra Ego" in GR, 81–96).
- 1990l. "Poèzija kak forma soprotivlenija real'nosti" in *Russkaja mysl'* "Special'noe priloženie" 3829 (25 May): i, xii.
- 1990m. "Posvjaščaetsja pozvonočniku." *Kontinent* 62: 233–44 (also published as "After a Journey" in GR, 62–81).
- 1990n. "Predstavlenie." *Kontinent* 62: 7–13.
- 1990o. *Primečanija paporotnika.* Bromma: Hylea.
- 1990p. *Razmerom podlinnika: Sbornik, posvjaščennyj 50–letiju I. Brodskogo.* Tallinn.
- 1990q. "The View from the Merry-Go-Round." *UNESCO Courier* (June): 31–6.
- 1991a. "August Rain." *Times Literary Supplement* (2 August): 4.
- 1991b. "Brise Marine." *Times Literary Supplement* (1 February): 4.
- 1991c. "Homage to Gerolamo Marcello." *New Yorker* (21 January): 30.
- 1991d. "An Immodest Proposal." *New Republic* (11 November): 31–6 (also published as "Laureate of the Supermarkets" in *Poetry Review* [Winter 1992]: 4–8, and GR, 198–212).
- 1991e. "The Muse Is Feminine and Continuous." *Literary – Half Yearly* 22/1 (January): 21–33.
- 1991f. Introduction to Najman 1991: vii–xi.
- 1991g. *Nazidanie.* Minsk: Èridan.
- 1991h. "North of Delphi." *Times Literary Supplement* (12 April): 21.
- 1991i. "Odysseus to Telemachus." *Partisan Review* (Fall): 680–1.
- 1991j. "Poets for Lithuania." *New York Times* (15 January): 17/19 (declaration signed by Brodsky with T. Venclova and C. Miłosz).
- 1991k. "Postcard from Lisbon." *Times Literary Supplement* (18 October): 4.
- 1991l. *Stixotvorenija.* Tallinn: Èèsti raamat/Aleksandra.
- 1991m. "Swiss Blue." *Times Literary Supplement* (11 January): 4.
- 1991n. "A Thousand Days of the 'Fatwa': The Rushdie Affair Reconsidered." *Times Literary Supplement* (8 November): 13.
- 1991o. "Tragičeskij èlegik: O poèzii Evgenija Rejna." *Znamja* 7: 180–4 (variants in "Predislovie" to Rejn, 1991, *Izbrannoe* of 1992 and introduction to Rejn translations, *Wilson Quarterly* [Autumn 1994]: 100–2.)
- 1991p. "Vertumnus." *Times Literary Supplement* (4 October): 16–17.

– 1991q. *Xolmy: Bol'šie stixotvorenija i poèmy*. St Petersburg: Kinocentr.
– 1992a. *Acqua Alta*. Paris: Gallimard.
– 1992b. *Bog soxranjaet vse*. Moscow: Mif.
– 1992c. "Bosnia Tune." *New York Times* (18 November): 17–27.
– 1992d. "Collector's Item: The Newer Meaning of Treason. Philby, England, Russia and a Postage Stamp." *New Republic* (20 April): 19–33 (also published in GR, 149–98).
– 1992e. "Fin de siècle." *Times Literary Supplement* (7 August): 8–9.
– 1992f. *Forma vremeni: Stixotvorenija, èsse, p'esy v dvux tomax*. Minsk: Èridan.
– 1992g. "Fossil Unwound." *Times Literary Supplement* (25 September): 11.
– 1992h. "Lines for the Winter Recess." *New Yorker* (4 May): 34.
– 1992i. *Naberežnaja neiscelimyx*. Moscow: Slovo.
– 1992j. "Poetry as a Form of Resistance to Reality." *PMLA* 107/2 (March): 220–5.
– 1992k. *Roždestvenskie stixi*. Moscow: Nezavisimaja gazeta.
– 1992l. "So Forth." *Times Literary Supplement* (9 October): 13.
– 1992m. "Song of Welcome." *Times Literary Supplement* (24 July): 4.
– 1992n. "Transatlantic." *New Yorker* (3 August): 32.
– 1992o. *Watermark*. New York: Noonday/ Farrar, Straus and Giroux (sections also published in *New York Review of Books* [11 June]: 30–2).
– 1992p. "What the Moon Sees." *Yale Review* 80/3 (July): 18–22.
– 1992–1996. *Sočinenija Iosifa Brodskogo* (1–4). St Petersburg: Puškinskij fond.
– 1993a. "Blood, Lies and the Trigger of History." *New York Times* (4 August): 15–19.
– 1993b. "Bosnia and the Future of Ethnic Cleansing." *World Affairs* 156/2 (Fall): 104–6 (open letter signed by Brodsky together with 110 other dignitaries, including Margaret Thatcher, George Shultz, and Czesław Miłosz).
– 1993c. Introduction to translations of C.P. Cavafy. *Wilson Quarterly* (Summer): 96–8.
– 1993d. "Daedalus in Sicily." *New York Review* (7 October): 14.
– 1993e. "Elegy." *Times Literary Supplement* (8 October): 5.
– 1993f. Introduction to translations of Z. Herbert. *Wilson Quarterly* (Winter): 112–14.
– 1993g. *Iosif Brodskij: Izbrannoe*. Moscow, Paris, New York, and Munich: Tret'ja volna/Nejmanis (Biblioteka novoj russkoj poèzii 1).
– 1993h. *Kappadokija*. St Petersburg: Peterburgskoe solo, vyp. 10.
– 1993i. Introduction to poems of W. Kees. *Wilson Quarterly* (Spring): 92–4.
– 1993j. "Lullaby." *New Yorker* (20 December): 104.
– 1993k. "New Life." *New Yorker* (26 April): 86–7.
– 1993l. "Profile of Clio." *New Republic* (1 February): 60–7 (also published in GR, 114–38).
– 1993m. Introduction to translations of Sextus Propertius. *Wilson Quarterly* (Autumn): 86–7.

- 1993n. "Venice Lido." *Times Literary Supplement* (14 May): 4.
- 1993o. *Vertumne at autres poèmes.* Paris: Gallimard.
- 1993p. "View from the Hill." *Times Literary Supplement* (26 November): 4.
- 1993q. *Znak wodny.* Kraków: Wydawnictwo Znak.
- 1994a. "Angel." *New Yorker* (10 January): 50.
- 1994b. "Cappadocia," "Persian Arrow." *Times Literary Supplement* (23 December): 7.
- 1994c. *Le Cauchemar du monde post-communiste* (avec V. Havel). Anatolia.
- 1994d. "Constancy." *Princeton University Library Chronicle.* LV/3 (Spring): 505.
- 1994e. "Gollandija est' ploskaja strana," "Ty ne skažeš' komaru," "V okrestnostjax Atlantidy," "Dedal v Sicilii," "Pesnja o krasnom svitere," "Novaja Anglija," "Posvjaščaetsja Čexovu," "Provincial'noe," "Itaka," "Iskija v oktjabre," "Ona nadevaet čulki, i nastupaet osen'," "Cvety," "Persidskaja strela," "Nadpis' na knige," ""Mir sozdan iz smešen'ja grjazi, vody, ognja," "Ne vyxodi iz komnaty, ne soveršaj ošibku," "Narjadu s otopleniem v každom dome," "Pamjati Klifforda Brauna," "Otvet na anketu," "Priglašenie k putešestviju," "Posleslovie k basne," "Čto ty delaeš', ptička, na černoj vetke," "Arxitektura." *Novyj mir* 5: 100–2.
- 1994f. "Homage to Marcus Aurelius" in Liberman: 28–60 (also published in GR, 267–99).
- 1994g. Introduction to poems of P. Huchel. *Wilson Quarterly* (Winter): 100–1.
- 1994h. *Izbrannye stixotvorenija: 1957–1992.* Moscow: Panorama.
- 1994i. "On Grief and Reason." *New Yorker* (26 September): 70–85 (also published in GR, 223–67).
- 1994j. "Porta San Pancrazio." *New Yorker* (14 March): 52.
- 1994k. "A Postcard," "A Photograph." *Times Literary Supplement* (28 October): 5.
- 1994l. "Primečanie k kommentariju" in V. Schweitzer, J.A. Taubman, P. Scotto, T. Babyonyshev, eds., *Marina Tsvetaeva: One Hundred Years.* Berkeley: Berkeley Slavic Specialities: 262–84.
- 1994m. Introduction to Translations of E. Rein (Rejn). *Wilson Quarterly* (Autumn): 100–2.
- 1994n. "To My Daughter." *Times Literary Supplement* (2 December): 4.
- 1994o. "Törnfallet." *New Yorker* (8 August): 46.
- 1995a. "At a Lecture." *New Republic* (8 May): 40.
- 1995b. "In Memory of Clifford Brown." *New Republic* (11 December): 40.
- 1995c. "Ischia in October," "Clouds." *Times Literary Supplement* (19 May): 10–11.
- 1995d. "Nobel Lecture." *Georgia Review* 49/1: 199–208.
- 1995f. *On Grief and Reason.* New York: Farrar, Straus and Giroux.
- 1995f. *Peresečennaja mestnost': Putešestvija s kommentarijami.* Moscow: Nezavisimaja gazeta.

- 1995g. "Remember Her." *Times Literary Supplement* (22 September): 19.
- 1995h. "View with a Flood." *Times Literary Supplement* (10 February): 23.
- 1995i. *V okrestnostnjax Atlantidy.* St Petersburg: Puškinskij fond.
- 1995j. "Wooing the Inanimate (Four Poems by Thomas Hardy)." *Partisan Review* (Summer): 351–71, 459–80 (also published as the introduction to *The Essential Hardy: Selected by Joseph Brodsky.* Hopewell: Ecco: 3–67, and GR, 312–76.)
- 1996a. "English Lessons from Stephen Spender." *New Yorker* (8 January): 58–67 (also published in GR, 459–84).
- 1996b. "Flourish" and "Love Song." *New Republic* (4 March): 39, 41.
- 1996c. "Folk Tune," "Elegy," "North Baltic," "May 24, 1980," "A Polar Explorer," "Dutch Mistress," "Tsushima Screen," "Seven Strophes," "Seaward," "Galtea Encore," "Belfast Tune," "To Urania," "A List of Some Observations...," "I Threw My Arms About Those Shoulders," "Letter to an Archaeologist." Collected on the Internet "Memorial Page" for Brodsky, starting 28 February. See Nossik, 1996.
- 1996d. *Pejzaž s navodneniem.* Dana Point: Ardis.
- 1996e. "Posleslovie" to D. Novikov, *Okno v janvare. Literaturnaja gazeta* (28 February): 5.
- 1996f. "The Russian Academy: Preliminary Notes." *New York Review of Books.* (21 March): 45.
- 1996g. "The Tale" and "Reveille." *Times Literary Supplement* (2 February): 29.
- 1996h. "Via Funari." *New York Review of Books* (1 February): 31.
- 1996i. "A Western Boyhood, in Russia" (adapted from the essay "Spoils of War"). *Harper's Magazine* (March): 29–34.
Brown, C. 1980. "The Best Russian Poetry Written Today." *New York Times Book Review* (7 September): 11, 16, 18 (e).
Brown, D. 1978. *Soviet Russian Literature since Stalin.* Cambridge: Cambridge University Press.
Brown, E.J. 1982. *Russian Literature since the Revolution.* Cambridge, Mass. and London: Harvard University Press: 340–1, 346, 354–8 (e).
- 1986. "Russian Literature Beyond the Pale." *Slavic and East European Journal,* 30/3: 380–8 (e, 380–1, 387).
Brown, P. and S.C. Levinson. 1987. *Politeness: Some Universals in Language Use.* Cambridge: Cambridge University Press.
Brumfield, W.C. 1993. *A History of Russian Architecture.* Cambridge: Cambridge University Press.
Brumm, A. – M. 1974. "The Muse in Exile: Conversations with the Russian Poet, Joseph Brodsky." *Mosaic* 8: 231–46.
Bucsela, J. 1972. "The Problems of Baroque in Russian Literature." *Russian Review* 31/3 (July): 260–72.
Burnett, L. 1990. "The Complicity of the Real: Affinities in the Poetics of Brodsky and Mandelstam" in Loseff and Polukhina, 1990: 12–34.

Byrns, R. 1976. "Aleksandr Blok and 'Hamlet.'" *Canadian Slavonic Papers* 6: 58–65.

Calabrese, O. 1992. *Neo-Baroque: A Sign of the Times.* Princeton: Princeton University Press.

Carlisle, O., ed. 1968. *Poets on Street Corners: Portraits of Fifteen Russian Poets.* New York: 400–21.

Cathcart, D. 1975. *Doubting Conscience: Donne and the Poetry of Moral Argument.* Ann Arbor: University of Michigan Press.

Cavafy, C.P. 1984. *Collected Poems.* London: Hogarth Press.

Cavalieri, G. 1992. "Joseph Brodsky: The Poet and the Poem. An Interview by Grace Cavalieri." *American Poetry Review* (November/ December): 51–4.

Celkov, O. 1987. "Dal že tebe Bog byt' potrjasajuščim russkim poètom." *Russkaja mysl'* 3698 (6 November): 9.

– 1996. "Proščaj, Iosif." *Russkaja mysl'* 4112 (8 February): 14–16.

Cervantes Saavedra, M. de 1964. *Don Quixote of La Mancha.* New York, Toronto, and London: Signet.

Chambers, A.B. 1961. "Goodfriday, 1613: Riding Westward. The Poem and the Tradition." *English Literary History* 28: 31–53 (reproduced in Roberts, 1978: 333–49).

Čeporov, È. 1992. "Derek Uolkott: 'Poèzija – pesn' čeloveka...'" *Literaturnaja gazeta* 43 (21 October): 7.

– 1996. "Iosif Brodksij: Vse skoro končitsja, no ran'še končus' ja." *Literaturnaja gazeta* (7 February): 9.

Činnov, I. 1992. "Ja sam s soboju govorju po-russki." *Ogonek* 9: 14.

Čiževskij, D. 1971. *A Comparative History of Slavic Literatures.* Nashville: Vanderbilt University Press.

Čukovskaja, L. 1987. "Pozdravljaju..." (telegram to Brodsky). *Russkaja mysl'* 3697 (30 October): 10.

– 1988. "Azbuka glasnosti." *Ogonek* 49: 26.

Cirio, R. 1995. "Galeotte furono le marionette." *L'Espresso* (12 May): 112–14.

Clark, K. 1981. *The Soviet Novel: History as Ritual.* Chicago and London: University of Chicago Press.

Coetzee, J.M. 1996. "Speaking for Language." *The New York Review* (1 February): 28–30.

Coffin, C.M. 1952. Introduction to Donne, 1952: xvii–xxxvi.

Cohen, A.A. 1973. Review of *Selected Poems. The New York Times Book Review* (30 December): 1–2.

Colie, R.L. 1964. "The Rhetoric of Transcendence." *Philological Quarterly* 43: 145–70 (reproduced in Roberts, 1978: 199–220).

Cooper, R.M., ed. 1979. *Essays on Richard Crashaw.* Salzburg: Institut für Anglistik und Amerikanistik (Elizabethan and Renaissance Studies 83).

Cowley, A. 1795. *The Works of the British Poets (Vol. 5)*, R. Anderson, ed. London and Edinburgh: J. and A. Arch / Bell and Bradfute / J. Mundell.

Cox, R.L. 1968. "The Two Sources of Christian Tragedy." *Antioch Review* 28: 67–89.

Crashaw, R. 1949. *The Verse in English of Richard Crashaw* (The 1646 text of "Steps to the Temple" and "The Delights of the Muses;" the 1652 text of "Carmen Deo Nostro;" the 1653 text of "A Letter from Mr. Crashaw to the Countess of Denbigh;" and the poems from manuscript). New York: Grove Press.

Cunnar, E.R. 1979. "Crashaw's Hymn 'To the Name above Every Name.' Background and Meaning": 102–29 in Cooper.

Curtis, J.M. 1975. "Shestov's Use of Nietzsche in his Interpretation of Tolstoy and Dostoevsky." *Texas Studies in Literature and Language* 17: 289–303.

"D.S." 1977. "Puškin i Brodskij." *Vestnik russkogo xristianskogo dviženija* 123/4: 127–39 (also published in L. Losev, 1986a: 207–19).

Daniel, M. 1996. "A Bard to Remember." *U.S. News* (2 February): 12.

Dante Alighieri, 1951. *La Divina Commedia.* Rome: Albrighi, Segati & C.

– 1980. *The Divine Comedy* (translated by C.H. Sisson). Manchester: Carcanet Press.

Dedjulin, S. 1986a. "Korotko o knigax: 'Römische Elegien und andere Gedichte.'" *Russkaja mysl'* 3615 (4 April): 10.

– 1986b. "Novye perevody stixov Brodskogo." *Russkaja mysl'* 3622 (22 May): 12–13.

– 1987a. "Brodskij po-francuzski." *Russkaja mysl'* 3702 (4 December): 9.

– 1987b. (as "S.D."?) "Otkliki na premiju." *Russkaja mysl'* 3697 (30 October): 10.

– 1988. (as "S.D."?) "Večer poèzii Iosifa Brodskogo v Leningrade." *Russkaja mysl'* 3722: 11 (e).

Dedjulin, S. and G. Superfin, eds. 1989. *Axmatovskij sbornik.* Paris: Institut d'Études Slaves.

de Mourgues, O. 1953. *Metaphysical, Baroque and Précieux Poetry.* Oxford: Oxford University Press.

Detkina, T. 1987. "Primite samye iskrennie i gorjačie pozdravlenija…" *Russkaja mysl'* 3697 (30 October): 11 (also signed by E. Kulinskaja, V. Pimonov, K. Popov, V. Senderov, V. Titov, and V. Šibaev).

Digges, C. 1996. "Joseph Brodsky an Exile by Choice." *St Petersburg Press* (19–25 March): 11.

Diment, G. 1990. "'Tolstoy or Dostoevsky' and the Modernists: Polemics with Joseph Brodsky." *Tolstoy Studies Journal* 3: 76–81.

– 1993. "English as Sanctuary: Nabokov's and Brodsky's Autobiographical Writings." *Slavic and East European Journal* 37/3: 346–61.

Dobin, E. 1968. *Poèzija Anny Axmatovoj.* Leningrad: Sovetskij pisatel'.

Dolgopolov, N. 1988. "V normandskoj derevuške Bornevill'…" *Komsomol'skaja pravda* (10 March):4.

Donatov, L. 1988. "Xvalu priemli ravnodušno." *Grani* 147: 82–91 (e, 86, 90).

Donne, J. 1952. *The Complete Poetry and Selected Prose of John Donne.* New York: Modern Library.

– 1963. Selected Verse with Introduction: 735–60 in Witherspoon and Warnke.

Döring-Smirnov, J.R. 1983. "'Uznat', čto budet ja, kogda...': Vergleichende Anmerkungen zu den Autobiographien von B. Pasternak und I. Brodskij." *Die Welt der Slaven* 28: 339–53 (e, 352–3).

Dostoevskij, F.M. 1973. *Idiot. Polnoe sobranie sočinenij v tridcati tomax (vol. 4).* Leningrad: Nauka.

"The Douglas Brothers." 1989. "Joseph Brodsky, Poet." *Esquire* (July): 66.

Dovlatov, S. 1979. *The Invisible Book (Epilogue).* Ann Arbor: Ardis (esp. 52–8).

Drage, C. 1978. *Russian Literature in the Eighteenth Century.* London: Published privately.

Driver, S. 1986. Review of Kreps, M. "O poèzii Iosifa Brodskogo." *World Literature Today* (Winter): 132–3.

Dru, A., ed. 1938. *The Journals of Søren Kierkegaard.* London: Oxford University Press.

Dufresne, B. 1990. "Lost in Transition: Literature after Censorship." *Commonweal* (9 November): 632.

Dunn, D. 1986. "In Whom the Language Lives." *Poetry Review* 76/3: 4–6 (e, 5).

Durant, W. 1953. *The Renaissance.* New York: Simon and Schuster.

Dyer, G. 1992. "Damp Courses." *New Statesman* (19 June): 24.

Eberstadt, F. 1986. "For Art's Sake." *Commentary* 82/5 (November): 74–6 (e).

Eder, R. 1980. "Joseph Brodsky in u.s.: Poet and Language in Exile." *New York Times* (25 March): 2 (e).

Edwards, J.R. 1981. "The Context of Bilingual Education." *Jounal of Multilingual and Multicultural Education* 2: 35 (as quoted in Romaine, 254).

Efimov, I. 1988. "Krysolov iz Peterburga: Xristianskaja kul'tura v poèzii Brodskogo." *Vestnik russkogo xristianskogo dviženija* 153: 118–35 (also published in Brodsky 1990p: 176–93).

Egeberg, E. 1987. "The Pilgrim, the Prophet and the Poet: Iosif Brodskij's 'Piligrimy':" 146–53 in P.A. Jensen, B. Lonnqvist, F. Bjorling, L. Kleberg, A. Sjoberg, eds., *Text and Context: Essays to Honor Nils Ake Nilsson.* Stockholm: Almqvist and Wiksell, Stockholm.

Egerton, K. 1994. "Grammatical Contrast in the Rhyme of Joseph Brodsky." *Essays in Poetics.* 19/1: 7–24.

Eliot, T.S. 1930. "Mystic and Politician as Poet: Vaughan, Traherne, Marvell, Milton." *The Listener* III (2 April): 509–91.

– 1950. "Lancelot Andrewes." *Selected Essays (New Edition).* New York: Harcourt Brace.

– 1963. "The Metaphysical Poets": 1061–65 in Witherspoon and Warnke.

– 1988. *Selected Poems: The Centenary Edition.* San Diego, New York and London: Harvest/Harcourt Brace and Jovanovich.

– 1993. *The Varieties of Metaphysical Poetry.* New York, San Diego and London: Harcourt Brace.

Èl'konin-Juxansen, I. 1987. "Pervyj den' Iosifa Brodskogo v Stokgol'me." *Russkaja mysl'* 3703 (11 December): 10.

Emmanuel, P 1967. "A Soviet Metaphysical Poet." *Quest* 52: 65–74.

Èpel'buan, A. 1991. "Evropejskij vozdux nad Rossiej" (interview with Brodsky). *Strannik* 1: 35–42.

Epstein, M. 1992. "Afterword": 271–87 in Johnson and Ashby.

Erlich, V. 1974. "A Letter in a Bottle." *Partisan Review* 41 (Fall): 617–21.

Erofeev, V. 1975. "'Ostaetsja odno: proizvol.' Filosofija odinočestva i literaturno – èstetičeskoe kredo L'va Šestova." *Voprosy literatury* 10: 153–89.

– 1988. "'Poèta daleko zavodit reč'..' Iosif Brodskij: Svoboda i odinočestvo." *Inostrannaja literatura* 9: 226–31 (e, 228).

– 1990. "Brodskij nužen, čtoby izlečit'sja ot nevežestva..." *Literaturnaja gazeta* 20/5294 (16 May): 6 (variant also in Erofeev, 1990: *V labirinte prokljatyx voprosou,* Moscow: Sovetskij pisatel': 206–21 [e, 206–7]).

Erwin, J.W. 1985. "Closure as Opening: Apocalyptic Marriage in Poetry" in A. Balakian, ed., *Proceedings of the Xth Congress of the International Comparative Literature Association.* New York and London: Garland: 24–8.

Ètkind, E. 1977. *Zapiski nezagovorščika.* London: 51–7, 116–9, 140–81, 364–70, 438–67.

– 1978. *Materija stixa.* Paris: Institut d'Études Slaves: 114–19.

– 1980. "Vzjat' notoj vyše, ideej vyše..." *Čast' reči* 1: 37–42 (e, 38).

– 1984. *Russiche Lyrik von der Oktober – Revolution zur Gegenwart Versuch einer Darstellung.* Munich: 209–16, 254–9 (e, 258).

– 1987. "Otkrytoe pis'mo sovetskim činovnikam." *Russkaja mysl'* 3697 (30 October): 8.

– 1988a. *Brodski ou Le Procès d'un Poète: Présentation et Commentaire d'Efim Etkind* (préface d'Hélène Carrère d'Encausse). Paris: Le Livre de Poche.

– 1988b. *Process Iosifa Brodskogo.* London: Overseas Publications Interchange.

Etkind, E., G. Nivat, I. Serman, and V. Strada, eds. 1990. *Histoire de la Littérature Russe: Le XXe siècle. Gels et dégels.* Paris: Fayard.

Ezerskaja, B. 1981. "Odin večer s Iosifom Brodskim." *Vremja i my* 63: 175–85 (also in Ezerskaja, B. *Mastera.* Tenafly: Èrmitaž 1982: 103–12).

Fisher, R. 1992. "A Noble Quixotic Sight": 291–309 in Polukhina, 1992b.

Fonjakov, I. 1996a. "Tom čertvertyj – ne poslednij..." *Literaturnaja gazeta* (28 February): 5.

– 1996b. "Vesti iz Sankt-Peterburga." *Literaturnaja gazeta* (12 June): 5.

Forbes, P. 1988. "Joseph Brodsky: The Acceleration of the Poet." *Poetry Review* 78/1: 4–5.

Forest, J. 1992. "Writes Poems, Will Travel." *Commonweal* (22 May): 6–7.

Forster, L. 1970. *The Poet's Tongues.* London, New York, Victoria, and Sydney: Cambridge University Press/ University of Otago Press.

France, P. 1982. *Poets of Modern Russia*. Cambridge: Cambridge University Press: 198–209 (e, 205–6).

– 1990. "Notes on the Sonnets to Mary Queen of Scots": 98–124 in Loseff and Polukhina, 1990.

Frank, V.S. 1964. "Brodsky's Trial." *Encounter* (November): 93–5.

Freccero, J. 1963. "Donne's 'Valediction Forbidding Mourning.'" *English Literary History* 30: 335–76 (reproduced in Roberts, 1978: 279–305).

Freer, C. 1979. "Mirth in Funeral: Crashaw and the Pleasures of Grief": 78–102 in Cooper.

Fridštejn, Ju. 1990. "Paradoksy Toma Stopparda." Afterword to Brodsky's translation "Rosencranc i Gil'denstern mertvy." *Inostrannaja literatura* 4 (1990): 83–135.

Friedrich, C.J. 1952. *The Age of the Baroque: 1610–1660*. New York: Harper and Bros.

Frost, R. 1956. *Robert Frost's Poems*. New York: Pocket Books.

Galackaja, N. 1990. "O rifmax odnogo stixotvorenija: Iosif Brodskij, 'Nočnoj polet.'" *Scando-Slavica* 36: 69–85.

Gandelevskij, S. 1996. "Genij odinočestva." *Ogonek* 6 (February): 75 (e).

Gandel'sman, V. 1996. "Pamjati poèta." *Russkaja mysl'* 4112 (8–14 February): 16.

Gardner, H. 1959. "The Argument about 'The Ecstasy'": 279–306 in H. Davis and H. Gardner, eds., *Jacobean Studies Presented to F.P. Wilson*. Oxford: Oxford University Press (reproduced in Roberts, 1978: 239–59).

– ed. 1985. *The Metaphysical Poets*. London: Penguin.

Gardzonio, S. 1993. "O nekotoryx čertax metaforizma russkogo barokko": 26–8 in Kurennaja et al.

Garfitt, R. 1974. "Near and Far East." *London Magazine* (June/ July): 104–7 (e, 105–6).

Gejro, R. 1988. "Ešče o Brodskom vo Francii." *Russkaja mysl'* 3750, "Literaturnoe priloženie 7" (11 November): 2.

Giddens, A. 1984. *The Constitution of Society*. Cambridge: Polity Press.

– 1991. *Modernity and Self-Identity*. Stanford: Stanford University Press.

Gifford, H. 1978. "The Language of Loneliness." *Times Literary Supplement* (11 August): 902–3 (e).

– 1980. "Idioms in Interfusion." *Times Literary Supplement* (17 October): 1159.

– 1986. "Of Petersburg, Poetry and Human Ties." *Times Literary Supplement* (19 September): 1019–20 (e, 1019).

– 1994. "Joseph Brodsky on Marina Tsvetaeva" in Wigzell: 117–30.

Gillespie, G. 1988. *The Garden and Labyrinth of Time: Studies in Renaissance and Baroque Literature*. Germanic Studies in America 56. New York, Berne, Frankfurt am Main, and Paris: P. Lang.

Gindin, S. 1993. "Russkij poètičeskij konstruktivizm: Barokko v kanun novogo Rima?" 30–2 in Kurennaja et al.

Ginzburg, A. 1987. "Kogda puskalis' na debjut..." *Russkaja mysl'* 3697 (30 October): 8.

‒ 1988. "'Ostat'sja samim soboj v situacii neestestvennoj': Iz vystuplenija Iosifa Brodskogo v Pariže." *Russkaja mysl'* 3749 (4 November): 10‒11.

Gioia, D. 1980‒1. Review of "A Part of Speech." *Hudson Review* 33/4 (Winter): 611‒13 (e).

Glad, J. 1987. (as Glèd, Dž.) "Nastignut' utračennoe vremja." *Vremja i my* 97: 164‒78 (also in J. Glad, 1993. *Conversations in Exile: Russian Writers Abroad.* Durham: Duke University Press: 21, 101‒13).

Godzich, W. 1995. "Brodsky and the Grounding of Poetry." *Georgia Review* 49/1: 209‒15.

Goldberg, C. 1994. "Culture: A Russian Tragedy." *Los Angeles Times* (19 February): A1, A12‒13.

Gorbanevskaja, N. 1983. "Byt' možet, samoe svjatoe, čto u nas est' ‒ èto naš jazyk...": Interv'ju s Iosifom Brodskim." *Russkaja mysl'* 3450 (3 February): 8‒9.

‒ 1987a. "Iosif Brodskij kommentiruet soobščenie o predstojaščej publikacii ego stixov v 'Novom mire.'" *Russkaja mysl'* 3701 (27 November): 9.

‒ 1987b. "Iz Stokgol'ma ‒ s ljubov'ju." *Russkaja mysl'* 3704 (18 December): 16.

‒ 1987c. "Ja tak rada, tak sčastliva..." *Russkaja mysl'* 3697 (30 October): 10.

‒ 1987d. "Pariž ‒ N'ju Jork, po telefonu." *Russkaja mysl'* 3700 (20 November): 11.

‒ 1991a. "Tri polovinki karmannoj lukovicy." *Russkaja mysl'* 3863: (25 January): 14.

‒ 1991b. "Iosif Brodskij ‒ razmerom podlinnika." *Russkaja mysl'* 387 (29 March): 13.

‒ 1992. "Subordination to the Language": 74‒94 in Polukhina, 1992b.

‒ 1996a. "Po ulice Brodskogo." *Russkaja mysl'* 4111 (1‒7 February): 16‒17.

‒ 1996b. "Iz cikla 'Novye vos'mistišija." *Russkaja mysl'* 4116 (March 7‒13): 13.

Gorbov, Ja. N. 1965. "Literaturnye zametki: Iosif Brodskij, Stixotvorenija i poèmy." *Vozroždenie* 8: 144‒50 (e, 149‒50).

Gorbovskij, G. 1991. *Ostyvšie sledy.* Leningrad: 217, 279‒81.

Gordin, Ja. 1989a. "Delo Brodskogo." *Neva* 2:134‒66.

‒ 1989b. "Dialog poètov: Tri pis'ma Axmatovoj k Brodskomu": 221‒4 in Dedjulin and Superfin (reproduced in R. Meyer, ed., *Anna Axmatova: My Half Century.* Ann Arbor: Ardis: 329‒32).

‒ 1990. "Drugoj Brodskij": 215‒22 in Brodsky, 1990p.

‒ 1992. "A Tragic Perception of the World": 29‒53 in Polukhina, 1992b.

‒ 1996a. "Strannik" in Brodsky, *Izbrannoe.* 5‒18 (reproduced from *Russian Literature* 1995/ 37: 227‒46).

‒ 1996b. "To, čto pišut segodnja o Brodskom" in "On prinimal vse stradanija." *Agumenty i fakty ‒ Peterburg* 22/144: 10.

Gorelov, P. 1988. "Mne nečego skazat'..." *Komsomol'skaja pravda* (10 March): 4 (e).

Gorjačeva, Ju. 1996. "Rannim utrom 28 janvarja..." *Nezavisimaja gazeta* (30 January): 1.

Gould, T. 1986. "Out of Russia." *New Society* (17 October): 29.

Gowda, H.H.A. 1995. "Joseph Brodsky and the Non-Russian Reader." *The Hindu* 03/09: 40.

Granqvist, R. 1996. "The Power of Poetry: Joseph Brodsky and Derek Walcott in Discussion" (taken from Nossik, 1996).

Graves, R. 1992. *The Greek Myths: Complete Edition.* London: Penguin.

Gray, P. 1987. "Lyrics of Loss, Theories of Gain." *Time* (2 November): 80 (e).

Green, J. 1974. "The Underground Life of a Russian Intellectual." *Detroit News* (28 April).

Grenander, M.E. 1960. "Holy Sonnets VIII and XVII: John Donne." *Boston University Studies in English* 4: 95–105 (reproduced in Roberts, 1978: 324–33).

Grierson, H.J.C. and G. Bullough, eds. 1934. *The Oxford Book of Seventeenth-Century Verse.* Oxford: Oxford University Press.

Grigor'janc, S. 1987. "Prisuždenie Nobelevskoj premii..." *Russkaja mysl'* 3697 (30 October): 11 (also in *Glasnost'* 10, 1987: xiv).

Grimes, T. 1996. "In Memoriam" (letter to the editor). *New Yorker* (25 March): 12.

Gross, M. 1981. "Born in Exile." *Observer* (25 October): 36–41.

Grout, D.J., ed. 1973. *A History of Western Music (Revised Edition).* London: J.M. Dent.

Grubišič, L. 1985. "Russkie pisateli v ignanii: Konferencija v Universitete Južnoj Kalifornii." *Russkaja mysl'* (23 May): 13.

Guibbory, A. 1975. "Francis Bacon's View of History: The Cycles of Error and the Progress of Truth." *Journal of English and Germanic Philology* 74 (July): 336–50 (quoted in Gillespie, 1988: 123).

Gul', R. 1978. "Soobščenija i zametki." *Novyj žurnal* 131: 285.

Guss, D.L. 1965. "Donne's Petrarchism." *Journal of English and Germanic Philology* 64: 17–28 (reproduced in Roberts, 1978: 150–61).

Haecker, T., ed. 1923. *Kierkegaard: Die Tagebücher* (In zwei Bänden ausgewählt und übersetzt von Th. Haecker).

Hafrey, L. 1986. "Love and the Analytic Poet." *New York Times Book Review* (13 July): 3.

Hall, R.L. 1993. *Word and Spirit: A Kierkegaardian Critique of the Modern Age.* Bloomington and Indianapolis: Indiana University Press.

Hamel-Schwulst, M. 1995. Review of "Campidoglio." *Library Journal* (15 February): 154–5.

Hamers, J.F. and M.H.A. Blanc. 1989. *Bilinguality and Bilingualism.* Cambridge: Cambridge University Press.

Hamill, S. 1990. "The Shadow and the Light." *American Poetry Review* (January/February): 19–22 (e).

Hass, R. 1980. "Lost in Translation." *New Republic* 182/25 (20 December): 35–7 (e, 35).

Hatzfeld, H. 1972. *The Rococo: Eroticism, Wit and Elegance in European Literature.* New York: Pegasus.

Heaney, S. 1987. Brodsky's Nobel: What the Applause was about." *New York Times Book Review* (8 November): 1, 63, 65 (e).

– 1996a. "Audenesque: In Memory of Joseph Brodsky." *Times Literary Supplement* (9 February): 11.

– 1996b. "The Singer of Tales: On Joseph Brodsky." *New York Times Book Review* (3 March): 31.

Heim, D. 1987. "Joseph Brodsky: Scrutinizing the Good." *The Christian Century* (11 November): 989–90 (e, 989).

Henderson, L. 1988. "Poetry in the Theater: An Interview with Joseph Brodsky." *Theater* 20/1 (Winter): 51–4.

Hilyard, J.P. 1979. "The Negative Wayfarers in Richard Crashaw's 'A Hymn in the Glorious Epiphanie':" 169–96 in Cooper.

Hinman, R.B. 1960. *Abraham Cowley's World of Order.* Cambridge, Mass.: Harvard University Press.

Hoffert, B. 1988. Review of "To Urania." *Library Journal* (15 May): 84.

Hofmann, M. 1986. "Measures of a Poet's Mind." *Guardian* (3 October): 11 (e).

Hollander, R. 1984. "Dante on Horseback?" *Italica* 61/4: 287–97.

Holt, E.G., ed. 1958. *A Documentary History of Art. Volume II: Michelangelo and the Mannerists; The Baroque and the Eighteenth Century.* New York: E.G. Holt/ Doubleday.

Hosking, G. 1992. "The Twentieth Century: In Search of New Ways, 1953–1980": 520–95 in C.A. Moser, ed., *The Cambridge History of Russian Literature.* Cambridge: Cambridge University Press: 591–94 (e, 594).

Howard, B. 1988. "Five Latitudes." *Poetry* (November): 106–9 (e).

Howard, D. 1981. *The Architectural History of Venice.* New York: Holmes and Meier.

Hudson, R.A. 1990. *Sociolinguistics.* Cambridge: Cambridge University Press.

Hughes, M.Y. 1934. "Kidnapping Donne." *Essays in Criticism (Second Series).* University of California Publications in English 4: 61–89 (reproduced in Roberts, 1978: 37–58).

– 1960. "Some of Donne's 'Ecstasies.'" *PMLA* 75: 509–18 (reproduced in Roberts, 1978: 259–71).

Hughes, R.E. 1968. *"The Progress of the Soul": The Interior Career of John Donne.* New York: Morrow and Co.

Husarska, A. 1987. "I Was Simply a Soviet: A Talk with Joseph Brodsky." *The New Leader* (14 December): 8–11.

Hutchison, P.E. 1992. Review of "Watermark." *Library Journal* (1 May): 80–1.

Innis, J. 1984. Review of M. Kreps, *O poèzii Iosifa Brodskogo. Russian Review* 45/ 2: 223–4.

– 1989. "Iosif Brodskij's 'Rimskie èlegii': A Critical Analysis." Ph.D. dissertation, Indiana University (e, vi, 17, 23, 43, 45, 51, 66, 136, 146, 153, 164, 189, 228, 230–2).

"Intellectuals and Writers since the Thirties." *Partisan Review* (Fall 1992): 531– 58.

Iskander, F. 1996. "Ja videl ego v Vašingtone..." in "On prinimal vse stradanija." *Agumenty i fakty – Peterburg* 22/ 144: 10.

Ivanov, V. 1988. "O Džone Donne i Iosife Brodskom." *Inostrannaja literatura* 9: 180–1.

Ivask, Ju. 1965. "Iosif Brodskij: Stixotvorenija i poèmy." *Novyj žurnal* 79: 297– 9.

– 1966. "Literaturnye zametki: Brodskij, Donn i sovremennaja poèzija." *Mosty* 12: 161–71.

– 1971. "Iosif Brodskij: Ostanovka v pustyne." *Novyj žurnal* 102: 294–7.

– 1986. "Poxvala rossijskoj poèzii." *Novyj žurnal* 165 (December): 112–28.

Jacobs, A.C. 1968–9. "A Russian-Jewish Poet." *Jewish Quarterly* 16/4 (Winter): 33.

Jacoby, S. 1994. "Joseph Brodsky in Exile." *Change* (September-October): 39– 43 (reprint from *Change* 1973 5/3: 58–63).

Jakimčuk, N. 1990. *Kak sudili poèta (Delo I. Brodskogo).* St Petersburg: Akvilon.

Jakovič, E. 1994. "Iosif Brodskij: 'Net pravyx i vinovatyx i nikogda ne budet.'" *Literaturnaja gazeta* (12 January): 5.

Janecek, G. 1986. "Brodskij čitaet 'Stixi na smert' T.S. Èliota':" 172–85 in L. Losev, 1986c (also published in *Russian Language Journal* 1980 34/118).

Javornik, M. 1990–1. "Interpretacija pesmi A.A. Ahmatovi J. Brodskega: In razmišljanje o pesniški evoluciji." *Jezik in Slovstvo* 36/1–2 (October-November): 21–5.

Johnson, B. 1928. "Classical Allusions in the Poetry of Donne." *PMLA* 43: 1098–1109 (reproduced in Roberts, 1978: 85–93).

Johnson, K. and S.M. Ashby, ed. 1992. *Third Wave: The New Russian Poetry.* Ann Arbor: University of Michigan Press.

Johnson, S. 1963. "The Metaphysical Poets": 1053–61 in Witherspoon and Warnke (taken from "Abraham Cowley," *The Lives of the Poets* [1779]).

Jolivet, R. 1951. *Introduction to Kierkegaard.* New York: Dutton.

Jones, C. 1993. "Rhyme and Joseph Brodsky: Making Connections." *Essays in Poetics.* 18/2: 1–11.

Julian-Baird, M. 1961. "Pasternak's Zhivago – Hamlet – Christ." *Renascence* 14: 179–84.

Kagan-Kans, E. 1975. *Hamlet and Don Quixote: Turgenev's Ambivalent Vision.* The Hague and Paris: Mouton.

Kalomirov, A. 1977 . "Problema sovremennoj russkoj poèzii." *Vestnik russkogo xristianskogo dviženija* 123/4: 140–51 (also published as "Iosif Brodskij [mesto]": 219–30 in L. Losev, 1986c).

– 1985. "Dvadcat' let novejšej russskoj poèzii: Predvaritel'nye zametki." *Russkaja mysl'* 3601, "Literaturnoe priloženie 2": 6–8.

Karabčievskij, Ju. 1990. *Voskresenie Majakovskogo.* Moscow: Sovetskij pisatel': 209–16 (e, 214).

Karlinsky, S. 1966. "Yevtushenko and the Underground Poets." *The Nation* 203/17 (November 21): 549–53.

Kasack, W. 1988a. "Brodsky, Iosif Aleksandrovich": 61–2 in *Dictionary of Russian Literature since 1917.* New York: Columbia University Press.

– 1988b. "Iossif Brodskij." *Osteuropa: Zeitschrift für Gegenwartsfragen des Ostens* 38/3 (March): 180–8 (e, 186).

Keast, W.R. 1950. "Johnson's Criticism of the Metaphysical Poets." *English Literary History* 17: 59–70 (reproduced in Roberts, 1978: 11–20).

Kelder, D. 1994. "The Campidoglio: A Historical Perspective" in Liberman, 199–205.

Kenner, H. 1996. "Between Two Worlds." *New York Times Book Review* (14 April): 14–15.

Kermode, F. 1957. "Dissociation of Sensibility." *Kenyon Review* 19: 169–94 (reproduced in Roberts, 1978: 59–84).

Kierkegaard, S. 1940. *Stages on Life's Way.* Princeton: Princeton University Press.

– 1941. *Journal (Extraits): 1834–1846.* Paris: Gallimard.

– 1957. *The Concept of Dread.* Princeton: Princeton University Press.

– 1964. *Repetition.* New York, Evanston, and London: Harper and Row.

– 1968. *Concluding Unscientific Postscript to the Philosophical Fragments.* Princeton: Princeton University Press.

– 1973. *Fear and Trembling/ The Sickness unto Death.* Princeton: Princeton University Press.

– 1978. *Two Ages.* Princeton: Princeton University Press.

– 1985. *Philosophical Fragments.* Princeton: Princeton University Press.

– 1987a. *Either/Or: Part One.* Princeton: Princeton University Press.

– 1987b. *Either/Or: Part Two.* Princeton: Princeton University Press.

– 1991. *Practice in Christianity.* Princeton: Princeton University Press.

Kline, G.L. 1965. "Elegy for John Donne." *Russian Review* 24: 341–53.

– 1971. "Religious Themes in Soviet Literature," in R.N. Marshal, ed., *Aspects of Religion in the Soviet Union: 1917–1967.* Chicago: University of Chicago Press: 157–86 (e).

– 1973a. Introduction and notes to *Joseph Brodsky: Selected Poems* (tr. G.L. Kline). Baltimore and Harmondsworth: Penguin.

– 1973b. "A Poet's Map of His Poem: An Interview by George L. Kline." *Vogue* 162 (September): 228, 30.

- 1973–4. "Translating Brodsky." *Bryn Mawr Now* (Spring): 1.
- 1974. "Russian Posy Throws Curve at American Poem Translator." *Pittsburgh Press* (31 October).
- 1977a. "A Bibliography of the Published Works of Iosif Aleksandrovich Brodsky": 159–75 in F. Moody, ed., *Ten Bibliographies of Twentieth Century Russian Literature*. Ann Arbor: Ardis.
- 1977b. "Working with Brodsky." *Paintbrush* IV/7–8: 25–7.
- 1980. "Brodsky, Iosif" in J.-A. Bidé and W.B. Edgertont, eds., *Columbia Dictionary of Modern European Literature*. New York: Columbia University Press: 121–2 (e, 121).
- 1989. "Revising Brodsky": 95–106 in D. Weissbort, ed., *The Double Labyrinth*. Iowa City: University of Iowa Press.
- 1990. "Variations on the Theme of Exile": 56–89 in Loseff and Polukhina, 1990.

Kline, G.L. and R.D. Sylvester. 1979. "Brodskii, Iosif Aleksandrovich" in H.B. Weber, and G. Breeze, eds., *Modern Encyclopedia of Russian and Soviet Literature*, Vol. III. Florida: Gulf Breeze: 129–37 (e, 135).

Klosty-Beaujour, E. 1984. "Prolegomena to a Study of Russian Bilingual Writers." *Slavic and East European Journal* 28/1: 58–75.
- 1989. *Alien Tongues: Bilingual Russian Writers of the "First" Emigration*. Ithaca and London: Cornell University Press.

Knox, J.E. 1978. Iosif Brodskij's Affinity with Osip Mandel'štam. Ph.D. dissertation, University of Texas at Austin (e, 44, 58, 97, 105, 224, 247, 325, 356, 370).
- 1986 (as Noks). "Ierarxija 'drugix' v poèzii Brodskogo": 160–72 in L. Losev, 1986c.

Koehler, W. 1953. *Rembrandt*. New York: H.N. Abrams.

Kolker, Ju. 1991. "Neskol'ko nabljudenij: O stixax Iosifa Brodskogo." *Grani* 44/162: 93–152.

Kondrašov (Direktor izd–va "Sovetskij pisatel'")/ Smirnov (Gl. redaktor). 1988. Letter of 1 October 1968 concerning Brodsky in "'Zimnjaja počta': K 20–letiju neizdanija knigi Iosifa Brodskogo." *Russkaja mysl'* 3750 "Literaturnoe priloženie 7" (11 November): 6.

Kopejkin, A. 1983. "Zametki o šestoj knige Iosifa Brodskogo." *Kontinent* 38: 387–93.
- 1984. "Kak popast' v specxran." *Russkaja mysl'* 3503 (9 February): 6.
- 1996. "Uroki poèta Iosifa Brodskogo." *Russkaja mysl'* 4116 (7–13 March): 13.

Korolevič, A. 1986. "Erofeev, Brodskij i drugie." *Russkaja mysl'* (4 April): 12.

Kosareva, N.S. (Zam. Sekretar' Pravlenija Len. Otd. Sojuza Pisatelej RSFSR) 1988. Letter of 30 September 1968 concerning Brodsky in "'Zimnjaja počta': K 20–letiju neizdanija knigi Iosifa Brodskogo." *Russkaja mysl'* 3750 "Literaturnoe priloženie 7" (11 November): 6.

Kostelanetz, R. 1987. Review of *Less than One*. *Boston Review* 12/4 (August): 9–30 (e).

Kovalenko, Y. and E. Polianovsky. 1988. "Joseph Brodsky's Nobel Prize" in "The Glasnost Papers. What the Soviets Are Saying About The Writers They Are Resurrecting." *The New Republic* (20 February): 38–40.

Kreps, M. 1984. *O poèzii Iosifa Brodskogo*. Ann Arbor: Ardis.

Krivulin, V. 1988. "Slovo o nobelitete Iosifa Brodskogo." *Russkaja mysl'* 3750, "Literaturnoe priloženie 7" (11 November): 2–3 (e, 3).

– 1989. "Russkij poèt – amerikanskij graždanin na francuzskom èkrane." *Russkaja mysl'* 3765 (3 March): 13 (e).

– 1991. "Teatr Iosifa Brodskogo." *Sovremennaja dramaturgija* 3: 15–17 (e, 16).

– 1992. "A Mask That's Grown to Fit the Face": 176–200 in Polukhina, 1992b.

Kroll, J. 1987. "Poetry's Laureate in Exile." *Newsweek* (2 November): 66 (e).

Kronik, J.W. 1992. "Editor's Column." *PMLA* (March): 217–19.

Kruglikov, V.A. 1990. "Meždu èpoxoj i prostranstvom: Podstupy k poètičeskoj filosofii I. Brodskogo": 88–97 in *Filosofija vozvraščennoj literatury*. Moscow: Akademija nauk SSSR, Ordena trudovogo krasnogo znameni institut filosofii (e, 88, 97).

Kublanovskij, Ju. 1983a. "Na predele lirizma." *Russkaja mysl'* 3477 (11 August): 10.

– 1983b. "Poka narod živ, živa i poèzija…" *Russkaja mysl'* 3475 (28 July): 9.

– 1990. "On postojanno vedet s Tvorcom svoego roda tjažbu." *Literaturnaja gazeta* 20/5294 (16 May): 6.

– 1991. "Poèzija novogo izmerenija." *Novyj mir* 2 (February): 242–6.

– 1992. "A Yankee in Russian Poetry": 200–15 in Polukhina, 1992b.

Kullè, V. 1990. "Struktura avtorskogo 'ja' v stixotvorenii Iosifa Brodskogo 'Niotkuda s ljubov'ju.'" *Novyj žurnal* 180: 159–72 (e, 166).

– 1992a. "…Tam, gde oni končili, ty načinaeš'." Introduction to Brodsky 1992, *Bog soxranjaet vse*: 5–6.

– 1992b. "The Linguistic Reality in Which We All Exist" (interviewed by V. Polukhina). *Essays in Poetics* 17/2: 72–83.

– 1993. "Brodskij glazami sovremennikov." *Grani* 167: 297–302.

– 1994. "Iosif Brodskij: Paradoksy vosprijatija (Brodskij v kritike Zeeva Bar-Selly)." *Structure and Tradition in Russian Society*. Slavica Helsingiensia: 64–82.

Kurennaja, N.M., L.A. Sofronova, and T.V. Civ'jan, eds. 1993. *Barokko v avangarde – avangard v barokko: Tezisy i materialy konferencii*. Moscow: Rossijskaja akademija nauk.

Kušner, A. 1966. *Nočnoj dozor*. Moscow and Leningrad: Sovetskij pisatel'.

– 1990a. "Cikl stixotvorenij": 234–9 in Brodsky, 1990p.

– 1990b. "Neskol'ko slov": 239–42 in Brodsky, 1990p.

– 1990c. "Poèt bezutešnoj mysli, edva li ne romatičeskogo otčanija." *Literaturnaja gazeta* 20/5294 (16 May): 6.

– 1991. "O Brodskom," "Zametki na poljax," "Protivostojanie." *Apollon v snegu*. Leningrad: 392–6, 438–45, 499–501.

– 1992. "The World's Last Romantic Poet": 100–13 in Polukhina, 1992b.

– 1996a. "Umer samyj dorogoj dlja menja poèt" in "Pamjati Iosifa Brodskogo." *Literaturnaja gazeta* (31 January): 3.

– 1996b. "My znaem, čto vnes Brodskij v russkuju poèziju" in "On prinimal vse stradanija." *Agumenty i fakty–Peterburg.* 22/144: 10.

– 1996c. "Iosif i ego Stikhotvoreniia." *Nevskoe vremja* (25 May): 4.

Kustarev, A. 1987. "Kul'tura kružka." *Sintaksis* 17: 155–60.

Kuzmin'skij, K. 1980–6. *The Blue Lagoon Anthology of Modern Poetry*. Newtonville (Vol. 1: 22–39; Vol. 2A: 106–7; 110–1; Vol. 2B: 177–91; 264–6; 272–3; Vol. 3B: 754–8).

– 1987. "Laureat 'Èriki,'" *Russkaja mysl'* 3697 (30 October): 11, 14.

LaBranche, A. 1966. "'Blanda Elegia': The Background to Donne's 'Elegies." *Modern Language Review* 61: 357–68 (reproduced in Roberts, 1978: 399–411).

Labriola, A.C. 1979. "Richard Crashaw's 'Schola Cordis' Poetry": 1–14 in Cooper.

Laird, S. 1988. "A Prize for Our Team." *Index on Censorship* 1: 7–11.

Lamont, R.C. 1974. "Joseph Brodsky: A Poet's Classroom." *Massachusetts Review* 15: 553–77.

– 1981. "Joseph Brodsky: A Part of Speech." *World Literature Today* 55/2 (Spring): 341–2 (e, 341).

Langeveld, A. 1983. "Iosif Brodski's 'Voor Jalta.'" *De Gids* 146/5: 404–12.

Lauterbach, A. 1988. "Genius in Exile." *Vogue* (February): 386–9, 434.

Lederer, J. 1946. "John Donne and the Emblematic Practice." *Review of English Studies* 22: 182–200 (reproduced in Roberts, 1978: 107–22).

Lehrer, J. 1994. "Joseph Brodsky." *NewsHour* (television interview). Broadcast on PBS (10 November).

– 1996. "Remembering a Poet." *NewsHour* (television interview with C. Miłosz and R. Hass). Broadcast on PBS (29 January).

Leishman, J.B. 1966. *The Art of Marvell's Poetry*. London: Hutchinson.

Lemxin, M. 1990. "Po maštabam istorii rossijskoj slovestnosti: Beseda Mixaila Lemxina s professorom Vjačeslavom Vsevolodovičem Ivanovym." *Russkaja mysl'* 3829, "Special'noe priloženie" (25 May): 11.

– 1996. "Edinstvennyj portret." *Russkaja mysl'* 4116 (7–13 March): 13.

Len, S. 1996. "Dvaždy proščal'noe poslan'e." *Literaturnaja gazeta* (7 February): 9.

Levinson, S. 1983. *Pragmatics*. Cambridge: Cambridge University Press.

Levitanskaja, E., A. and O. Levitanskaja. 1996. "Sem'e Iosifa Brodskogo." *Russkaja mysl'* 4111 (1–7 February): 16.

Levinton, G. 1996. "Smert' poèta." *Russkaja mysl'* 4116 (7–13 March): 12–13.

Levy, A. 1972. "Think it Over Brodsky, but Decide Now." *Saturday Review* (8 July): 6–8.

Lewalksi, B.K. 1979. *Protestant Poetics and the Seventeenth-Century Religious Lyric.* Princeton: Princeton University Press.

Liberman, A. and J. Brodsky. 1994. *Campidoglio: Michelangelo's Roman Capitol.* New York: Random House.

– 1994. "Experiencing the Campidoglio" in *Campidoglio:* 14–22.

Lilly, I.K. 1993. "The Metrical Context of Brodsky's Centenary Poem for Axmatova." *Slavic and East European Journal* 37/2: 211–19.

Limonov, È. 1984. "Poèt – Buxgalter: Neskol'ko jadovityx nabljudenij po povodu fenomena I.A. Brodskogo." *Muleta: Semejnyj al'bom 'A.'"* Paris: Edition Vivrisme: 132–5 (e, 135).

Lindsey, B. 1978. "Iosif Brodskij: Konec prekrasnoj èpoxi." *World Literature Today* (Winter): 129–30 (e, 130).

Links, J.G. 1977. *Canaletto and His Patrons.* New York: New York Unversity Press.

"Lisbon Conference on Literature: A Round Table of Central European and Russian Writers." *Cross-Currents* 1990 9: 77–124.

"Literature in Languages Other than English: A Conversation among Joseph Brodsky, Raymond Federman, José Ferrater-Mora, and Richard Kostelanetz": 343–65 in R. Kostelanetz, ed., 1991: *American Writing Today.* New York: Whitston.

Lixačev, D.S. 1973. *Razvitie russkoj literatury X-XVII vekov: Èpoxi i stili.* Leningrad: Nauka.

Lönnqvist, B. and M. Vincent. 1989. "En Lovsång Till Mötet." *Bonniers Litterara Magasin* 58/1 (February): 19–24.

Loseff, L. 1984. *On the Beneficence of Censorship: Aesopian Language in Modern Russian Literature.* Arbeiten und Texte zur Slavistik 31; Herausgegeben von Wolfgang Kasack. Munich: Verlag Otto Sagner in Kommission: 12, 82–4, 248 n19, 257–8 n34.

– 1985. Review of B. Ezerskaja, *Mastera. The Russian Review* 44/2: 198–9.

– 1989. "Iosif Brodskii's Poetics of Faith": 188–201 in McMillin, ed., *Aspects of Modern Russian and Czech Literature,* Columbus.

– 1990a. "Politics/Poetics": 34–56 in Loseff and Polukhina, 1990.

– 1990b. "Joseph Brodsky (né en 1940)," 725–40, 988–9, 1039–40 in Etkind and Nivat.

– 1992a. "Home and Abroad in the Works of Brodskii": 25–41 in A. McMillin, ed. *Under Eastern Eyes: The West as Reflected in Recent Russian Émigré Writing.* New York: St Martin's Press (e, 25, 29).

– 1992b. "A New Conception of Poetry": 113–40 in Polukhina, 1992b.

Loseff, L. and V. Polukhina, eds. 1990. *Brodsky's Poetics and Aesthetics.* Houndmills and London: Macmillan.

Losev, A. (L.) 1977. "Niotkuda s ljubov'ju... Zametki o stixax Iosifa Brodskogo." *Kontinent* 14: 307–31 (e, 320).

- 1978. "Iosif Brodskij: Posvjaščaetsja logike." *Vestnik russkogo xristianskogo dviženija* 127: 124–30.
- 1980a. "Anglijskij Brodskij." *Čast' reči* 1: 53–60.
- 1980b. "Iosif Brodskij. Predislovie." *Èxo* 1: 23–30.
- 1981–2. "Pervyj liričeskij cikl Iosifa Brodskogo." *Čast' reči* 2/3: 63–8.

Losev, L. 1983. "Poka narod živ, živa i poèzija" (interview with Jurij Kublanovskij). *Russkaja mysl'* 3475 (28 July): 9.

- 1984. "Ironičeskij monument: P'esa Iosifa Brodskogo 'Mramor.'" *Russkaja mysl'* 3521 (24 July): 10.
- 1986a. "Brodskij: ot mifa k poètu": 7–16 in L. Losev, 1986c.
- 1986b. "Čexovskij lirizm u Brodskogo": 185–98 in Losev, L. 1986c.
- 1986c. *Poètika Brodskogo: Sbornik statej pod redakciej L.V. Loseva.* Tenafly: Èrmitaž.
- 1987. "Prazdnik spravedlivosti." *Russkaja mysl'* 3697 (30 October): 9.
- 1989. "Moj drug idet po lesu..." *Russkaja mysl'* (16 June): 8–9.
- 1996. "V poslednie nedeli žizni Iosif byl vesel." *Nezavisimaja gazeta* (January 30): 1 (reprinted as "Na Brodskom zakončilas' russkaja poèzija, kakoj my znali ee s XVIII veka." *Russkaja mysl'* 4111 [1–7 February]: 17).

Losskaja, V. 1987. "Ja v polnom vostorge ot Nobelevskoj premii Iosifu Brodskomu..." *Russkaja mysl'* 3697 (30 October): 11.

Lotman, M. 1988. "Russkij poèt – Laureat nobelevskoj premii po literature." *Družba narodov* 8: 184–6.

Lotman, M. Ju. and Ju. M. Lotman. 1990. "Meždu vešč'ju i pustotoj: Iz nabljudenij nad poètikoj sbornika Iosifa Brodskogo 'Uranija.'" *Učenye zapiski Tartuskogo Universiteta*, 883: 170–87 (e, 175, 180, 182).

Lourie, R. 1971. "Brodsky, Joseph: Ostanovka v pustyne." *Russian Review* (30 April): 202.

Love, H. 1966. "The Argument of Donne's 'First Anniversary.'" *Modern Philology* 64: 125–31 (reproduced in Roberts, 1978: 355–68).

Lur'e, S. 1990. "Svoboda poslednogo slova." *Zvezda* 8: 142–6 (e, 143–5). (Also published in Brodsky, 1990p: 165–76, as well as Brodsky 1991, *Xolmy*: 350–7.)

Mahony, P. 1969. "The 'Anniversaries': Donne's Rhetorical Approach to Evil." *Journal of English and Germanic Philology* 68: 407–13 (reproduced in Roberts, 1978: 363–8).

Maksimov, V. 1987. "Poèt Bož'ej milost'ju." *Kontinent* 54: 375–8 (e, 378). (Also partially reproduced in *Russkaja mysl'* 3697 [October]: 10.)

Maksimova, O. 1986. "Ja tebja ljublju, no ty mne ne nraviš'sja." *Strana i mir* 7: 89–96.

Malcolm, N. 1990. "Voting for the Revolution." *Times Literary Supplement* (2–8 November): 1180.

Mambrino, J. 1988. "Joseph Brodsky: Poète de la Patrie Humaine." *Études* 368/4, (April): 485–91 (e, 488).

Mandel'štam, N. 1982. *Moe zaveščanie i drugie èsse.* New York: Serebrjanyj vek.

Manevič, G. and È. Štejnberg. 1996. "Na smert' Iosifa Brodskogo." *Russkaja mysl'* 4111 (1–7 February): 16.

Maramzin, V. 1987. "Naš sverstnik." *Russkaja mysl'* 3697 (30 October): 9.

Marcus, J. 1992. "Gondola Dreams." *New York Times Book Review* (31 May): 32.

Marotti, A.F. 1986. *John Donne, Coterie Poet.* Madison: Univeristy of Wisconsin Press.

Martin, B., ed. 1970. *Great Twentieth–Century Jewish Philosophers: Shestov, Rosenweg, Buber.* London: Macmillan.

Martin, J.R. 1977. *Baroque.* London: Allen Lane.

Martz, L.L. 1959. "Donne and the Meditative Tradition." *Thought* 34: 269–78 (reproduced in Roberts, 1978: 142–50).

Massie, S. 1972. *The Living Mirror: Five Young Poets from Leningrad.* New York: Doubleday: 215–99.

Matich, O. 1984. "Is There a Russian Literature Beyond Politics?" 180–7 in O. Matich and M. Heim, eds. *The Third Wave: Russian Literature in Emigration.* Ann Arbor. Ardis

May, J. 1989. "Poets' Round Table: 'A Common Language.'" *PN Review* 15/4: 39–47.

McFadden, R. D. 1996. "Joseph Brodsky, Exiled Poet Who Won Nobel, Dies at 55." *New York Times* (31 January): A1/B5 (e).

McMillin, A. 1994. "Bilingualism and Word Play in the Work of Russian Writers of the Third Wave of Emigration: The Heritage of Nabokov." *Modern Language Review* 89/2: 417–26.

Medvedev, F. 1988. "Čeloveka možno vsegda spasti." *Ogonek* 31: 28–9.

Mejlax, M. 1990. "Russkie poèty – druz'ja sèra Isaji Berlina: Beseda s Iosifom Brodskim i Anatoliem Najmanom." *Russkaja mysl'* 3822, "Literaturnoe priloženie 9" (6 April): 5.

– 1992 (as Meilakh). "Liberation from Emotionality": 158–76 in Polukhina, 1992b.

– 1996. "In Memoriam." *Russkaja mysl'* 4112 (8–14 February): 16.

Melaga, G. 1994. "L'accademia, Nerone e io." *L'Espresso* (24 June): 110–11.

Mendelson, E. 1986. "Against the Limits of Language." *Book World: Washington Post* (25 May): 7 (e).

Mikhnik, A. 1995. "Conversation of Joseph Brodsky with Adam Mikhnik." *Gazeta Wyborcza* (February; translation by D. Gorelkov taken from Nossik, 1996).

Miloslavskij, Ju. 1996. "V prodolženie poslednej četverti uxodšego ot nas dvadcatogo stoletija…" in "Pamjati Iosifa Brodskogo." *Literaturnaja gazeta* (31 January): 3.

Miłosz, C. 1980. "A Struggle against Suffocation." *New York Review of Books* 27/13 (14 August): 23–5 (e).

– 1988. "O Josifie Brodskim." *Zeszyty Literackie* 22: 5–14.

– 1992. "A Huge Building of Strange Architecture": 325–41 in Polukhina, 1992b.

Maxton, H. 1983. "Joseph Brodsky and 'The Great Elegy for John Donne'; A Note." *The Crane Bag* 7/1: 62–4 (e, 62).

McCanles, M. 1966. "Paradox in Donne." *Studies in the Renaissance* 13: 266–87 (reproduced in Roberts, 1978: 220–39).

Miner, E. 1969. *The Metaphysical Mode From Donne to Cowley.* Princeton: Princeton University Press.

– 1971. *The Cavlier Mode from Jonson to Cotton.* Princeton: Princeton University Press.

Mirčev, A. 1989. "Interv'ju s Brodskim." *15 Interv'ju.* New York: Izdate'stvo imeni A. Platonova: 21–34.

Mitchell, W.J. 1972. "From Russia with Very Mixed Emotions: Iosif Alexandrovich Brodsky, Poet in Exile." *Detroit Free Press* (17 September): 13.

Molčalova, V. 1993. "Soglasnoe nesoglasie, ili nesoglasnoe soglasie: Barokko i avangard": 4–7 in Kurennaja et al.

Molon, È. and Ricci, D. 1993. "Barokko v ital'janskom avangarde: K arxitektonike futurizma": 32–5 in Kurennaja et al.

Monas, S. 1983a. "Iosif Brodskij: Rimskie èlegii." *World Literature Today* 57/2 (Spring): 309–10.

– 1983b. "Words Devouring Things: The Poetry of Joseph Brodsky." *World Literature Today* 57/2 (Spring): 214–18 (e, 214).

Montenegro, D. 1987. "An Interview with Joseph Brodsky." *Partisan Review* 54/4: 527–40.

Montgomery, M.R. 1991. "Joseph Brodsky, the People's Poet." *Boston Globe* (2 October): 39, 44 (e, 44).

Morassi, A. 1955. *G.B. Tiepolo: His Life and Work.* London: Phaidon.

Morozov, A. 1962. "Problema barroko v russkoj literature XVII – načala XVIII veka: Sostojanie voprosa i zadači izučenija." *Russkaja literatura* 3: 3–39.

Morson, G.S. 1992. "Russian Cluster." *PMLA* (March): 226–31.

Muldoon, P. 1996. "The Hug (In Memory of Joseph Brodsky)." *Times Literary Supplement* (9 February): 31.

Murav'eva, I. 1996. "Slova proščanija." *Russkaja mysl'* 4112 (8–14 February): 16.

Muravnik, M. 1987. "'Kontinent' 51." *Russkaja mysl'* 3685 (7 August): 10.

Murray, P. 1971. *Piranesi and the Grandeur of Ancient Rome.* London: Thames and Hudson.

Murray, W.A. 1959. "What Was the Soul of the Apple?" *Review of English Studies* 10: 141–55 (reproduced in Roberts, 1978: 462–75).

"Naberežnaja neiscelimyx": *Progulki s I. Brodskim (Čast' pervaja).* 1994 television broadcast: Ostankino (4 August).

Najman, A. 1968 (as "N.N."). "Zametki dlja pamjati." Introduction to *Ostanovka v pustyne*: 7–15.

- 1989. "Četyre stixotvorenija." *Literaturnoe obozrenie* 5: 110–12.
- 1990. "Veličie poètičeskogo zamysla." *Russkaja mysl'* 3829, "Special'noe priloženie" (25 May): 2–3 (e, 2). (Also printed as "Prostranstvo Uranii," *Oktjabr'* 1990 12: 193–18.)
- 1991 (as A. Nayman). *Remembering Anna Akhmatova.* New York: John Macrae/H. Holt: 5, 41, 51, 66–7, 75, 85, 103, 130–5, 138, 140, 145, 157, 159, 205, 207, 215, 219, 224 n23.
- 1992 (as A. Naiman). "A Coagulation of Linguistic Energy": 1–29 in Polukhina, 1992b (also published in Brodsky, 1990p: 127–54.)
- 1993. "Bukvy, prostupajuščie na stene." *Literaturnaja gazeta* (21 April): 6.
- 1996. "28 janvarja 1996 goda." *Russkaja mysl'* 4112 (8–14 February): 17.
Nandy, P., ed. 1969. *New Underground Russian Poets.* Calcutta: Dialogue Calcutta Anthology Eight/ Satyabrata Pal.
Navrozov, L. 1981. "Russian Literature in Exile and the New York Times." *The Rockford Papers* 6/1 (January): 1–16.
Neizvestnyj, È. 1996. "Junyj Iosif Brodskij..." in "Pamjati Iosifa Brodskogo." *Literaturnaja gazeta* (31 January): 3.
Nekrasov, V. 1989. *Stixi iz žurnala.* Moskva: 6, 8, 38.
Nelson, L. 1961. *Baroque Lyric Poetry.* New Haven and London: Yale University Press.
- 1993. "Mannerism": 732–3 in A. Preminger and T.V.F. Brogan, eds., *The New Princeton Encyclopedia of Poetry and Poetics.* Princeton: Princeton University Press.
Nethercott, A.H. 1931. *Abraham Cowley: The Muse's Hannibal.* London: Oxford University Press.
Newlove, D. 1974. Review of *Selected Poems. The Village Voice* (14 March): 26–7.
Nicolson, M.H. 1960. *The Breaking of the Circle: Studies in the Effect of the "New Science" upon Seventeenth-Century Poetry.* New York and London: Columbia University Press.
Nivat, G. 1986. "Portrait de Joseph Brodsky." *La Quinzaine Littéraire* 469 (1–15 September): 19–20 (e).
- 1988a. "Le Destin de Brodsky." *L'Autre Europe* 17–19: 12–37 (e, 12, 21).
- 1988b (as Dž Niva). "Kvadrat, v kotoryj vpisan krug večnosti." *Russkaja mysl'* 3750, "Literaturnoe priloženie" (11 November): 1–2 (e, 1).
- 1990. "The Ironic Journey into Antiquity": 89–98 in Loseff and Polukhina, 1990.
Norwich, J.J. 1982. *A History of Venice.* New York: A.A. Knopf.
Nossik, A. 1996. "Na poxorony xvatit: 01/31/96." Taken from Nossik and Barbarash, "Memorial Page."
Nossik, A. and S. Barbarash, eds. 1996."Memorial Page" for Brodsky, compiled on the Internet on January 28: http://zaraza.netmedia.net.il/Nossik/brodsky/
Ochs, E. 1992. "Introduction": 1–17 in B.B. Schieffelin and E. Ochs, ed., *Language Socialization across Cultures.* Cambridge: Cambridge University Press.

Ornstein, R. 1956. "Donne, Montaigne and Natural Laws." *Journal of English and Germanic Philology* 5: 213–19 (reproduced in Roberts, 1978: 129–42).

Ovid. 1984. *Metamorphoses*. Loeb Classical Library. Cambridge, Mass. and London: Harvard University Press and W. Heinemann.

Ozerov, L. 1992. "Nu, kak tam Flavij?" *Literaturnaja gazeta* (3 June): 16.

Pann, L. 1996. "Proščanie s poètom (N'ju – Jork prostilsja s I. Brodskim)." *Russkaja mysl'* 4113 (15–21 February): 12.

Panova, V. 1988. "Iosif Brodskij 'Zimnjaja počta.' Sbornik stixotvorenij (1967)" in "'Zimnjaja počta': K 20–letiju neizdanija knigi Iosifa Brodskogo." *Russkaja mysl'* 3750 "Literaturnoe priloženie 7" (11 November): 5.

Paramonov, B. 1983. "Soglasno Jungu." *Kontinent* 37: 275–81.

Parfitt, G. 1985. *English Poetry of the Seventeenth Century*. London and New York: Longman.

– 1989. *John Donne: A Literary Life*. Houndmills: Macmillan.

Parrish, P.A. 1979. "Crashaw's Funeral Elegies": 50–78 in Cooper.

Parshchikov, A. 1992. "Absolute Tranquility in the Face of Absolute Tragedy": 261–276 in Polukhina, 1992b.

Parshchikov, A. and A. Wachtel. 1992. "Introduction": 1–13 in Johnson and Ashby.

Pasternak, B. 1957. *Doktor Živago*. Milan: Feltrinelli.

Patterson, D. 1978. "Sestov's Second Dimension: 'In Job's Balances.'" *Slavic and East European Journal* 22/2: 141–53.

– 1993. "From Exile to Affirmation: The Poetry of Joseph Brodsky." *Studies in Twentieth Century Literature* 17/2 (Summer): 365–83 (e, 365). (Subsequently included in *Exile: The Sense of Alienation in Modern Letters*. University Press of Kentucky.)

Pawel, E. 1968. "The Poetry of Joseph Brodsky." *Midstream* 14/5: 17–22.

Persky, S. 1996. "A Poetic Challenge that Repays the Effort." *Globe and Mail* (30 March): C7.

Peters, A.M. and Boggs, S.T. 1992. "Interactional Routines as Cultural Influences upon Language Acquisition": 80–97 in B.B. Schieffelin and E. Ochs, eds. *Language Socialization across Cultures*. Cambridge: Cambridge University Press.

Peterson, D.L. 1959. "John Donne's 'Holy Sonnets' and the Anglican Doctrine of Contrition." *Studies in Philology* 56: 504–18 (reproduced in Roberts, 1978: 313–24).

Petro, P. 1993. "Apropos Dostoevsky: Brodsky, Kundera and the Definition of Europe": 76–90 in L. Miller, K. Petersen, P. Stenberg, and K. Zaenker, eds. *Literature and Politics in Central Europe. Studies in Honour of Markéta Goetz – Stankiewicz*. Columbia, S.C.: Camden House.

Petruk, A. 1988. "Na poroge Leman – kolledža N'ju – Jorkskogo universiteta…" *Komsomol'skaja pravda* (10 March): 4.

Phillips, W. 1987. Review of "Less than One." *Partisan Review* 1: 139–45.

Pignatti, T. 1958. *Carpaccio.* Lausanne: Éditions d'Art Albert Skira.

Pikač, A. 1990. "Citaja Brodskogo": 242–50 in Brodsky, 1990p.

Pilshchikov, I.A. 1993. "Brodsky and Baratynsky": 214–28 in V. Polukhina, J. Andrew, and R. Reid, eds. *Literary Tradition and Practice in Russian Culture. Papers from an International Conference on the Occasion of the Seventieth Birthday of Y.M. Lotman. Russian Culture/Structure and Tradition: Studies in Slavic Literature and Poetics 20.* Amsterdam/Atlanta: Rodopi.

Pirog, G. 1995. Review of Bethea, Joseph Brodsky and the Creation of Exile. *Slavic Review* (Fall): 743–4.

Pitkethly, L. (dir.). 1989. "Joseph Brodsky: A Maddening Space." Television broadcast. New York and London: New York Center for Visual History/ Channel Four.

Polonin, M. 1987. "Večer 'Strel'ca' v Lozanne." *Russkaja mysl'* 3697 (30 October): 14.

Polukhina, V. 1979. "The 'Strange Theme' in J. Brodsky's Poetry." *Essays in Poetics* 4/1: 35–54 (e, 40).

– 1985. "The Poetry of Joseph Brodsky: A Study of Metaphor." Ph.D. dissertation, Keele University.

– 1986a. "Grammatika metafory i xudožestvennyj smysl": 63–97 in L. Losev, 1986c.

– 1986b. "A Study of Metaphor in Progress. Poetry of Joseph Brodsky." *Wiener Slawisticher Almanach* 17: 149–85 (e, 158, 164).

– 1987a. "Paradoksy Brodskogo." *Russkaja mysl'* 3705, "Literaturnoe priloženie 5" (25 December): 1 (e).

– 1987b. "Vsevidjaščee oko slov." *Russkaja mysl'* 3697 (30 October): 9.

– 1989a. *Joseph Brodsky: A Poet for Our Time.* Cambridge: Cambridge Univeristy Press.

– 1989b. "Axmatova i Brodskij: K probleme pritjaženij i ottalkivanij" in Dedjulin and Superfin, 143–53 (e, 147).

– 1990a. "An Interview with Bella Akhmadulina": 198–205 in Loseff and Polukhina, 1990.

– 1990b. "On smotrit na mir s točki zrenija Vremeni." *Literaturnaja gazeta* 20/ 5294 (16 May): 6.

– 1990c. "Similarity in Disparity": 152–80 in Loseff and Polukhina 1990.

– 1992a. "Brodsky's Poetic Self-Portrait": 122–37 in S.D. Graham, ed., *Selected Papers from the Fourth World Congress for Soviet and East European Studies, Harrogate.* New York: St Martin's Press (e, 123, 126, 133, 135 n8).

– 1992b. *Brodsky through the Eyes of His Contemporaries.* New York: St Martin's Press.

– 1993. "Landšaft liričeskoj ličnosti v poèzii Iosifa Brodskogo": 229–45 in V. Polukhina, J. Andrew, and R. Reid, eds. *Literary Tradition and Practice in Russian Culture. Papers from an International Conference on the Occasion of the*

Seventieth Birthday of Y.M. Lotman. Russian Culture/Structure and Tradition: Studies in Slavic Literature and Poetics 20. Amsterdam/Atlanta: Rodopi.

– 1994. "The Myth of the Poet and the Poet of the Myth: Russian Poets on Brodsky" in Wigzell, 139–59 (e, 149).

Poženckij, K. 1987 "Uvenčanie neslomlennoj Rossii." *Russkaja mysl'* 3705, "Literaturnoe priloženie 5" (25 December): 2 (e).

"Pravoslavnye xristiane iz SSSR." 1984. "Xristoprodavcy." *Kontinent* 43: 380–1.

Praz, M. 1951. "The Critical Importance of the Revised Interest in Seventeenth-Century Metaphysical Poetry": 158–66 in C.L. Wrenn and G. Bullough, eds. *English Studies Today.* London: Oxford University Press (reproduced in Roberts, 1978: 3–11).

Prelin, I. 1996. "Na smert' poèta." *Pravda.* (8 February): "Pravda Rossii": 4.

Presson, R. 1992. "A Redemptive Reality." *New Letters* 59/1: 139–51.

Proffer, È. 1987. "My očen' gordimsja tem..." *Russkaja mysl'* 3697 (30 October): 9.

Proffer, K. 1986. "Ostanovka v sumašedšem dome: poèma Brodskogo 'Gorbunov i Gorčakov'": 132–41 in L. Losev, 1986c (also published in *Russian Literature Triquarterly* 1971 1).

Porotov, E. (dir.). 1996. "Iosif Brodskij: Nemnogo o sebe." Television broadcast, 26 May. St Petersburg: Pjatyj Kanal.

Puškin, A.S. 1957. *Polnoe sobranie sočinenij v desjati tomax (Izdanie vtoroe).* Moscow: Izdatel'stvo Akademii Nauk.

"Questions and Answers after Brodsky's Reading, 21 February 1978." *Iowa Review* (Summer 1978): 4–9.

Quinn, D. 1969. "Donne's 'Anniversaries' as Celebration." *Studies in English Literature* 9: 97–105 (reproduced in Roberts, 1978: 368–74).

Rajs, È. 1965. "Leningradskij Gamlet: O stixax I. Brodskogo." *Grani* 59: 168–72.

Rančin, A.M. 1993a. "Filosofskaja tradicija Iosifa Brodskogo." *Literaturnoe obozrenie* 3–4: 3–13.

– 1993b. "'Rimskij tekst' Iosifa Brodskogo.'" *Russian Literature* 34: 471–86 (e, 472, 478–9, 482).

Rannit, A. 1980. "Zametka o Rossii i Iosife Brodskom." *Čast' reči* 1: 61–6.

Ravnum, I.M. 1991. "Josif Brodskij: En Poetisk Kosmopolitt." *Vinduet* 45/1: 62–7.

Ray, M.K. 1989. "Joseph Brodsky: Poet." *New Quest* 73 (January-February): 48–52 (e).

Rayfield, D. 1986. "Grist to the Mill." *Times Higher Education Supplement* (10–18 October) (e).

Raxmanov, L. 1988. "Pervaja kniga I. Brodskogo 'Zimnjaja počta'..." in "'Zimnjaja počta': K 20–letiju neizdanija knigi Iosifa Brodskogo." *Russkaja mysl'* 3750 "Literaturnoe priloženie 7" (11 November): 5.

Reavey, G. 1966. *The New Russian Poets: 1953–1966.* New York: 255–69, 291–2.

"Redakcija žurnala 'Kontinent.'" 1976. "Dorogoj Iosif!" (Telegram). *Kontinent* 9: 418.

– 1987. "Toržestvo russkoj poèzii." *Kontinent* 54: rear cover.

– 1990. "24 maja 1990: Iosifu Brodskomu ispolnitsja 50 let." *Kontinent* 63: rear cover.

"Redaktorskaja gruppa 'Èkspress-Xroniki.'" 1987. "Primite pozdravlenija v svjazi s prisuždeniem Vam Nobelevskoj premii." *Russkaja mysl'* 3697 (30 October): 11 (e).

Reddaway, P., ed. 1972. *Uncensored Russia: Protest and Dissent in the Soviet Union.* New York, St Louis, San Francisco, and Toronto: American Heritage Press.

Reeder, R. 1995. "Joseph Brodsky: Arrest and Exile": 432–45 in *Anna Akhmatova, Poet and Prophet.* London: Allison and Busby.

Reeve, F.D. 1975. "Additions and Losses." *Poetry* 127 (October): 42–4.

– 1981. "On Joseph Brodsky." *American Poetry Review* (July/ August): 36–7.

Rejn, E. 1987. "Prošu peredat' Iosifu moju ljubov'..." *Russkaja mysl'* 3697 (30 October): 10.

– 1988. Introduction to "Iosif Brodskij: Stixi raznyx let." *Družba narodov* 8: 175–86.

– 1990. *Temnota zerkal: Stixotvorenija i poèmy.* Moscow: Sovetskij pisatel'.

– 1991. *Protiv časovoj strelki.* Tenafly: Èrmitaž.

– 1992a (as Rein). "The Introduction of the Prosaic into Poetry": 53–74 in Polukhina, 1992b.

– 1992b. "Na izlete romantizma" (interview with T. Rasskazova). *Literaturnaja gazeta* (26 August): 5.

– 1996. "K navsegda razlučennomu drugu." *Russkaja mysl'* 4111 (1–7 February): 17.

Remnick, D. 1996. "Perfect Pitch." *New Yorker* (12 February): 38–45.

Rezek, J., ed. 1975. *Three Slavic Poets.* Chicago: Elpenor.

Rišina, I. 1993. "Prorok? Eretik? Dezertir?" *Literaturnaja gazeta* (7 April): 3.

Roberts, J.R., ed. 1978. *Essential Articles for the Study of John Donne's Poetry.* Hamden: Harvester/ Archon.

Robertson, G. 1968. *Giovanni Bellini.* Oxford and London: Oxford University Press.

Romaine, S. 1993. *Bilingualism.* Oxford and Cambridge, Mass.: Blackwell.

Rooney, W.J. 1976. "'The Canonization' – The Language of Paradox Reconsidered." *English Literary History* 23: 36–47 (reproduced in Roberts, 1978: 271–9).

Rosenberg, J. 1968. *Rembrandt: Life and Work.* London and New York: Phaidon.

Ross, B. 1990. "Nostalgia and the Child Topoi: Metaphors of Disruption and Transcendence in the Work of Joseph Brodsky, Marc Chagall and Andrei Tarkovsky." *Analecta Husserliana* 28: 307–23 (e, 307, 309–10).

Röthlisberger, M. 1977. "Le Paysage Comme Idéal Classique": introductory essay in *Tout l'Œuvre Peint de Claude Lorrain*. Paris: Flammarion.

Rowe, E. 1975. "Pushkin, Lermontov and 'Hamlet.'" *Texas Studies in Literature and Language* 17: 337–47.

Roždestvenskij, V. 1988. "Iosif Brodskij 'Zimnjaja počta': Sbornik stixov, 1966" in "'Zimnjaja počta': K 20–letiju neizdanija knigi Iosifa Brodskogo." *Russkaja mysl'* 3750 "Literaturnoe priloženie 7" (11 November): 4.

Rublev, I. 1996. "Pominaja Brodskogo, 40–j den'." *Russkaja mysl'* 4118 (21–27 March): 17.

Russell, N. 1986. "Interview: Noel Russell Talks to Joseph Brodsky." *Literary Review* (January): 10–2.

Russkij PEN-centr. 1996. "Vosled tebe gljadja, vo vse vremena" in "Pamjati Iosifa Brodskogo." *Literaturnaja gazeta* (31 January): 3.

Ruthven, K.K. 1969. *The Conceit*. London: Methuen.

Ryan, D. 1993. "Joseph Brodsky and the Fictions of Poetry, Including Vers Libre." *Lituanus* 39/2: 70–7.

Rybakov, V. 1978. "Jazyk – edinstvennyj avangardist: Iosif Brodskij v 'Russkoj mysli.'" *Russkaja mysl'* 3188 (26 January): 8.

Sacks, P. 1986. "The Evolution of 'The Elegy'" in *Key Reporter* (Spring): 51/3.

Safonov, A. 1996. "Alex Safonov's Collection/Iosif Brodsky Translated into English" in Nossik, 1996.

Sapiets, J. 1968. "Introduction" to K. Bosley, *Russia's Other Poets*. xxii–iii.

Savitski, D. 1987. "Brodski, c'est Byzance." *Libération* (23 October): 38–9.

– 1987. "Et la Néva va..." *Libération* (9 December): 42.

Sazonova, L.I. 1991. *Poèzija russkogo barokko: Vtoraja polovina XVII–načalo XVIII v.* Moscow: Nauka.

Scarpetta, G. 1978. "Joseph Brodsky: Poésie et Dissidence." *Tel Quel* 76 (Summer): 54–9.

Schaarschmidt, G. 1988. "Multilingualism and the Problem of Literary Style." *Zagadnienia Rodzajów Literackich* 31/1–2: 75–87.

Scherr, B. 1980. "Russian and English Versification: Similarities, Differences, Analysis." *Style* 14/4 (Fall): 353–78.

– 1986a. *Russian Poetry: Meter, Rhythm, and Rhyme*. Berkeley, Los Angeles, and London: University of California Press.

– 1986b (as Šerr). "Strofika Brodskogo": 97–121 in L. Losev, 1986c.

– 1990. "Beginning at the End: Rhyme and Enjambment in Brodsky's Poetry": 180–98 in Loseff and Polukhina, 1990.

Schmidt, M. 1980. "Time of Cold." *New Statesman* (17 October): 25.

Scott, J. 1994. "Beside the Bible, a Book of Poetry to Soothe the Weary Traveler." *New York Times* (15 March): B1, B4.

Sedakova, O. 1992. "A Rare Independence": 237–61 in Polukhina, 1992b.

Segal', M. 1988. "Po povodu stat'i Z. Bar-Selly 'Poèzija i pravda.'" 22/61: 218–19.

Segel, H.B. 1973. "Baroque and Rococo in Eighteenth – Century Russian Literature." *Canadian Slavonic Papers/ Revue Canadiene des Slavistes* 15/4 (Winter): 556–66.

– 1974. *The Baroque Poem: A Comparative Survey.* New York: E.P. Dutton.

Sellin, P.R. 1983. *John Donne and 'Calvinist' Views of Grace.* Amsterdam: VU Boekhandel/Uitgeverij.

Serke, J. 1981. "Die Verbanneten Dichter: Die Kraft der Ersten Lüge." *Stern* (1 October): 137–48 (e, 148).

Shakespeare, W. 1938. *The Complete Works of William Shakespeare Gathered in One Volume.* New York: Oxford University Press.

Šajtanov, I. 1988. "Predislovie k znakomstvu." *Literaturnoe obozrenie* 8: 55–64.

Šargorodskij, S. 1985. "Igry v sadu: Ob odnom stixotvorenii Brodskogo." *Dvadcat' dva* 40: 205–13.

Sharp, R.L. 1940. *From Donne to Dryden: The Revolt Against Metaphysical Poetry.* Chapel Hill: University of North Carolina Press.

Šaruga, L. 1987. "Esli ljubov'…" *Russkaja mysl'* 3701 (27 November): 9 and continued in 3702 (4 December): 9 (translated from Polish).

Šefner, V. 1988. "O rukopisi Iosifa Brodskogo 'Zimnjaja počta' (9 ijulja 1967)" in "'Zimnjaja počta': K 20–letiju neizdanija knigi Iosifa Brodskogo." *Russkaja mysl'* 3750 "Literaturnoe priloženie 7" (11 November): 5.

Shein, L.J. 1967. "Lev Shestov: A Russian Existentialist." *Russian Review* 26/3: 278–86.

– 1991. *The Philosophy of Lev Shestov (1866–1938): A Russian Existentialist.* Toronto Studies in Theology 57. Lewiston, Queenston, and Lampeter: Edwin Mellen Press.

Šelkovskij, I. 1987. "Sovetskij sojuz deržit absoljutnyj rekord…" *Russkaja mysl'* 3698 (6 November): 9 (e).

Šemjakin, M. 1996. "Dlja menja uxod Iosifa Brodskogo bol'šoe ličnoe gore" in "Pamjati Iosifa Brodskogo." *Literaturnaja gazeta* (31 January): 3.

Sheppard, R.Z. 1986. "Notes from a Poet in His Prime." *Time* (7 April): 70 (e).

Sherwood, T.G. 1984. *Fulfilling the Circle: A Study of John Donne's Thought.* Toronto, Buffalo and London: University of Toronto Press.

Šestov, L. 1911a. *Dobro v učenii gr. Tolstogo i F. Nitše: Filosofija i propoved'. Sobranie sočinenij.* St. Petersburg: Sipovnik (vol. 2).

– 1911b. *Šekspir i ego kritik Brandes. Sobranie sočinenij.* St Petersburg: Šipovnik (vol. 1).

– 1922. *Dostoevskij i Nitše: Filosofija tragedii.* Berlin: Skify.

– 1929. *Na vesax Iova: Stranstvovanija po dušam.* Paris: La Société Nouvelle d'Éditions Franco-Slaves.

– 1939. *Kirgegard i èkzistencial'naja filosofija: Glas vopijuščego v pustyne.* Paris: Dom knigi.

– 1951. *Afiny i Ierusalim.* Paris: YMCA.

– 1964. *Umozrenie i otkrovenie.* Paris: YMCA.

– 1971. *Apofeoz bezpočvennosti*. Paris: YMCA reprint of 1911 *Sobranie sočinenij* vol. 4. St Petersburg: Šipovnik.

– 1978. *Načala i koncy: Sbornik statej*. Ann Arbor: Ardis reprint of 1908 St Petersburg: Stasjulevič.

Šraer-Petrov, D. 1989. *Druz'ja i teni: Roman s učastiem avtora*. New York: Liberty (separate chapter on Brodsky, 273–83).

Shrayer, M.D. 1993. "Two Poems on the Death of Akhmatova: Dialogues, Private Codes, and the Myth of Akhmatova's Orphans." *Canadian Slavonic Papers/ Revue canadienne des slavistes* 35/1–2 (March-June): 45–68.

Štern, L. 1990. "Brodskij – geolog": 250–1 in Brodsky, 1990p.

Šunejko, A.A. 1994. "No my živy, pokamest est' proščenie i šrift: Vzgljad na mire Iosifa Brodskogo." *Russkaja reč'* 2: 15–21.

Švarc, E. 1992 (as Shvarts). "Coldness and Rationality": 215–37 in Polukhina, 1992b.

Simon, J. 1986. "Promoter of Meaning." *National Review* (24 October): 54–6.

– 1988. "Whence This?" *National Review* (14 October): 54–6.

Skelton, R., ed. 1970. *The Cavalier Poets*. London: Faber and Faber.

Skirne, P.N. 1978. *The Baroque: Literature and Culture in Seventeenth-Century Europe*. London: Methuen.

Slavinskij, E. 1987. "Moja pervaja reakcija byla..." *Russkaja mysl'* 3698 (6 November): 9.

Sloan, T.O. 1963. "The Rhetoric in the Poetry of John Donne." *Studies in English Literature* 3: 31–44 (reproduced in Roberts, 1978: 190–8).

Smirnov (Gl. redaktor). 1988. Letter to Brodsky of 12 December 1966 in "'Zimnjaja počta': K 20–letiju neizdanija knigi Iosifa Brodskogo." *Russkaja mysl'* 3750 "Literaturnoe priloženie 7" (11 November): 5.

Smirnov, I.P. 1979. "Barokko i opyt poètičeskoj kul'tury načala XX v.": 335–62 in A.I. Rogov, A.V. Lipatov, and L.A. Sofronova, eds. *Slavjanskoe barokko: Istoriko – kul'turnye problemy èpoxi*. Moscow: Nauka.

Smirnov (Predsedatel')/ Uspenskaja (Sekretar'). 1988. "Protokol redso-veščanija ot 26 ijulja 1966g" in "'Zimnjaja počta': K 20–letiju neizdanija knigi Iosifa Brodskogo." *Russkaja mysl'* 3750, "Literaturnoe priloženie 7" (11 November): 4.

Smith, A.J. 1956. "An Examination of Some Claims for Ramism." *Review of English Studies* 7: 348–59 (reproduced in Roberts, 1978: 178–89).

Smith, G. 1983. "Brodsky, Iosif Aleksandrovich": 104–5 in A. Bullock and R.B. Woodings, eds., *Fontana Biographical Companion to Modern Thought*. London.

– 1986a. "More than Brodsky." *New York Times Book Review* (7 September): 37.

– 1986b. "Versifikacija v stixotvorenii I. Brodskogo 'Kellomjaki':" 141–60 in L. Losev, 1986c.

– 1987. "Another Time, Another Place." *Times Literary Supplement* (26 June): 692–4 (e, 692).

- 1989. "Russian Poetry Outside Russia since 1970: A Survey": 179–87 in A. McMillin, ed., *Aspects of Modern Russian and Czech Literature*, Columbus (e, 185).
- 1990. "'Polden' v komnate'": 124–35 in Loseff and Polukhina, 1990.
- 1992. "England in Russian Emigré Poetry: Iosif Brodskii's 'V Anglii':" 17–24 in A. McMillin, ed., *Under Eastern Eyes: The West as Reflected in Recent Russian Emigré Writing.* New York: St Martin's Press.
- 1993. *Contemporary Russian Poetry* (selected, with an Introduction, Translations, and Notes by G.S. Smith). Bloomington and Indianapolis: Indiana University Press.

Sobčak, A. 1996. "S Iosifom Broskim u menja svjazana vsja studenčeskaja žizn'" in "On prinimal vse stradanija." *Agumenty i fakty–Peterburg.* 22/144: 10.

Sodružestvo sojuzov pisatelej. 1996. "Prišla skorbnaja vest'" in "Pamjati Iosifa Brodskogo." *Literaturnaja gazeta* (31 January): 3.

Sokolov, V. 1988. "Tvorčestvo Iosifa Brodskogo ne odnoznačno oceniva-etsja..." *Komsomol'skaja pravda* (10 March): 4.

Solov'ev, V. 1988. "Iosif Brodskij – Literaturnyj otščepenec i nobelevskij laureat." *Vremja i my* 101: 185–97 (e, 190).

Soprovskij, A. 1982. "Konec prekrasnoj èpoxi." *Kontinent* 32: 335–54.

Sorokin, V. 1989. "Svoi čužie." *Nas sovremennik* 8: 168–78 (e, 169, 172).

Speh, A. 1992. "The Poet as Traveller: Joseph Brodsky's Mexican and Roman Poems." Ph.D. dissertation, Bryn Mawr College (e, 18, 85–6, 98, 116, 152, 161, 164–7, 176, 187, 193–4, 200, 205, 214–20, 243–4, 247–8).

Spender, S. 1973. "Bread of Affliction." *New Statesman* (14 December): 915–16 (e, 915).

Sproede, A. 1989. "Una Poetica della Memoria con Iosif Brodskij." *Belfagor. Rassegna di Varia Umanita* 44/3 (31 May): 263–72 (e, 263, 265, 270).
- 1992. "La Poésie d'Amour chez Iosif Brodskij: Observations sur les 'Élégies Romaines':" 169–85 in L. Heller, ed., *Amour et Érotisme dans la Littérature Russe du XXe Siecle/Ljubov' i èrotika v russkoj literature XX–go veka.* Berne: P. Lang.

Stanwood, P.G. 1971. "'Essential Joye' in Donne's 'Anniversaries.'" *Texas Studies in Literature and Language* 13: 227–38 (reproduced in Roberts, 1978: 387–96).

Stapleton, L. 1958. "The Theme of Virtue in Donne's Verse Epistles." *Studies in Philology* 55: 187–200 (reproduced in Roberts, 1978: 451–62).

Steckler, I.M. 1982. "The Poetic Word and the Sacred Word: Biblical Motifs in the Poetry of Joseph Brodsky." Ph.D. dissertation, Bryn Mawr College (e, 1,3, 10, 11, 54, 57, 62, 85, 93–5, 112, 125–7, 170, 183–5, 195, 200, 245, 362).

Stefanovič, A. 1988. "Stokgol'm. Dekabr'. 1987." *Junost'* 8: 66.

Steiner, W. 1982. "A Cubist Historiography": 521–47 in P. Steiner, M. Cervenka, and R. Vroon, eds., *The Structure of the Literary Process. Studies Dedicated to the Memory of Felix Vodicka.* Amsterdam and Philadelphia: John Benjamin.

Stern, M. 1976. "Brodsky: Dissident Poet." *Midstream* (June/ July): 87–8.

Stoppard, T. 1991. *Rosencrantz and Guildenstern Are Dead.* New York: Evergreen/Grove Weidenfeld.

Struve, G. 1964 (as "G. Stukov"). "Poèt – 'Tunejadec' – Iosif Brodskij." Introduction to *Stixotvorenija i poèmy.* 5–15.

Struve, N. 1987. "Proslavlenie russkoj poèzii." *Russkaja mysl'* 3697 (30 October): 10 (e).

Sviridova, A. 1996. "Proščanie s poètom (Rot zakryt...)" *Russkaja mysl'* 4113 (15–21 February): 12.

Sweedler, U. 1989. Review of "Marbles." *Library Journal* (15 April): 75.

Sylvester, R. 1975. "The Poem as Scapegoat: An Introduction to Joseph Brodsky's 'Halt in the Wilderness.'" *Texas Studies in Literature and Language* 17: 303–27 (e, 327).

– 1980 (as R. Sil'vestr). "Ostanovivšijsja v pustyne." *Čast' reči* 1: 42–52 (e, 51).

Talbot-Rice, T. 1967. *A Concise History of Russian Art.* New York and Washington: F.A. Praeger.

Tapié, V.-L. 1960. *The Age of Grandeur: Baroque and Classicism in Europe.* London: Weidenfeld and Nicolson.

Tavis, A. 1988. "A Journey from Petersburg to Stockholm: Preliminary Biography of Joseph Brodsky." *Slavic Review* 47: 499–501.

Teleženskij, V. (A. Rastorguev). 1990. "Novaja žizn', ili Vozvraščenie k kolybel'noj": 193–215 in Brodsky, 1990p.

Ternovskij, E. 1976. "Soimennik i imjarek: Poèt i kul'tura." *Grani* 100: 424–38.

Tertz, A. 1960. *On Socialist Realism.* New York: Pantheon.

Thomas, D.M. 1981. "Lift-Off." *Poetry Review* 70/4: 47–50 (e, 47, 49).

Tietze, H. 1948. *Tintoretto: The Paintings and Drawings.* London: Phaidon.

Timmer, C.B. 1964. "Een Russiche Dichter in de u.s.s.r." *Tirade* 8: 645–7.

Timofeev, L. 1987. "Nobelevskaja premija Iosifu Brodskomu – dlja nas v Rossii sobytie i radostnoe i gor'koe." *Russkaja mysl'* 3697 (30 October): 11 (e). (Also in *Glasnost'* 10, 1987: 14.)

Tolstaya, T. 1996. "On Joseph Brodsky (1940–1996)." *New York Review* (29 February): 7, 53 (e).

Tomaševskaja, Z. 1996. "Kak-to my govorili s Iosifom o pamjatnikax" in "On prinimal vse stradanija." *Agumenty i fakty–Peterburg* 22/144: 10.

Turgenev, I.S. 1964. "Gamlet i Don Kixot." *Polnoe sobranie sočinenij v dvadcati vos'mi tomax* (vol. 8). Moscow and Leningrad: Nauka.

Ufljand, V. 1989. "Intellgencija. Nekotorye soobraženija terminologii." *Russkaja mysl'* 3757 (6 January): 11.

– 1990a. Introduction to Brodsky 1990, *Osennij krik jastreba:* 3–4.

- 1990b. "Ot poèta k mifu": 163–5 in Brodsky, 1990p.
- 1990c. "Parnas, Iosifomu Brodskomu (Stixotvorenie)": 162 in Brodsky, 1990p.
- 1990d. "Belyj peterburgskij večer 25 maja." *Avrora* 12: 129–35.
- 1991. "Šest'desjat minut demokratii." *Russkaja mysl'* 3888 (19 July): 13.
- 1990e. "Mogučaja piterskaja xvor'." *Zvezda* 1: 179–84.
- 1992a. Introduction to Brodsky, 1992, *Forma vremeni*: 6–12.
- 1992b. "One of the Freest Men": 140–58 in Polukhina, 1992b.
- 1996. "Bessmertnye tože smertny." *Russkaja mysl'* 4111 (1–7 February): 17.
Unbegaun, B.O. 1956. *Russian Versification*. Oxford: Oxford University Press.
Updike, J. 1992. "Mandarins." *New Yorker* (13 July): 84–5.
Urnov, D. 1990. "Sudit' segodnja o poèzii Brodskogo tol'ko kak o poèzii – zatrudnitel'no." *Literaturnaja gazeta* 20/5294 (16 May): 6 (e).
Ushakova, E. 1992. "A Poet of Intense Thought": 94–100 in Polukhina, 1992b.
Vajl', P. 1992. "Roždestvo: točka otsčeta: Beseda Iosifa Brodskogo s Petrom Vajlem": 50–61 in Brodsky, 1992, *Roždestvenskie stixi*.
- 1995. "Prostranstvo kak vremja": 184–95 in Brodsky, *Peresečennaja mestnost'*.
Vajl', P. and A. Genis. 1986. "Ot mira – k Rimu": 198–207 in L. Losev, 1986c.
- 1990. "V okrestnostjax Brodskogo." *Literaturnoe obozrenie* 8: 23–9 (e, 23–4).
Vat, A., Z. Xerbert, and C. Miloš. 1976. "Pol'skoe poèty v perevodax Iosifa Brodskogo." *Kontinent* 8: 7–11.
Veit, B. 1992. "Ich bin wie ein Hund, oder besser: wie eine Katze." *Neue Rundschau*, 103/4: 99–117.
Velikson, B. 1996. "Umer Brodskij." INFO-RUSS Posting (taken from Nossik, 1996).
Venclova, T. 1976. "Pamjati poèta. Variant" (translated by Brodsky). *Kontinent* 9: 5–6.
- 1984. "'Litovskij divertisment' Iosifa Brodskogo": 191–201 in O. Matich and M. Heim, eds., *The Third Wave: Russian Literature in Emigration*. Ann Arbor: Ardis (also published in Venclova, 1988. *Neustojčivoe ravnovesie: Vosem' russkix poètičeskix tekstov.* New Haven: Yale Center for International and Area Studies.)
- 1990a. "Čuvstvo perspektivy: Razgovor Tomasa Venclovy s Iosifom Brodskim." *Vil'njus* 7: 111–26.
- 1990b. "A Journey from Petersburg to Istanbul": 135–52 in Loseff and Polukhina, 1990.
- 1992. "Development of Semantic Poetics": 276–91 in Polukhina, 1992b.
Verheul, K. 1968. "Poetry and Syntax": 153–64 in A.G.F. van Holk, ed., *Dutch Contributions to the Sixth International Congress of Slavicists.* The Hague: Mouton.
- 1973. "Iosif Brodsky's 'Aeneas and Dido.'" *Russian Literature Triquarterly* 7: 490–501 (also published in L. Losev, 1986c: 121–32).

– 1976. "Het persoonlijke konflikt van Iosif Brodski." *Verlaat Debuut.* Amsterdam: 53–8.

– 1987 (as K. Verxejl). "Èta premija prisuždena..." *Russkaja mysl'* 3697 (30 October): 11.

– 1991 (as K. Verxejl). "Kal'vinizm, poèzija i živopis': Ob odnom stixotvorenii I. Brodskogo." *Zvezda* 8: 195–98.

Vigdorova, F. 1964. "East and West: Trial of a Young Poet. The Case of Joseph Brodsky." *Encounter* 23 (September): 84–91.

– 1965. "Zasedanie suda Dzeržinskogo rajona goroda Leningrada." *Vozdušnye puti: Al'manax* 4: 279–303 (also in *Ogonek*, 1988 49: 26–31 and Gordin, 1989).

Vinokurova, I. 1988. "Zamečatel'nyj lirik N." *Oktjabr'* 7: 203–7.

– 1989. "A Case of Struggle against Suffocation." *Soviet Literature* 2: 150–4 (e, 151).

– 1990. "Iosif Brodskij i russkaja poètičeskaja tradicija." *Russkaja mysl'* 3834, "Literaturnoe priloženie" (6 July): 8 (e).

Virgil. 1986. *The Aeneid: Virgil in Two Volumes.* Loeb Classical Library. Cambridge, Mass. and London: Harvard University Press and Heinemann (used in conjunction with 1944 *The Aeneid*: translated by John Dryden. New York: Heritage).

Vitale, S. 1986. "La Voce di Brodskij contro un Mondo di Uomini-Fossili." *La Stampa* (5 April): 5.

Vitale, T. 1985–6. "A Conversation with Joseph Brodsky." *Ontario Review* 23 (Fall/Winter): 7–14.

Vol'ckaja, T. 1996. "On sdelal vse, čto mog ..." *Nevskoe vremja* (25 May): 4.

Volkov, S. 1980. "N'ju-Jork: Pejzaž poèta. Interv'ju Solomona Volkova s Iosifom Brodskim." *Čast' reči* 1, 27–36.

– 1981–2. "Venecija: Galzami Stixotvorca. Dialog s Iosifom Brodskim." *Čast' reči* 2–3, 175–87.

– 1987. "Vspominaja Annu Axmatovu: Razgovor s Iosifom Brodskim." *Kontinent* 53: 337–82 (also published as *Brodskij ob Axmatovoj: Dialogi s S. Volkovym.*" Moscow: Nezavisimaja gazeta 1992).

– 1995. *St. Petersburg: A Cultural History.* New York: Free Press: 420, 470–82, 508–21, 540, 547–9 (e, 513).

Volkova, M. and S. Volkov. 1990. *Iosif Brodskij v N'ju-Jorke: Fotoportrety i besedy s poètom.* New York: Slovo.

Vološinov, V.N. 1973. *Marxism and the Philosophy of Language.* Cambridge, Mass.: Harvard University Press.

"Vozljublennoe otečestvo." 1994. *Progulki s I. Brodskim (Čast' vtoraja).* Television broadcast: Ostankino (8 August).

Wachtel, E. 1993. Radio interview with Brodsky on *Writers and Company*, Canadian Broadcasting Company (originally broadcast May 1993; repeated 4 February 1996).

Wainwright, J. 1987. "The Art of Estrangement." *Poetry Nation Review* 14/2: 36–8 (e).

Walcott, D. 1988. "Magic Industry." *The New York Review* (24 November): 35–9.

– 1992. "A Merciless Judge": 309–25 in Polukhina, 1992b.

Wallace, R. 1970. *The World of Bernini: 1598–1680*. New York: Time.

Warnke, F.J. 1972. *Versions of Baroque*. New Haven and London: Yale University Press.

Warnock, M. 1970. *Existentialism*. London, Oxford and New York: Oxford University Press.

Warren, A. 1939. *Richard Crashaw: A Study in Baroque Sensibility*. Baton Rouge: Louisiana State University Press.

– 1963. "Baroque Art and the Emblem": 1077–83 in Witherspoon and Warnke.

Webb, W.L. 1996. "Joseph Brodsky: Poet against an Empire." *The Guardian* (January 29, taken from Nossik: edia.net.il/Nossik/brodsky/obituary/webbobit.html [e]).

Weil, M. 1996. "Nobel-Winning Poet Joseph Brodsky, 55, Dies." *Washington Post* (29 January): B4.

Weiner, A. 1994. "Influence as Tribute in Joseph Brodsky's Occasional Poems: A Study of His Links to Modern English-Language Poets." *Russian Review* 53 (January): 36–58 (e, 45).

Weisberg, J. 1994. "Brodsky's Venice." *Partisan Review* (Spring): 325–7.

Weissbort, D. (ed. and tr.). 1974. *Post-War Russian Poetry*. Harmondsworth: Penguin.

– 1989. "Translating Brodsky: A Postscript": 221–7 in D. Weissbort, ed., *The Double Labyrinth*. Iowa City: Univeristy of Iowa Press.

– 1996 (as D. Vejsbort). "Iosifu Brodskomu s ljubov'ju." *Russkaja mysl'* 4112 (8–14 February): 17.

Wellek, R. 1963. "The Concept of Baroque in Literary Scholarship": 69–115 in *Concepts of Criticism*. New Haven and London: Yale University Press.

Wigzell, F., ed. 1994. *Russian Writers on Russian Writers*. Oxford and Providence: Berg.

Wilde, J. 1974. *Venetian Art from Bellini to Titian*. Oxford: Oxford University Press.

Wilk, S. 1978. *The Sculpture of Tullio Lombardo: Studies in Sources and Meaning*. New York and London: Garland.

Willey, B. 1962. *The Seventeenth Century Background: Studies in the Thought of the Age in Relation to Poetry and Religion*. New York: Columbia University Press.

Wind, E. 1969. *Giorgione's "Tempesta," with Comments on Giorgione's Poetic Allegories*. Oxford and London: Oxford Univeristy Press.

Witherspoon, A.M. and F.J. Warnke, eds. 1963. *Seventeenth-Century Prose and Poetry*. New York, Chicago, San Francisco and Atlanta: Harcourt, Brace and World.

Wittgenstein, L. 1958. *Philosophical Investigations.* New York: MacMillan.

Wölfflin, H. 1979. *Renaissance and Baroque (1888).* Ithaca: Cornell University Press.

Woll, J. and V. Treml, eds. 1978. *Soviet Unofficial Literature: Samizdat. An Annotated Bibiliography of Works Published in the West.* Durham: Duke University Center for International Studies.

Wu, D. 1986. "Translation as Exile." *Literary Review* (October): 38–9 (e).

Xazanov, B. "S točki zrenija voron." *Literaturnaja gazeta* (22 May): 6.

Xejfec, M. 1986. "K istorii napisanija stat'i 'Iosif Brodskij i naše pokoleneie':" 230–9 in L. Losev, 1986c.

Xlebnikov, O. 1996. "Iosifu Brodskomu." *Literaturnaja gazeta* (28 February): 5.

Zabaluev, A. 1990. "Konošskij period poèta": 154–62 in Brodsky, 1990p.

Zand, N. 1996. "Joseph Brodsky: Le prix Nobel de littérature 1987, poète d'origine russe." *Le Monde* (30 January): 18.

Zaslavskij, G. and Zotov, I. 1996. "Buduščee vsegda nastanet." *Nezavisimaja gazeta* (30 January): 1.

Zeeman, P. 1983. "Leegte in Licht, Iosif Brodski." *De Gids* 146: 392–9.

Zelinsky, B. 1987. "Dido und Aneas bei Anna Achmatova und Iosif Brodskij. Zwei Möglichkeiten der lyrischen Aneignung eines tradierten Stoffes": 265–78 in G. Geisemann and H. Jelitte, eds., *Jubilaumsschrift zum 25-jahrigen Bestehen des Instituts fur Slavistik der Universitat Gessen,* New York: P. Lang (e, 274).

Žažojan, M. 1996. "Na smert' Iosifa Brodskogo." *Russkaja mysl'* 4112 (8–14 February): 16.

Žerdeckij, S. 1996. "Otkrytka iz Florencij." *Russkaja mysl'* 4116 (7–13 March): 13.

Žigačeva, M.V. 1992. "Ballada v rannem tvorčestve Iosifa Brodskogo." *Vestnik Moskovskogo Universiteta* 9/4 (July/August): 51–6 (e, 51).

Zholkovsky, A. 1986a (as Žolkovskij). "'Ja vas ljubil...' Brodskogo: Interteksty, invarianty, tematika i struktura": 38–63 in L. Losev, 1986c.

– 1986b. "Writing in the Wilderness: On Brodskij and a Sonnet." *Slavic and East European Journal* 30/3: 404–19 (e, 404, 406).

Zissermann, N. 1966. "Yosif Brodsky." *Landfall* 78: 150–5.

Zunder, W. 1982. *The Poetry of John Donne: Literature and Culture in the Elizabethan and Jacobean Period.* Towota: Harvester/ Barnes and Noble.

Index

Ar'ev, A. 201–2
Auden, W.H. 29–30, 33, 170
Azadovskij, K. 196–7
Axmatova, A. 33, 201

Bacon, F. 9, 12–13
Bakhtin, M. 20
Bainton, R.L. 32
Baroque: in history, 7–8; in painting, 10–12; as parallel to the avant-garde, 14, 17–20; as parallel to contemporary society, 16–17; in philosophy, 8–10; in the poetry of Crashaw, 100–2; as recurrent phenomenon, 20–1; in semiotics, 15–16; in spatio-temporal perception, 12–13
Bazin, G. 11 -12, 132
Begunov, Ju. 195–6
Bellini, G. 178–83
Benčič, Z. 14
Bernini, P. 10–11, 101, 132
Birkerts, S. 42, 60, 104, 153, 163, 174
Blitzer, C. 8
Bobyšev, D. 201

Bourdieu, P. 22–3
Brodsky, J.: and the absurdity of faith, 39–42, 55–7; and architecture, 178–89 *passim*; and bilingualism, 191–3; and the consequences of Donne's influence, 102–4; and the dialectic of body/soul, 112–13; and the dialectic of flora/fauna, 104–12; and the dialectic of poetic form/content, 113–14; and the dialectic of poetry/prose, 124–6; and the dialectic of space/time, 114–19, 139–44; and the dialectic of vision/sound, 119, 139–44; and discourse as life, 82–8; and the elegiac tradition, 90–3; and ethics, 37–9, 53–5, 151–5; and existential limitlessness, 42; and literary versus mathematical eternity, 137–9; and nomadism, 158–61, 171–3, 175–8; and particularity, 43; and perception in profile or full-face, 144–8; in posthumous biographies, 193–203; and probabilism, 76; and the relationship of naming to ontology,